Discovering America

Discovering America

Essays on the Search for an Identity

Edited by David Thelen and Frederick E. Hoxie

University of Illinois Press
Urbana and Chicago

© 1994 by the Board of Trustees of the University of Illinois
Published by arrangement with the Organization of American Historians.
Manufactured in the United States of America
P   5   4   3   2   1

This book is printed on acid-free paper.

Library of Congress Cataloging-in-Publication Data

Discovering America : essays on the search for an identity / edited by
   David Thelen and Frederick E. Hoxie.
      p. cm.
   Includes index.
   ISBN 0-252-06384-8 (paper)
   1. United States—Civilization. 2. Learning by discovery—Social
aspects—United States. I. Thelen, David P. (David Paul)
II. Hoxie, Frederick E., 1947– .
E169.1.D547 1994
973—dc20   93–33604
                                                      CIP

Contents

Preface

The editors and editorial board of the *Journal of American History* hoped that the quincentennial commemoration held in 1992 would produce more than successive rounds of self-congratulation and self-criticism. Anticipating that the anniversary of the voyages of Columbus would inspire waves of offense and barrages of defense, we sought a more constructive and illuminating approach. After considering a variety of proposals, we decided to take up Fred Hoxie's suggestion that a group of articles on "discovery" examine how and why Americans have told stories about themselves that emphasize freshness, rejuvenation, and invention. How do events become discoveries? Why are some events elevated to that realm and not others? What are the consequences of this tradition? In 1991, we invited a group of historians to contribute topical essays reflecting on such questions to a special issue of the journal, slated for December 1992.

As the essays began to appear, we realized that we had embarked on an enterprise with the potential for raising issues that lay far beyond the reputation of Christopher Columbus. The voyages of 1492 provide, after all, only one metaphor for the ways Americans think of themselves and their history. The first drafts of many essays made clear that other American discoveries—for example, of nature, of landscape, of self, and of language—suggested other metaphors and other ways in which Americans have shaped their identities. Discussion among the authors (particularly at a lively editorial conference at the Newberry Library in the winter of 1992) brought this lesson home.

As the issue neared completion we found that a set of common concerns informed the contributions: Taken together, the essays confronted issues raised by recent theoretical writings in literary and cultural theory. How are historians to reconcile the postmodern respect for the authenticity of all stories as they are told with the traditional demand that stories be accurate accounts of what happened in the past? How can different witnesses and chroniclers construct different meanings from the same texts or events? Does the past leave witnesses and documents that should constrain the stories we tell? How can we assess their credibility? How can we use witnesses and documents in ways that are sensitive to the different degrees, and even different kinds, of credibility? We hoped that the approaches to such questions in the following essays would help historians define spaces where they can stand in the debates opened by recent theoretical scholarship.

The enthusiastic response to that special issue reinforced our sense that the authors succeeded in provocatively exploring how Americans discovered other people, an unfamiliar nature, and their own evolving language and culture. The authors all showed that as Americans made discoveries, they shaped distinctive identities. The authors simultaneously illustrated current disagreements about the extent to which discovery is subjective—some presenting the discoveries they recounted as free-floating inventions imposed on reality, some showing how people and nature in the past were able to contest inventions. They explored how discoveries and identities grew out of bitter conflicts: sometimes they were shaped by negotiation, sometimes by the imposition of force; sometimes they reflected terrible lies and sometimes courageous truth.

Acknowledgments

This book is the work of many people. It began with a vision by Fred Hoxie. It took shape in the essays by these authors and moved toward its final form at an editorial conference hosted by the Newberry Library and supported by that institution and the Organization of American Historians. It moved through editing and publication by the staff of the *Journal of American History* and the Capital City Press. And those staffs cooperated with the University of Illinois Press to produce this volume.

Discovering America

An allegorical engraving of America, which served as the frontispiece in Arnoldus
Montanus's *Nieuwe en Onbekende Weereld* (Amsterdam, 1671).

Discovering America: An Introduction

Frederick E. Hoxie

By custom, the voyages of Christopher Columbus define the beginning of our national narrative. Even though scholars characterize the achievements of the Italian admiral in many ways and cast him in an array of costumes, everyone seems to agree that he and his trip were important. Why? Clearly, 1492 marks something deeper than the arrival on an island of a man in a boat: It enshrines discovery as the founding myth of America.

The idea that Columbus's journey was a "discovery" had many consequences. It defined this continent as a new land and cast its past into "prehistoric" time. It enabled both the participants in subsequent events and the historians who told their tales to set themselves apart from previous experience, to see themselves as new people living out a new history in a new place. In the centuries that followed, an ever-broadening array of humanity constructed communities here, invented new identities, and recorded new histories. Discoveries have been asserted in connection with each of these processes. Discoveries have set off contests over land and territory, but they have also legitimized political regimes and sustained new social relationships.

The passage from the precontact world to the contemporary United States has not only entailed shifts in technology and landownership, it has also brought forth a distinctive cultural tradition. Central to that tradition has been a persistent faith that existing things can be found anew, and that, once defined as new, they can serve as icons of identity, justifications for conflict, or sources of community life. The quincentennial reveals that we belong to a society with a remarkable faith in the idea of discovery.

Historians—chroniclers of this unruly American enterprise—have grappled with the task of framing our actions and ideas in an image of continuity. This effort itself has required discovery and conflict, for scholars, like their subjects, have repeatedly claimed that this continent holds something new. In their search for narratives that

Frederick E. Hoxie is director of the D'Arcy McNickle Center for the History of the American Indian at the Newberry Library.

reveal coherence in individual lives and distinctiveness in collective experience, historians of the United States have also celebrated discovery. Their discoveries have been used to structure didactic and popular versions of the national past and to fuel a public rhetoric that celebrates the actions of pioneers, founders, entrepreneurs, and visionaries. In the twentieth century, many of our colleagues have based their lifework on the assumption that a single group or factor best reveals the distinctive-ness of the national story—be it the Puritans, the frontier, the struggle of the people against the interests, the appeal of consensus, or white supremacy. Having discov-ered these propositions, scholars then turn to exploring them. Thus, whatever else he may have carried onto that beach in the Caribbean, Columbus brought "dis-covery" to America.

Eyeing the tradition of discovery and contest inaugurated by Columbus's first voyage and reflecting on the American attraction to things new, we asked several historians to explore how Americans have discovered nature and landscape, race and class, citizenship and language, even Columbus himself. We were delighted to find that many of the contributors shared, not a common method or conclusion, but a common curiosity about the process of discovery itself. Their essays and reflections on discovery provide an especially American arena for reflecting on the quincenten-nial as well as engaging current debates in literary and cultural theory about how meanings are made.

We asked authors to consider their topics on three levels. First, how have the reali-ties Americans were "discovering" or the context of those discoveries constrained the concepts they devised to describe unfamiliar people, ideas, places, and cultures? As contemporary theories of language suggest, is our written history a story of uncon-strained cultural invention, a series of free-floating stories that bear no relationship to the realities they describe? If not, how did nature and people contest those in-ventions?

Second, how should historians weigh their traditional commitment to accuracy as they encounter interpretive approaches that emphasize the roles of interpreters and readers? How can scholars reconcile a faith in accurate renderings of the past with a recognition that both historians and consumers of history need stories that authenticate their social allegiances and personal identities? How can our need for a history that is authentic in the present square with our commitment to an accurate picture of the past? These concerns are closely related to the question of invention, for they lead us to ask how memories, witnesses, artifacts, and documents contest and shape the meanings historians attach to the past.

Third, how have the myriad discoveries of individuals and groups meshed into a larger whole? What has *one from many* meant in American practice? In a post-modern world in which some see only interpretations and multiple perspectives, should we, indeed, *can* we find impulses or values that point toward unity? Is Amer-ican history a story of diversity and fragmentation or of common experiences and shared perspectives? We asked authors to explore what people have shared as Americans in this discovered space, as well as what has generated American diversity.

We hope that these explorations will help historians engage theoretical debates over how to reconcile the existence of invention with the claims of reality, the need for authenticity with our commitment to accuracy, the diversity of perspectives with hopes for a unifying understanding.

From the initial invention of Indians as savages onward, many Americans have imposed inventions without regard to the realities they were "discovering." In the American classic *Walden,* Henry David Thoreau used the pretense of describing an encounter with a woodchuck to release what Richard White characterizes as completely "loony" inventions about the meaning of the "wild." With little interest in the actual woodchuck, Thoreau simply invented nature to meet his own needs.

Two other essays illustrate that the process of inventing American qualities may be more important in the history of the United States than the content of those inventions. Carroll Smith-Rosenberg shows how American political leaders created a new national self, or subject, by drawing on conflicting tendencies in late eighteenth-century culture and by defining themselves (white, male, and middle class) as different from women and people of color. The subject they created would simultaneously proclaim liberty and speak for a new empire. The result was an ongoing construction of unstable and fanciful identities for the new American self. Michael Rogin explores how Hollywood movies in the 1920s invented American identity. White ethnic performers and audiences used blackface and racial cross-dressing to proclaim their Americanness while leaving race as the defining feature of national identity. Indeed, Smith-Rosenberg's and Rogin's stories may illustrate that what is distinctively American is precisely a drive to try out many identities, to try out different people's clothes, and to achieve a common identity amid conflicts and divisions by make believe. Born in a tradition that turned travel into discovery, that insisted on new products, new governments, and new ideas, Americans have acted as though discoveries were indeed inventions, creations unconstrained by reality.

But, as these essays make clear, discoveries are not inventions. For one thing, the time, place, and social and political circumstance of a discovery shaped its course. Just as Americans in the 1780s discovered a special American subject to fit their new government, so in the early seventeenth century—as Ronald Takaki shows—they racialized an earlier belief that others were savages to fit their claims to new lands. Similarly, promoters of Columbus's greatness began making their case in the eighteenth century but—as Thomas J. Schlereth shows—only when the admiral's reputation became linked to significant political and social currents did he rise to prominence.

Further, preexisting categories can shape discoveries, hiding their freshness and their challenge to contemporary conditions. Frederick E. Hoxie shows, for example, that much of modern Indian identity was formed amid severe political and economic restriction. Consequently those searching for new ways of being Indian in the twentieth century often clung to the words of the United States Constitution, proclaimed their allegiance to the authoritarian rules of the Office of Indian Affairs, and pledged to live peacefully alongside white neighbors. "We like church," one leader of the peyote religion declared in the 1920s. "We want to meet every Sunday . . . and then we want to work and farm." In a similar way, as James R. Barrett shows, early twentieth-century industrial workers articulated their demands in a language that echoed management's growing obsession with "Americanization."

Finally, the reality that they discovered talked back to discoverers, challenging them to reshape their findings. Richard White shows how investigations of nature in America have formed an evolving and shifting conception of geography and the environment that is neither wholly an invention nor wholly an accumulation of data. He sees a "long and complicated" conversation about American nature in which physical realities often disproved and limited grand theories and inventions.

The discovery of what went before can deepen and expand one's imagination. Patricia Nelson Limerick traces discoveries of landscapes that "shake the soul" as they reveal the layers of meaning and memories encrusted on particular spots by the successive events that took place in them. In places where people have striven and suffered, such as the camps where Japanese Americans were detained during World War II, the altered landscape becomes an artifact, resonant with moral and aesthetic meanings.

Historical memories can also be challenged by the voices of those who witnessed discoveries. Reminders of how limited our authoritative texts of exploration can be appear in Richard White's description of Gonzalo Fernández de Oviedo's tendency to confuse new American species with known European plants and animals, and Hoxie's account of Native Americans who collaborated with early anthropologists to shape a positive picture of their tribes. Both undermine what James Clifford has called the "mode of modern fieldwork," the notion that "you are there . . . because I was there."[1] Enhancing the perspective of a single text is a chorus of voices from those who were objects of discovery and exploration. They include people like the Virginia Indian who declared that the English had "come from under the world," the Omaha women who identified specimens for the botanist John Bradbury, and Belinda, a slave, whose eighteenth-century attack on human bondage was framed and distorted by the Federalist publisher Mathew Carey.

In addition to demonstrating how the constraints of time, nature, and memory have limited the free play of invention, these essays show that the tradition of discovery has left us with a legacy of suppression and evasion. As some actors have spoken in new voices, others have been silenced. For example, Kenneth Cmiel's account of the discovery of American language in the nineteenth century takes on a new meaning when read in the wake of Ronald Takaki's analysis of William Shakespeare's play *The Tempest*. In the play, the European Prospero reminds the non-European Caliban that he had taught him a European language and that earlier he "wouldst gabble like a thing most brutish." Caliban's angry retort captures

---

[1] James Clifford, *The Predicament of Culture: Twentieth-Century Ethnography, Literature, and Art* (Cambridge, Mass., 1988), 22.

the lie at the heart of his discoverer's triumph: "You taught me language, and my profit on't is, I know how to curse. The red plague rid you for learning me your language."

Likewise, the discovery of an American citizen-subject that Carroll Smith-Rosenberg describes was inseparable from the invention of women and femininity as threats to male republicanism. In a republic that banned women from the public sphere, women figured prominently in political discourse as emblems of consumption run amok, and elite Federalists were quick to characterize their Shaysite opponents as effeminate. The self-discovery of citizens for the new empire of liberty required the simultaneous discovery and silencing of others whose "absent presence"—in Rogin's powerful phrase—enabled unparalleled opportunities for freedom and invention for European men. As Rogin observes, "Discovery makes the discovered into passive objects, and discoverers into autonomous subjects."

In Rogin's analysis of Hollywood films from the 1920s and 1930s, the discovery of the modern American subject entails the suppression of memory and the subjugation of others. His story of "racial cross-dressing" is a reminder of the creativity of twentieth-century American popular culture, which thrives by drawing vitality from ethnic and racial subcultures. Rogin's essay is also a disturbing account of how early Hollywood film producers from immigrant backgrounds manipulated racial imagery to offer their ethnic audiences—and themselves—the opportunity to "pass" as lily-white Americans. In this regard, Rogin's story provides a sinister backdrop to Barrett's essay on immigrant working-class Americanization from the bottom up. But even more important, Rogin's unraveling of the multiple identities of the cross-dressing, blackfaced, and sexually ambiguous American Adams flickering on movie screens in the interwar years puts a terrifying process of evasion at the center of this country's national identity. In Rogin's account, there is no heroic self discovered underneath the burnt cork and the transvestite garb, only a Hollywood version of Melville's Confidence Man. In these films, Rogin argues, the newly liberated ethnic subject is ready to appropriate the power and identity of the excluded, but he cannot admit complicity in the lies and brutality that produced such exclusion. Rogin concludes, "the freedom promised immigrants to make themselves over points to the vacancy, the violence, the deception and the melancholy at the core of American self-fashioning."

The essays in this volume offer dozens of separate American voices that begin to articulate a new conception of the whole. And who better to help us hear that wholeness amid apparent chaos than the poet of democratic upheaval, Walt Whitman? Whitman, more than any other figure in these essays, celebrated both the unruliness and the coherence of American culture. His approach to the English language, so vividly portrayed in Cmiel's essay, was a metaphor for his view of American life. Just as he believed English was "not a fossil language" but should embrace new idioms and expressions, so he celebrated the disjuncture and variety all around him. Connecting language to a democratic outlook, Cmiel explains, Whitman refused to exclude any dialect or reject any phrase just as he refused to exclude any group from his democratic nation. But Cmiel also makes plain that Whitman was no anarchist. He believed that language, like America itself, had a larger coherence. The best English, he wrote, "breaks out of the little laws to enter truly the higher ones." He envisioned an order beyond the cacophony around him.

Modern historians rightly fear the notion that there are higher laws at work in human history because these have so often been instruments of ideology and self-interest. The alternative, the idea that diverse experience cannot cohere, is equally disturbing because it suggests that historical writing is ultimately a fruitless enterprise. Cmiel proposes an alternative, that historians try to follow the example of Walt Whitman's "perfect writer" who bears witness to the diversity of American experiences. Alert to the details of cultural difference and the power of human creativity, Whitman argues, that writer should seek to "make words sing, dance, kiss, do the male and female act, bear children, weep, bleed, rage, stab, steal, fire cannon, steer ships, sack cities, or do any thing that man or woman or the natural powers can do." The theme of discovery has led contributors to this issue to chronicle a dizzying variety of inventions, encounters, and struggles, but it has also allowed them to take up a side of Whitman's challenge that is frequently overlooked: to embrace variety and difference as a means to a new, unified vision. "The best of America," Whitman declared, "is the best cosmopolitanism."

Inspired by Whitman, Cmiel speaks for many of us:

> Whitman did not see any contradiction between disorder and order, between the elaboration of difference and an embrace of the whole. . . .
>
> . . . .
>
> Is it possible that current theory has once again blinded us? That efforts to expose the limits of language have ironically limited our own sense of how people might live together—limited, in other words, our own democratic horizon? Perhaps the dance of language and linguistics will have to take a new turn, with facts, once more, speaking to theory.

Our essays make clear that historians' efforts can overcome American forms of evasion and denial. In new conversations between discoverers and discovered, America might still be discovered.

Dis-Covering the Subject of the "Great Constitutional Discussion," 1786–1789

Carroll Smith-Rosenberg

On June 18, 1783, George Washington resigned as commander in chief of the armies of the United States of America. A victorious war had been fought, he wrote the governors of the several states in a congratulatory and self-congratulatory tone. Americans had secured their liberty and independence; they had won their right to empire. Without the slightest touch of self-conscious irony, Washington declared that the war that had freed Americans from colonial domination had also transformed them into one of the world's great colonizing peoples. "The citizens of America, placed in the most enviable condition, as the lords and proprietors of a vast tract of continent, comprehending all the various soils and climates of the world, and abounding with all the necessaries and conveniences of life, are now, by the late satisfactory pacification, acknowledged to be possessed of absolute freedom and independence. They are from this period to be considered as actors on the most conspicuous theatre, which seems to be peculiarly designed by providence for the display of human greatness and felicity."[1] What is perhaps most striking about Washington's letter is that it situates Americans as imperialists first and as independent republicans second.

Carroll Smith-Rosenberg is Term Professor in the Humanities in the Department of History, University of Pennsylvania.

The generous support I received from many scholars and scholarly institutions has made this essay possible. To them all, thank you: the American Council of Learned Societies, the Institute for Advanced Study, the University of Pennsylvania, the Newberry Library. Most especially I wish to thank the director and staff of the Library Company of Philadelphia, David Thelen, Frederick E. Hoxie and my fellow contributors to this volume, Nina Auerbach, Houston Baker, Evelyn Brooks Higginbotham, Elin Diamond, Linda Hart, Julia Epstein, Frances Furguson, Margaret Jacobs, Ann R. Jones, Linda Kerber, Mark Poster, Peter Stallybrass, and my other colleagues in that most valuable of all intellectual groups, the Seminar on the Diversity of Language and the Structure of Power, University of Pennsylvania. Above all, I am indebted to Alvia Golden, Phyllis Rackin, and Gabrielle Spiegel for their cogent criticism, wise counsel, and unfailing support. An early version of this paper, presented at the colloquium, "The American Imaginary," Laboratoire de Recherche sur l'Imaginaire Americain, Foundation de la Maison des Sciences de l'Homme, Paris, was published as "Red, Black, and Female: Constituting the American Subject," in *Social Science Information*, 30 (June 1991), 341–57.

[1] "A circular Letter from his Excellency General Washington, Commander in chief of the Armies of the United States of America, addressed to the Governors of the several States, on resigning his Command, and retiring from public Business, June 18, 1783," *American Museum*, 1 (May 1787), 388.

The great seal of the United States, adopted by Congress only three years later, similarly fused American independence and American imperialism. "The escutcheon or shield is borne on the breast of an American eagle without any other supporters, to denote that the United States of America ought to rely on their own virtue," the designers explained. "The eagle itself," they continued, reinforcing their adoption of a well-known Roman symbol, "is a symbol of empire." In the same spirit, a popular South Carolinian orator praised "the fathers of our independence" as the founders "of our infant empire" and denominated the Fourth of July as "the natal anniversary" of that empire.[2]

Americans' self-fashioning as an autonomous and a powerful people rested solidly upon their self-image as the legitimate heirs both of Britain's republican political beliefs and Britain's North American empire. Colonizer and republican fused in their revolutionary and new national identities and rhetoric. Do those fusions represent a moment of collective hypocrisy? The cloaking of expansionist self-interest in patriotic platitudes? I would not be the first to suggest such an interpretation, but it is far too simple. The fusions and confusions of independence and colonialism were not self-conscious stratagems but products and representations of the deep-rooted inconsistencies and contradictions that characterized the new nation's political ideologies and rhetoric.

Why do I think of that rhetoric and ideology as inconsistent and contradictory? How could they have been otherwise? Both ideology and rhetoric took their forms gradually during a century that began in the shadow of the Glorious Revolution and ended with the French Revolution, a century formed and informed by radical economic change, a war for colonial independence, imperial expansion west-ward. Conflicting arguments, attitudes, and assumptions, rhetorically elaborated, emerged as embattled discourses: civic and liberal humanism, religious enthusiasm and enlightened deism, mercantilism and pietism. Acquiring slightly different meanings depending on whether they were spoken with a colonial or a cosmopolitan accent, those discourses contested one another, layering political rhetoric and beliefs with diverse meanings and values, molding perceptions and behaviors.[3] Informed by these multiple conflicting discourses, late eighteenth-century British North Americans imagined a new nation, constituted a new government—and constructed new identities as subjects of that nation and to that Constitution.

Nations, constitutions, and subjects form and inform one another in processes that are subtle, intricate, and never ending. The "external frontiers of the state," the eighteenth-century political theorist Johann Fichte tells us, must become the "internal frontiers" of the citizen. The late twentieth-century theorist Étienne

---

[2] "The device of the Armorial Atchievement, appertaining to the United States . . . forms the Great Seal for the United States, in Congress assembled. . . ," *Columbia Magazine and Monthly Miscellany*, 1 (Sept. 1786), 33–34; "Dr. Ladd's oration on the Anniversary of American independence," *American Museum*, 2 (Oct. 1787), 333.

[3] For particularly cogent discussions of the complexities and contradictions in the new nation's political rhetoric and ideological heritages, see Joyce Appleby, "Republicanism and Ideology," *American Quarterly*, 37 (Fall 1985), 461–73; and Isaac Kramnick, "The 'Great National Discussion': The Discourse of Politics in 1787," *William and Mary Quarterly*, 45 (Jan. 1988), 3–32. The title of my essay is a misreading and rewriting of Kramnick's title.

Balibar concurs, arguing that a nation "only reproduces itself as a nation to the extent that, through a network of apparatuses and daily practices, the individual is instituted as *homo nationalis*." For a nation to live, its heterogeneous, often contentious, inhabitants must experience themselves as national subjects, that is, as integral parts of a collective "people," no matter how artificially constructed that collectivity and sense of belonging are. Otherwise the nation would exist only as "an arbitrary abstraction: patriotism's appeal would be addressed to no one."[4] Without national subjects, there can be no nation. To forge Virginia and Rhode Island, Georgia and Pennsylvania into one nation, British-American patriots had not only to write a new constitution. They had to constitute a new American identity, one that Virginia planters, Rhode Island merchants, Georgia farmers, and Pennsylvania artisans would internalize as their own and in that process become subjects of and to the new nation. That process is the subject of my essay.

Is it a process of discovery? This essay appears as part of a special issue examining "discovery," an issue that deliberately plays the tropes of "discovery" and "invention" against one another. Yet, ironically perhaps, I refuse both tropes. I do not believe European and Asian immigrants "discovered" American identities on this continent. Yet neither does the trope of invention work for my essay, for two reasons. Its original Renaissance meaning (which the word must always evoke for the historian) was, quite simply, "to discover." To substitute *invent* for *discover,* therefore, advances our argument not one whit. On the other hand, more recent notions of *invent,* those suggested by the unabridged *Oxford English Dictionary* (*OED*) and Michael Rogin's essay, for example—"to compose as a work of imagination or literary art. . . . To devise something false or fictitious"—suggest too finished an act and too identifiable a group of self-conscious inventors to describe the process I seek to uncover. I prefer the trope "production," using it to suggest the laborious ongoing process of making. Raymond Williams argues that we "understand society because we have made it . . . we understand it not abstractly but in the process of making it . . . the activity of language is central in this process."[5] If we accept Williams's argument, then to understand American society and Americans we must trace the processes by which America as a concept and the American subject were made as old religious rituals and new political practices, old political rhetoric and the new technologies and genres of popular culture inscribed on the imaginations of disparate groups a common identity and loyalty that they, in turn, worked to internalize and own.[6]

---

[4] For Johann Fichte's statement in *Reden an die deutsche Nation* (Addresses to the German People, 1808), see Étienne Balibar, "The Nation Form: History and Ideology," trans. Immanuel Wallerstein and Chris Turner, *Review, Fernand Braudel Center,* 13 (Summer 1990), 329–61, 347–48. *Ibid.,* 345–51, esp. 345, 349.

[5] *The Oxford English Dictionary,* 2d ed., s.v. "invent." I am indebted to Ann R. Jones, of Smith College, and Phyllis Rackin, of the University of Pennsylvania, for "discovering" the original meaning of invent. Michael Rogin, "Making America Home: Racial Masquerade and Ethnic Assimilation in the Transition to Talking Pictures," *Journal of American History,* 79 (Dec. 1992), 1050–77; Raymond Williams, *Marxism and Literature* (New York, 1977), 23.

[6] The comments do little more than skim over the complexities suggested by the overlapping of meanings assigned to the three terms *discovery, invention,* and *production.* For instance, could I say that, as a historian, I have *discovered* the processes by which an American subject was *produced?* No, for I can never distance my self from

The story historians traditionally tell of how the new Constitution was adopted obscures the story of how the new American subject was constituted. We can dispel at least some of this obscurity by turning to the new nation's popular press and exploring the ways an American subjectivity was constructed on its pages, especially on those of the new political magazines that spoke to and for the nascent urban middle classes. During the very years that those magazines, reaching out to an emergent mercantile and professional urban readership, successfully urged the establishment of a new American nation and a new federal constitution, they also strove to constitute a new *homo nationalis,* a new *homo Americanus,* at least among their urban and would-be urbane readers. Despite Americans' racial, ethnic, class, and gender diversity, the new American subject was male, white, and, increasingly, middle-class. His parochial beginnings notwithstanding, he would come to dominate the national imagination. And, like Washington's letter to the several governors, like the great seal of the United States, he would always embody the fundamental contradictions that characterize American political rhetoric.

American historians and political theorists have traditionally situated this emergent political subject and the conflicted rhetoric that produced him within the larger framework of the evolution of eighteenth-century republican discourses and the history of ideas.[7] Defining the subject of their studies as the evolution of republican political thought, they have plotted its intellectual genealogies, dissected its component parts. In doing so, they have focused on political issues and canonical

---

the production process. In dis-covering past American subjects, I produce present subjects—myself, perhaps my readers. As Michel Foucault warns, the will to knowledge produces not knowledge but knowers, and as Étienne Balibar points out, historians are central actors in the construction of modern nationalism and national identities. For explorations of these issues, see Balibar, "Nation Form," trans. Wallerstein and Turner, 329; Michel Foucault, *The Archeology of Knowledge and the Discourse on Language,* trans. A. M. Sheridan Smith (New York, 1972); and Michel Foucault, *The History of Sexuality,* vol. I: *An Introduction,* trans. Robert Hurley (New York, 1978).

   [7] A survey of the historiography of American republican discourses reads like the who's who of great American historians: J. G. A. Pocock, *The Machiavellian Moment: Florentine Political Thought and the Atlantic Republican Tradition* (Princeton, 1975); Bernard Bailyn, *The Ideological Origins of the American Revolution* (Cambridge, Mass., 1967); Gordon S. Wood, *The Creation of the American Republic, 1776–1787* (Chapel Hill, 1969); Isaac Kramnick, *Bolingbroke and His Circle: The Politics of Nostalgia in the Age of Walpole* (Cambridge, Mass., 1968); Isaac Kramnick, "Republican Revisionism Revisited," *American Historical Review,* 87 (June 1982), 629–64; Joyce Oldham Appleby, *Economic Thought and Ideology in Seventeenth-Century England* (Princeton, 1978); Joyce Appleby, *Capitalism and a New Social Order: The Republican Vision of the 1790s* (New York, 1984); Joyce Appleby, "Republicanism in Old and New Contexts," *William and Mary Quarterly,* 43 (Jan. 1986), 20–34; C. B. Macpherson, *The Political Theory of Possessive Individualism: Hobbes to Locke* (Oxford, 1962); Albert O. Hirschman, *The Passions and the Interests: Political Arguments for Capitalism before Its Triumph* (Princeton, 1977); Istvan Hont and Michael Ignatieff, eds., *Wealth and Virtue: The Shaping of Political Economy in the Scottish Enlightenment* (Cambridge, Eng., 1983); Drew R. McCoy, *The Elusive Republic: Political Economy in Jeffersonian America* (Chapel Hill, 1980). Still others have explored the impact of gender, religion, and middle-class values upon republican rhetoric: Linda K. Kerber, *Women of the Republic: Intellect and Ideology in Revolutionary America* (New York, 1986); Linda K. Kerber, "The Republican Ideology of the Revolutionary Generation," *American Quarterly,* 37 (Fall 1985), 474–95; Linda K. Kerber et al., "Beyond Roles, Beyond Spheres: Thinking about Gender in the Early Republic," *William and Mary Quarterly,* 46 (July 1989), 565–85; J. E. Crowley, *This Sheba, Self: The Conceptualization of Economic Life in Eighteenth-Century America* (Baltimore, 1974); Sean Wilentz, *Chants Democratic: New York City and the Rise of the American Working Class, 1780–1850* (Oxford, 1984); Ruth H. Bloch, *Visionary Republic: Millennial Themes in American Thought, 1756–80* (Cambridge, Eng., 1985); Ruth Bloch, "The Gendered Meanings of Virtue in Revolutionary America," *Signs,* 13 (Autumn 1987), 34–58.

texts, debating subtle shades of meaning and turns of phrase. While it could be argued that individually and as participants in bitter scholarly debates, historians and political scientists have created a complex picture of the gradual evolution of the republican political and the liberal economic subject, they have not done so self-consciously nor have they directly addressed themselves to the issue of subjectivity. For us to do so now, we must contextualize the history of political theory in the history of subjectivity and enlarge our understanding of Lockean liberalism by relating it to the evolution of the liberal humanist subject. If we are to understand emergent nationalisms, as Fichte urged us to, we must shift the focus of our historical analysis from the writing of a new constitution to the *constitution* of new political subjects. In short, we must move from political theory to cultural theory, from the history of political ideas to the history of political *rhetoric*.

To reposition, however, is not to substitute. It is rather to enrich one form of analysis with the insights of another—the intellectual and political with the cultural. Doubly visioned, we will then be able to see more clearly the ways America's divergent discourses, under the pressure of independence and national sovereignty, interacted to constitute a series of new political and economic subjectivities whose forms, like amber, immortalized the imperfections that marked their birth.

Since historians of America infrequently address the issue of subjectivity, let me clarify my use of the term. I use the word *subjectivity* to refer to psychologically internalized identities associated with specific subject positions or, more correctly, composites of subject positions. One such composite might consist of, for example, the brave soldier / productive farmer / virtuous republican. The respectable bourgeois matron / pious mother / white American might constitute a second. Neither subject positions nor the resultant subjectivities are biologically rooted or psychologically inherent to individuals. Rather, being ideologically constructed and socially normative, they circulate within the popular culture—where they are produced and reproduced in religious sermons, political orations, newspaper articles, and popular fiction—and through social interactions and, ultimately, are enforced by the political power of the state. It is thus as subjects to and of popular and political culture that individuals internalize and affirm a particular subjectivity as "naturally" their own. Neither static nor monolithic, subjectivities change over time. We can see this most simply on a personal and familial level: rebellious sons, for example, not infrequently become demanding fathers. Even greater dynamic instability characterizes national and political subjectivities, for they are produced by interweaving diverse and often contradictory ideologies. In producing a republican subjectivity in late eighteenth-century North America, for example, the new urban magazines drew upon both civic humanist and liberal humanist discourses, the rhetoric and beliefs of the European and the Scottish Enlightenment, evangelical Protestantism, romanticism, civil law, concepts of national sovereignty, and British imperialism. These discourses and ideologies were both rent with internal contradictions and strident in their discord with one another. The term *cacophony* or the image of a crazy quilt in-process-of-becoming far more accurately represents the composition of this subject than the Cartesian insistence on the subject as "the conscious and coherent originator of meanings and actions."[8]

Internally fragmented subjectivities assume a coherence when they have it not, by being juxtaposed to multiple others—especially negative (feared or hated) others. The more contradictory and unstable the ideologies that construct subjectivities, the more insistent the mechanisms constructing these others become. Internal contradictions, rejected or hated aspects of the subject, are projected outward onto negatively constructed others who exist in "Manichaean" opposition to a now empowered and purified self, serving as foils against which the uncertain subject is consolidated and mobilized. At the same time, more positive aspects of those others may be appropriated in a process we might call selective identification or symbiosis. The result, a subjectivity conceived in alienation, yet one cathected with desire. Every affirmation of self necessarily confirms a sense of loss and the desire for connectedness, for the other, which desire, in the instant, is repressed. A charged emotional complexity binds subject and others together, a complexity, the historian might well argue, that racism and nationalist xenophobia repeatedly enact.[9]

These complexities and contradictions produce subjectivities that are not only ideologically, linguistically, and psychologically decentered but socially destabilized as well. Because subjectivities are formed and reformed in interaction with particular historically rooted sets of social relations and material forces, significant alterations in these relations and forces not only destabilize subject positions and subjectivities, they also provide the basis for resisting and subverting those subjectivities.[10] Certainly this was true of late eighteenth-century America, ruptured by a series of

---

[8] Paul Smith, *Discerning the Subject* (Minneapolis, 1988), xxviii. Debates about subjectivity pervade contemporary scholarship. For two excellent overviews, see *ibid.*; and Mark Poster, *Critical Theory and Poststructuralism: In Search of a Context* (Ithaca, 1989). For influential literary studies, see Stephen Greenblatt, *Renaissance Self-Fashioning: From More to Shakespeare* (Chicago, 1980); and Catherine Belsey, *The Subject of Tragedy: Identity and Difference in Renaissance Drama* (London, 1985). For a cogent feminist analysis, see Teresa de Lauretis, *Technologies of Gender* (Bloomington, 1987), esp. 1–30. On subjectivity in relation to colonialism and postcolonialism, see Homi K. Bhabha, "The Other Question: Difference, Discrimination, and the Discourse of Colonialism," in *Literature, Politics, and Theory: Papers from the Essex Conference, 1976–84*, ed. Frances Barker et al. (London, 1986), 148–72.

[9] On the role of Manichaean opposition in subject formation, see Abdul R. JanMohamed, "The Economy of Manichean Allegory: The Function of Racial Difference in Colonialist Literature," in *"Race," Writing, and Difference*, ed. Henry Louis Gates, Jr. (Chicago, 1985), 78–106. I am indebted to Alvia G. Golden for drawing my attention to the process of selective identification. Jacques Lacan's work raises the issue of desire in the relation between subject and other. See, especially, Jacques Lacan, *Escrits: A Selection*, trans. Alan Sheridan (London, 1966); and Jacques Lacan, *The Four Fundamental Concepts of Psycho-analysis*, trans. Alan Sheridan, ed. Jacques-Alain Miller (New York, 1981). For appreciations of Lacan's theories of subjectivity that also deal with Lacan's sexism, see Stephen Heath, "'Difference,'" *Screen*, 19 (Autumn 1978), 51–112; Teresa de Lauretis, "Eccentric Subjects: Feminist Theory and Historical Consciousness," *Feminist Studies*, 16 (Spring 1990), 115–50; and Laura Kipnis, "Feminism: The Political Conscience of Postmodernism?" in *Universal Abandon? The Politics of Postmodernism*, ed. Andrew Ross (Minneapolis, 1989).

[10] Increasingly, feminist scholars, especially those concerned with the operation of racism and colonialism, have refused the determinism embedded in the notion of ideologically constituted subjectivities. Insisting that languages are *social* acts, that meaning takes form through the dialogic interaction of many speaking subjects, we seek to constitute a middle ground between traditional empiricist and materialist history and the abstractions of deconstruction. For a sophisticated history of post-structuralism and the articulation of a middle ground, see Gabrielle M. Spiegel, "History, Historicism, and the Social Logic of the Text in the Middle Ages," *Speculum*, 65 (Jan. 1990), 59–86.

political, economic and social revolutions that, triangulating, informed and transformed one another and the American subjects subject to them.

Let me provide a simplified example of what I mean. During the closing decades of the eighteenth century, economic and demographic changes associated with the commercial revolution interacted with social discourses and normative expectations imported from England to constitute an emerging American middle class. This resulted, in turn, in the increasing exclusion of white middle-class women from the workplace, their confinement to the domestic sphere, their economic dependence — and, concomitantly, in growing social and familial commitments to their eduction. Female literacy increased, as did the need for cheap public education — read: low-paid teachers. New economic opportunities arose for middle-class women as teachers, popular writers, magazine editors, and religious missionaries. In the meantime, changing technology intensified material and discursive change. Religious and political dissent escalated, and pious domestic women emerged as political agitators at war with the culture that produced them, altering that culture. The assignment of primary causality to any single factor in this complex chain of actions and reactions, even supposing such an assignment possible, seems far less interesting than the careful mapping of their exquisitely patterned interaction.

Before it is complete, however, such a mapping must account for more factors still. To dis-cover the American subject, we must further reposition that subject within the frame of colonial and postcolonial discourses. Doing so will foreground the issue of race or, rather, races.[11] British North Americans stridently represented their revolution as a struggle for *colonial* independence from British *imperial* oppression. But what an unusual colonial and consequently postcolonial discourse they spoke — one in which, unlike those of colonial and postcolonial Africa and India, race did not distinguish the colonized from the colonizer, signifying the colonial's inferiority. Claiming not only a common political heritage and legal rights but also a common "race" and color with their "imperial tyrants," British-American revolutionaries adamantly refused the hierarchical distinction of center and margins embedded in the discourses of colonialism. Stridently they insisted that they, pure white colonists, spoke the political and imperial mother tongue with greater authenticity and purity than their imperial oppressors.[12]

Yet even after we have racially problematized British Americans' postcolonial discourses, we have yet to exhaust the complexities and contradictions embedded in the new national rhetoric. As Washington's letter so emphatically claims, British Americans were simultaneously colonists struggling for national liberation and im-

---

[11] The paradigmatic texts on colonial and postcolonial discourses and subjectivities are: Edward Said, *Orientalism* (New York, 1978); and Frantz Fanon, *Black Skin, White Masks*, trans. Charles Lam Markmann (New York, 1967). On the interdependency of colonialism and sexism, see Gayatri Chakravorty Spivak, "Imperialism and Sexual Difference," *Oxford Literary Review*, 8 (nos. 1–2, 1986), 225–40; and Gayatri Chakravorty Spivak, "Three Women's Texts and a Critique of Imperialism," in *"Race," Writing, Difference*, ed. Gates, 262–80. See also Sander L. Gilman, "Black Bodies, White Bodies: Toward an Iconography of Female Sexuality in Late Nineteenth-Century Art, Medicine, and Literature," *ibid.*, 223–61.

[12] See, especially, Pocock, *Machiavellian Moment*, ch. 14, 15.

perialists ambitious to assert their suzerainty over an entire continent. Whatever else it may have been, the American Revolution was not a war against imperialism per se, only a war against *British* imperialism.[13] Victory made Britain's former white colonists heirs to Britain's North American empire and to its subject peoples — made white Americans simultaneously postcolonial and colonizing subjects. American patriots faced in two directions. Looking east, they called themselves Sons of Liberty, true heirs of Augustan republicanism and the Scottish Enlightenment. Facing west, they became lords and proprietors of a vast continent. In a relation presumed by Washington but left unspoken, they faced south as well, where they lived masters in a land of slavery. The Manichaean economy of colonial and postcolonial discourses doubly enriched them, simultaneously constituting the citizen of the United States white subject to red savage / black brute and pure republican subject to degenerate British tyrant. Refusing the simple European dichotomies of colonizer and colonized, civilized and savage, the cultivated white American inhabited a privileged middle ground between metropolitan and wild, feudal and free worlds — a middle ground illuminated by the "whiteness" of his skin. Colors, red and black, framed and set off this whiteness.

A new American subject took form at the matrix of three novel subject positions: that of the republican citizen, the United States national, and the middle-class actor. Emergent, not fully formed, representing but one moment in a long and on-going battle among a host of protean discourses, they partook, as well, of a second order of instability. By their nature all were liminal, that is, between, and therefore outside of, traditional categories. The republican citizen balanced between the dependent status of a monarch's subject and the anarchy of man in a state of nature. We have already seen that the American national was intensely liminal. Perched on the lip of a red continent, the white descendants of European settlers denied their European-ness at the very time they insisted on a privileged position in relation to those Other Americans: American Indians and African Americans. The middle class, proclaimed liminal by its very name, not only existed between the upper and the lower classes, it situated its identity, its unique institutions and constructions (the "private" sector of the economy, the voluntary association, the coffeehouse, the newspaper, and the novel) between older understandings of public and private space and so constituted new social space. A space it then employed in its efforts to replace J. Hector St. John Crèvecoeur's yeoman farmer as the truly liminal American subject, equipoised between degenerate European aristocrats and savages native to America's woods. Singly and triangulated, poised between social categories and centuries, all three subject positions — those of republican citizen, American na-

---

[13] On British North Americans' involvement in British imperialism in the West Indies, Latin America, Africa, and Asia, see Peggy K. Liss, *Atlantic Empires: The Network of Trade and Revolution, 1713–1826* (Baltimore, 1983); and Marc Egnal, *A Mighty Empire: The Origins of the American Revolution* (Ithaca, 1988). On the interaction of nationalism and imperialism in a colonial and postcolonial context, see Benedict Anderson, *Imagined Communities: Reflections on the Origin and Spread of Nationalism* (London, 1983).

tional, and middle-class actor—existed at the threshold of new conjunctions, new formations: a new America.

Constructed out of contradictory discourses, each depended on discursively constructed negative others to demarcate and confine its boundaries. While the number of negative others proliferated during the turbulent closing decades of the eighteenth century, from their number, three principal figures emerge: the white middle-class woman, the American Indian warrior, and the enslaved African American. Predictably, like the subjects they existed to support, these negative others were interdependent, self-contradictory, and protean.

Subjects and their others were as much a product of the social and technological changes that marked late eighteenth-century America as they were of its discordant discourses. Economic and political revolutions formed and reformed one another, transforming society as cities doubled and quadrupled in size, a new professional middle class emerged, and wage labor changed the lives of working Americans. The new popular press—newspapers, the growing number of urban (and urbane) magazines, advice books, and novels—played a critical role as a bellwether product and producer of these changes. Certainly the pages of the popular press were a principal site for the production and enactment of our three new subject positions and their negative others. Here, new urban dwellers were constituted as virtuous republicans, honest shopkeepers, white Americans through the rhetorical device of direct address, through appeals to patriotism and industry, through satires of those no reader would wish to be—as well as through the dissemination of information essential to the new urban, economic subject (the arrivals and departures of ships, trade news from foreign ports, public announcements and court decisions). Here, as well, they debated their ambiguous relations with the negative others who reaffirmed their new and uncertain senses of self.[14]

It is the twined construction and intense interaction of subjects and others that I seek to explore. I will examine the initial representations of subjects and others that appeared in the new urban political and literary magazines published at the time of the great constitutional debate, the spring and summer of 1787. A somewhat narrow view, perhaps, but one that permits the close inspection of the ways national and middle-class identities fuse and confuse one another and the political subject who embedded them.[15]

---

[14] On the printing industry, see, for example, Isaiah Thomas, *The History of Printing in America,* ed. Marcus A. McCorison (New York, 1970); Stephen Botein, "'Meer Mechanics' and an Open Press: The Business and Political Strategies of Colonial American Printers," *Perspectives in American History,* 9 (1975), 130–211; and G. Thomas Tanselle, "Some Statistics on American Printing, 1764–1783," in *The Press and the American Revolution,* ed. Bernard Bailyn and John B. Hench (Boston, 1981). On a key publisher, see James N. Green, *Mathew Carey: Publisher and Patriot* (Philadelphia, 1985). Each magazine I examined began with a statement to the readers/subscribers by the editor(s), which was interesting in projecting a writer/reader relation. An essay entitled "Thoughts on reading a Newspaper" declared: "Of all literary production, there are not better calculated to make a deep impression on the mind, and convince us of the instability . . . of all earthly things, than a news-paper. . . . The medley of terrors, amusements, misery, disease, and pleasures, etc. is so mingled into one mass, that . . . [at one moment] the heart shudders . . . [the next] we sigh at the inequality of human beings . . . [or] again we weep and melt into pity." *Pennsylvania Packet and General Advertiser,* May 13, 1788, n.p.

[15] This study is based on those issues of the following urban magazines that appeared during the constitutional

The Republican Citizen

The pages of America's burgeoning urban press represented the ideal American as a virtuous republican subject who, bravely breaking the "shackles" of tyranny, embraced liberty with reason and "moderation." Courageous, the republican subject was "independent," "self-reliant," "enlightened," and "commanding." A "man of judgment" and of the mind, he controlled his passions, restrained his baser instincts, acted with "forethought," "determination," and "dignity." Led and inspired by great heroes, he despised self-interest and served the general good. But he was equally a liberal economic actor. As such, sure of his self-interest, he "calculated" his investments wisely, was fiscally responsible and productive. An aspiring member of the nascent middle classes, he sought to cloak his productivity with urbanity—and increasingly with evangelical piety and bourgeois moral conventions.[16]

Taking form at the nexus of conflicting discourses, the American political subject was simultaneously an empowered and a divided subject. The very layout of journal issues and newspaper pages illustrates these rhetorical and conceptual contradictions and conflicts. Essays celebrating American liberty were framed by newspaper ads offering slaves for sale ("TO BE SOLD, A LIKELY Negro Girl . . . very tender to children. Enquire of SAMUEL MOORE, brewer") or seeking runaway indentured servants ("FOUR DOLLARS REWARD" for returning "an Irish servant girl named ANN HENRY . . . so that her master may have her again"). Fulminations against extravagance and foreign luxuries nestled among ads for the taffetas and silks of the Indies.[17] Praise for ancient heroes alternated with essays that validated the refinements commerce made possible and debunked the golden age as an age of physical violence. The new American republican's independence was linked simultaneously to the brave defiance of British tyrants and to the fiscal responsibility of urban merchants and shopkeepers who paid their debts promptly and lived within their means. Virtue could refer equally to the hero's renunciation of class comforts during war and to the middle-class woman's prudent maintenance of her sexual reputation.

---

debates: *American Museum* (Philadelphia, 1786–1789); *Columbian Magazine and Monthly Miscellany* (Philadelphia, 1787–1788); *American Magazine* (New York, 1787–1788); *Massachusetts Magazine* (Boston, 1788–1789); *New Jersey Magazine and Monthly Advertiser* (New Brunswick, 1786).

[16] The political characteristics permeate the political essays in the new urban magazines. See, for example, "The Evil Consequences of Party Spirit," *American Museum*, 1 (March 1787), 203–5; "A View of the Federal Government of America. Its defects and a proposed remedy. Letter I," *ibid.* (April 1787), 294–98; "A View of the Federal Government of America. . . . Letter II," *ibid.*, 298–303; "Letters written in the American Camp," *ibid.*, 339–45; "Miscellanies. On the Establishment of Free Schools," *ibid.*, 326–29; "To the Freemen of America," *ibid.* (June 1787), 491–95; An Old Soldier, "Essays on Paper-Money," *ibid.*, 2 (July 1787), 36–38; and "Portrait of General Washington," *Columbian Magazine and Monthly Miscellany* (henceforth, *Columbian Magazine*), 1 (Jan. 1787), 227–29. Predictably, many essays fused civic and liberal humanist rhetoric. See, for example, Joel Barlow, "An Oration, delivered at the North Church in Hartford, at the Meeting of the Connecticut Society of the Cincinnati, July fourth, 1787 . . . ," *American Museum*, 2 (Aug. 1787), 135–36. For accounts of the liberal economic actor, see Benjamin Franklin, "Of the Employment of Time and of Indolence, particularly as respecting the state at large," *ibid.*, 1 (Feb. 1787), 112–13; "Moral Essays. On the Advantage of depending upon our own Exertions," *ibid.*, 170–72; "Letter III. On American Manufactures," *ibid.* (March 1787), 211–16; and "Wholesome Scraps," *ibid.* (Jan. 1787), 84.

[17] *Dunlap's Pennsylvania Packet or the General Advertiser,* April 4, 1777. White as well as black children were offered for sale in these revolutionary newspapers. See, for example, *ibid.*, Feb. 11, 1777, Oct. 25, 1773, Jan. 4, Feb. 1, Feb. 18, May 6, May 13, 1777. On extravagance, see *ibid.*, Oct. 28, Dec. 23, 1771.

Pleas to fund the revolutionary war debt at full value (a decidedly commercial republican concern) came draped in the rhetorical flourishes of civic humanism.[18]

Political subjectivity, rent by such ideological contradictions, was a new, unstable site of ideological contestations, contestations that spilled over into the rhetoric of the constitutional debates as Federalists attacked the Articles of Confederation in the language of failed subjectivity and sought to recuperate a rational and coherent political subject with a new unified constitution. The Congress under the old Articles of Confederation, the new Federalists asserted, constituted a "weak, imperfect and distracted government," "ineffective . . . disjointed." "Where the 'supreme power' is said to be lodged . . . we . . . are represented by thirteen voices." Its laws were "like the weak commands of a superannuated matron." Anthropomorphized, Congress was also sexualized, as in the complaint of another author: "if any thing can be added to this description of the impotence of our federal government, it must be a total want of authority over its own members." In contrast, "vigour, energy, and . . . unanimity" characterized the new government as did "an ardent zeal for . . . honor and prosperity." That energy, embodied in its subjects, became explicitly virile. Federalists rallied one another "to know our danger, to face it like men, to triumph over it by constancy and courage." "The malevolence, which may, for a time, be directed against an honest, spirited and patriotic citizen [by critics of the new constitution]," Federalist judges informed jurors in directives Federalist publishers reprinted for their magazine subscribers, "is like the harmless hissing of serpents who cannot bite. He will soon triumph over their impotent clamour."[19]

A critical ideological slippage informed this Federalist use of the language of liberal humanist subjectivity to represent the new republic and its republican subject. Fusing the identities of state and individual, the Federalists refused — or rather inverted — civic humanism's presumption of a hierarchical relation of power and authority between the state and its individual subjects (that is, its subject individuals). Analogies such as "Honest nations, like honest men," "Contracting nations . . . like individuals," which were commonplace on the pages of urban political and literary

[18] "Political Sketches inscribed to his excellency, John Adams . . . by a citizen of the united states," *American Museum*, 2 (Sept. 1787), 220–48; John Quincy Adams, "An Oration, delivered at the Public Commencement, in the University of Cambridge, in New England, July 18, 1787," *Columbian Magazine*, 1 (Sept. 1787), 625–28.

[19] "A View of the Federal Government of America. . . . Letter I," 294–98, esp. 295; "A View of the Federal Government of America. . . . Letter II," 298–99, 303–6; Harrington, "Address to the Freemen of America," *American Museum*, 1 (June 1787), 491–95, esp. 495; "An Inquiry into the Principles on which a Commercial System for the United States of America should be founded . . . Read before the Society for Political Enquiries convened at the house of his Excellency Benjamin Franklin . . . May 11, 1787," *ibid.*, 496–514; "Thoughts on the present Situation of Public Affairs," *ibid.* (April 1787), 306–10, esp. 310; "On the Philadelphia Convention," *ibid.* (May 1787), 420–23, esp. 421; "Account of a deputation from Congress to the assembly of New Jersey," *ibid.*, 2 (Aug. 1787), 153–58, esp. 157; "Thoughts on the Present Situation of Public Affairs," *ibid.*, 1 (April 1787), 306–10. See, Pocock's discussion of the association of civic virtue with *virtu*, Spartan asceticism, and military valor, *Machiavellian Moment*, esp. ch. 14, 15. For an example of Federalist judges' role, see "Political Economy. Part of Judge Pendelton's Charge to the Grand Jurors of Gagetown . . . in the State of Carolina," *American Museum*, 1 (June 1787), 483–88, esp. 486–87. I am using the term *interpellate* as Louis Althusser does, to mean the way a text/orator leads a reader/audience to internalize an ideologically constructed subjectivity. See Louis Althusser, "Ideology and Ideological State Apparatuses," in Louis Althusser, *Lenin and Philosophy, and Other Essays*, trans. Ben Brewster (London, 1977), 121–73.

magazines that summer, suggested, not a traditional civic humanist relation of state authority and subject deference, but an inversion of traditional hierarchical distinctions. As a result, the political state not only became like its individual subjects; it became subject to and modeled upon specific kinds of economic subjects— merchants, shopkeepers, money dealers. As one Federalist political commentator, interpellating his reader as a middle-class economic actor, advised: "Societies, sir, become respectable on the same principles by which the character of an individual is maintained. Dishonesty in either is equally opposed to wisdom, and equally pernicious to their true interest."[20]

In making the new American state subject to its own economic and political subjects, Federalists politically authorized a highly problematic liberal economic subject who refused both the republican (and popular) association of political virtue with economic autonomy and the equally common republican association of the political state with the public and the economic individual (or subject) with the private. Permit me to explicate a point that may at first appear complex.[21]

If the eighteenth-century businessman was only as good as his credit, that is, if his autonomy was always compromised by his dependence on others to admit his credibility and hence create his credit-ability, and if the contracting nation was like the contracting businessman, then the nation's political independence and powers must be similarly compromised.[22] Like men of commerce, the new nation would become subject to the judgment of its "public," that is, its private economic creditors, who were subject in their turn to the judgment of *their* creditors in an endless chain of dependency and interdependency. In these ways, Federalist rhetoric made subjectivity, like money, interchangeable (that is, exchangeable). It made men of commerce actors, as actors were men of commerce. The private citizen became the crediting "public"; the state became subject to its subjects; and those subjects, in their turn, became the audience and consumers of the state.[23]

---

[20] "On Public Faith," *American Museum*, 1 (May 1787), 405–12; "Circular Letter transmitted by the United States in Congress Assembled, to the Governors of the respective states, April, 1787," *ibid.*, 397–401; "On the Redemption of Public Securities," *ibid.*, 415–17; "On Establishing a Sinking Fund in Pennsylvania . . . ," *ibid.* (June 1787), 487–91; "Thoughts on the Present Situation of Public Affairs," 306–10; "Speech of a Member of the General Court of Massachusetts, on the Question whether the Public securities should be redeemed at their Current Value," *American Museum*, 1 (May 1787), 412–17, esp. 412–13.

[21] "Maxims for republics," *American Museum*, 2 (July 1787), 80–82, esp. 81, provides a classic example of the civic humanist vision of man's relation to the general good and to his family. "The first duty we owe is to God—the second to our country—and the third to our families. The man who inverts the gradation of these duties, breaks in upon the order of nature, established by God for the happiness and freedom of the world." A very different view of the power and authority of the state was presented by an author who denied that the civil state had any power to affect the economy, issues of prosperity, the amount of money in circulation, or prices. See "On the Establishment of a Mint in Rhode Island," *ibid.*, 1 (April 1787), 311–13.

[22] "Thoughts on the Present Situation of Public Affairs," 306–10; "On Establishing a Sinking Fund in Pennsylvania," 487–89; "Reply to the Essay on Public Credit," *American Museum*, 1 (May 1787), 409–12; "An Inquiry into the Principles on which a Commercial System . . . should be founded," 496–514.

[23] I am grateful to Frances Furguson, of Johns Hopkins University, for suggesting the "chain of dependency and interdependency." This paragraph and the next draw on her suggestions. Frances Furguson, comments on an early draft of this essay, University of Pennsylvania Seminar on the Diversity of Language and the Structure of Power, 1992 (in Carroll Smith-Rosenberg's possession).

By insisting upon a credit-conscious state, Federalist rhetoric had endowed the state with what Frances Furguson has called "a derived identity," an identity that depended more upon reception than upon intentions or even actions. That is, the new nation's legitimacy no longer rested simply on the consent of its political subjects, but upon its capitalist economic subjects' "repeated gesture of imagining the government as if it were an individual whose credit-worthiness one were continually assessing." They assessed the nation as eighteenth-century men continually assessed the credibility of the virtue of a middle-class woman who had entered the marriage market, in the same way as that woman's identity as virtuous depended upon the reception accorded her.[24] But women, all eighteenth-century political discourses agreed, could never claim a legitimate political subjectivity.

Diminishing (by feminizing) the political state's relation to its economic subjects, Federalist rhetoric similarly diminished the political subject's relation to the political state. In doing so, Federalist rhetoric radically reversed revolutionary rhetoric's insistence that political sovereignty resided in the political subject—and that the political representative, representing that subject, was subject to his directives. (Voters during the Revolution, for example, presumed and at times exercised their right to direct the specific votes of their legislators.) As the constitutional debates grew more bitter, however, and as Federalists rallied to oppose propositions for a bill of rights, Federalist editors sought to reverse this power relationship, arguing that the political representative represented, not the political subject, but the sovereign state. Part of the body politic, the representative assumed the prestige and qualities of the state he represented. Noah Webster, in particular, insisted that the political subject was subject to his political representative, arguing that as the bride and her husband became one following the marriage, so the political subject and his representative, following an election, became one (with one voice and one will) and that the one was the representative. Judicious and well-informed, seeing beyond the special interests of his constituents, he served, not their interests, but the general good. He must guide and govern them, as the paterfamilias governed his wife and children. Webster forcefully expressed this position in an *American Magazine* essay in January 1788:

> I am sensible that it is a favorite idea in this country, bandied about from one demagogue to another, that rulers are the servants of the people. . . . The truth is, a Representative . . . as a Representative of a State, . . . is invested with a share of the sovereign authority, and is so far a Governor of the people. In short, the collective body of Representatives . . . are . . . masters, rulers, governors.

---

[24] This invocation of the sexual and the feminine in analyzing Federalist repositionings of the male political subject is supported by the magazines' rhetoric. See, for example, how one advocate coupled the adoption of the Constitution with redemption of paper money: "When the promise is once plighted [paper money printed, bonds issued], government that moment descends to the rank of an individual and all it has to do, is to fall on some effectual measures to fulfill its engagements." "Political Sketches inscribed to his excellency John Adams . . . ," 230; "Speech of a member of the General Court of Massachusetts . . . "; "On the Question whether the Public Securities should be redeemed at their Current Value," *American Museum,* 1 (May 1787), 412–17.

As with the political state, so with the political subject, feminization accompanied disempowerment. The new Federalist magazines bestowed on the political subject characteristics republican rhetoric had traditionally defined as feminine. Political subjects were represented as passionate and irrational, ill-informed and ill-educated, easily duped, confined by their parochial knowledge and interests, as the wife was confined to her home.[25]

As a result of this intricate series of fusions, inversions, and subjugations, the political subject, whom Washington's letter had empowered with "absolute freedom and independence," had become decentered and disempowered, rendered subject to a political representative, who as representative of the political state was subject to the state's economic subjects. Dividing and displacing the individual subject's political authority and subjectivity, Federalists had rhetorically privatized (parochialized and domesticated) the public/political subject while making private/economic subjects (such as jobbers in congressional bonds and paper money) the state's "public" judges and guides.

Republican Others

So contradictory and divided a republican subject sought definition from an array of negative others. Shays's Rebellion produced one such other—the riotous debtor farmer of New England. "Pulled from plough-tail and dram-shop," "the fellow student and companion of his oxen," the Shaysite farmers constituted the antithesis of the rational, restrained, and educated ideal republican. Honored with self-government, they had degenerated into wild men and wilder mobs. As "Camillus" told his Philadelphia readers, the "philosophic observer" of the recent Massachusetts' uprisings "will behold men who have been civilized returning to barbarism, and threatening to become fiercer than the savage children of nature."[26] If only on the pages of the new urban press, the Shaysite defined and refined the republican subject as urbane and philosophical.

That the Federalist Philadelphia press represented Shaysite farmers as dumb oxen and savage anarchists should not surprise us. What might startle the twentieth-century reader is that the same press depicted them as degenerate revelers in luxury—as effeminate. Yet none other than Benjamin Franklin reported to his fellow Philadelphians that what had impoverished the Shaysites was indulgence in luxurious dress and extravagant imported trifles. "Mr. Printer," he wrote, evoking his own artisan past, "I saw a man [bring] a lamb to market.—Lambs command cash and cash pays taxes—but the good countryman went to a store and bought a feather—5 shillings for a feather, Mr. Printer. Sugar, coffee, gauzes, silks, feathers,

[25] Giles Hickory [Noah Webster], "Government," *American Magazine,* 1 (Jan. 1788), 75–80, continued *ibid.* (Feb. 1788), 137–45.

[26] Camillus, "Observations on the late insurrection in Massachusetts . . . Letter I," *American Museum,* 2 (Oct. 1787), 315–18, 316.

and the whole life of baubles and trinkets," Franklin continued, "what an enormous expence! . . . My countrymen are all grown very tasty."[27]

A number of other essayists mimicked Franklin's satire of farmers who caused "hard times" and threatened eighteenth-century social order by dressing like urban(e) merchants and professional men. "The other day I went to see some farmers who owed me a trifle," the author of "On Hard Times," wrote. "I found them in the field at work: one was clad in a velvet vest and breeches, and fine worsted stockings; the other in sattinet vest and breeches, stockings like his companion, and a fine holland shirt, with a ruffle at the bosom. I asked them for the money they owed me; and received payment in the solid coin of 'money is exceedingly scarce: the times are very hard: and it is an impossible thing to get money.'" Rather than representing the decline in the use of homespun as evidence of the extension of a cash/consumer economy into rural America, an event essential to the commercialization of America that Philadelphia merchants and industrialists so much desired, this essay, in a fascinating conflation of class and gender, represented it as a female-like indulgence of the appetites and as an inappropriate aping of social superiors by their natural inferiors. "For a few years past," he continued distastefully, "the farmers have, to appearance, been vying with the merchants in dress. They have neglected to manufacture their own wearing apparel because, say they, our own manufactures are not so handsome as foreign. . . . By this means they have reduced themselves to poverty, and now loudly complain of the hardness of the times."[28]

Not only did Franklin and his fellow essayists draw upon civic humanist rhetorical devices, which had originally been deployed by the early eighteenth-century Augustan gentry to criticize the British court and men of commerce, to serve the liberal humanist aim of establishing a strong, commercially sound state, they achieved two other significant rhetorical displacements. As members of America's new commercial classes (as Franklin and the magazine's publisher, Mathew Carey, were), they projected criticism initially directed against the new commercial classes onto the ruined farmers of western Massachusetts and thereby refused Shaysite farmers' self-reproductions as heroic patriots and republican critics of the new commercialism and the new Federalism.

The charges of effeminacy directed against the Shaysite rebels underscore the centrality of gender in the construction of the republican citizen. Both civic and liberal humanism fused masculinity and republicanism as the defining characteristics of the new American subject. His reason, independence, bravery, moderation, produc-

[27] An Industrious Man [Benjamin Franklin], "On Redress of Grievances," *ibid.*, 1 (Feb. 1787), 114–16. Franklin expressed similar sentiments in another essay: Tom Thoughtful [Benjamin Franklin], "The Devil is in You," *ibid.*, 116–19.

[28] "On Hard Times," *ibid.* (June 1787), 536–38. On the debate about the extent of commercialization in late eighteenth-century American agricultural areas, see Allan Kulikoff, "The Transition to Capitalism in Rural America," *William and Mary Quarterly,* 46 (Jan. 1989), 120–44. See also Bettye Hobbs Pruitt, "Self-Sufficiency and the Agricultural Economy of Eighteenth-Century Massachusetts," *ibid.*, 41 (July 1984), 333–64; Mary McKinney Schweitzer, "Elements of Political Economy in the Late Eighteenth Century: The Backcountry of Pennsylvania and the Shenandoah Valley of Virginia," paper presented at the Philadelphia Center for Early American Studies, University of Pennsylvania, Oct. 19, 1990 (Philadelphia Center for Early American Studies, Philadelphia, Pa.).

tivity, and fiscal responsibility were demarcated against the other, the irrational, extravagant, passionate, seductive, dependent woman.

Federalist rhetoric linked women to Shaysite farmers in two distinct moves. First, Federalists attributed economic hard times to unrestrained desires for feathers, gauzes, and ribbons, both the lack of restraint and the specific objects of desire being conventionally associated with foolish women. Federalists, second, discredited any negative discussion of those hard times and of political disorder (discussions that were quite widespread following Shays's rebellion) as feminine and foolish. At times this second rhetorical move took the form of broad but brutal humor. In the very issue in which Carey had condemned the weak-nerved and the factious and which was otherwise filled with serious economic and political essays, he printed a rather odd piece of satire entitled "On the Fear of Mad Dogs." The essay lampooned old women for spreading false alarms of dogs gone mad and consequently of disturbing the peace of "the capitol" (a word loaded and rent with multiple meanings: the seat of government, Philadelphia, and with the slightest change in spelling, productive commercial wealth). It is not that dogs had gone mad (or that capitol, or capital, and the times had gone bad), Carey argued, but that hysterical women gossips had done both. Comparing gossiping women to old witches, scolds, and ludicrous animals, Carey not only associated the rumors of hard times with devalued women, he constituted woman as an irrational and ridiculous other to the sagacious middle-class male citizen, represented by the essay's narrator. "When epidemic terror is . . . excited, every morning comes loaded with some new disaster," the *American Museum*'s essay began portentously. "A lady, for instance, in the country, of very weak nerves, has been frighted by the barking of a dog; the story spreads . . . grows more dismal . . . and, by the time it has arrived . . . at the capitol the lady is described . . . running mad upon all fours, barking like a dog, biting her servants, and at last smothered between two beds." As if this was not sufficient to convict women as irrational and politically dangerous, Carey's magazine repeated the story in only a slightly altered guise, now told to the narrator, a sensible and bemused observer, by his landlady. "A mad dog . . . , she assured me, had bit a farmer, who soon becoming mad, bit a fine brindled cow; the cow, foaming at the mouth, went about upon her hind legs, sometimes barking like a dog, and sometimes attempting to talk like the farmer."[29]

Twice-told tales promise many meanings. This one depicts the circulation of stories that lack currency because they cannot be redeemed in the solid coin of hard facts just when the credit of postrevolutionary America's fiscal currency was critically in doubt.

The association of the lack of credi(ta)bility with women's gossip suggests additional questions. The popular press had frequently been accused of fomenting fac-

[29] "Thoughts on Mobs . . . Causes of Popular Discontents . . . ," *American Museum*, 1 (March 1787), 205–7, esp. 205; "A Word of Consolation for America," *ibid.*, 1, 207–11, esp. 210–11. See also "The Evil Consequences of Party Spirit . . . ," *ibid.*, 203–6; and "A View of the Federal Government of America. . . . Letter II," 298–303; "Humour. On Fear of Mad Dogs," *American Magazine*, 1 (March 1787), 262–64. I am indebted to Phyllis Rackin, of the University of Pennsylvania, for her suggestions for reading this essay.

tions and of feeding public fears with scandal and rumor. Might Carey's journal have sought not simply to discredit the fearful by associating them with foolish women but also to displace criticisms leveled against the popular press itself by foregrounding a wise narrator, who, discrediting women's gossip, credited the new commercial economy and the new political press? One is tempted to speculate that the woman who "bit . . . her [public?] servants . . . and [was] at last smothered between two beds [of type?]" had been constituted other not only to the newly polished, judicious, and urban(e) male voter but also to Carey, the politically credible printer/publisher.

The effort to control the threat women posed to the public sphere, either in their own right or as the feminine principle displaced onto the absent aristocrat, the indebted farmer, or the demagogic printer served to mobilize and consolidate the republican citizen's divided and conflicted subjectivity. The very women who confirmed the male republican's subjectivity, however, undermined the middle-class subjectivity so closely allied to it.

The Middle-Class Subject

The middle class that began to emerge during the new national period was a commercial class concerned in international trade, the domestic production of consumer items, the spread of a cash economy.[30] Its economic success was rooted in commerce and desire; its social status, in exhibitionist display. You would know it by its brick houses and marble stoops, its rugs and furniture, its porcelain and silver, its books and clothing, its elaborate etiquette, correct grammar, and social polish. Yet, locked as they were in political dialogue with civic humanism, the commercial middle classes rooted their political virtue in the rhetoric of productive industry and talent, frugality and self-control. "Frugality is . . . necessary to the happiness of the world," the new urban press declared. "Happiness, or content, (for the terms are synonymous)," an essay, "On Contentment," continued, "depends much less on the acqui-

---

[30] Social and economic historians have traditionally rooted class identity in socioeconomic experiences. While I think of class as tied to material practices, I also see it as discursively constituted. We must search for the origins of British North America's class identities not only in economic changes but as well in the discourses Americans inherited from eighteenth-century England. As Gareth Stedman Jones argues, class is a "contested point between many competing, overlapping or simply differing forms of discourse." Gareth Stedman Jones, *Languages of Class: Studies in English Working Class History, 1832–1982* (Cambridge, Eng., 1983), esp. "Introduction." See also Stuart M. Blumin, "The Hypothesis of Middle-Class Formation in Nineteenth-Century America: A Critique and Some Proposals," *American Historical Review*, 90 (April 1985), 299–338; and Herbert G. Gutman, *Work, Culture, and Society in Industrializing America: Essays in American Working-Class and Social History* (New York, 1976). For social histories of American class development, see, for example, Stuart M. Blumin, *The Emergence of the Middle Class: Social Experience in the American City, 1760–1900* (Cambridge, Eng., 1989); Anthony F. C. Wallace, *Rockdale: The Growth of an American Village in the Early Industrial Revolution* (New York, 1978); Billy G. Smith, "Inequality in Late Colonial Philadelphia: A Note on its Nature and Growth," *William and Mary Quarterly*, 41 (Oct. 1984), 629–45; and John K. Alexander, "Poverty, Fear, and Continuity: An Analysis of the Poor in Late Eighteenth-Century Philadelphia," in *The Peoples of Philadelphia: A History of Ethnic Groups and Lower-Class Life, 1790–1940*, ed. Allen F. Davis and Mark H. Haller (Philadelphia, 1973). On consumerism, see Beatrice B. Garvan, *Federal Philadelphia, 1785–1825* (Philadelphia, 1987), the catalog of an exhibition of domestic arts and crafts held at the Philadelphia Art Museum in 1987.

An eighteenth-century allegorical engraving of America, artist unknown.
Courtesy Library Company of Philadelphia.

sition of what we have not than on the enjoyment of what we actually have. Those conditions . . . where content is universally supposed . . . to dwell, . . . absolutely exclude all ideas . . . of luxuriances and refinements."[31] In these myriad ways, then, the signs of class *identity* and the signs of class *virtue* battled one another — presumably not only on the pages and in the rhetoric of the urban press but in the homes and the consciousness of the new middle-class citizens.

As the feminine lurked beneath the masculine facade of the commercially credible state, so it informed the emerging identity of the productive middle class. Women were in many ways the producers of the new middle class. It was women's desires in the form of domestic consumption that drove much of America's import trade and enriched America's great merchants, small shopkeepers, industrious artisans — and indeed printers as the trade in novels, literary magazines, and devotional literature proliferated. Enriching the men of their class, middle-class women also embodied their status. Elite men within the new middle class used the elite women's personal elegance in clothing and in speech and her familiarity with things cultural to display their own economic security and sense of cultural superiority.[32]

Yet just as woman's desires and display of self produced her class, so they threatened her class's survival — or at the very least served to express merchants', shopkeepers', and master craftsmen's fears in an uncertain, indeed revolutionary, economy. Hundreds of essays warned husbands of the dangers their wives' ambitions and desires posed to their class's fiscal virtue and social security. Philadelphia's "men of sense" knew only too well that it was the wives of Massachusetts farmers who had lured their husbands into extravagant purchases of feathers and gauzes and thence into bankruptcy and anarchy. It was the desire of shopkeepers' wives to shine socially, to serve their butter to one another at elegant teas rather than to sell it behind their husbands' counters, that bankrupted so many promising young men and created a sense that "the times were hard." Addressing the conflict between a discursive commitment to frugality and a material commitment to production and consumption, the constitutors of the new American middle class projected their class fears and contradictions on to their representations of middle-class white women.[33]

---

[31] This advice was standard in the eighteenth-century press. "Moral Essays. On Contentment," *American Museum*, 1 (Feb. 1787), 71. Cf. "Frugality," *ibid.* (Jan. 1787), 82–84. A bit earlier, see "A Philosopher's Advice to his Son, on Entering the World," *Pennsylvania Packet and the General Advertiser*, Dec. 16, 1771; and "Philosophy. A Poem," *ibid.*, Dec. 18, 1771, n.p.

[32] For an example of an essay associating middle-class women with a civilizing influence, see "Queries submitted to our Correspondents for a fair and Candid Discussion," *Columbian Magazine*, 1 (Sept. 1786), n.p. Although historians of American men disagree as to whether we can talk of a class structure in eighteenth-century America, historians of American women almost never question the emergence of a class structure by that time. One reason for this difference may well be the role women played both in signing the new middle class and in forming much of the new wage-labor class (domestic servants, washerwomen, or members of the needle trades). Furthermore, the wives of merchants, shopkeepers, and professionals were far more likely than their husbands to have immediate contact with members of the working class since they employed and worked intimately with domestics and seamstresses. Perhaps as a reflection of these cross-class experiences, the problematization of class constituted a central issue in women's fiction during the late eighteenth and early nineteenth centuries. See Carroll Smith-Rosenberg, "Domesticating Virtue: Rebels and Coquettes in Young America," in *Literature and the Body: Essays on Populations and Persons*, ed. Elaine Scarry (Baltimore, 1988).

[33] See, for example, [Benjamin Franklin], "Cause of, and cure for, hard times. A Farmer," *American Museum*,

An essay entitled "Consequences of Extravagance" elaborately expressed the economic anxieties of Philadelphia's small shopkeepers—and larger merchants—and demonstrated the ways those anxieties were displaced onto white middle-class women. The author identified himself as the ideal American entrepreneur, that is, as a young man recently come to Philadelphia from the country with four hundred pounds. "Frugality and strict attention to a little shop, in which I did business to advantage, made me a happy man." But his display of prosperity began to conflict with the happiness that was wedded to contentment. Women, of course, introduced temptation and extravagance into the young shopkeeper's frugal Eden. "As soon as our neighbours found we were thriving, visitors crowded from all the houses in the square, to pay their respects to my wife. This gave me great satisfaction at first; but was afterwards the occasion of much disquiet to me." From being a contented and productive helpmeet, his wife became an increasingly willful middle-class matron, urging him to more ambitious ventures, refusing any longer to stand behind his counter. Continually badgered by wife and daughter, he wrote, "I commenced merchant extensively; was concerned in ships; wrote at offices, without fear, every risque that offered," rented a large house, hired a full complement of servants, and purchased a carriage. The chambermaid tried to seduce him, bankruptcy loomed, until his wife suddenly freed herself from the unnatural influence of the "club" of fashionable women who had misled her, dismissed the servants, and "determined to live happy with her family as usual."[34]

A pointed lesson for the *American Museum*'s many middle-class women readers, his essay also represented men's sense of powerlessness in a rapidly expanding and uncertain economy. Interestingly, author and publisher represented (and perhaps experienced) that economy as driven by the desires of strong autonomous women who, gathered in "clubs," constituted an alternative form of social organization. The message of the essay, like the message of the class itself, was highly ambivalent. Admonitions and titillation jostled for ascendancy as the essayist detailed his extravagant social arrangements. He simultaneously warned his readers of the dangers for small shopkeepers of imitating the luxurious extravagance that had become fashionable among Philadelphia's richest merchants, aroused those shopkeepers' desires by the tale of his own extravagances, and instructed them on the makeup of an

---

1 (Jan. 1787), 13–15; and Franklin, "Of the Employment of Time . . . ," 112–13. Virtually all references to women in the *American Museum* were satirical *and* judgmental, criticizing women for being extravagant, luxury loving—and foolish. See "Satire and Humour. Plan for the establishment of a Fair of Fairs, or Market of Matrimony," *American Museum*, 1 (Feb. 1787), 152–54; and "Humour. An Account of a Buyer of Bargains," *ibid.* (April 1787), 345–48. Women were also satirized for being too sexually reproductive. See "Speech of a Miss Polly Baker before a Court of the Judicature, in Connecticut, where she was persecuted for the Fifth Time for having a Bastard Child," *ibid.* (March 1787), 243–45; and Q. S., "For the Massachusetts Magazine. The Reformer. No. II on Scandal—An oblique Hint to Females, and the Accusations of Idlers," *Massachusetts Magazine,* 1 (March 1789), 141–42. For a contrasting denunciation of a woman religious leader for being masculine in her dress and authoritative in her *self*-presentation, see "Account of Jemimah Wilkinson, Etc.," *American Museum*, 1 (Feb. 1787), 165–69, continued *ibid.* (April 1787), 333–38, and *ibid.* (May 1787), 462–67. One reader responded in angry defense of Wilkinson: "Defense of Jemimah Wilkinson," *ibid.* (March 1787), 251–56. Such satire and denouncements seem poorly designed to help women readers develop a sense of themselves as rational and virtuous republican citizens.
34 "Consequences of Extravagance," *American Museum*, 1 (June 1787), 549–52.

upper middle-class household (which fashionable possessions were essential, what constituted a fashionable complement of servants, what exceeded rational self-interest).

At the same time that the middle-class woman's ambition, desires, and exhibitionism symbolized her class's *social status,* her lack of desire, that is, her sexual purity, symbolized her class's *respectability.* The same woman whose physical visibility and consumptions signed her class and drove its economy was also asked to embody the emergent middle-class virtues through her domesticity and sexual purity. Idealized as a republican mother, she was demurely to refine her husband and to instruct her sons in virtue. Literally and figuratively, the middle-class woman was to reproduce her emergent economic class—by being unlike the white middle-class man, his different, defining other. The male author of "On the Happy Influence of Female Society" announced that "the elements are differently mixed in women than what they are in men . . . they are almost of different sorts." To be different from men on the pages of men's magazines meant to be elegant, polished of manners and speech. It meant as well to be emotional, not rational; dependent, not autonomous; submissive, not courageous; to be other—and dangerous.[35]

Women, like commerce, that other highly problematized refiner of men, were seductive. "In their forms lovely," women "ben[t] the haughty stubbornness of man . . . an insinuating word . . . or even a smile, . . . conquered Alexander, subdued Caesar and decided the fate of empires and of kingdoms." Fearful of "the power of women to bend the stronger sex to their will," this author warned: "to enjoy any pleasure in perfection, we must never be satiated with it." But could the middle-class man ever distance himself sufficiently from these women who produced, reproduced, displayed—and seduced—his class? As if in answer to that question, one male contributor to the *Pennsylvania Packet* in the 1770s had begged his love to "despise the tricks of female art; / And pride in nothing but a tender heart." To be good, women must not only be unlike men, they must renounce their own femaleness and take pride in little or "nothing."[36]

Since white middle-class women served their class as both sign and scapegoat, their subjectivities were too marred by internal contradiction, too deeply implicated in the ideological inconsistencies of their class, to do other than reinforce the middle-class man's sense of instability. White middle-class spokesmen, therefore,

[35] On changing eighteenth-century representations of female virtue, see Bloch, "Gendered Meanings of Virtue." For the initial depicting of "republican motherhood," see Kerber, *Women of the Republic.* On shifting attitudes toward female sexuality, see Mary P. Ryan, *Cradle of the Middle Class: The Family in Oneida County, New York, 1790–1865* (Cambridge, Eng., 1981), 18–60; and John D'Emilio and Estelle B. Freedman, *Intimate Matters: A History of Sexuality in America* (New York, 1988). On differences between men and women, see "Sentimental and Moral. Comparison between the Sexes," *American Museum,* 1 (Jan. 1787), 72–74, esp. 74; and "On the Happy Influence of Female Society," *ibid.,* 74–75. On eighteenth-century attitudes toward women as the refiners of men, see John Dwyer, *Virtuous Discourse: Sensibility and Community in Late Eighteenth-Century Scotland* (Edinburgh, 1987).

[36] "On the Happy Influence of Female Society," 76. For an earlier but quite typical expression of fear of women, see a parable about two female eagles who deplumed and blinded an ambitious young male owl. *Pennsylvania Packet and the General Advertiser,* Feb. 17, 1772, n.p. *Supplement to the Pennsylvania Packet and the General Advertiser,* Feb. 15, 1772.

turned to a second negative other against whom to stabilize their own subjectivity—
the African-American slave. Not surprisingly, however, the African-American slave
proved as contradictory and destabilizing an other as the white middle-class
woman.[37]

To begin with, his very existence convicted white middle-class republicans of
hypocrisy. Their acceptance of slavery belied their liberal *political* belief that all men
should be free and undermined their self-representation as victorious resisters of
British "enslavement." How could Americans, whose political subjectivity was
rooted in their republican resistance to British enslavement, enslave others? Echoing
the doubts privately expressed by such republican leaders as Thomas Jefferson and
Benjamin Rush, "Humanus" wrote in the *American Museum:* "I am still distressed
to see our printers continue to advertise negroe slaves for sale in their newspapers. . . . I think it holds out to the world that we are inconsistent people. . . .
In reading such an advertisement (if habits of cruelty had not blinded our eyes or
hardened our hearts) we should naturally ask—what has this man done to subject
himself to be sold for life? . . . the advertisement says [only]—he is sold—for no
fault!!!"[38]

Slavery also challenged the liberal *economic* presumption that the individual was
"the proprietor of his own person or capacities," free to sell his own labor.[39] A petition presented to the Massachusetts state legislature by Belinda, a slave, presents
this argument. Mathew Carey reprinted part of that petition in his *American
Museum:* "The laws rendered her incapable of receiving property and though she
was a free moral agent, accountable for her own actions, yet never had she a moment
at her own disposal! Fifty years her faithful hands have been compelled to ignoble
servitude for the benefit of an Isaac Royall," the petition continued, "by the laws
of the land, she is denied the enjoyment of one morsel of that immense wealth,
a part whereof hath been accumulated by her own industry, and the whole aug-
mented by her servitude." Echoing American arguments against parliamentary

---

[37] Race combined with enslavement was apparently such a strong demarcator of otherness and inferiority that
gender played virtually no role in these early discussions of African Americans. Consider the following quote: "Two
or three negroes and a white woman were killed." "Description of a water-spout," *American Museum,* 2 (July 1787),
79. For a sophisticated analysis of why gender was so insignificant in eighteenth-century white male representations
of African Americans, see Hortense J. Spillers, "Mama's Baby, Papa's Maybe: An American Grammar Book," *Di-
acritics,* 16 (Summer 1987), 65–81.

[38] See, for example, Harrington [pseud.], "Address to the Freemen of America," *American Museum,* 1 (June
1787), 491–95; "Satire and Humour, On Trifles," *ibid.* (May 1787), 444–50; St. George Tucker, "Reflections on the
policy and necessity of encouraging the commerce of the citizens of the united states of America . . . ," *ibid.,* 2
(Sept. 1787), 263–76; Sylvius, "Letter VI. Further Remarks on an Excise . . . ," *ibid.,* 2 (Aug. 1787), 125–29; and
"Address to the Heart, on the Subject of American Slavery," *ibid.,* 1 (June 1787), 541–45, esp. 541. Humanus,
"On Slavery," *ibid.* (May 1787), 471.

[39] Macpherson, *Political Theory of Possessive Individualism,* 3. Slavery also violated mercantilist sentiments because the purchase of slaves necessitated the export of bullion from the United States to Great Britain. See, for
example, "Political Economy. Part of Judge Pendleton's Charge to the Grand Jury of Gagetown . . . ," *American
Museum,* 1 (June 1787), 484; and Black Beard, "Ludicrous Plan for the Benefit of R*** I****," *ibid.,* 2 (Aug. 1787),
171–72, esp. 171. For a discussion of earlier British benevolent and mercantilist opposition to slavery, see Crowley,
This Sheba, Self, 32–33.

efforts to tax the colonies during the 1760s and 1770s, Carey ended his selection with the argument that slavery violated "the just returns of honest industry."[40]

One issue of Carey's *American Museum* brought the overlap between African-American and white middle-class American subjectivities almost to consciousness, thus making them too dangerous to be maintained. The issue—which also demonstrated the overall fragility and inconsistency of America's new subjectivities—began with a patriotic refutation of the British denigration of all things American. America's landscapes were noble, Carey's journal insisted, and her painters sold and received high prices for their paintings in London. The second essay in this issue can be read as a further effort to address such attacks by displacing them onto Americans other than the *Museum*'s Philadelphia readers—in this case onto white, southern slaveholders. The essay, entitled "Manner of Living of the Different Ranks of Inhabitants of Virginia," represents that nearby state in the very terms that, as Mary Pratt argues, imperialist narratives used in representing "deepest Africa," its climate exotic, its inhabitants utter strangers to northern ways. Its wealthy planters resembled not hard-working Yankees but effete and corrupt British colonials. They rose at nine o'clock, visited their stables, and spent the rest of the day in languid ease. In a description evoking eighteenth-century pornographic art, the scantily dressed planter "lay down on a pallet with a negro at his head and another at his feet to fan him." Middling planters worked not much more and were given to strong drink; their wives did not drink tea. The essay contrasted these white nonproducers to "the poor Negro slaves [who] alone work hard." Virtually everything produced in the South is produced by them. "It is astonishing and unaccountable . . . what an amazing degree of fatigue these poor . . . wretches undergo." The productive black proved southern whites degenerate and unproductive. The enslaved black proved them inhuman and brutish as well. Tyrants, they mutilated slaves who acted in just self-defense. Evoking language only recently directed toward British invaders, the pages of Philadelphia's popular press condemned white overseers as the "unfeeling sons of barbarity."[41]

A dangerous slippage accompanied this deployment of African-American slaves to constitute southern whites as other to the northern white middle class. This essay, especially when read alongside Belinda's brief, threatened to establish too close a bond between the productive and freedom-loving northern white American producer and the equally productive and enslaved African American. The essayist had then to extricate himself from his dangerous erosion of racial difference by re-emphasizing the slave's distinctive racial nature. If the slave, economically oppressed

[40] Belinda, "Petition of an African Slave, to the Legislature of Massachusetts," *American Museum*, 1 (June 1787), 538–40.

[41] "Miscellanies. Manner of Living of the Different Ranks of Inhabitants of Virginia. Hardships of Negro Slaves. Traits of their Character. Their Passion for Music and Dancing," *ibid.* (March 1787), 245–48. For patriotic claims about American culture, see, for example, "Miscellanies. On American Genius," *ibid.*, 234–38. On the role of early travel narratives in colonialist discourses, see Mary Louise Pratt, "Scratches on the Face of the Country; or, What Mr. Barrow Saw in the Land of the Bushmen," in *"Race," Writing, and Difference*, ed. Gates, 138–62.

and deprived of all political freedoms, were really like the northern white republican, he should have been emotionally depressed. Instead, he was unnaturally
happy. "Notwithstanding [the] . . . degrading situation and rigid severity to which
fate has subjected this wretched race, they are . . . devoid of care . . . jovial, contented and happy. Fortunate . . . for them that they are [so] . . . blessed . . . else
human nature must sink." The African American did not, after all, share the same
human nature as the northern white free producer. Equally industrious, the black
slave was not equally freedom-loving. Northern white freemen and African slaves
were not alike. They did not even share a similar physical constitution. The slave
had an unnatural vigor and an animalistic desire to dance. At the end of a day of
killing labor, did he sink to the ground as the white man would? On the contrary,
he walked twelve miles and danced the night away.[42]

Issue after issue of Philadelphia's, Boston's, and New York's political magazines
inscribed and reinscribed this tortured ambivalence, representing American slave
owners as brutal and venal, Africans and African Americans as noble victims,
romantic heroes, almost like freedom-loving white Americans, but then again not
quite like them — or alternatively, as brutes, or yet again as lower than animals, the
perverse offspring of unnatural matings between Hottentots and orangutans. The
ideal resolution to this ambivalence, a number of essayists suggested, again
representing widely held beliefs, was to return African Americans to Africa.
Removing African Americans would both reaffirm Americans' unalloyed whiteness
and transform the American South into the American North — in short, efface
difference and make the new, northern middle-class subject the true American
subject.[43]

Relations between the middle-class white man's principal defining others were
as intense and complex as those between them and him. A complex triangularity
far better describes this overall pattern than parallel constructions of difference and
inferiority. Certainly many characteristics link the white middle-class woman and
African Americans of both genders. Both are depicted as intellectually inferior to
the white man, as more emotional and passionate and less controlled, more like
children, closer to nature, especially to animal nature. White women and all enslaved African Americans were equal — in their lack of legal and political subjectivity. Indeed, if anything, the logic of eighteenth-century middle-class discourses
privileges the African-American slave over the white middle-class woman by representing the African American as productive, the middle-class woman, the signature
of her class, as unproductive. Only racial difference, that other great discursive construction, elevated the white middle-class woman above the African-American slave
on the discursive map of the new urban press during this age of revolution, leading

---

[42] "Miscellanies. Manner of Living . . . ," 250.

[43] "Observations on the Gradation in the Scale of Being between human and Brute Creation. Including some
curious Particulars respecting Negroes. (From a late History of Jamaica)," *Columbian Magazine*, 2 (Jan. 1788),
14–22, esp. 14; A Friend to the Fair Sex, "Marriage Ceremonies of different Countries Compared," *ibid.*, 1 (1787),
491–97, esp. 493; "Address to the Heart, on the Subject of American Slavery," 541–42; "For the Columbia Magazine," *Columbian Magazine*, 1 (Sept. 1786), 3–6, esp. 5.

us to realize that a society's construction of gender can never be understood apart from its construction of race.[44]

The American National Subject

As productivity and race, gender and gentility simultaneously confirmed and compromised the white middle-class man's political and economic subjectivity, so similar discursive slippages and ironies fused and confused the American national subject and the multiple negative others that defined him.

One of the most obvious of these ironic fusions and confusions was the rhetorical ploy that permitted British Americans to refuse their British progenitors as politically tyrannical and economically corrupt and simultaneously to represent themselves as the legitimate heirs of Britain's republican and imperial heritage. Militarily and politically, the American War of Independence had violently distinguished North American settlers from their British forebears. The rhetorical battles that surrounded that war, however, did not constitute all Britons as other — only the English court and its dependents. Indeed, as J. G. A. Pocock has so definitively demonstrated, British-American attacks upon a corrupt and tyrannical British court adopted the very rhetorical devices the British gentry had developed in the long years that lay between James Harrington and the American Revolution.[45] It was the colonists, British-American colonists claimed, not Britain's corrupt courtiers, who embodied Britain's glorious republican tradition; it was the colonists, not the metropolitan elite, who spoke Britain's republican discourses with the purest accent. Race permitted British Americans to refuse the subordinate position associated with the colonized other and to assert their rights as the legitimate (blood) heirs to Britain's political and legal systems — to insist upon their cultural identification as British while refusing a political identification as British.

The revolutionary generation had to maintain such an ambivalent relation to their European forefathers, else how were they to distinguish themselves from that racial and political other, the original American, the American Indian? The otherness of the American Indian surprisingly proved more difficult to sustain than the otherness of British tyrants — if only because white Americans routinely had to purchase the land they would build their empire upon from American Indian tribal councils. If the American Indian was not a true American, why did he (or, as was often the case, she) "own" America's western lands?[46] European Enlightenment

---

[44] "A Tract on the Unreasonableness of the Law of Britain in regard to Wives," *Columbian Magazine*, 2 (April 1788), 186–89; A Friend to the Fair Sex, "Marriage Ceremonies of different Countries Compared."

[45] Pocock, *Machiavellian Moment*, ch. 15; and J. G. A. Pocock, *Virtue, Commerce and History: Essays on Political Thought and History, Chiefly in the Eighteenth Century* (Cambridge, Eng., 1983), ch. 4, 7. See also Wood, *Creation of the American Republic.*

[46] The issue of American Indian women's "ownership" of cultivated lands remains controversial. For studies arguing the affirmative, see Eleanor Leacock, "Women in Egalitarian Societies," in *Becoming Visible: Women in European History*, ed. Renate Bridenthal and Claudia Koonz (Boston, 1977); and Ramon A. Gutierrez, *When Jesus Came, the Corn Mothers Went Away: Marriage, Sexuality, and Power in New Mexico, 1500–1846* (Stanford, 1991).

rhetoric further complicated the Euro-American claim to a middle ground between venal Europeans and savage Indians by depicting American Indians as noble savages, virile fighters for liberty, free from corruptions of luxury and commercial dependency—in short, as virtuous republicans. How could America's Sons of Liberty, fighters against European tyranny and corruption, deny their brotherhood with this son of nature—especially since white Americans' formal treaty language incorporated the red American trope that all the inhabitants "of this great island" were "children of a common mother"?[47]

The difficulty with which urban magazine editors denied such brotherhood paralleled their rhetorical ambivalence toward the productive African American. Advocating ruthless expansion into western lands one moment and at the next depicting the holders of those lands as noble republicans, the new nation's political magazines continued to muddy the discursive picture, fusing and thus confusing the identities of "the children of a common mother," inscribing the tense balance of rejection and desire that characterized the subject/other relation. "The[ir] laws . . . in point of reason and equity, stand on a footing with those of most civilized nations," Noah Webster's *American Magazine* told its readers one month, "in point of execution and observance, their administration would do honor to any government." Another issue predicted a golden age "where the tawny natives of America and the descendants of those who fled hither from the old world shall forget their animosities." Yet at the same time, Webster insisted that American Indians were too savage to construct complex fortifications and were superstitious devil worshippers. During these same years, Webster and other magazine editors could condemn whites for murdering American Indian women and children in one essay and in another praise just such attacks. In a single essay, the editorial "we" could inscribe the sameness of "the children of a common mother" (when defending against the attacks on American nature by Georges Louis Leclerc, comte de Buffon) and a paragraph later, disassociate Euro-Americans, as men of science, from superstitious and tawny "natives."[48]

---

[47] I am indebted to Richard White for calling this rhetorical convention to my attention. On Euro-American representations of American Indians, see, for example, Richard Slotkin, *Regeneration through Violence: The Mythology of the American Frontier, 1600–1860* (Middletown, 1973), Ch. 8–11; James Axtell, *The Invasion Within: The Contest of Cultures in Colonial North America* (New York, 1985); and Robert Berkhofer, Jr., *Salvation and the Savage: An Analysis of Protestant Missions and American Indian Response, 1787–1862* (Lexington, Ky., 1965).

[48] For favorable views of Indians, see "Morality," *American Magazine,* 1 (July 1788), 526–30; and Thomas Dawes, jun. Esq., "Part of an Oration, delivered at Boston, on the 4th of July, 1787," *ibid.* (Aug. 1788), 619–23, esp. 620. The first essayist (perhaps the *American Magazine's* editor, Noah Webster) used American Indians' love of liberty to condemn southern and West Indian slaveholders, and the Indians' reputation for relentless honesty to criticize the corrupt values of the commercial North. In another essay, Webster made Pocahontas (who, he stressed, was a Christianized Indian maiden married to an American planter) a symbol of Euro-American innocence victimized by British imperialism. "A Letter from Capt. John Smith to the Queen," *ibid.* (Oct. 1788), 776–78. For unfavorable views of Indians, see Noah Webster, "Antiquity. Copy of a letter from Mr. Webster, to the Rev. D. Stiles, President of Yale College, dated Philadelphia, October 22, 1787," *ibid.* (Dec. 1787), 15–16. The debate that this letter began continued throughout the run of the magazine (one year). Ezra Stiles steadily refuted Webster's obsessively repeated argument that only white men could have constructed the elaborate structures and fortifications in pre-Columbian America. See also Noah Webster, "Education," *ibid.,* 22–26; "Curiosities," *ibid.,* 49–52; "History. Smith's History of Virginia," *ibid.* (July 1788), 537–41, esp. 537. On whites' attacking Indians,

Such rhetorical ambivalence hindered efforts to legitimate the new nation's physical possession of America's land. Only if white Americans were the true Americans and American Indians inhuman outcasts could white Americans justify their seizure of the name American and their exercise of political suzerainty. Nor was landownership an abstract issue in the 1780s, as revolutionary veterans demanded land promised them as payment for military service. Drawing upon the military crises in the Ohio Valley and on the Pennsylvania frontier in the 1780s, American expansionists constructed a series of military and captivity narratives that represented the American Indians' inhumanity and incivility. Yet even these military and captivity narratives, which the Philadelphia publisher, Mathew Carey, published in large numbers in the 1780s and 1790s, were unable to completely repress the new "Americans'" ambivalence toward and identification with the old Americans.[49] On the pages of the new political magazines, self and other continued to fuse with and confuse one another.

One magazine story makes this quite explicit. It reported the response of a western Pennsylvania community on finding two American Indians near a white farmer's field. Fearful of "marauding Indians," the story explains, an elderly white farmer had moved his family to the protection of a local fort. No American Indians having been reported one day, he sent his sons out to farm and, at noon, went to join them. No sooner had the farmer come to his fields, however, than he spied two American Indians. The farmer began to run, the Indians to chase him. Finding flight impossible, the farmer turned, shot one of the Indians, and grappling with the other, gouged out his eye, bit off his ear, and drove a knife deep into his stomach. The farmer then ran for help. Neighboring farmers found the injured man hiding in a tree. "'How do do broder, how do do broder?'" the American Indian called down to them. "Alas, poor savage," the narrator reported, "their brotherhood to him extended only to tomahawking, scalping, and, to gratify some peculiar feelings of their own, skinning them both; and they have their skins now in preparation for drum heads."[50]

Sex and gender color this narrative. The elderly farmer appears at first more like the protagonist of a classic captivity narrative (typically a white woman forced to witness the murder of her children) than an archetypal republican political hero, forceful and daring. Like a woman, the farmer hid himself in the enclosed space of the fort, sending his sons out as proxies. Having seen American Indians, he did

see "Eloquence of the Natives of this Country, from Mr. Jefferson's Notes on Virginia, with notes by N. W.," *ibid.* (Jan. 1788), 106–8; "American Intelligence," *ibid.* (July 1788), 598–602; "An Essay on the Advantages of Trade and Commerce," *American Museum*, 2 (Oct. 1787), 328–30; and "Remarkable encounter of a white man with two Indians. In a letter to a gentleman of Philadelphia," *ibid.* (July 1787), 79–80. [Thomas Jefferson], "Comparative view of the Animals of America and those of Europe,— being a Refutation of Mr. Buffon's Assertion. . . . ," *Columbian Magazine*, 2 (April 1787), 366–69.

[49] For one such collection published by Mathew Carey, see *Affecting History of the Dreadful Distresses of Frederic Manheim's Family. To which are added, the Sufferings of John Corbly's Family. An Encounter between a White Man and Two Savages. . . .* (Philadelphia, 1794). See also "Review of New Publications," *American Magazine*, 1 (Oct. 1788), 799–804.

[50] "Remarkable encounter of a white man with two Indians," 79–80.

not run to protect his sons but rather, through flight, abandoned them. But at the moment of combat the narrative's implicit engendering reverses. Now it is the elderly farmer, become brave, who penetrates the American Indian; the Indian, like a woman, who is penetrated. In a final conflation of subjectivities, the white farmers, having rejected the American Indian's pleas for brotherhood, enact the savage behavior white narratives traditionally associated with savage American Indians — a savage brotherhood the narrator foregrounded with his ambivalent discussion of white necrophilia. As they had with African Americans, urban (and urbane?) editors sought through racism to embody the illusive differences that would distinguish white American from red as the true American, the legitimate possessor of America's lands.[51]

In ironic tension with this tale, they made the American Indian's savagery his identifying sign. Significantly, it is one of Philadelphia's leading republican patriots, physician and scientist Benjamin Rush, famed for his sympathetic interest in white women and African Americans, whom we associate with one of the most extreme examples of such racism. Perhaps reacting to violence along the Pennsylvania frontier, perhaps in response to veterans' demands, Rush refused American Indians even the qualified humanity Jefferson, Franklin, and other republicans had earlier granted them. In an essay entitled "An Account of the Vices peculiar to the Savages of North America," Rush denounced "the European fashion" "to celebrate the virtues of the savages of America." They were inhuman, he argued, beasts of the field — not rational political subjects. To support his argument, he presented as their "natural history" a list of their principal vices, almost all of which foregrounded their body and sexuality and which began with two words that were most commonly used to connote female sexual impurity. These were "UNCLEANNESS" (by which he meant bestiality) and "NASTINESS" (which the *OED* defines as "foulness of person . . . moral foulness or impurity, . . . obscenity"). The list ended by again reversing gender. Having implicitly conflated American Indians' and women's sexual impurities, Rush then attacked American Indians for debasing their own women. "The infamy of the Indian character," Rush concluded, "is completed by the low rank to which they degrade their women." Completely misreading American Indian culture and gender parity, Rush (and many others) translated American Indian women's ownership of land and control of the means of agricultural production as sign, not of their empowerment, but of their debasement and exploitation.[52]

---

[51] A satire on British imperialism presented African Americans as black cattle, valuable for their "Offal" and American Indians as "wild beasts," whose uncontrollable desire for "molasses" (liquor) led them to perform debasing "tricks" for bemused and sadistic whites. "The Foresters. An American Tale, being a Sequel to the History of John Bull, the Clothier," *Columbian Magazine*, 1–2 (1787, 1788), *passim*. Other essays represented American Indians as inferior to beavers. See "The Force of Instinct exemplified in the Natural History of the Beaver," *American Magazine*, 1 (Aug. 1788), 653–57. Note also the repeated deployment of the term "natural history" in essays debasing American Indians.

[52] [Benjamin Rush], "An Account of the Vices peculiar to the Savages of North America," *Columbian Magazine*, 1 (Sept. 1786), 9–11. For typical condemnations of American Indians as savage torturers and molesters of women, see "The Narrative of Capt. Isaac Steward," in *Affecting History of the Dreadful Distresses of Frederic Manheim's Family;* and "Thoughts on the present Situation of Public Affairs," *American Museum*, 1 (April 1787), 306–10. *The Oxford English Dictionary*, 2d ed., s.v. "nastiness."

The Arrival of Vespucci in the New World, an engraving by Theodore Galle (c. 1600).

Rush's concluding evocation of women points to a last and perhaps most telling complication in the displacement of the American Indian as representative American and as emblem of the new continent. It underscores the role the construction of gender played in colonialism and in the construction of race.

The American republican, the Son of Liberty, the frontiersman, the empire builder obviously had to be male. Carey's dedication of the first volume of the *Columbian Magazine* to the marquis de Lafayette, the glorification of Washington, the endless articles celebrating America's military heroes and Founding Fathers confirmed the American republican subject in his masculinity. Formal iconographic tradition, on the other hand, represented nations as women. European iconography, in particular, represented America as a naked Indian woman.[53] How could Amer-

---

[53] On the origins and development of this tradition, see Bernadette Bucher, *Icon and Conquest: A Structural Analysis of the Illustrations of de Bry's Great Voyages,* trans. Basia Miller Gulati (Chicago, 1981); Hugh Honour, *The New Golden Land: European Images of America from the Discoveries to the Present Time* (New York, 1975); Peter Hulme, "Polytropic Man: Tropes of Sexuality and Mobility in Early Colonial Discourse," in *Europe and Its Others: Proceedings of the Essex Conference on the Sociology of Literature, July, 1984,* ed. Francis Barker et al. (2 vols., Colchester, 1985); E. McClung Fleming, "The American Image as Indian Princess, 1765–1783," *Winterthur Portfolio,* 2 (1965), 65–81; Clare Le Corbeiller, "Miss America and Her Sisters: Personifications of the Four Parts of the World," *Metropolitan Museum Bulletin,* 19/20 (1960), 209–23; Gary B. Nash, "The Image of the Indian in the Southern Colonial Mind," *William and Mary Quarterly,* 29 (April 1972), 197–230.

ican men respond? As Linda Kerber has so tellingly argued, they made Columbia, demurely garbed, the ideal republican mother surrounded by her unmistakably white children, the emblem of the new nation.[54] As a representation of America, Columbia with Minerva or Columbia with Clio brought far fewer contradictions to the foreground than William Blake's famous and enticing Europe surrounded by America and Africa.

But did she? Given men's problematic representation of women and of the feminine, even Columbia evoked too many discursive conflicts and ideological anxieties. Indeed, the male engravers employed by America's nascent press complicated the iconographic representation of America in ways that went far beyond what even the generic use of feminine icons entailed. To demonstrate my point let us look at the first two volumes of the fashionable new journal, the *Columbian Magazine and Monthly Miscellany*. The editors of the *Columbian Magazine* inaugurated their first issue with a frontispiece of the magazine's namesake, Columbia, blessed by Minerva, representing a victorious American republic. Mature women dominate this engraving. Minerva—arrayed in military garb, her arm resting on a pedestal, holding a staff of office, her other hand stretched forth blessing Columbia and her children—occupies the authoritative and authorizing position. Men are represented only by Columbia's young son, the smallest figure present, and a diminutive farmer far in the background of the picture.

Yet is this engraving quite so transparent? Let us reexamine the two main figure, Columbia and Minerva. They are decidedly women, it is true, but equally decidedly, they are women who refer back clearly and forcefully to men. Columbia is the namesake of an Italian/Spanish navigator, Christopher Columbus; Minerva, motherless, was born from the head of Zeus. Champion of the matricide, Orestes, she spelled the downfall of three female deities, the Furies. Furthermore, is not the diminutive white farmer far in the back of the engraving the fulcrum of the engraving, the center point upon which all else balances? And so we find the engraving transparent only if we see through surfaces to its underlying *pentimenti*. But even then, what is it that we finally see: Male subjects in female drag? Women enacting men? Indeterminate—and divided—subjects?[55]

The frontispiece for the *Columbian Magazine's* second volume reiterated the ambivalence of America's iconographic feminization. Again female figures dominate. Two classically garbed feminine figures occupy the foreground, addressed by a highly androgynous adolescent putto, his front demurely shielded from our view. In the background we see a Greek temple crowned by three guardian female figures: Liberty, Justice, and Peace. Father Time, again quite diminutive and distant, appears the only other male.

But have I described what we are actually looking at? If we read the engraving's subtext, we find that the central figure in the triad before the temple is not a female

---

[54] We are all absolutely indebted to Linda K. Kerber for her formulation of the generative concept of Columbia as the "Mother of the Republic." Kerber's *Women of the Republic* is filled with telling illustrations of just this point.
[55] Cf. Rogin, "Making America Home."

Frontispiece from the *Columbian Magazine and Monthly Miscellany,*
1 (1786). *Courtesy Library Company of Philadelphia.*

after all but "Concord, fair Columbia's son." Why, one asks, did the engraver represent "fair Columbia's son" in such a feminine manner? Neither his dress nor his phy-
sique distinguish him from Clio, kneeling, pen in hand, at his side. His hair is
dressed exactly as hers is; his pelvis is thrust slightly forward, again in a quite feminine manner. But then the editors add still one more layer of confusion. Apparently
they did not feel that the engraving's subtext adequately represented their intention. In an "Address to the Public" that followed the title page, they provided a further gloss. Here "fair Columbia's son" becomes a woman, CONCORD, invited by
the "winged youth" to enter the temple that is the American government. Again,
twice-told tales hold multiple meanings. What ambivalence surrounds the feminine
iconographic representation of the virile and virtuous American Republic!

Frontispiece from the *Columbian Magazine and Monthly Miscellany,*
2 (1787). *Courtesy Library Company of Philadelphia.*

The magazine's editors then counter their obsessive representation of America as Columbia with a host of patriotic male icons. The American eagle, balding and apparently quite male, numerous generals similarly represented, all were called forth to counter the charms of Columbia. But this was not enough. Essay after essay sets the American's two most problematic others—the middle-class white woman and the American Indian warrior—against each other as savage Indians abducted, tortured, and murdered "Columbia" and her children.[56] In this way male publicists

---

[56] See, for example, "Cruelty of Savages," *American Museum,* 1 (April 1787), 329–32; and "Thoughts on the present Situation of Public Affairs," 307.

reduced the fearful woman of sexual, economic, and iconographic power to a mutilated victim while they used women's sexual victimization to prove the savagery and hence the inhumanity of the American Indian.

As she had when rhetorically triangulated with the productive African American, the white woman confirmed the white man's superiority to the negative others who defined and contested his subjectivity. Momentarily, at least, he had subjugated the unruly figures that threatened his coherence. Black, red, and female, they framed him in their discursive embrace.

Discovering Nature in North America

Richard White

Americans are constantly discovering nature, and through it, or so they think, themselves. But what they discover and how they discover it are hardly simple matters. The very concept of nature, as Raymond Williams has argued, "contains, though often unnoticed, an extraordinary amount of human history." We carry that history with us whenever we go discovering. No new land, no new place is ever *terra incognita*. It always arrives to the eye fully stocked with expectations, fears, rumors, desires, and meanings.[1] And even as discoverers claim new knowledge from direct and unmediated experience with nature, history intervenes, filtering and imposing meaning on their experiences in the natural world.

Originally, and in the older scholarship, the annals of discovery posed as the replacement of ignorance with knowledge, but this was too simple. Postmodernists have deconstructed the texts of discoverers as a deployment of various linguistic tropes in which even "substantial bodies: artifacts, animals, plants, ore — Indians" dissolve "into multiple references back into the order of language." But this also is too simple. Discoverers did deploy representations derived from the Old World over the New, but to say so states only the beginning, rather than the end, of a complicated process. Such representations often could not contain the actual plants, animals, and landscapes they pretended to reveal. There was, and remains, a tangible physical world that sometimes affirmed but often mocked the representations designed to constrain it. For all the power of the postmodernist critique, it neglects this physical, tangible world, a world of substantial bodies, and trivializes our experience in it.[2]

Richard White is McClelland Professor of History at the University of Washington. He would like to thank Thomas Hankins and Keith Benson for reading sections of this article. He would also like to thank the other authors in the volume for their help and criticism.

[1] Raymond Williams, *Problems in Materialism and Culture: Selected Essays* (London, 1980), 67. For ancient and early modern European meanings of nature, see Carolyn Merchant, *The Death of Nature: Women, Ecology, and the Scientific Revolution* (San Francisco, 1980), xix.

[2] Mary C. Fuller, "Ralegh's Fugitive Gold: Reference and Deferral in the *Discoverie of Guiana*," *Representations*, 33 (Winter 1991), 47. For Fuller "the material" is but a "catachrestic trope"; see *ibid.*, 62. This issue of *Representations* can serve as an example of postmodern treatments of discovery. I am adopting a concept of experience from Charles Birch and John B. Cobb, Jr., *The Liberation of Life: From the Cell to the Community* (Cambridge, Eng., 1981), 104–5, 131.

Inevitably, because both nature and experience are reduced to language in the texts of discovery, the representations dominate. But because beyond the representations, plants and animals are accessible to direct human experience, the domination of language is tentative, insecure, and always open to challenge. The recognition that "knowledge and meaning are not discoveries, but constructions" has yielded a new reductionism—in John E. Toews's words, "the reduction of experience to the meanings that shape it"—which denies that

> in spite of the relative autonomy of cultural meanings, human subjects still make and remake the worlds of meaning in which they are suspended and . . . these worlds are not creations ex nihilo but responses to, and shapings of, changing worlds of experience ultimately irreducible to the linguistic forms in which they appear.[3]

To analyze the discovery of nature, one must try to resurrect the linguistically irreducible—the plants, the animals, the human experience with them—buried within the narratives of discovery, while denying the conventional pose of the texts of discovery as simply a reflection of the truths of nature as revealed by experience.

Walden, because it is the classic text of self-discovery through nature, can serve as an example of how we might approach such texts and the world and experiences that they claim to represent. Henry David Thoreau, that "self-appointed inspector of snow-storms and rain-storms," presented *Walden* as a wisdom derived from direct experience in the natural world. He ostentatiously stripped himself of the material baggage of his society, but the cultural baggage was less easily discarded. As a result, rarely has so little experience with nature supported so elaborate a representation of nature. Take Thoreau's encounter with a woodchuck, described in the chapter "Higher Laws." It yields one of the looniest and yet most revealing meditations in American nature writing. Thoreau reported that his glimpse of a woodchuck one evening gave him a "thrill of savage delight." The experience produced an immediate temptation to devour the animal raw and prompted his famous declaration that "I love the wild not less than the good."[4]

But love of the wild is only the beginning of the chapter; the woodchuck, and Thoreau's experience, have weightier burdens to bear. The desire to consume raw, wild meat gave way to a belief that preserving the "higher or poetic faculties" required abstaining from animal food and following an internal and more spiritual genius. The woodchuck, not surprisingly, provided insufficient material for this lesson, and Thoreau buttressed his point with quotations from "the Ved" and "Thseng-tseu." The desire to devour the woodchuck raw yielded to a "wonder" that humans can "live this slimy, beastly life, eating and drinking."[5]

The man who at the beginning of the chapter loved the wild now wondered how we can repress the animal—the "reptile and sensual"—within us. Thoreau quoted

---

[3] John E. Toews, "Intellectual History after the Linguistic Turn: The Autonomy of Meaning and the Irreducibility of Experience," *American Historical Review,* 92 (Oct. 1987), 882, 906.

[4] Henry David Thoreau, *Walden; or, Life in the Woods* (Boston, 1929), 232, 233.

[5] *Ibid.,* 237, 240, 241.

Mencius; he quoted the Ved again. "Chastity," he proclaimed, "is the flowering of man." Uncleanliness and sloth are the enemies. "Nature is hard to be overcome, but she must be overcome." We have moved far from the woodchuck (sex unknown) as the male celibate Thoreau struggles to overcome gendered, female, sensual nature. The sentiments and the markers have become conventional, the disgust with the body manifest, revulsion at the human condition pervasive. Whatever the source of all this, these seem unlikely lessons learned from a woodchuck or from Thoreau's experience at Walden Pond. Carrying so heavy a freight of meaning would have crushed a woodchuck like so much road kill.[6]

In the text of *Walden*, Thoreau's "Nature"—historically constituted at a given time as a set of competing meanings—intrudes on and dominates the natural world. Recognizing nature as a shifting historical construct blocks any return to an older view of discovery as simply the progressive replacement of ignorance with knowledge. And this is as true of larger voyages of exploration as of personal journeys such as *Walden*. We are tempted to think that all our old discoveries of nature reduce to texts like *Walden*, where language chases only its own tale, where woodchucks and ponds are fraught with imported meaning and we can glimpse only the meanings.

And yet, in a sense, I can mock Thoreau only through the woodchuck. Because I and tens of thousands of other incredulous readers have both seen woodchucks and read Thoreau, nature speaks back. Precisely because others have access to experiences with woodchucks and ponds, Thoreau's musings are open to contestation. That they are so rarely contested speaks to the continuing cultural power of Thoreau's representation of nature. His account of Walden Pond has so thoroughly shaped our perceptions of the place that we go there not so much to see Walden Pond (for far more interesting ponds are readily available) but to see the meaning of the pond. Thoreau started a conversation that continues, and in that conversation he musters his woodchucks and I muster mine. In all seriousness, woodchucks too have a say.

What we need to maintain are real woodchucks, real encounters—"a glimpse of a woodchuck stealing across my path"—and, if Thoreau can be trusted, real and visceral human reactions. That the cultural baggage Thoreau carried to such encounters shaped them is uncontested, but all such baggage did not necessarily survive all such encounters. Instead, received meanings found themselves up for grabs in a world of experience, competing meanings, and changing physical realities. Meanings changed or persisted in ways that, as Toews has said, cannot be explained by reference to a hermeneutics whose premise is that there is no accessible world beyond meanings.[7]

And we must complicate things still more. As Europeans defined and redefined nature in their heads, they shaped it with their hands. By introducing new species,

---

6 *Ibid.*, 232–46, esp. 243, 244.
7 Toews, "Intellectual History after the Linguistic Turn," 882, 885.

eliminating existing ones, and changing the physical conditions in which life maintained itself, Europeans profoundly changed the natural world of the Western Hemisphere. They altered what they discovered well before they fully learned what was there. Europeans created a series of what Alfred W. Crosby has called Neo-Europes in lands that had once held very different natural communities.[8]

The more deeply we examine the process of discovery, the less it seems either a catalog of facts or a collection of meanings imposed on a malleable nature. Instead the acts classed as discovery seem parts of a protean conversation involving Europeans, and later Euro-Americans, Native Americans (though far more rarely), and nature. The conversation is protean because both the speakers and what they speak of have changed constantly as the conversation has proceeded. Yet it is still a conversation because what is said remains linked to what was said before. Like Thoreau, Americans have defined themselves and their continent in terms of nature while quarreling over what nature contains and what it means. But because nature represents both ideas in human heads and an actual world of plants and animals, changes in the natural world have shaped such meanings, even as changes in meaning have brought changes in the natural world. The conversation is a long and complicated one. What follows is a set of illustrative moments.

Christopher Columbus was both the first creator of Neo-Europes in the Americas and the first European to speak with nature in the Americas and preserve his conversation. The conversation is retained, if only as a palimpsest, in his fascinating and problematic *Diario*. (The *Diario* is not Columbus's journal but Bartolomé de las Casas's summary of the now-lost journal of the first voyage.) Columbus at first conceived of his discovery as a continuation of a known nature, a place where the land and sea would speak to him in the usual ways. Columbus, in effect, entered into a conversation with the unseen Indies while still far out at sea. The natural world gave signs he could decipher. The habits of birds, the flotsam on the ocean formed the locution of the land. But, ironically, either the land misspoke, or Columbus misread the signs. The land was not near.[9]

When Columbus first reached the Indies, it was as if the land spoke a new tongue. Columbus recognized that both human and nonhuman were different from what he knew in Europe, and they excited wonder, but ultimately the *Diario* is a testimony to his ability to absorb and represent the wondrous within accustomed pat-

[8] Alfred W. Crosby, *Ecological Imperialism: The Biological Expansion of Europe, 900–1900* (New York, 1986).

[9] Christopher Columbus, *The Diario of Christopher Columbus's First Voyage to America, 1492–1493*, ed. and trans. Oliver Dunn and James E. Kelley, Jr. (Norman, 1989), 44–45, 50–51, 54–57. On textual problems and interpreting the *Diario* as a historical document, see David Henige, "Text, Context, Intertext: Columbus' *diario de a bordo* as Palimpsest," *Americas,* 46 (July 1989), 17–40. For the view that "Columbus was less an intense observer than an intense reader of signs," see Stephen Greenblatt, *Marvelous Possessions: The Wonder of the New World* (Chicago, 1991), 86. For Columbus's misreading, see Tzvetan Todorov, *The Conquest of America: The Question of the Other,* trans. Richard Howard (New York, 1981), 20.

terns of signs. The subtext of his narrative is the discovery of the familiar within the exotic.[10]

At first he saw "many trees very different from ours." There were "a thousand kinds of plants" of which "nothing was recognized except this aloe." The "fish are so different from ours that it is a marvel," while animals seemed almost entirely absent. This initial disorientation yielded, not dismay, but wonder. "The Admiral says that he never saw such a beautiful thing, full of trees all surrounding the river, beautiful and green and different from ours, each one with its own kind of flowers and fruit."[11]

Yet the Indies, for all the wonder they inspired, for all their original exoticism, became a mirror that reflected a grander version of the European original. The very newness of the nature Columbus saw brought to his mind the corresponding newness of European nature in spring. Difference created analogies, and analogies made the New World familiar. The breezes were as sweet as April in Seville; the groves and vegetation were like April in Andalusia. The perfection of the Indies paralleled the perfect season of Spain. By the time he reached Hispaniola, Columbus saw "very large valleys and farmlands and extremely high mountains all very similar to Castile." Although until then he "had not seen a fish resembling those of Spain," the sailors now fished and caught mullet and sole "and other fish like those of Castile." And he walked among cultivated lands, and nightingales sang, and he saw "other little birds like those of Castile." And he found "myrtle and other trees and plants like those of Castile." He was in a Castile of greater perfection, and he named the island Hispaniola — the Spanish island. Discovery had yielded the familiar. And the familiar was a humanized landscape. Columbus never presented the Indies as a wilderness. In the landscape of Hispaniola, Columbus found the expected marks of humans. Hispaniola was "in appearance all very intensively cultivated."[12]

Columbus expected nature to display the marks of humanity, but he did not expect humanity to display so openly the marks of nature. The Indians went naked. Nudity became the central fact about Indians for Columbus, and nudity became the human expression of nature in the diary. The world *natura,* as used by Columbus, referred not to nature but to human genitalia, which the Indians barely covered or openly displayed. Columbus struggled to place Indian society within parallel European forms, but he repeatedly was dismayed and frustrated by the Indians' nakedness, by their open display of nature/*natura.* He equated clothing with intelligence and intelligence with commerce. He grew more hopeful both about his own prospects and about the Indians' intelligence when he saw women on one island

[10] The *Diario*'s treatment of nature is capable of numerous and contradictory readings. See, for example, Todorov, *Conquest of America,* trans. Howard, 17–23; Antonello Gerbi, *Nature in the New World: From Christopher Columbus to Gonzalo Fernandez de Oviedo,* trans. Jeremy Moyle (Pittsburgh, 1985), 13–25; and Stuart B. Schwartz, *The Iberian, Mediterranean, and Atlantic Traditions in the Formation of Columbus as a Colonizer* (Minneapolis, 1986).

[11] Columbus, *Diario,* ed. and trans. Dunn and Kelley, 89–91, 110–11, 116–17.

[12] *Ibid.,* 54–55, 104–5, 152–55, 172–73, 208–15, esp. 212–13; Gerbi, *Nature in the New World,* trans. Moyle, 18; Greenblatt, *Marvelous Possessions,* 88.

wearing "in front of their bodies a little thing of cotton that scarcely covers their genitals." Columbus reacted to Indian nudity by partially naturalizing Indians in a way that set them off from Europeans. Prepared for a linkage between humans and nature displayed in the body of the land, the landscape, Columbus was disconcerted by a linkage displayed in the human body.[13]

Columbus's *Diario* begins the dialogue with nature, but it is at first in part an interior dialogue because the boundaries between humans and nature are neither clear nor firm. For Columbus, humans were part of an organic nature less because humans were naturalized than because nature was humanized. Nature was not yet "out there," it was not yet "decisively seen as separate from men." Within this view, it was initially impossible to separate the European discovery of nature in the New World from the European discovery of Indian peoples, for two seemingly opposite reasons: first, because Columbus discerned an organic landscape that incorporated both humans and other forms of life; but second, because the Indians' nakedness, their display of their *natura,* associated them with nature in a way that distanced them from Europeans.[14]

The *Diario* contained, some in embryonic form, some nearly full-blown, most of the techniques and problems that confronted later discoverers. It recorded attempts to perceive and comprehend American nature through strategies of difference/similarity and presence/absence. It recorded attempts to find both meaning and commodities.

Initially, the familiar was most amenable to commodification. Antonello Gerbi has pointed out that as Columbus discovered familiar natural objects in the Indies, he commodified them. He

> recognizes . . . noble pines straight as spindles which he can already see sawn into planks for caravels or raised as masts for the largest ships in Spain. The forest becomes a fleet. The virgin timber of the American woods is already raw material, merchandise for the mother country.

Conditioned by his previous experience in the Mediterranean and Atlantic worlds of commerce, Columbus had come to the Indies in search of gold, spices, and slaves. His discovery consisted, in part, of verifying the presence or absence of gold, spices, and slaves.[15]

This search for commodities shaped Columbus's course in the Indies, and it also shaped what he saw. Columbus saw what he wished so ardently to see. He brought back pepper, which was not pepper; cinnamon, which was not cinnamon; aloes, which were not aloes; and ginger, which was not ginger. Columbus's presences translated themselves into absences when they arrived in Europe. But if these were not pepper, cinnamon, aloes, and ginger, then what were they?[16]

---

[13] Columbus, *Diario,* ed. and trans. Dunn and Kelley, 89, 212–13. For Columbus's use of *natura,* see *ibid.,* 453.
[14] Williams, *Problems in Materialism and Culture,* 79; Merchant, *Death of Nature,* 1–41.
[15] Gerbi, *Nature in the New World,* trans. Moyle, 18.
[16] Schwartz, *Iberian, Mediterranean, and Atlantic Traditions,* 14–17; Todorov, *Conquest of America,* trans.

By recording perception and categorization, the *Diario* put its representation of nature at risk against the physical world—part of which Columbus carted back to Europe with him. Columbus's spices that were not spices mocked him; just as, nearly a century later, when the British explorer Martin Frobisher carted back gold that was not gold, the very rocks of the New World mocked him. Nature spoke back.[17]

Delineating the varied and extraordinary interplay between meaning and experience during the centuries immediately following Columbus's voyages involves moving away from the usual American sources. English-speaking peoples initially proved too timid to dominate discovery. They came late and hugged the coasts while the Spanish and the French ventured inland. They were also intellectually backward in their attempts to comprehend the nature of the New World. Like all Europeans, they traveled to the countries of other people and called their travels discoveries, but they usually arrived on the long-distant heels of other Europeans. Not only in the Americas in general but also in the present confines of the United States, the Spanish and the French were the first Europeans to discover an American nature.[18]

The cosmography the first Europeans carried in their heads when they reached the Western Hemisphere combined the known natural world of Europe and an array of fantastic creatures recorded in popular tradition and by writers from Pliny to John Mandeville. "This assembly of the fantastic and familiar," as Anthony Pagden has written, "amounted to a belief that the new could always be described by means of some simple and direct analogy with the old." Like Columbus, such explorers established equivalence and then turned equivalence into identity. Although Gonzalo Fernández de Oviedo, the first great chronicler of New World nature, began to distinguish relatively quickly between the New World and the Old, he initially made pumas into lions and jaguars into tigers.[19]

This cosmography encouraged the search for "known" entities, whether monsters and mermaids or gold and silver. In particular, Europeans looked for the presence of known European commodities. But experience in the New World complicated such discoveries. The natural world could speak back; it could also deceive. Simple and direct analogies led discoverers astray. Columbus had not, after all, been able accurately to decide when pepper was pepper or when rhubarb was rhubarb. And the inability to discern created the possibility of purposeful deceptions and oppor-

---

Howard, 8–12; David Beers Quinn, "New Geographical Horizons: Literature," in *First Images of America: The Impact of the New World on the Old,* ed. Fredi Chiappelli (2 vols., Berkeley, 1976), II, 637–38.

[17] On Martin Frobisher and his shipments of gold that were not gold, see Samuel Eliot Morison, *The European Discovery of America: The Northern Voyages* (New York, 1971), 510, 517, 529–31, 544–45.

[18] The phrase on traveling to other people's countries and calling it discovery is borrowed from Raymond Williams, *The City and the Country* (New York, 1973), 120.

[19] Anthony Pagden, *The Fall of Natural Man: The American Indian and the Origins of Comparative Ethnology* (Cambridge, Eng., 1982), 10–12; Gerbi, *Nature in the New World,* trans. Moyle, 280–82, 284. Such a tendency to diminish differences and to assert a common substance and a single species for similar animals was, as Keith Benson pointed out to me, common in the Aristotelian tradition of natural history.

coverers saw often could not be seen by those who followed. Some deceived themselves; others lied; but what is interesting is the pattern of the deceptions and lies. Like the first Spanish explorers, seventeenth-century French and Spanish discoverers sought the familiar and civil, not the exotic and wild.

Perhaps the most important decision Europeans made about American nature in the centuries following Columbus was that they were not part of it, but Indians were. Europeans removed themselves from the natural world and claimed technical mastery over it. They defined Indians as "natural" men, distinct from the "civil" men of Europe. America came to stand for nature, and Indians stood for the natural. An American voyage became by definition a voyage into nature. The humanized landscapes of Columbus did not disappear, but they increasingly receded into the unseen interior of the continent. And even when they encountered obviously human landscapes, Europeans tended to deny that Indians could have created them. The actual Indians encountered and naturalized became inferior to the people who had risen above nature, those who were civil, that is, to Europeans.[23]

The connections Europeans forged between Indians and nature make it hard to distinguish cleanly between the discovery of nature and the discovery of Indians as Europeans advanced into North America. In New Mexico, the techniques of using Old World analogies to establish similarity and difference remained for a time virtually identical to those of Columbus.

> Francisco Vásquez de Coronado named Cíbola "Granada," "because it has some similarity to it." A Piro pueblo was named Sevilleta because it resembled Seville. The trees of New Mexico were "like those of Castile," observed Hernando de Alvarado in 1640. Kivas were "mosques," dark-skinned Indians were "Turks," their bows and arrows "Turkish bows," and their wives "Moorish women."

But in this landscape of European equivalents, the equation of nudity, nature, and savagery marked Indians even more strongly as natural and inferior. So compelling was the linkage that the discoverers of New Mexico disregarded the obvious marks of Indian civility their own senses proclaimed. In 1540, for example, Coronado doubted whether the Zuñi could "have the judgment and intelligence needed to be able to build these houses in the way in which they are built, for most of them are entirely naked." Such assertions—"fantasmatic representation[s] of authoritative certainty in the face of spectacular ignorance"—formed much of the colonial discourse of discovery. By definition, naturalized humans could not have produced a civil society and a human landscape.[24]

---

[23] Tzvetan Todorov makes this formulation, but he points out that Jean-Jacques Rousseau and François René, vicomte de Chateaubriand, usually cited as the major exponents of "natural men" and "le bon sauvage" held much more complicated views. Tzvetan Todorov, *Nous et les autres: La réflexion française sur la diversité humaine* (Paris, 1989), 310–29.

[24] Ramón A. Gutiérrez, *When Jesus Came, the Corn Mothers Went Away: Marriage, Sexuality, and Power in New Mexico, 1500–1846* (Stanford, 1991), 44–45; Greenblatt, *Marvelous Possessions*, 90.

tunities for the tens of thousands of liars and speculators who offered their own versions of the New World.

Experience necessitated markings of difference that extended beyond the creation of analogies. But precise measures of differences require certain standards, certain classificatory schemes. How is something different, and what is it different from? In creating such schemes, the standard continued to be Europe. European chroniclers and discoverers almost universally resorted to comparison: "the observation of generic similarities and specific differences." They discovered an American nature — they delineated the new — by deciding which aspects of nature in the Indies were like European flora, fauna, and land forms and which aspects were different. American nature, like the American language Kenneth Cmiel discusses, took on its particular identity and meaning by being compared to that of Europe.[20]

This move from analogy and equivalence to a demarcation of difference proceeded most rapidly among the Spanish and Italians who dominated the early natural history of the New World. At the end of the sixteenth century, José de Acosta recognized that American nature had its own distinctive characteristics and that reducing American species to European types by analogy was "like calling an egg a chestnut." Europeans recognized difference, wondered at it, but, metaphor and analogy having failed them, lacked a language to describe it. Discoverers resorted to drawing pictures and to transporting specimens back to Europe, where naturalists realized that such new finds represented different forms from those handed down by the ancients and deserved their own place on the *scala naturae*.[21]

The eventual triumph of the systematizers gradually moved the site of discovery of American nature from the New World to the Old. As specimens, representatives of an American nature, accumulated in Europe, they were there systematized into a new framework, a new descriptive system. The project of recognizing and incorporating the exotic had its halting beginnings in the private collections and early cabinets of the seventeenth century, but new systems did not fully triumph until the eighteenth century. Such systematizing, in which the classifier validated what discoverers brought back and revealed its true place and significance in a universal order, eroded the old basis for legitimizing discovery, in which the discoverer bore witness to "the truth of what might otherwise be deemed incredible."[22]

During the seventeenth century, the discoverer who mediated between Europeans and what lay out beyond their sight remained dominant. But what the dis-

---

[20] Gerbi, *Nature in the New World*, trans. Moyle, 8; Kenneth Cmiel, "'A Broad Fluid Language of Democracy': Discovering the American Idiom," *Journal of American History*, 79 (Dec. 1992), 913–36.

[21] Pagden, *Fall of Natural Man*, 10–12. There is a long argument about whether Europeans invented America, most notably between Edmundo O'Gorman, *The Invention of America: An Inquiry into the Historical Nature of the New World and the Meaning of Its History* (Bloomington, 1961); and Gerbi, *Nature in the New World*, trans. Moyle, 7–10. I prefer Gerbi's view. See also Todorov, *Conquest of America*, trans. Howard, 17–19, 23, 247–48, 251; and J. H. Elliott, *The Old World and the New, 1492–1650* (London, 1970), 5, 20–21, 41. I owe information on the reaction of European naturalists to Keith Benson.

[22] On systematizers, see John E. Lesch, "Systematics and the Geometrical Spirit," in *The Quantifying Spirit in the Eighteenth Century*, ed. Tore Frangsmyr, J. L. Heilbron, and Robin E. Rider (Berkeley, 1990), 73–112. Greenblatt, *Marvelous Possessions*, 122.

In denying civility to most Indians whom they actually knew, sixteenth- and seventeenth-century Europeans fixed their eyes on the horizon, hoping to discover the more civil people and the more humanized landscape that must lie beyond. The more they encountered nature, the more they sought civilization. In the European imagination, the continent grew less wild, less natural as one traveled into it.

This discovery of the humanized interior took place in ways that we now dismiss as fraud or delusion, and further experience discredited it. But at the time such discoveries yielded knowledge held to be as reliable as that provided by what we regard as valid expeditions. Those discoveries, though their "knowledge" is now forgotten or discounted, are also important, for they remind us that discovering and forgetting are allied as well as opposite acts.

Although it may seem paradoxical, the discovery of the New World by Europeans has also been an act of forgetting. The discoveries we now commemorate once existed, without particular pride of place, alongside other discoveries since purged from maps and nearly from memories but once validated by witnesses. Mermaids swam in the Caribbean, and giants lived on its islands. Mother María de Jesús followed Coronado across the Plains. The Eokoros, the Essanapes, and Mozeemlek lived alongside the Sioux. Once, the Rio Buenaventura ran beside the Missouri and the Columbia. All these things and more were once discoveries. Ways of knowing change; categories of what can be known emerge and fade. What is "found" and then forgotten has also been part of the shaping of a known place.

Of these now nearly forgotten journeys into the interior, two—the visionary discoveries of Mother María de Jesús and the fabricated discoveries of Louis-Armand de Lom d'Arce, baron de Lahontan—are representative because they touch the mystical and rationalist poles of the seventeenth-century European imagination. Mother María de Jesús de Agreda, a Spanish nun, reported that beginning in 1620 she had been miraculously transported to New Mexico to preach "our holy Catholic faith." The Jumano Indians, who lived on the Great Plains and near the junction of the Conches and the Rio Grande, were actively seeking missionaries in New Mexico. They verified her visits. Shown a picture of another Spanish nun, Luisa de Carrion, they reported: "A woman in similar garb wanders among us over there, always preaching, but her face is not old like this but young." Other Indians, Quiviras and Xapies, followed, and they, too, claimed to have seen Mother María. The Franciscans credited their conversions east of the Rio Grande to her and those west of the river to Mother Luisa. Stories of Mother María extended as far as the Texas coast where Tejas reported as late as 1690 that she had been among them "in times past." Mother María de Jesús herself claimed to have journeyed far beyond the known peoples bordering New Mexico. And for a century or more, her travels had wide credence among the missionaries of New Mexico and Texas. When visited by the Franciscan missionary, Alonso de Benavides, she validated her knowledge by describing to him, as he put it, "all the things in New Mexico as I have seen them myself."[25]

[25] On María de Jesús, see Frederick Fray Alonso de Benavides, *Fray Alonso de Benavides' Revised Memorial of 1634,* ed. and trans. W. Hodge, George P. Hammond, and Agapito Rey (Albuquerque, 1945), n. 136, 95, 316–18.

Mother María described a continent that grew more civil and less wild—more familiar and similar to Europe—as one proceeded. The kingdom of Titlas, "very large and very densely populated," was ruled by a king whose people worked in precious metals. She described her visionary geography "in the most vivid details," and the Franciscans of New Mexico, far from being skeptical, thought, as Benavides wrote, that "it is very probable that in the continued exploration of New Mexico and the conversion of those souls, a kingdom called Tidan will soon be reached. . . . If by chance, the cosmography could be erroneous, it would be helpful to take note of three other kingdoms, called Chillescas, Guismanes, and Aburcos, respectively, which border on the said kingdom of Tidan."[26]

To pair the baron de Lahontan (anti-Catholic, rationalist, male, French, and with years of experience in the North American woods) with Mother María (devout, mystical, female, Spanish, and without any physical experience in North America) may at first seem odd. But Lahontan attached to his actual experiences in the Great Lakes in the late seventeenth century a fabricated journey beyond the Mississippi. What makes this journey surprising is not that it was imagined rather than actually experienced, or that, like similar journeys, it created a mapped landscape that survived for a century or more. Rather, it is odd because Lahontan, the creator in his conversations with the Huron Adario of an archetype of the *bon sauvage,* had his Indians grow progressively less *sauvage,* less "natural," and less Indian as he proceeded up his invented Long River. When he meets the Mozeemlek, he mistakes them for the Spanish: "I could not imagine that they were Savages." There was so much "honor and politeness" in their conversation that he thought he spoke with Europeans. And beyond them lay the Tahuglauk who lived in six noble cities, each surrounded by stone walls, and who made copper axes and cloth.[27]

Neither the Tahuglauk nor the Tidans nor any of the "civil" Indian peoples imagined by Europeans ever appeared. Experience eliminated them, but Europeans replaced civil Indians with a rational nature at the heart of the continent. Except perhaps for the English, clinging to the Atlantic coast, who were the most timid and fearful of the imperial Europeans, there was no heart of darkness beating in the interior of North America. And eventually the English and Anglo-Americans, too, came to imagine a beneficent and abundant female nature, symmetrically and usefully arranged, waiting to be discovered, improved, perfected, and exploited.

By the eighteenth and nineteenth centuries, witnessing was providing an increasingly insufficient basis for discovering nature. The discoverer, once supreme, became no more than an adventurous collector. Representative samples of nature had to be preserved, carried back, cataloged, and later photographed for the museum-based expert. When this was impossible, specially trained and validated witnesses—

---

[26] Benavides, *Benavides Memorial of 1634,* ed. and trans. Hodge, Hammond, and Rey, 142, 96, 93.
[27] Louis-Armand de Lom d'Arce, baron de Lahontan, *New Voyage to North America by the Baron de Lahontan,* ed. Reuben Gold Thwaites (2 vols., Chicago, 1905), II, 193–95, xxxviiii.

scientists and naturalists—had to be transported to the discovery to give testimony. Discoverers had always, of course, tried to carry back some physical evidence of the wonders they had seen, but now they had to do so systematically and to submit them to the rigorous examination of others.

Discovery became less a final achievement and more obviously a constantly repeated process. The range of possible discoveries broadened. Even geographical discovery was no longer accomplished by a single passage. It became refined as, for example, explorers surveyed and measured the same land again and again to find first where boats, then wagons, then trains could or could not go in the American West. But it was, above all, in the discovery of commodified nature and in the search for self-discovery through nature that the possibilities of repeated discoveries in the same place seemed to ramify indefinitely as industrialization proceeded. No single pass over the land could exhaust the possibilities. The number of presences being checked always increased; the absences were always tentative. Very familiar places, very settled places—even Walden Pond—were always open to new discoveries. Exploration had become, in William Goetzmann's words, "a social process of seeking—not necessarily and finally discovering."[28]

Together the demands for a validation beyond witnessing and the widening scope of discovery yielded the two markers of the second great age of explorations: systematization and empiricism. In the eighteenth century, the great systematizers of natural history examined, ordered, and classified the relics of discovery. Building on earlier attempts, they created new frameworks for ordering knowledge of nature, and in doing so they created new standards for proclaiming something a discovery. In animate nature, what counted as a discovery was something new according to the botanical and zoological systems. Those new systems made both the site of discovery and the identity of the discoverer ambiguous. Was the site the point of collection or the laboratory where difference was determined? Was the discoverer the collector or the systematizer, who might never have actually seen American nature?

The new systems also changed what counted as new and, therefore, as a discovery. As specimens of new species from around the world flooded into Europe, Enlightenment systematizers—particularly Linnaeus and Georges Louis Leclerc, comte de Buffon, but also Michel Adanson and Antoine-Laurent de Jussieu—finally abandoned Europe as the ultimate standard for comparison. Although Buffon and the others attacked the Linnaean system as artificial, Linnaeus, like them, sought a natural system of classification based on the study of the entire organism and all variations in nature. Linnaeus rejected earlier systems because in his own examination of nature he "saw her striving against the opinions of the savants." Like Buffon, he sought a single natural system, but both he and Buffon had to settle for the creation of useful systems based on select criteria derived from a relatively small sample of species. Linnaeus classified plants according to their sexual organs since he thought

---

[28] William Goetzmann, *New Lands, New Men: America and the Second Great Age of Discovery* (New York, 1986), 179–81. On commodification, see William Cronon, *Nature's Metropolis: Chicago and the Great West* (New York, 1991), 176, 177.

that the flowers had within themselves the plan of the natural system. Since Europeans had just established that plants reproduced sexually, Linnaeus borrowed from the heavily metaphorical language of European sexuality in proposing his system. In classifying plants Linnaeus differentiated between "public" and "clandestine" marriages, between "legitimate" or "illegitimate" nuptial relationships. Technically, these systems of botanical and zoological classification avoided making European species the standard against which others were measured, but nature did not impose its own system. Nature spoke, but the language of nature was partially the language of European sexuality and gender.[29]

The new systems aspired to reflect nature and to be universal, but they were, in fact, ideologically charged.[30] As on one level, they moved away from a definition of New World nature based simply on its similarity to or difference from Old World nature, on another level, they repeated the old comparisons. Above all, the comte de Buffon thought his systematic study of nature revealed the inferiority of the New World to the Old. He explicitly answered the question that the older comparisons only implicitly asked: Which was better, the New World or the Old?

Buffon argued that the New World was quite literally new. Having more recently risen from the waters than the Old World, North America was wet, cold, and miasmal. Nature "had not had time to carry out all her plans." Those species native to it were smaller in size, and many American species were not distinct at all, but rather degenerate forms of European types. Nature deteriorated in the Western Hemisphere. Buffon was optimistic about America in the long run: the climate would evolve toward European norms, and species would conform to their ideal type, but the short-term outlook was not good. And not all Buffon's disciples were so sanguine. Cornelius de Pauw extended Buffon's arguments to humans, native and immigrant, making a case for American degeneration and inferiority.[31]

American naturalists shared the desire of Buffon and other French naturalists for a natural system, but they could not accept his judgment of a degenerate American nature. With the birth of the American republic, issues of the inferiority or superiority of American nature became particularly significant both ideologically and politically. Like the discovery of an American subject and the discovery/invention of an American language, the discovery of an American nature now bore the burden of validating the republican experiment and supporting the possibility of infinite human progress.[32]

---

[29] On systematics, see Lesch, "Systematics and the Geometrical Spirit," 73–112. On the natural system, see Paul L. Farber, "Buffon and the Concept of Species," *Journal of the History of Biology,* 5 (Fall 1972), 261; Sten Lindroth, "The Two Faces of Linnaeus," in *Linnaeus: The Man and His Work,* ed. Tore Frangsmyr (Berkeley, 1983), 21; and Charlotte M. Porter, *The Eagle's Nest: Natural History and American Ideas, 1812–1842* (University, Ala., 1986), 2–17.

[30] Such systems privileged numerical and spatial qualities of their objects and the visual sense, and systematizers who went abroad usually served imperial interests. See Lesch, "Systematics and the Geometrical Spirit," 77, 79. Gerbi, *Nature in the New World,* trans. Moyle, 3–8.

[31] For Buffon and species, see Farber, "Buffon and the Concept of Species," 259–84. For Buffon and the American discovery of nature, see Porter, *Eagle's Nest,* 16–25; and Goetzmann, *New Lands, New Men,* 62–64.

[32] For French advocates of natural classification and ultimate parallels with Linnaeus, see Lesch, "Systematics and

In the late eighteenth and early nineteenth centuries, as Charlotte M. Porter has shown, the refutation of Buffon formed the intellectual heart of the American discovery of nature. In the midst of a search for a natural order, comparisons with Europe reasserted themselves. Thomas Jefferson himself set the agenda in his *Notes on the State of Virginia;* American naturalists eagerly followed it; and the Great Captains, Meriwether Lewis and William Clark, were part of the campaign. American naturalists sought to demonstrate both an abundance of American species (to refute Buffon's claim that the number of such species was quite limited) and large animals (to refute Buffon's claim that the American fauna consisted of degenerate, and thus smaller, forms than their European counterparts). The American West, as made known by expeditions of discovery, provided a particular cornucopia of new species. American naturalists realized, however, that the refutation of Buffon provided only a Pyrrhic victory, for they had reverted to measuring American nature against European standards. In 1808 Alexander Wilson, in the first volume of his *American Ornithology,* twitted Buffon while urging naturalists to go beyond hemispheric comparisons.

> This eternal reference of every animal of the new world to that of the old, if adopted to the extent of this writer Buffon, with all the transmutations it is supposed to have produced, would leave us in doubt whether even the Ka-te-dids of America were not originally Nightingales of the old world degenerated by the inferiority of the food and climate of this upstart continent. . . . Let us examine better into the operations of nature, and many of our mistaken opinions, and groundless prejudices will be abandoned for a more just, enlarged, and humane mode of thinking.[33]

The refutation of Buffon ceased to be a matter of much concern after 1815, but Wilson's belief that greater knowledge of nature could cure mistaken opinions and groundless prejudices enunciated a deeper sense that nature itself could supply not only order but also meaning. In their discontent with the "fog of technicalities thrown on [nature] by the Linnaean school," American naturalists ironically echoed Buffon himself as well as English naturalists. All searched for a "natural" system of classification that would be the "uncontaminated gift of Nature."[34]

The American naturalists who sought a natural system proved remarkably immune to seeking one, as they logically might have, among the "natural men"—the Indians. What Indian peoples had discovered about nature outside of favored routes or sources of water and game remained of minor interest to Europeans. John Brad-

---

the Geometrical Spirit," 79–81. See Cmiel, "'A Broad Fluid Language of Democracy'"; and Carroll Smith-Rosenberg, "Dis-Covering the Subject of 'The Great Constitutional Discussion,' 1786–1789," *Journal of American History,* 79 (Dec. 1992), 841–73.

[33] For Alexander Wilson's statement, see Porter, *Eagle's Nest,* 50. On new species, see *ibid.,* 35–39, 49, 76; on new systems, *ibid.,* 75, 94. The irony is that Buffon shared the desire for a natural system. See Farber, "Buffon and the Concept of Species," 261–62.

[34] Porter, *Eagle's Nest,* 34, 61–62.

bury, who accompanied the overland expedition of the Pacific Fur Company part way up the Missouri in 1810, found the Omahas very interested in his plant collecting. They asked, in French, if the plants were for food or medicine. When Bradbury replied that they were for medicine, the women, calling him Wakendaga, asked him into their lodges. He refused but allowed them to examine his collected specimens, "for all of which I found they had names." When, later, others collected such names, they did so as part of a study of Indians, not of plants. At the turn of the century, Melvin Randolph Gilmore recognized among the Indian peoples of the Missouri River "the beginning of taxonomy" and a "faint sense of the relationship of species to species." His informants show "the incipiency of phytogeography, plant ecology, and morphology." But this was only, he decided, aborted discovery, "the beginnings of a system of natural science which never came to maturity."[35]

Like Thoreau, American naturalists did succeed in discovering order and meaning in nature, but they predictably did so largely on the level of ideology. From the late eighteenth century, through the nineteenth and early twentieth centuries, Euro-American naturalists, explorers, scientists, and ideologues found that nature reflected the current condition of the Republic. To the great American naturalist, William Bartram, nature was, in Charlotte Porter's words, "a beautiful, vulnerable state in which democracy finds precedent in the relationships of plants and animals." American nature taught American republicanism; its exhibition in Charles Willson Peale's famous Philadelphia Museum demonstrated "self-sufficiency and egalitarianism." And as the century progressed, Americans found a Paris-based natural history less congenial than a natural history that stressed natural theology. Asa Gray and John Torrey sought to read nature in a way that reconciled the seeming divergence of accounts offered by Christianity and natural science. They described nature in a language religious Americans could read. By the late nineteenth century, William Graham Sumner read capitalism and a more sanguinary progress in Darwinian nature. In the twentieth century, Frederic Clements had the Great Plains and an ecological nature preaching community and cooperation.[36]

These ideological constructs arose alongside a process of discovery that was being transformed by an increasingly inclusive empiricism. Part of this empiricism sprang from the old commodification of the natural world—the translation of trees into lumber, mountains into ore, grass into hay. The more nature was commodified, the

[35] John Bradbury, *Travels in the Interior of America in the Years, 1809, 1810 and 1811. . . .* in *Early Western Travels, 1748–1846,* ed. Reuben Gold Thwaites (32 vols., Cleveland, 1904–1907), V, 88–89. Bradbury thought Wakendaga meant physician but the Omaha word wakandagi means "something supernatural." They may have been equating him more with a priest than a doctor; these were quite separate statuses among the horticultural tribes of the Missouri. See Melvin Randolph Gilmore, *Uses of Plants by the Indians of the Missouri River Region: Thirty-Third Annual Report of the Bureau of American Ethnology, 1911–1912* (Washington, 1919), 54–55, 137–38.

[36] Porter, *Eagle's Nest,* 5, 7, 51, 155–56; Ronald C. Tobey, *Saving the Prairies: The Life Cycle of the Founding School of American Plant Ecology, 1895–1955* (Berkeley, 1981), 208–9; Richard Hofstadter, *Social Darwinism in American Thought* (Boston, 1955). Here, as elsewhere in this section, I owe much to Keith Benson.

more resources existed, and the more discoveries there were to make. The same ground could be gone over again and again with new eyes looking for new things.[37]

But the new empiricism went well beyond the search for furs or gold or water routes to Asia. A more and more broadly defined nature became the object of discovery. And discovery was equated with cataloging what was found. In the eighteenth century, Capt. James Cook and his scientists had as their object "the nature of the soil and the produce thereof; the Animals and Fowls that inhabit or frequent it; the Fishes that are to be found in the Rivers or upon the Coasts," as well as mines, minerals, trees, shrubs, plants, fruits and grains, and human inhabitants. All of these fell within what was seen as a complete cataloging of the earth. It was part of what another explorer, George Vancouver, referred to as "the arduour of the present age . . . to discover and delineate the true geography of the earth." Knowledge for such explorers, as James Ronda has pointed out, was to be a pure artifact of experience.[38]

The proud empiricism of the age remained, of course, part of a larger package. Discovery had become an enterprise of increasing scale and sophistication: the government surveys blended imperialism, economic development, and science into one formidable package. The claim that these expeditions were purely empirical exercises was largely self-deception and thus an easy target for later scholars. The true geography that Vancouver and Cook and Lewis and Clark pursued, for example, was not to be written on a blank slate. The idea of the Northwest Passage, which each in some form sought, had been "conditioned for three centuries by the logical assumptions and teleological positiveness that would not die." Europeans had long believed that something so useful and desirable must exist, but by the eighteenth century they had gone beyond desire and divine beneficence: a rational nature demanded its existence. By "the concept of symmetrical geography," the rivers of the unknown western part of the continent would mirror in form those of the eastern part. This conjectural geography shaped the course of much British and American exploration. But empiricism did invite nature to speak, and nature insisted on talking back. Experience first reduced the passage from an oceanic pathway to an easy portage across a "height of land" between rivers draining into the Atlantic and Pacific and then, eventually, killed it entirely.[39]

Throughout what William Goetzmann has called the second great age of discovery in the nineteenth century, empiricism demanded that Europeans and Euro-Americans quite consciously put their ideological formulations of nature at risk in the physical world. The great exploring expeditions of the late eighteenth and nine-

[37] Goetzmann, *New Lands, New Men*, 179–81.

[38] James Ronda, "'A Knowledge of Distant Parts': The Shaping of the Lewis and Clark Expedition," *Montana*, 41 (Autumn 1991), 8–9, 14.

[39] John Logan Allen, *Passage through the Garden: Lewis and Clark and the Image of the American Northwest* (Urbana, 1975), xxi, xxi–xxv, 18, 30, 44. See also Goetzmann, *New Lands, New Men*, 97–108. Clarence King's and John Muir's differing versions of glaciation suggest that once imposed on nature, concepts become at risk. See Michael Smith, *Pacific Visions: California Scientists and the Environment, 1850–1915* (New Haven, 1987), 72–73, 102–3.

teenth centuries yielded a "flood of new specimens, new data, and new information." But they did more. Discovery of nature helped nurture a "world in which
science itself and its basic categories were continually being redefined."[40]

Yet discovery also changed in even a more fundamental way, for it increasingly
took on a temporal dimension. Such a process was in one sense old. For many earlier
discoverers, the Indians, whether as representatives of a golden age before history
or as modern representatives of the barbaric ancestors of the Europeans, had
provided access to the past. Joseph-François Lafitau, in his early eighteenth-century
study of the customs of American Indians, argued that Europeans confronted part
of their own past when they confronted Indians. Buffon, although not an evolu-
tionist, had introduced a temporal dimension into natural history since over time
his species could degenerate from, or improve toward, a fixed ideal type. By the
nineteenth century, geology had become the most clearly temporal science. At the
height of the second great age of discovery, many nineteenth-century explorers had
become time travelers. Discoverers traveled in the present, but they saw the past.
The exploration of American nature had also become an exploration of the past.[41]

But time—history as it were—proved subversive. It began to unravel the very systematics that had helped bring time to the forefront of discovery. The ultimate ambition of systematics was to detail a natural order that would reveal the order of creation. Such an order would reveal essences, and essences do not change. Systematics
produced extensive efforts at cataloging, among them Charles Darwin's voyage on
the *Beagle*. The "discoveries" of Darwin eventually helped to topple the ideological
formulations of the systematic classifying that had spawned Darwin's research.

In undermining the old systematics, Darwin also unintentionally helped re-
invigorate the older role of the discoverer. Simultaneously collector and scientist,
Darwin was both a man who directly experienced the natural world being discovered
and a man who made a great discovery. As in anthropology and other disciplines,
observation and interpretation became reunited in the natural sciences during the
twentieth century. Experience, though less than earlier, once more became a validation of interpretation. In the late twentieth century, in the exploration of smaller
and smaller components of nature and in travel beyond the planet, the relation between experience and interpretation became more ambiguous. How an observer
could experience a subatomic world was not clear, and when they travel outside the
planet, explorers seem to become mere collectors once more.

The discovery of nature, including an American nature, still goes on, but with
several ironic twists. Our capacity to alter has outrun our capacity to discover. Losing

[40] Goetzmann, *New Lands, New Men*, 1–2; Robert M. Young, *Darwin's Metaphor: Nature's Place in Victorian Culture* (Cambridge, Eng., 1985), 79–125.

[41] I would like to thank Thomas Hankins for his help on this section of the paper, especially for help in clarifying the role of Buffon. On the golden age, see Gerbi, *Nature in the New World*, trans. Moyle, 30, 53–55. For the classic comparison of Indians with ancients, see Joseph-François Lafitau, *Customs of the American Indians Compared with the Customs of Primitive Times*, ed. and trans. William Fenton and Elizabeth Moore (2 vols., Toronto, 1974–1977).

nature, not finding it, has become our central concern. As a result, like Lahontan or María de Jesús, we let our imaginations run ahead of us. For us, species die unsaved in the Amazon basin much as the souls that María de Jesús sought died unsaved in the heart of North and South America. We lament that we lose species before we have ever discovered them, and we regret a world of experience that we will no longer have. The difference that astounded and worried Columbus still astounds and worries us, but where he sought to erase difference in nature, we seek to preserve it. He, unintentionally, began a process that erased biological diversity; we, lamenting as we go, accelerate the process. And we, perhaps most peculiarly of all, seem to think that our lamentations make us superior to the discoverers who went before.[42]

---

[42] See, for example, E. O. Wilson, ed., *Biodiversity* (Washington, 1988).

The Tempest in the Wilderness: The Racialization of Savagery

Ronald Takaki

"O brave new world that has such people in't," they heard Miranda exclaim. It was 1611 and London theatergoers were attending the first performance of William Shakespeare's *The Tempest*. In the early seventeenth century, the English were encountering what they viewed as strange inhabitants in new lands. Those experiences determined the meaning of the utterances they heard. A perspicacious few in the audience could have seen that this play was more than a story about how Prospero was sent into exile with his daughter, Miranda, took possession of an island inhabited by Caliban, and redeemed himself by marrying Miranda to the king's son.[1]

Indeed, *The Tempest* can be approached as a fascinating tale about the creation of a new society in America. Seen in that light, the play invites us to view English expansion not only as imperialism but also as a defining moment in the making of an English-American identity based on race. For the first time in the English theater, an Indian character was being presented. What did Shakespeare and his audience know about the native peoples of America, and what choices were they making when they characterized Caliban? Although they saw him as a "savage," did they racialize savagery? Was the play a prologue for America?

The Tempest studied in relationship to its context can help us answer those questions. *Othello* also offers us an opportunity to analyze English racial attitudes, as Winthrop Jordan has demonstrated so brilliantly, but our play is a more important

Ronald Takaki is professor of ethnic studies at the University of California, Berkeley.

I wish to express my appreciation to Frederick E. Hoxie and David Thelen for helping me develop the critical contours of my analysis.

[1] William Shakespeare, *The Tempest*, ed. Louis B. Wright and Virginia A. Lamar (New York, 1971), 81. *The Tempest* has recently been swept into the storm over "political correctness." George Will issued a scathing attack on "left" scholars and their "perverse liberation" of literature, especially their interpretation of *The Tempest* as a reflection of "the imperialist rape of the Third World." Shakespeare specialist Stephen Greenblatt responded: "This is a curious example—since it is very difficult to argue that *The Tempest* is *not* about imperialism." Such an authoritative counterstatement clears the way for a study of the play in relationship to its historical setting. See George Will, "Literary Politics: 'The Tempest'? It's 'really' about imperialism. Emily Dickinson's poetry? Masturbation," *Newsweek*, April 22, 1991, p. 72; and Stephen Greenblatt, "The Best Way to Kill Our Literary Inheritance Is to Turn It into a Decorous Celebration of the New World Order," *Chronicle of Higher Education*, June 12, 1991, pp. B1, B3. As Adam Begley has recently noted, Stanley Fish reminds us that "the circumstances of an utterance determine its meaning." See Adam Begley, "Souped-Up Scholar," *New York Times Magazine*, May 3, 1992, p. 52. The ideas on race and ethnicity presented in this article are further developed in Ronald Takaki, *A Different Mirror: A History of Multi-Cultural America* (Boston, forthcoming).

window for understanding American history, for its story is set in the New World. Moreover, the timing of that first performance of *The Tempest* was crucial: It came after the English invasion of Ireland but before the colonization of New England, after John Smith's arrival in Virginia but before the beginning of the tobacco economy, and after the first contacts with Indians but before full-scale warfare against them. In that historical moment, the English were encountering "other" peoples and delineating the boundary between *civilization* and *savagery.* The social constructions of both those terms were dynamically developing in three sites— Ireland, Virginia, and New England.[2]

One of the places the English were colonizing in 1611 was Ireland, and Caliban seemed to resemble the Irish. Theatergoers were familiar with the "wild Irish" on stage, for such images had been presented in the plays *Sir John Oldcastle* (1599) and *Honest Whore* (1605). Seeking to conquer the Irish in 1395, Richard II had condemned them as "savage Irish, our enemies." In the mid-sixteenth century, the government had decided to bring all of Ireland under its rule, and to that end, it encouraged private colonization projects.[3]

Like Caliban, the Irish were viewed as "savages," a people living outside of "civilization." They had tribal organizations, and their practice of herding seemed nomadic. Even their Christianity was said to be merely the exterior of strongly rooted paganism. "They are all Papists by their profession," claimed Edmund Spenser in 1596, "but in the same so blindly and brutishly informed for the most part as that you would rather think them atheists or infidels." To the English colonists, it seemed that the Irish lacked "knowledge of God or good manners." They had no sense of private property and did not "plant any Gardens or Orchards, Inclose or improve their lands, live together in settled Villages or Townes." The Irish were described as lazy, "naturally" given to "idleness," and unwilling to work for "their own bread." Dominated by "innate sloth," "loose, barbarous and most wicked," and living "like beasts," they were also thought to be criminals, an underclass inclined to steal from the English. The colonists complained that the Irish savages were not satisfied with the "fruit of the natural unlaboured earth" and therefore continually "invaded the fertile possessions" of the "English Pale."[4]

The English colonizers established a two-tiered social structure. According to sixteenth-century English law, "every Irishman shall be forbidden to wear English

[2] Winthrop Jordan, *White over Black: American Attitudes toward the Negro, 1550–1812* (Chapel Hill, 1968), 37–40. *Othello* was first performed in 1604, before the founding of Jamestown. Jordan overlooked the rich possibility of studying *The Tempest.*

[3] Nicholas P. Canny, "The Ideology of English Colonization: From Ireland to America," *William and Mary Quarterly,* 30 (Oct. 1973), 585; David B. Quinn, *The Elizabethans and the Irish* (Ithaca, 1966), 161; Francis Jennings, *The Invasion of America: Indians, Colonialism, and the Cant of Conquest* (New York, 1976), 7. George Frederickson, *White Supremacy: A Comparative Study in American and South African History* (New York, 1971), 13, describes the conquest of Ireland as a "rehearsal."

[4] Canny, "Ideology of English Colonization," 585, 588; Howard Mumford Jones, *O Strange New World: American Culture, the Formative Years* (New York, 1965), 169; Keith Thomas, *Man and the Natural World: A History of the Modern Sensibility* (New York, 1983), 42; Jennings, *Invasion of America,* 46, 49; James Muldoon, "The Indian as Irishman," *Essex Institute Historical Collections,* 111 (Oct. 1975), 269; Quinn, *Elizabethans and the Irish,* 76.

apparel or weapon upon pain of death. That no Irishman, born of Irish race and brought up Irish, shall purchase land, bear office, be chosen of any jury or admitted witness in any real or personal action." To reinforce this social separation, British laws prohibited marriages between the Irish and the colonizers. The new world order was to be one of English over Irish.[5]

The Irish also became targets of English violence. "Nothing but fear and force can teach duty and obedience" to this "rebellious people," the invaders insisted. The sixteenth-century English were generally brutal in waging war, but they seemed to have been particularly cruel toward the Irish. The colonizers burned the villages and crops of the inhabitants and relocated them on reservations. They slaughtered families, "man, woman and child," justifying their atrocities by arguing that families provided support for the rebels. After four years of bloody warfare in Munster, according to Edmund Spenser, the Irish had been reduced to wretchedness. "Out of every corner of the woods and glens they came creeping forth upon their hands, for their legs would not bear them. They looked anatomies of death; they spake like ghosts crying out of their graves." The death toll was so high that "in short space there were none almost left and a most populous and plentiful country suddenly left void of man and beast." The "void" meant vacant lands for English resettlement.[6]

The invaders took the heads of the slain Irish as trophies. Sir Humphrey Gilbert pursued a campaign of terror: He ordered that "the heads of all those . . . killed in the day, should be cut off from their bodies and brought to the place where he encamped at night, and should there be laid on the ground by each side of the way leading into his own tent so that none could come into his tent for any cause but commonly he must pass through a lane of heads. . . . [It brought] great terror to the people when they saw the heads of their dead fathers, brothers, children, kinsfolk, and friends." After seeing the head of his lord impaled on the walls of Dublin, Irish poet Angus O'Daly cried out:

> O body which I see without a head,
> It is the sight of thee which has withered up my strength.
> Divided and impaled in Ath-cliath,
> The learned of Banba will feel its loss.
> Who will relieve the wants of the poor?
> Who will bestow cattle on the learned?
> O body, since thou art without a head,
> It is not life which we care to choose after thee.[7]

The English claimed that they had a God-given responsibility to "inhabit and reform so barbarous a nation" and to educate the Irish "brutes." They would teach

[5] Muldoon, "Indian as Irishman," 284; Quinn, *Elizabethans and the Irish,* 108.

[6] Canny, "Ideology of English Colonization," 593, 582; Jennings, *Invasion of America,* 153; Frederickson, *White Supremacy,* 15; Quinn, *Elizabethans and the Irish,* 132–33.

[7] Canny, "Ideology of English Colonization," 582; Jennings, *Invasion of America,* 168; Quinn, *Elizabethans and the Irish,* 44.

them to obey English laws and to stop "robbing and stealing and killing" one another. They would uplift this "most filthy people, utterly enveloped in vices, most untutored of all peoples in the rudiments of faith." Thus, although they saw the Irish as savages and although they sometimes described this savagery as "natural" and "innate," the English believed that the Irish could be civilized, improved through what Shakespeare called "nurture." In short, the difference between the Irish and the English was a matter of culture.[8]

As their frontier advanced from Ireland to America, the English began making comparisons between the Irish and the Indian "savages" and wondering whether there might be different kinds of "savagery."

The parallels between English expansionism in Ireland and that in America were apparent. Sir Humphrey Gilbert, Lord De La Warr, Sir Francis Drake, and Sir Walter Raleigh—all participated both in invading Ireland and in colonizing the New World. The conquest of Ireland and the settlement of Virginia were bound so closely together that one correspondence, dated March 8, 1610, stated: "It is hoped the plantation of Ireland may shortly be settled. The Lord Delaware [Lord De La Warr] is preparing to depart for the plantation of Virginia." Commander John Mason conducted military campaigns against the Irish before he sailed for New England, where he led troops against the Pequots of Connecticut. Samuel Gorton wrote a letter to John Winthrop, Jr., connecting the two frontiers: "I remember the time of the wars in Ireland (when I was young, in Queen Elizabeth's days of famous memory) where much English blood was spilt by a people much like unto these [Indians]. . . . And after these Irish were subdued by force, what treacherous and bloody massacres have they attempted is well known."[9]

The first English colonizers in the New World found that the Indians reminded them of the Irish. Capt. John Smith observed that the deerskin robes worn by the Indians in Virginia did not differ much "in fashion from the Irish mantels." Thomas Morton noticed that the "natives of New England [were] accustomed to build themselves houses much like the wild Irish." Roger Williams reported that the thick woods and swamps of New England gave refuge to the warring Indians "like the bogs to the wild Irish." Thus, in their early encounters, the English projected the familiar onto the strange, their images of the Irish onto the native people of America. Initially, "savagery" was defined in relationship to the Irish, and Indians were incorporated into this definition.[10]

The Tempest, the London audience knew, was not about Ireland but about the New World, for the reference to the "Bermoothes" (Bermuda) revealed the location of the island. What was happening on stage was a metaphor for English expansion

---

[8] Canny, "Ideology of English Colonization," 588; Jennings, *Invasion of America*, 46, 49; Quinn, *Elizabethans and the Irish*, 76; Shakespeare, *Tempest*, ed. Wright and Lamar, 70.

[9] Quinn, *Elizabethans and the Irish*, 121; William Christie MacLeod, "Celt and Indian: Britain's Old World Frontier in Relation to the New," in *Beyond the Frontier: Social Process and Cultural Change*, ed. Paul Bohannan and Fred Plog (Garden City, 1967), 38–39; Jennings, *Invasion of America*, 312.

[10] Quinn, *Elizabethans and the Irish*, 121; Muldoon, "Indian as Irishman," 270; MacLeod, "Celt and Indian," 26. See also Canny, "Ideology of English Colonization," 576.

into America. The play's title was inspired by a recent incident. Caught in a violent storm in 1609, the *Sea Adventure* had been separated from a fleet of ships bound for Virginia and had run aground in the Bermudas. Shakespeare knew many of the colonizers, including Sir Humphrey Gilbert and Lord De La Warr. One of his personal friends was the geographer Richard Hakluyt, author of widely read books about the New World. The future of Englishmen lay in America, proclaimed Hakluyt, as he urged them to "conquer a country" and "to man it, to plant it, and to keep it, and to continue the making of Wines and Oils able to serve England."[11]

The description of the play's setting evoked the mainland near the "Bermoothes"—Virginia. "The air breathes upon us here most sweetly," the theatergoers were told. "Here is everything advantageous to life." "How lush and lusty the grass looks! how green!" Impressed by the land's innocence, Gonzalo of *The Tempest* depicted it as an ideal commonwealth where everything was as yet unformed and unbounded, where letters, laws, metals, and occupations were yet unknown. Both the imagery and the language revealed America as the site of Prospero's landing: It was almost as if Shakespeare had lifted the material from contemporary documents about the New World. Tracts on Virginia had described the air as "most sweet" and as "virgin and temperate," and its soil as *"lusty"* with meadows "full of *green grass."* In *A True Reportory of the Wracke,* published in 1609, William Strachey depicted Virginia's abundance: "no Country yieldeth goodlier *Corn,* nor more manifold increase . . . we have thousands of goodly *Vines."* Here was an opportunity for colonists to enhance the "fertility and pleasure" of Virginia by "cleansing away her woods" and converting her into "goodly meadow."[12]

Moreover, the play provided a conclusive clue that the story was indeed about America: Caliban, one of the principal characters, was a New World inhabitant. "Carib," the name of an Indian tribe, had come to mean a savage of America, and the term *cannibal* was a derivative. Shakespeare sometimes rearranged letters in words ("Amleth," the name of a prince in a Viking tale, for example, became "Hamlet"), and here he had created another anagram in "Caliban."[13]

The English had seen or read reports about Indians who had been captured and brought to London. Beginning with Christopher Columbus, European visitors to the New World had brought back Indians. Columbus himself had displayed Indians. During his first voyage, he wrote: "Yesterday came [to] the ship a dugout with

[11] Shakespeare, *Tempest,* ed. Wright and Lamar, 13, 81; Frank Kermode, "Introduction," in William Shakespeare, *The Tempest,* ed. Frank Kermode (London, 1969), xxvii; Robert R. Cawley, "Shakespeare's Use of the Voyagers in *The Tempest,"* PMLA, 41 (Sept. 1926), 699–700, 689; Frederickson, *White Supremacy,* 22; Shakespeare, *Tempest,* 13. See also Leo Marx, *The Machine in the Garden: Technology and the Pastoral Ideal in America* (New York, 1964), 34–75.

[12] Shakespeare, *Tempest,* ed. Wright and Lamar, 27–28, 31; Cawley, "Shakespeare's Use of the Voyagers in *The Tempest,"* 702–4; Kirkpatrick Sale, *The Conquest of Paradise: Christopher Columbus and the Columbian Legacy* (New York, 1990), 102. For analysis of America imaged as a woman, see Carolyn Merchant, *Ecological Revolutions: Nature, Gender, and Science in New England* (Chapel Hill, 1989), 101; and Annette Kolodny, *The Lay of the Land: Metaphor as Experience and History in American Life and Letters* (Chapel Hill, 1975).

[13] Shakespeare, *Tempest,* ed. Wright and Lamar, xxxviii; Kermode, "Introduction," xxiv. For the anagram of Hamlet, see dedication to William Shakespeare at Kronborg Castle, Denmark.

six young men, and five came on board; these I ordered to be detained and I am bringing them." When Columbus was received by the Spanish court after his triumphal return, he presented a collection of things he had brought back, including gold nuggets, parrots in cages, and six Indians. On his second voyage, in 1493, Columbus again sent his men to kidnap Indians. On one occasion, a captive had been "wounded seven times and his entrails were hanging out," reported Guillermo Coma of Aragon. "Since it was thought that he could not be cured, he was cast into the sea. But keeping above water and raising one foot, he held on to his intestines with his left hand and swam courageously to the shore . . . . The wounded Carib was caught again on shore. His hands and feet were bound more tightly and he was once again thrown headlong. But this resolute savage swam more furiously, until he was struck several times by arrows and perished." When Columbus set sail with his fleet to return to Spain, he took 550 Indian captives with him. "When we reached the waters around Spain," Michele de Cuneo wrote matter-of-factly, "about 200 of those Indians died, I believe because of the unaccustomed air, colder than theirs. We cast them into the sea."[14]

English explorers also engaged in the practice of kidnapping Indians. When Capt. George Waymouth visited New England in 1605, he lured some Abenakis to his ship; taking three of them hostage, he sailed back to England to display them. An early seventeenth-century pamphlet stated that a voyage to Virginia was expected to bring back its quota of captured Indians: "Thus we shipped five savages, two canoes, with all their bows and arrows." In 1614 the men on one of Capt. John Smith's ships captured several Indians on Cape Cod. "Thomas Hunt," Smith wrote, "betrayed four and twenty of these poor savages aboard this ship, and most dishonestly and inhumanely . . . carried them with him to Maligo [Malaga] and there for a little private gain sold . . . those savages for Rials of eight." In 1611, according to a biographer of William Shakespeare, "a native of New England called Epenew was brought to England . . . and 'being a man of so great a stature' was showed up and down London for money as a monster." In *The Tempest* Stephano considered capturing Caliban: "If I can recover him, and keep him tame, and get to Naples with him, he's a present for any emperor." Such exhibitions of Indians were "profitable investments," literary scholar Frank Kermode noted, and were "a regular feature of colonial policy under James I. The exhibits rarely survived the experience."[15]

To the spectators of these "exhibits," Indians personified "savagery." They were depicted as "cruel, barbarous and most treacherous." They were thought to be cannibals, "being most furious in their rage and merciless . . . not being content only

[14] Samuel Eliot Morison, ed., *Journals and Other Documents on the Life and Voyages of Christopher Columbus* (New York, 1963), 126; Sale, *Conquest of Paradise*, 126; Morison, ed., *Journals and Other Documents*, 238, 226–27.

[15] Kenneth M. Morrison, *The Embattled Northeast: The Elusive Ideal of Alliance in Abenaki-Euramerican Relations* (Berkeley, 1984), 22–23; Leonard A. Adolf, "Squanto's Role in Pilgrim Diplomacy," *Ethnohistory*, 11 (Fall 1964), 247–48; Cawley, "Shakespeare's Use of the Voyagers in *The Tempest*," 720, 721; Shakespeare, *Tempest*, ed. Wright and Lamar, 41, 40; Shakespeare, *Tempest*, ed. Kermode, 62.

Inhabitants of the Americas, as depicted by Laevinus Hulse, in his illustrated transcription of Sir Walter Raleigh's account of Guiana (Frankfurt, 1601).

to kill and take away life, but delight to torment men in the most bloody manner . . . flaying some alive with the shells of fishes, cutting off the members and joints of others by piecemeal and broiling on the coals, eating the collops of their flesh in their sight whilst they live." According to Sir Walter Raleigh, Indians had "their eyes in their shoulders, and their mouths in the middle of their breasts." In *Nova Brittania,* published in 1609, Richard Johnson described the Indians in Virginia as "wild and savage people," living "like herds of deer in a forest." One of their striking physical characteristics was their skin color. John Brereton described the New England Indians as "of tall stature, broad and grim visage, of a blacke swart complexion."[16]

Indians seemed to lack everything the English identified as civilized — Christianity, cities, letters, clothing, and swords. "They do not bear arms or know them, for I showed to them swords and they took them by the blade and cut themselves through ignorance," wrote Columbus in his journal, noting that the Indians did not have iron. George Waymouth tried to impress the Abenakis: He magnetized a sword "to cause them to imagine some great power in us; and for that to love and fear us."[17]

[16] William Bradford, *Of Plymouth Plantation: 1620–1647* (New York, 1967), 26; Frederickson, *White Supremacy,* 11; Roy Harvey Pearce, *Savagism and Civilization: A Study of the Indian and the American Mind* (Baltimore, 1967), 12; Colin G. Calloway, ed., *Dawnland Encounters: Indians and Europeans in Northern New England* (Hanover, 1991), 33.

[17] Shakespeare, *Tempest,* ed. Wright and Lamar, 70; Wilcomb Washburn, ed., *Indian and White Man* (New

Like Caliban, the native people of America were viewed as the other. European culture was delineating the border, the hierarchical division between civilization and wildness. Unlike Europeans, Indians were allegedly dominated by their passions, especially their sexuality. Amerigo Vespucci was struck by how the natives embraced and enjoyed the pleasures of their bodies: "They . . . are libidinous beyond measure, and the women far more than the men. . . . When they had the opportunity of copulating with Christians, urged by excessive lust, they defiled and prostituted themselves." Caliban personified such passions. Prospero saw him as a sexual threat to the nubile Miranda, her "virgin-knot" yet unbroken. "I have used thee (filth as thou art) with humane care," Prospero scolded Caliban, "and lodged thee in mine own cell till thou didst seek to violate the honor of my child." And the unruly native snapped: "O ho, O ho! Would't had been done! Thou didst prevent me; I had peopled else this isle with Calibans."[18]

To the theatergoers, Caliban represented what Europeans had been when they were lower on the scale of development toward civilization. To be civilized, they believed, required denial of wholeness—the repression of the instinctual forces of human nature. Prospero, personification of civilized man, identified himself as mind rather than body. His epistemology relied on the visual rather than the tactile and on the linear knowledge of books rather than the polymorphous knowledge of experience. With the self fragmented, Prospero was able to split off his rationality and raise it to authority over the other—the sensuous part of himself and everything Caliban represented.[19]

But could Caliban, the audience wondered, ever become Christian and civilized? The sixteenth-century Spanish lawyer Juan Gines de Sepulveda had justified the Spanish conquest of Indians by invoking Aristotle's doctrine that some people were "natural slaves." The condition of slavery, Sepulveda argued, was natural for "persons of both inborn rudeness and of inhuman and barbarous customs." Thus what counted was an ascriptive quality based on a group's nature, or "descent."[20]

On the other hand, Pope Paul III had proclaimed that Indians as well as "all other people" who might later be "discovered" by "Christians" should not be deprived of their liberty and property, even though they were outside the Christian faith. Christopher Columbus had reported that Indians were "very gentle and without knowledge of . . . evil." He added: "They love their neighbors as themselves, and have the sweetest talk in the world, and gentle, and always with a smile." In the

---

York, 1964), 4–5; Morrison, *Embattled Northeast,* 22–23. On the significance of the sword, see Riane Eisler, *The Chalice and the Blade: Our History, Our Future* (New York, 1988).

[18] Shakespeare, *Tempest,* ed. Wright and Lamar, 85; Washburn, ed., *Indian and White Man,* 4, 5, 7.

[19] Shakespeare, *Tempest,* ed. Wright and Lamar, 62, 18, 19.

[20] Frederickson, *White Supremacy,* 9. The terms "descent" and "consent" are from Werner Sollors, *Beyond Ethnicity: Consent and Descent in American Culture* (New York, 1986), 6. Sollors minimizes the significance of race, arguing that it is "merely one aspect of ethnicity." Sollors, *Beyond Ethnicity,* 36. I take the opposite position here as well as in Ronald Takaki, "Reflections on Racial Patterns in America," in *From Different Shores: Perspectives on Race and Ethnicity in America,* ed. Ronald Takaki (New York, 1987), 26–38; and Ronald Takaki, *Iron Cages: Race and Culture in Nineteenth-Century America* (New York, 1979).

play, Gonzalo told theatergoers: "I saw such islanders . . . who, though they are of monstrous shape, yet, note, their manners are more gentle, kind, than of our human generation you shall find many—nay, almost any." Thus, Indians were not always viewed as brutish by nature: Already capable of morality and gentleness, they could be acculturated, become civilized through "consent."[21]

Indeed, Caliban seemed educable. Prospero had taught him a European language: "I . . . took pains to make thee speak, taught thee each hour one thing or other. When thou didst not, savage, know thine own meaning, but wouldst gabble like a thing most brutish." Defiantly, the native retorted: "You taught me language, and my profit on't is, I know how to curse. The red plague rid you for learning me your language." A Virginia tract stated that the colonists should take Indian children and "train them up with gentleness, teach them our English tongue." In the contract establishing the Virginia Company in 1606, the king endorsed a plan to propagate the "Christian Religion to such people" who as yet lived in "darkness and miserable ignorance of the true knowledge and worship of God." Three years later, the Virginia Company instructed the governor of the colony to encourage missionaries to convert Indian children. They should be taken from their parents if necessary, since the parents were "so wrapped up in the fog and misery of their iniquity." A Virginia promotional tract stated that it was "not the nature of men, but the education of men" that made them "barbarous and uncivil." Every man in the new colony had a duty to bring the savage Indians to "civil and Christian" government.[22]

In 1611 these cultural constructs of Indians were either the fantasy of Shakespeare or the impressions of policy makers and tract writers in London. What would happen to these images on the stage of history?

The first English settlement in the New World was in Virginia, the home of fourteen thousand Powhatans. An agricultural people, they cultivated corn—the mainstay of their subsistence. Their cleared fields were large—one-hundred-acre fields were not uncommon—and they lived in palisaded towns, with forts, storehouses, temples, and framed houses covered with bark and reed mats. They cooked their foods in ceramic pots and used woven baskets for storing corn; some of their baskets were constructed so skillfully they could carry water in them. The Powhatans had a sophisticated numbering system for evaluating their harvests. According to John Smith, they had numbers from one to ten, after which counting was done by tens to one hundred. There was a word for "one thousand." The Powhatan calendar had five seasons: "Their winter some call *Popanow,* the spring *Cattaapeuk,* the sommer *Cohattayough,* the earing of their Corne *Nepinough,* the harvest and fall of the leafe *Taquitock.* From September until the midst of November are the chief Feasts and sacrifice."[23]

[21] Sollors, *Beyond Ethnicity,* 36–37; Frederickson, *White Supremacy,* 8; Morison, ed., *Journals and Other Documents,* 92, 136; Shakespeare, *Tempest,* ed. Wright and Lamar, 57.
[22] Shakespeare, *Tempest,* ed. Wright and Lamar, 19; Cawley, "Shakespeare's Use of the Voyagers in *The Tempest,*" 715; Frederickson, *White Supremacy,* 12; Pearce, *Savagism and Civilization,* 9, 10.
[23] James Axtell, *After Columbus: Essays in the Ethnohistory of Colonial North America* (New York, 1988), 190;

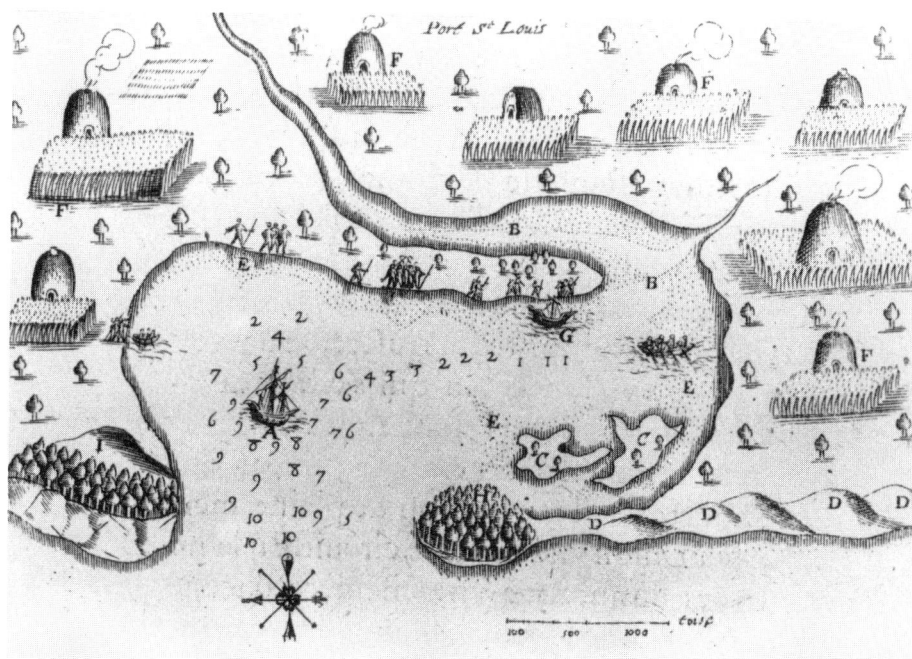

Samuel de Champlain's map of Wampanoag villages on Cape Cod. He wrote, "All along the shore [there was] a great deal of land cleared up and planted with Indian corn."
Des Sauvages: ou Voyage de Samuel de Champlain de Brouage faict en la France Nouvelle (Paris, 1604).

In Virginia the initial encounters between the English and the Indians opened possibilities for friendship and interdependency. The first colonists arrived and set up camp in 1607. There were 120 of them. Then, John Smith reported, came "the starving time." A year later, only 38 still lived, hanging precariously on the very edge of survival. The New World had been depicted as a garden; the reality of America was something else. Descriptions of its natural abundance turned out to have been exaggerated. Many of the English were not prepared for survival in the wilderness. "Now was all our provision spent . . . all help abandoned, each hour expecting the fury of the savages," Smith wrote. Fortunately, in that "desperate extremity," the Powhatans brought food to the starving strangers.[24]

A year later, several hundred more colonists arrived; again they quickly ran out of provisions. They were forced to eat "dogs, cats, rats, and mice," even "corpses" dug from graves. "Some have licked up the blood which hath fallen from their weak

Helen C. Rountree, *The Powhatan Indians of Virginia: Their Traditional Culture* (Norman, 1990), 44, 45, 46, 49, 60, 63.
[24] Mortimer J. Adler, ed., *Annals of America,* vol. I: *Discovering a New World* (Chicago, 1968), 21, 26, 22.

fellows," a survivor reported. "One [member] of our colony murdered his wife, ripped the child out of her womb and threw it into the river, and after chopped the mother in pieces and salted her for his food, the same not being discovered before he had eaten part thereof." "So great was our famine," John smith stated, "that a savage we slew and buried, the poorer sort took him up again and ate him; and so did diverse one another boiled and stewed with roots and herbs."[25]

Hostilities soon broke out as the English tried to extort food supplies by attacking the Indians and destroying their villages. In 1608 an Indian declared: "We hear you are come from under the World to take our World from us." A year later Gov. Thomas Gates arrived in Virginia with instructions that the Indians should be forced to labor for the colonists and also make annual payments of corn and skins. The orders were brutally carried out. During one of the raids, the English soldiers attacked an Indian town, killing fifteen people and forcing many others to flee. Then they burned the houses and destroyed the cornfields. According to a report by Commander George Percy, they marched the captured queen and her children to the river where they "put the Children to death . . . by throwing them overboard and shooting out their brains in the water."[26]

Indians began to doubt that the two peoples could live together in peace. One young Indian told Capt. John Smith: "[We] are here to intreat and desire your friendship and to enjoy our houses and plant our fields, of whose fruits you shall participate." But he did not trust the strangers: "We perceive and well know you intend to destroy us." Chief Powhatan had come to the same conclusion; he told Smith that the English were not in Virginia to trade but to "invade" and "possess" Indian lands.[27]

Indeed, Smith and his fellow colonists were encouraged by their culture of expansionism to claim entitlement to the land. In *The Tempest* the theatergoers were told by Sebastian: "I think he [the king of Naples] will carry this island home in his pocket and give it his son for an apple." Prospero declared that he had been thrust forth from Milan and "most strangely" landed on this shore "to be the lord on't." Projecting his personal plans and dreams onto the wilderness, he colonized the island and dispossessed Caliban. Feeling robbed, Caliban protested: "As I told thee before, I am subject to a tyrant, a sorcerer, that by his cunning hath cheated me of the island." But the English did not see their taking of the land as robbery. In *Utopia* (1516), written almost one hundred years before English colonization of America began in earnest, Sir Thomas More had provided a rationale for the appropriation of Indian lands: Since the natives did not "use" the soil but left it "idle and waste," the English had "just cause" to drive them from the territory by force. In 1609 Robert Gray declared that "the greater part" of the earth was "possessed

[25] Gary Nash, *Red, White, and Black: The Peoples of Early America* (Englewood Cliffs, 1974), 58; Adler, ed., *Annals of America*, I, 26.

[26] Cotton Mather, *Magnalia Christi Americana*, books I and II (Cambridge, 1977), 116; Frederickson, *White Supremacy*, 24; Sale, *Conquest of Paradise*, 277.

[27] Jennings, *Invasion of America*, 66; Nash, *Red, White, and Black*, 57.

and wrongfully usurped by wild beasts . . . or by brutish savages." A Virginia pamphlet argued that it was "not unlawful" for the English to possess "part" of the Indians' land.²⁸

But the English soon wanted more than just a "part" of Indian territory. Their need for land was suddenly intensified by a new development — the cultivation of tobacco as an export crop. In 1613 the colony sent its first shipment of tobacco to London, a small but significant four barrels' worth. The exports grew dramatically: 2,300 pounds in 1616, 19,000 the following year, 60,000 by 1620. The colonists increasingly coveted Indian lands, especially already cleared fields. Tobacco agriculture stimulated not only territorial expansion but also immigration. During the "Great Migration" of 1618–1623, the colony grew from 400 to 4,500 people.

In 1622 the natives tried to drive out the intruders, killing some three hundred colonists. John Smith denounced the "massacre" and described the "savages" as "cruel beasts," who possessed "a more unnatural brutishness" than wild animals. The English deaths, Samuel Purchas argued, established the colonists' right to the land: "Their carcasses, the dispersed bones of their countrymen . . . speak, proclaim and cry, This our earth is truly English, and therefore this Land is justly yours O English." Their blood had watered the soil, entitling them to the land. "We, who hitherto have had possession of no more ground than their [Indian] waste, and our purchase . . . may now by right of War, and law of Nations," the colonists declared, "invade the Country, and destroy them who sought to destroy us." They felt they could morally sweep away their enemies and even take their developed lands. "We shall enjoy their cultivated places . . . . Now their cleared grounds in all their villages (which are situated in the fruitfulest places of the land) shall be inhabited by us."²⁹

In their fierce counterattack, the English waged total war. "Victory may be gained in many ways," a colonist declared: "by force, by surprise, by famine in burning their Corn, by destroying and burning their Boats, Canoes, and Houses . . . by pursuing and chasing them with our horses, and blood-hounds to draw after them, and mastives to tear them." In 1623 Capt. William Tucker led his soldiers to a Powhatan village, presumably to negotiate a peace treaty. After he concluded the treaty, he persuaded the Indians to drink a toast, serving them poisoned wine. An estimated two hundred Indians died instantly; Tucker's soldiers then killed another fifty and "brought home part of their heads." In 1629, a colonist reported, the English forced hostile Indians to seek peace by "continual incursions" and by "yearly cutting down, and spoiling their corn." The goal of the war was to "root out [the Indians] from being any longer a people."³⁰

²⁸ Merchant, *Ecological Revolutions*, 22; Shakespeare, *Tempest*, ed. Wright and Lamar, 29, 80, 52; Thomas More, *Utopia* (New Haven, 1964), 76; Thomas, *Man and the Natural World*, 42; Cawley, "Shakespeare's Use of the Voyagers in *The Tempest*," 715.

²⁹ Jennings, *Invasion of America*, 78, 80; Sale, *Conquest of Paradise*, 295.

³⁰ Nash, *Red, White, and Black*, 62, 63; Sale, *Conquest of Paradise*, 293, 294; Jennings, *Invasion of America*, 153.

What happened in Virginia, while terrible and brutal, was still based largely on the view that Indian "savagery" was cultural. Like the Irish, Indians were identified as brutal and backward, but they were not yet seen as incapable of becoming civilized because of their race, or "descent." Their heathenism had not yet been indelibly attached to distinctive physical characteristics such as their skin color. So far at least, "consent" was possible for Indians. What occurred in New England was a different story, however, and here again *The Tempest* was preview.[31]

Although the theatergoers were given the impression that Caliban could be acculturated, they also received a diametrically opposite construction of his racial character. They were told that Caliban was "a devil, a born devil" and that he belonged to a "vile race." "Descent" was determinative: his birthmark signified an inherent moral defect. On the stage, they saw Caliban, with long shaggy hair, personifying the Indian. He had distinct racial markers. "Freckled," covered with brown spots, he was "not honored with human shape." Called a "fish," he was mockingly told: "Thy eyes are almost set in thy head." "Where should they be set else? He were a brave monster indeed if they were set in his tail." More important, his distinctive physical characteristics signified intellectual incapacity. Caliban was "a thing of darkness" whose "nature nurture [could] never stick." In other words, he had natural qualities that precluded the possibility of becoming civilized through "nurture," or education. The racial distance between Caliban and Prospero was inscribed geographically. Prospero forced the native to live on a reservation located in a barren region. "Here you sty me in this hard rock," he complained, "whiles you do keep from me the rest o' the island." Prospero justified this segregation, charging that the "savage" possessed distasteful qualities "which good natures could not abide to be with. Therefore wast thou deservedly confined into this rock, who hadst deserved more than a prison." The theatergoers saw Caliban's sty located emblematically at the back of the stage, behind Prospero's "study," signifying a hierarchy of white over dark and cerebral over carnal.[32]

This deterministic view of Caliban's racial character would be forged in the crucible of New England. Five years after the first performance of *The Tempest*, Capt. John Smith sailed north from Virginia to explore the New England coast; again he found not wild men but farmers. The "paradise" of Massachusetts, he reported, was "all planted with corn, groves, mulberries, savage gardens." "The sea Coast as you pass shews you all along large Corne fields." Indeed, while the Abenakis of Maine were mainly hunters and food gatherers dependent on the natural abundance of the land, the tribes in southern New England were horticultural. For example, the Wampanoags, whom the Pilgrims encountered in 1620, were a farming people, with a political system of governance and representation as well as a division of labor with workers specializing in arrow making, woodwork, and leathercraft.[33]

---

[31] Sollors, *Beyond Ethnicity,* 6, 36, 37.

[32] Shakespeare, *Tempest,* ed. Wright and Lamar, 70, 15–16, 18, 19, 29, 50. For the location of Caliban's sty, see Shakespeare, *Tempest,* ed. Kermode, 63.

[33] Howard S. Russell, *Indian New England before the Mayflower* (Hanover, 1980), 11; Adler, ed., *Annals of America,* I, 39.

Corner detail from John Smith's map of Virginia showing Powhatan's "court." Smith quotes a Powhatan Indian, "[We] are here to intreat and desire your friendship and to enjoy our houses and plant our fields, of whose fruits you shall participate." *Generall Historie of Virginia, New-England, and the Summer Isles . . . .* (London, 1624).

it be in our granaries." Contrary to the stereotype of Indians as hunters and therefore savages, these Indians were farmers.[35]

However, many colonists in New England disregarded this reality and invented their own representations of Indians. What emerged to justify dispossessing them was the racialization of Indian "savagery." The Indians' heathenism and alleged lazi-

---

[35] Russell, *Indian New England,* 10, 11, 166; Merchant, *Ecological Revolutions,* 80; Peter A. Thomas, "Contrastive Subsistence Strategies and Land Use as Factors for Understanding Indian-White Relations in New England," *Ethnohistory,* 23 (Winter 1976), 10; Roger Williams, *A Key into the Language of America* (Detroit, 1973), 170; Butler, "Algonkian Culture and the Use of Maize," 15, 17. For a study of the Abenakis as hunters, see Merchant, *Ecological Revolutions,* 29–68.

The Wampanoags as well as the Pequots, Massachusets, Nausets, Nipmucks, and Narragansets cultivated corn. As the main source of life for these tribes, corn was the focus of many legends. A Narraganset belief told how a crow had brought this grain to New England: "These Birds, although they do the corn also some hurt, yet scarce one *Native* amongst a hundred will kill them, because they have a tradition, that the Crow brought them at first an *Indian* Grain of Corn in one Ear, and an *Indian* or French bean in another, from the Great God *Kautantouwits* field in the Southwest from whence . . . came all their Corn and Beans." A Penobscot account celebrated the gift of Corn Mother. During a time of famine, an Indian woman fell in love with a snake in the forest. Her secret was discovered one day by her husband, and she told him that she had been chosen to save the tribe. She instructed him to kill her with a stone axe and then drag her body through a clearing. "After seven days he went to the clearing and found the corn plant rising above the ground. . . . When the corn had born fruit and the silk of the corn ear had turned yellow he recognized in it the resemblance of his dead wife. Thus originated the cultivation of corn."[34]

These Indians had a highly developed agricultural system. Samuel de Champlain found that "all along the shore" there was "a great deal of land cleared up and planted with Indian corn." Describing their agricultural practices, he wrote: "They put in each hill three or four Brazilian beans [kidney beans]. . . . When they grow up, they interlace with the corn . . . and they keep the ground very free from weeds. We saw there many squashes, and pumpkins, and tobacco, which they likewise cultivate." Thomas Morton noted the Indian practice of "dung[ing] their ground" with fish to fertilize the soil and increase the harvest. After visiting the Narragansets in Rhode Island, John Winthrop, Jr., noted that, although the soil in that region was "sandy & rocky," the people were able to raise "good corn without fish" by rotating their crops. "They have every one 2 fields," he observed, "which after the first 2 years they let one field rest each year, & that keeps their ground continually [productive]." According to Roger Williams, when the Indians were ready to harvest the corn, "all the neighbours men and women, forty, fifty, a hundred," joined in the work and came "to help freely." During their green corn festival, the Narragansets erected a long house, "sometimes a hundred, sometimes two hundred feet long upon a plain near the Court . . . where many thousands, men and women" gathered. Inside, dancers gave money, coats, and knives to the poor. After the harvest, the Indians stored their corn for the winter. "In the sand on the slope of hills," according to Champlain, "they dig holes, some five or six feet, more or less, and place their corn and other grains in large grass sacks, which they throw into the said holes, and cover them with sand to a depth of three or four feet above the surface of the ground. They take away their grain according to their need, and it is preserved as well as

[34] Eva L. Butler, "Algonkian Culture and the Use of Maize in Southern New England," *Bulletin of the Archeological Society of Connecticut* (no. 22, Dec. 1948), 6; Speck, "Penobscot Tales and Religious Beliefs," *Journal of American Folk-lore,* 48 (Jan.–March 1915), 75; Merchant, *Ecological Revolutions,* 72.

ness came to be viewed as inborn group traits that rendered them naturally incapable of civilization. This process of dehumanizing the Indians developed a peculiarly New England dimension as the colonists associated Indians with the devil. Indian identity became then a matter of "descent": Their racial markers indicated ineradicable qualities of savagery.

This social construction of race occurred within the economic context of competition over land. The colonists argued that only those who used the land were entitled to it. Native men, they claimed, pursued "no kind of labour but hunting, fishing and fowling." Indians were not producers. "The *Indians* are not able to make use of the one fourth part of the Land," argued the Puritan minister Francis Higginson in 1630, "neither have they any settled places, as Towns to dwell in, nor any ground as they challenge for their owne possession, but change their habitation from place to place." In the Puritan view, Indians were lazy. "Fettered in the chains of idleness," they would rather starve than work, complained William Wood of the Massachusetts Bay colony in 1634. Indians were sinfully squandering America's resources. Under their irresponsible guardianship, the land had become "all spoils, rots," and was "marred for want of manuring, gathering, ordering, etc." Like the "foxes and wild beasts," Indians did nothing "but run over the grass."[36]

The Puritan possession of Indian lands was facilitated by the invasion of unseen pathogens. When the colonists began arriving in New England, they found that the Indian population was already being reduced by European diseases. Two significant events had occurred in the early seventeenth century: Infected rats swam to shore from Samuel de Champlain's ships, and some sick French sailors were shipwrecked on the beaches of New England. By 1616 epidemics were ravaging Indian villages. Victims of "virgin soil epidemics," the Indians lacked immunological defenses against the newly introduced diseases. Between 1610 and 1675, the Indian population declined sharply—from 12,000 to a mere 3,000 for the Abenakis and from 65,000 to 10,000 for the southern tribes.[37]

Describing the sweep of deadly diseases among the Indians, William Bradford reported that the Indians living near the trading house at Plymouth "fell sick of the small pox, and died most miserably." The condition of those still alive was "lamentable." Their bodies were covered with "the pox breaking and mattering and running one into another, their skin cleaving" to the mats beneath them. When the sick Indians turned over, "whole sides" of their skin flayed off. In this terrible way, they died "like rotten sheep." After one epidemic, Bradford recorded in his diary: "For it pleased God to visit these Indians with a great sickness and such a mortality that of a thousand, above nine and a half hundred of them died, and many of them did rot above ground for want of burial."[38]

[36] Johnson, *Wonder-working Providence*, 262; William Cronon, *Changes in the Land: Indians, Colonists, and the Ecology of New England* (New York, 1983), 55, 56; William Wood, *New England's Prospect*, ed. Alden T. Vaughn (Amherst, 1977), 96.

[37] Alfred W. Crosby, "Virgin Soil Epidemics as a Factor in the Aboriginal Depopulation in America," *William and Mary Quarterly*, 33 (April 1976), 289; Dean R. Snow, "Abenaki Fur Trade in the Sixteenth Century," *Western Canadian Journal of Anthropology*, 6 (no. 1, 1976), 8; Merchant, *Ecological Revolutions*, 90.

[38] Bradford, *Of Plymouth Plantation*, 270–71.

Leaders of the Massachusetts Bay colony interpreted these Indian deaths as divinely sanctioned opportunities to take the land. John Winthrop declared that the decimation of Indians by smallpox manifested a Puritan destiny: God was "making room" for the colonists and "hath hereby cleared our title to this place." After an epidemic had swept through Indian villages, John Cotton claimed that the destruction was a sign from God: When the Lord decided to transplant his people, he made the country vacant for them to settle. Edward Johnson pointed out that epidemics had desolated "those places, where the English afterward planted."[39]

Indeed, many New England towns were founded on the very lands the Indians had used before the epidemics killed them. The Plymouth colony itself was located on the site of the Wampanoag village of Pawtuxet. The Pilgrims had noticed that the village was empty and the cornfields overgrown with weeds. "There is a great deal of Land cleared," one of them reported, "and hath beene planted with Corne three or foure yeares agoe." The original inhabitants had been decimated by the epidemic of 1616. "Thousands of men have lived there, which died in a great plague not long since," another Pilgrim wrote; "and pity it was and is to see so many goodly fields, and so well seated, without men to dress and manure the same." During their first spring, the Pilgrims went out into those fields to weed and manure them. Fortunately, they had some corn seed to plant. Earlier, when they landed on Cape Cod, they had come across some Indian graves and found caches of corn. They considered this find, wrote Bradford, as "a special providence of God, and a great mercy to this poor people, that here they got seed to plant them corn the next year, or else they might have starved." The pallid strangers probably would have perished had it not been for the seeds they found stored in the Indian burial grounds. Ironically, Indian death came to mean life for the Pilgrims.[40]

However, the Puritans did not see it as irony but as the destruction of devils. They had demonized the native peoples, condemning Indian religious beliefs as "diabolical, and so uncouth, as if . . . framed and devised by the devil himself." In 1652 Thomas Mayhew, who was a missionary to the Wampanoags of Martha's Vineyard, wrote that they were "mighty zealous and earnest in the Worship of False gods and Devils." They were under the influence of "a multitude of Heathen Traditions of their gods . . . and abounding with sins."[41]

To the colonists, the Indians were not merely a wayward people: They personified something fearful within Puritan society itself. Like Caliban, a "born devil," Indians failed to control their appetites, to create boundaries separating mind from body. They represented what English men and women in America thought they were not and, more important, what they must not become. As exiles living in the wilderness

[39] Roy Harvey Pearce, "The 'Ruines of Mankind': The Indian and the Puritan Mind," *Journal of the History of Ideas,* 13 (1952), 201; Peter Carroll, *Puritanism and the Wilderness: The Intellectual Significance of the Frontier, 1629–1700* (New York, 1969), 13; Johnson, *Wonder-working Providence,* 40.

[40] Cronon, *Changes in the Land,* 90; Alfred W. Crosby, "God . . . Would Destroy Them, and Give Their Country to Another People," *American Heritage,* 29 (Oct./Nov. 1978), 40; Bradford, *Of Plymouth Plantation,* 65–66.

[41] William S. Simmons, "Cultural Bias in the New England Puritans' Perception of Indians," *William and Mary Quarterly,* 38 (Jan. 1981), 70, 62.

far from "civilization," the English used their negative images of Indians to delineate the moral requirements they had set up for themselves. As sociologist Kai Erikson explains, "deviant forms of behavior, by marking the outer edges of group life, give the inner structure its special character and thus supply the framework within which the people of the group develop an orderly sense of their own cultural identity. . . . One of the surest ways to confirm an identity, for communities as well as for individuals, is to find some way of measuring what one is *not*." By depicting Indians as demonic and savage, the colonists, like Prospero, were able to define more precisely what they perceived as the danger of becoming Calibanized.[42]

. The Indians presented a frightening threat to the Puritan errand in America. "The wilderness through which we are passing to the Promised Land is all over fill'd with fiery flying serpents," warned the Puritan minister Cotton Mather in 1692. "Our Indian wars are not over yet." The wars were now within Puritan society and the self; the dangers were internal. Self-vigilance against sin was required, or else the English would become like Indians. "We have too far degenerated into Indian vices. The vices of the Indians are these: They are very lying wretches, and they are very lazy wretches; and they are out of measure indulgent unto their children; there is no family government among them. We have [become] shamefully Indianized in all those abominable things."[43]

To be "Indianized" meant to serve the Devil. Cotton Mather thought this had happened to Mercy Short, a young girl who had been a captive of the Indians and who was suffering from tormenting fits. According to Mather, Short had seen the Devil. "Hee was not of a Negro, but of a Tawney, or an Indian colour," she said; "he wore an high-crowned Hat, with straight Hair; and had one Cloven-foot." During a witchcraft trial, Mather reported, George Burroughs had lifted an extremely heavy object with the help to the Devil, who resembled an Indian. Puritan authorities hanged an Englishwoman for worshipping Indian "gods" and for taking the Indian devil-god Hobbamock for a husband. Significantly, the Devil was portrayed as dark-complected and Indian.[44]

For the Puritan, to become Indian was the ultimate horror, for they believed Indians were "in very great subjection" to the Devil, who "kept them in a continual slavish fear of him." Governor Bradford harshly condemned Thomas Morton and his fellow prodigals of the Merrymount settlement for their promiscuous partying with Indians: "They also set up a maypole, drinking and dancing about it many days together, inviting the Indian women for their consorts, dancing and frisking together like so many fairies." Interracial cavorting threatened to fracture a cultural and moral border—the frontier of Puritan identity. Congress of bodies, white and

[42] Kai Erikson, *Wayward Puritans: A Study in the Sociology of Deviance* (New York, 1966), 13, 64. See also Pearce, *Savagism and Civilization*, 8.

[43] Cotton Mather, *On Witchcraft: Being, the Wonders of the Invisible World* (New York, n.d.), 53. This treatise was originally published in 1692. Simmons, "Cultural Bias," 71.

[44] Richard Slotkin, *Regeneration through Violence: The Mythology of the American Frontier, 1600–1860* (Middletown, 1973), 132, 142, 65.

"tawney," signified defilement, a frightful boundlessness. If the Puritans were to become wayward like the Indians, it would mean that they had succumbed to savagery and failed to shrivel the sensuous parts of the self. To be "Indianized" meant to be de-civilized, to become wild men.[45]

But they could not allow this to happen, for they were embarking on an errand to transform the wilderness into civilization. "The whole earth is the Lord's garden and he hath given it to the sons of men [to] increase and multiply and replentish the earth and subdue it," asserted John Winthrop in 1629 as he prepared to sail for New England. "Why then should we stand starving here for the places of habitation . . . and in the meantime suffer a whole Continent as fruitful and convenient for the use of man to lie waste without any improvement."[46]

Actually, Indians had been farming the land, and this reality led to conflicts over resources. Within ten years after the arrival of Winthrop's group, twenty thousand more colonists came to New England. This growing English population had to be squeezed into a limited area of arable land. Less than twenty percent of New England was useful for agriculture, and the Indians had already established themselves on the prime lands. Consequently, the colonists often settled on or directly next to Indian communities. In the Connecticut Valley, for example, they erected towns such as Springfield (1636), Northhampton (1654), Hadley (1661), Deerfield (1673), and Northfield (1673) adjacent to the Indian agricultural clearings at Agawam, Norwottuck, Pocumtuck, and Squakheag.[47]

Over the years, the expansion of English settlement sometimes led to wars that literally made the land "vacant." During the Pequot War of 1637, some seven hundred Pequots were killed by the colonists and their Indian allies. Describing the massacre at Fort Mystic, an English officer wrote: "Many were burnt in the fort, both men, women, and children. . . . There were about four hundred souls in this fort, and not above five of them escaped out of our hands. Great and doleful was the bloody sight." Commander John Mason explained that God had pushed the Pequots into a "fiery oven," "filling the place with dead bodies." By explaining their atrocities as divinely driven, the English were sharply inscribing the Indians as a race of devils. This was what happened during King Philip's War of 1675–1676. About a thousand English were killed during this conflict, and over six thousand Indians died from combat and disease. Altogether about half of the total Indian population had been destroyed in southern New England. Again, the colonists quickly justified their violence by demonizing their enemies. The Indians, Increase Mather observed, were "so *Devil driven* as to begin an unjust and bloody war upon the English, which issued in their speedy and utter extirpation from the face of God's earth." Cotton Mather explained that the war was a conflict between the devil and God: "The Devil decoyed those miserable savages [to New England] in hopes that the Gospel of the

---

[45] Johnson, *Wonder-working Providence*, 263; Bradford, *Of Plymouth Plantation*, 205.
[46] John Winthrop, *Winthrop Papers*, vol. II: *1623–1630* (Boston, 1931), 139.
[47] Thomas, "Contrastive Subsistence Strategies and Land Use," 4.

Lord Jesus Christ would never come here to destroy or disturb His *absolute empire* over them."[48]

Indians, "such people" of this "brave new world," to use Shakespeare's words, personified the devil and everything the Puritans feared — the body, sexuality, laziness, sin, and the loss of self-control. They had no place in a "new England." This was the view trumpeted by Edward Johnson in his *Wonder-Working Providence*. Where there had originally been "hideous Thickets" for wolves and bears, he proudly exclaimed in 1654, there were now streets "full of Girls and Boys sporting up and down, with a continued concourse of people." Initially, the colonists themselves had lived in "wigwams" like Indians, but now they had "orderly, fair, and well-built houses . . . together with Orchards filled with goodly fruit trees, and gardens with variety of flowers." The settlers had fought against the devil who had inhabited the bodies of the Indians, Johnson observed, and made it impossible for the soldiers to pierce them with their swords. But the English had violently triumphed. They had also expanded the market, making New England a center of production and trade. The settlers had turned "this Wilderness" into "a mart." Merchants from Holland, France, Spain, and Portugal were coming to it. "Thus," proclaimed Johnson, "hath the Lord been pleased to turn one of the most hideous, boundless, and unknown Wildernesses in the world in an instant . . . to a well-ordered Commonwealth."[49]

But all of these developments had already been acted out in *The Tempest*. Like Prospero, the English colonists had sailed to a new land, and like him, many of them felt they were exiles. They viewed the native peoples as savages, as Calibans. The strangers occupied the land, believing they were entitled to be "the lord on't."[50]

The English possessed tremendous power to define the places and peoples they were conquering. As they made their way westward, they developed an ideology of "savagery," which was given form and content by the political and economic circumstances of the specific sites of colonization. Initially, in Ireland, the English had viewed savagery as something cultural, or a matter of "consent." They assumed that the distance between themselves and the Irish, or between civilization and savagery, was quantitative rather than qualitative. The Irish as "other" were educable: They were capable of acquiring the traits of civilization. But later as colonization reached across the Atlantic and as the English encountered a new group of people, many of them believed that savagery for the Indians might be inherent. Perhaps the Indians might be different from the English in kind rather than degree; if so, then the native people of America might be incapable of improvement because of their race. To use Shakespeare's language, they might have a "nature" that "nurture" would never be able to "stick" to or change. Race or "descent" might be destiny.[51]

---

[48] Charles M. Segal and David C. Stineback, eds., *Puritans, Indians & Manifest Destiny* (New York, 1977), 136–37, 111; Sherburne F. Cook, "Interracial Warfare and Population Decline among the New England Indians," *Ethnohistory*, 20 (Winter 1973), 19–21; Simmons, "Cultural Bias," 67; Segal and Stineback, eds., *Puritans, Indians & Manifest Destiny*, 182.

[49] Johnson, *Wonder-working Providence*, 71, 168, 211, 247–48; see Cronon, *Changes in the Land*, 166–67.

[50] Shakespeare, *Tempest*, ed. Wright and Lamar, 76.

[51] Shakespeare, *Tempest*, ed. Wright and Lamar, 70; Sollors, *Beyond Ethnicity*, 6–7, 36–37.

What happened in America in the actual encounters between the Indians and the English strangers was not uniform. In Virginia, Indian savagery was viewed largely as cultural: Indians were ignorant heathens. In New England, on the other hand, Indian savagery was racialized: Indians came to be condemned as a demonic race, their dark complexions signifying an indelible and inherent evil. Why was there such a difference between the two regions? Possibly the competition between the English and the Indians over resources was more intense in New England than in Virginia where there was more arable land. More important, the colonists in New England had brought with them a greater sense of religious mission than the Virginia settlers. For the Puritans, theirs was an "errand into the wilderness"—a mission to create what John Winthrop had proclaimed as "a city upon a hill" with the eyes of the world upon them. In this economic and cultural framework, a "discovery" occurred: the Indian other became a manifest devil. Thus savagery was racialized as the Indians were demonized, doomed to what Increase Mather called "utter extirpation." That process of cultural construction contributed to the making of a national identity.[52]

Over the centuries, the significance of this cultural construction of race grew even broader, more dynamic, and more inclusive. The play could harbor broader constructions, too, for Caliban's racial identity was ambiguous. Caliban could also have been African. "Freckled," dark-complected, a "thing of darkness," Caliban was the son of Sycorax, a witch who had lived in Africa. "Have we devils here?" declared Stephano in *The Tempest*. "Do you put tricks upon's with savages and men of Inde, ha?" As this reference to India suggests, Caliban could also have been Asian.[53]

[52] Perry Miller, in Miller, *Errand into the Wilderness* (New York, 1964), 1–15; John Winthrop, "A Model of Christian Charity," in Perry Miller, ed., *The American Puritans: Their Prose and Poetry* (New York, 1956), 79–84; Simmons, "Cultural Bias," 67. Miller's metaphor and theme originally came from Samuel Danforth's sermon, delivered on May 11, 1670, "A Brief Recognition of New England's Errand into the Wilderness."

[53] Shakespeare, *Tempest*, ed. Wright and Lamar, 15, 41.

"A Broad Fluid Language of Democracy": Discovering the American Idiom

Kenneth Cmiel

"Of course the English Language must take on new powers in America," one popular book of the 1850s claimed. "Was it supposed that the English Language was finished? But there is no finality to a Language! The English has vast vista in it — vast vista in America."[1]

Between the Revolution and the Civil War, the idea of an American English was invented. It was an idea hotly debated, for not everyone thought a national idiom was either a good thing or even possible. American literature might be doomed to the second-rate, the *North American Review* feared, because our language was from a nation "totally unlike our own." The difficulties were acute: "How tame will his language sound, who would describe Niagara in language fitted for the falls at London bridge, or attempt the majesty of the Mississippi in that which was made for the Thames?"[2]

Debating the category "American English" was part of an effort to imagine a nation, to construct some cohesive "thing" called the United States of America. Into fights over words, writers might pour all their profoundest hopes and deepest angst about the American nation. At stake was nothing less than control over the nation's public identity.

But if discussions of American English were bound up in nineteenth-century ideologies of nationalism, they also revealed something even deeper in Western cultural life — something about the relationship of invention to discovery in modern theories of knowledge. To invent, as the eighteenth-century rhetorician Hugh Blair noted, is to make something new; to discover is to find what's there but hidden. Galileo invented the telescope; William Harvey discovered the circulation of blood.[3]

Kenneth Cmiel is visiting associate professor in the rhetoric department at the University of California, Berkeley.

Thanks are due to the other participants in this issue for their helpful comments as well as to the Project on the Rhetoric of Inquiry seminar at the University of Iowa. Special thanks also have to go to Rebecca Rogers, Tom Lutz, Marianne Constable, John Peters, and William Thomas.

[1] William Swinton, *Rambles among Words: Their Poetry, History, and Wisdom* (New York, 1859), 287.
[2] "Essay on American Language and Literature," *North American Review*, 1 (Sept. 1815), 309.
[3] Hugh Blair, *Lectures on Rhetoric and Belles Lettres* (1783; reprint, London, 1823), 100.

John Locke had argued that humans invent language. That belief, which was part of larger changes in attitudes toward knowledge, underlay much eighteenth- and early nineteenth-century discussion of language. The attitude was expressly instrumental, assuming that the earth was almost infinitely malleable and that the task of humanity was to shape the world to its will. Crystal clear language was one tool needed for this project, and it needed inventing.

Mid-nineteenth-century romantic philologists, however, had a decidedly different approach. Instead of thinking about how words should be invented to help master a pliable world outside, they argued that language, properly understood, might help us feel a part of that world, help us feel at home here. Locke's linguistic instrumentalism, in their eyes, had generated a sense of "rootlessness" that must be combated. Romantic philologists tried to recover the deep spiritual truths buried in our words, truths that might tell us who we were. They turned, in other words, from invention to discovery. In nineteenth-century linguistics, "discovery" became one response to the fears generated by modernity's culture of invention.

While language debates were connected to issues of nationalism and the culture of invention, they also were tied to the liberating implications of democracy. Early modern language theories all suggested ways of ordering the language. Lockean or anti-Lockean, nationalist or anti-nationalist — each declared what language "was," in its essence. Consequently, each identified something outside the pale, something that would no longer be "English." Specifics varied. For one theory the illegitimate might be Americanisms; for another, words that were too imprecise; for still a third, English derived from the Latin. But whatever the differences, all theory accepted the idea that language had to be controlled, disciplined.

But while theory tried to bind language, the facts of language spoke against such discipline. Didn't words that were imprecise, unidiomatic, or vulgar tumble merrily into the flow of discourse regardless of whether theory called them English? In the early nineteenth century, this debate between theory and fact, linguistics and language, was complicated by politics. Once the idea of democracy, however imperfectly realized, began framing the political horizon, theory intent on disciplining language became problematic.

The poet Walt Whitman was one of the first to grasp this. His fragmentary writings on English in the late 1850s marked a real turning point. Whitman dreamt of an unbound American language. He urged Americans to enjoy the unruly words erupting all around them, to revel in the plebeian, the sensual, the crude. In this way, Whitman thought, earlier debates might be transcended. Americans would discover who they were by inventing a speech. And by warmly accepting all English, the national would become cosmopolitan. In the 1850s, at least, Whitman fervently believed a liberated language would create an American English that would sing in harmony — a native grand opera. While many of Whitman's specifics are ignored today, his commitment to an unbounded language persists — in some ways right into contemporary post-structural theory.

Europeans had commented on the new diction of American colonists in the eighteenth century. But such comments swelled after the 1780s. Not surprisingly, it was then that the phrases "American English" and "American language" appeared.[4] Americans, the argument ran, were adding new words to the language or adding new meanings to old words: political terms like *gubernatorial, presidential,* and *caucus;* strange neologisms like *lengthy, belittle,* and *illy.* By the middle of the century the list of Americanisms (real or imagined) ran into the thousands, including terms like *banter, budge, calculate* (guess), *carry on, fellow countrymen, full blast, hurry up, lickspittle,* and *odoriferous.* And there were hundreds of others that are utterly alien to us today, words like *giraffed* (humbugged), *puckerstopple* (embarrass), and *squinch* (quench).

Between the 1790s and the 1830s, Americans who wrote on language responded to the innovation in two broad ways. One group defended a linguistic cosmopolitanism that was skeptical of any idiomatic nationalism. Journals like the *Monthly Anthology,* the *Port-Folio,* and the *Knickerbocker Magazine* jumped to condemn any "freeborn *Boozer*" or "*citizen* Sambo" who, "'independent' of precedent and rule," dared to "*clip the King's English.*"[5] On the other side were those linguistic nationalists who dreamt of a uniquely American idiom.

Most of both groups, however, shared certain assumptions, one of the most important being that language was a social convention. This was the linguistic version of social contract theory. Locke, in his *Essay Concerning Human Understanding,* had made the argument, counterposing it to the idea that language was directly given to humans by God. The notion that there was some sort of "natural" connection between words and things has a long history, ultimately reaching back to Plato's *Cratylus.* While God had given us the capacity to speak, Locke argued, particular forms of language were arbitrary and conventional. The primary purpose of language was to express ideas. Since we expressed them to others, however, our words had to have a common currency. Words acquired meaning, however imperfectly, from the "tacit Consent" of all speakers. Ideas about the conventional nature of language, while not universally accepted, percolated through educated thought, becoming a staple of much eighteenth-century linguistics, including the very important tradition of Scottish rhetoric.[6]

By the 1750s, the language-as-convention theory also translated into a distrust of universal grammar (also known as philosophical grammar), the notion that there

---

[4] Allen Walker Read, "British Recognition of American Speech in the Eighteenth Century," *Dialect Notes,* 6 (part 6, 1933), 313–34. Joseph Medard Carrière, "Early Examples of the Expressions 'American language' and 'langue américaine'," *Modern Language Notes,* 75 (June 1960), 485–88. The phrase "American dialect" has been found as early as 1740, but that was an unusual usage. Sir William A. Craigie and James R. Hulbert, eds., *A Dictionary of American English* (Chicago, 1968), s.v. "American."

[5] "Domestic Occurrences," *Port-Folio,* July 11, 1801, p. 223.

[6] John Locke, *An Essay Concerning Human Understanding,* ed. Peter N. Nidditch (Oxford, 1975), 402–8. For the phrase "tacit Consent," see *ibid.,* 408. Wilbur Samuel Howell, *Eighteenth-Century British Logic and Rhetoric* (Princeton, 1971).

were universal rules governing all languages. (This idea remains alive today in the linguistics of Noam Chomsky.) Theories of universal grammar can be traced back to thirteenth-century scholastic philosophy; they posit a basic connection between syntax and reason. While almost all late eighteenth-century linguists continued to believe there was something called philosophical grammar, by the middle of the century there was a new and widespread sense that it had no place in practical linguistics. Discussion of universal grammar was relegated to speculative philosophy.[7]

Locke's ideas about language were part of a wider shift in Western epistemology. Charles Taylor has observed that after Galileo, partisans of the new began picturing knowledge as representational. Whereas knowledge had been connected with discovering the order God put into the universe, it now was associated with *building* an accurate picture of external reality. For Locke and René Descartes, knowledge was a product of an active mind. This epistemological shift, notes Taylor, was tied to a new and grandiose faith in the ability of humans to manipulate reality. Locke's contention that language was not a gift from God but a human invention was but one illustration of that new conception of knowledge.[8]

Such thinking put a premium on clarity. For a Lockean, presenting a perfectly accurate picture of our ideas became the first linguistic virtue. Precision was a god.[9] And since language was a human invention, made by fallible people in the course of their intersubjective dealings, it was especially important to guard against vagueness. Here too Locke is an example — several chapters of *An Essay Concerning Human Understanding* discuss the imperfections of words. But this notion was by no means Locke's alone. Through the eighteenth century, key rhetorics, grammars, and dictionaries simply assumed that the language had to be watched. If not disciplined, language might degenerate, its mirrorlike character tarnished by imprecision.[10]

Provincialisms were one sort of illegitimate language. The very word *provincialism*, conjuring up distance from the center, an enclosed existence, conveyed a message at odds with eighteenth-century elite cosmopolitanism.[11] Such words had to be resisted. David Hume had worried about his Scotticisms in the 1740s; John Witherspoon invented the term *Americanism* in 1781; *provincialism* itself dates from 1770.[12]

[7] See Murray Cohen, *Sensible Words: Linguistic Practice in England, 1640–1785* (Baltimore, 1977), 88–96.

[8] Charles Taylor, *Sources of the Self: The Making of the Modern Identity* (Cambridge, Mass., 1989), 144, 149–55, 165–68. For a discussion of the same shift in the American cultural context, see Larzer Ziff, *Writing in the New Nation: Prose, Print, and Politics in the Early United States* (New Haven, 1991).

[9] As Martin Heidegger pointed out, this was new: "Greek science was never exact, precisely because, in keeping with its essence, it could not be exact and did not need to be exact." Martin Heidegger, *The Question Concerning Technology and Other Essays*, tr. William Lovitt (New York, 1977), 117; for an example, see Aristotle, *The Ethics of Aristotle*, ed. J. A. K. Thomson (Baltimore, 1953), 27–28.

[10] Locke, *Essay Concerning Human Understanding*, 475–524; Kenneth Cmiel, *Democratic Eloquence: The Fight over Popular Speech in Nineteenth-Century America* (New York, 1990), 31–39. See also Sterling Andrus Leonard, "The Doctrine of Correctness in English Usage, 1700–1800" (Ph.D. diss., University of Wisconsin, 1929). For the variations introduced by common-sense philosophy, see Michael P. Kramer, *Imagining Language in America: From the Revolution to the Civil War* (Princeton, 1992), 125–30.

[11] See Thomas J. Schlereth, *The Cosmopolitan Ideal in Enlightenment Thought* (Notre Dame, 1977). On eighteenth-century hostility to linguistic provincialisms, see Leonard, "Doctrine of Correctness," 151, 177–79.

[12] John Clive and Bernard Bailyn, "England's Cultural Provinces: Scotland and America," *William and Mary*

The debate over the newly emerging American language was filtered through such categories. Conservatives who decried the invention of an American language in the early nineteenth century regularly drew attention to the problems of provincialisms. Provincialisms were "food for local prejudices," one southern writer noted in 1837. The New Englander John Pickering, in his 1816 book on American provincialisms, described them as "corruptions [that] have crept into our English." Three decades later John Bartlett of Rhode Island, in his *Dictionary of Americanisms,* called them "perversions."[13]

Behind these thoughts, not surprisingly, were other fears. Language theory merged into politics. It is no surprise that Pickering was a Federalist and later a Whig. For those critical of the emerging American English, language was contributing to the disintegrating forces of the times. It "is remarkable how debased the language has become in a short period in America," one British visitor claimed in 1839. One year later the *Knickerbocker Magazine* reported that the "greatest danger" to the language was "innovation." Americans would be "wise" to listen to British critics of American English.[14]

National stereotypes being formulated in the early nineteenth century were seen as embodied in the language. One of the more galling Americanisms was the verb *progress*. As a noun, the word was legitimate, but as a verb it was more than suspect. That its use as a verb surfaced in the United States in the 1790s was just too much of a coincidence to be ignored. It annoyed many Brits and made numerous Americans uncomfortable. As a verb, *to progress* indicated an activity, an ongoing process. It was a state of being ("they are progressing") instead of the more limited and specific act that was the noun ("they made progress"). To its critics, *to progress* was ugly in itself, a declension from a more precise usage, but it also was a depressing sign of an emerging way of life, indicative of the inability of Americans to sit still.[15]

But if key terms had sinister resonance, it was not primarily the esoteric hermeneutics of words like *progress* that raised questions. The problem was the whole drift of the dialect. Accent, grammar, spelling, vocabulary—all were ugly and vague, all muddied communication. New Yorkers, according to one British visitor, had "a snivel and a drawl, which, I confess, to my ear, is by no means laudable on the score of euphony." Another visitor, Frances Trollope, reported that she rarely

---

Quarterly, 11 (April 1954), 210–11; Mitford M. Mathews, ed., *Dictionary of Americanisms on Historical Principles* (Chicago, 1951), s.v. "Americanism"; R. W. Burchfeld, ed., *Supplement to the Oxford English Dictionary* (Oxford, 1972), s.v. "provincialism."

[13] Simeon Smallfry, "Improprieties of Speech," *Southern Literary Messenger,* 3 (April 1837), 222; John Pickering, *A Vocabulary, or Collection of Words or Phrases Which Have Been Supposed to be Peculiar to the United States of America* (Boston, 1816), 11; John Bartlett, *Dictionary of Americanisms: A Glossary of Words and Phrases Usually Regarded as Peculiar to the United States* (New York, 1848), iv, xviii.

[14] Capt. Marryat, *A Diary in America* (New York, 1839), 146; "The English Language," *Knickerbocker Magazine,* 15 (March 1840), 214, 216.

[15] On *to progress,* see H. L. Mencken, *The American Language: An Inquiry into the Development of English in the United States, Supplement I* (New York, 1945), 28, 47, 86, 88, 122, 137, 225. Using *progress* as a verb was common in England between about 1590 and 1670. It then became obsolete. In the 1790s, Americans began using the term once again. Only after 1800 did British usage follow. See Craigie and Hulbert, eds., *Dictionary of American English,* s.v. "progress."

"heard a sentence . . . correctly pronounced from the lips of an American." Something in the expression or accent always jarred "the feelings" and shocked "the taste." James Fenimore Cooper in 1838 complained that "false accentuation" was common in America (*engine* pronounced "engyne," *virtue* became "virtoo," and *fortune,* "fortin"). Charles Augustus Murray, still another visitor from Britain, reported after visiting Easton, Pennsylvania: "It would kill a grammatical purist to spend a week in that vicinity."[16]

In the early years of the nineteenth century, cosmopolitan critics equated native provincialisms with "American." And a number thought that there was a real danger that a new language, incomprehensible to England, would eventually surface in the United States. One typical foreign observer worried in the early 1830s that unless Americans changed their habits their speech would eventually become "utterly unintelligible" to the English. The Americans "have only to '*progress*' in their present course," he added, "and their grandchildren bid fair to speak a jargon as novel and peculiar as the most patriotic American linguists can desire."[17]

This was a common fear in the early years of the century. Mutual incomprehension, if not imminent, loomed in the not too distant future. To the Bostonian John Pickering, who was among the fearful, this would hurt the United States far more than Britain. Americans would not be able to read British authors, Pickering thought. American literature, in turn, would have limited appeal. Even worse, according to Pickering, American science, commerce, law, and religion would all be cut off from "the language of the nation, from which we are descended."[18]

Such worries stemmed from a conception of dialect far different from ours. In the early nineteenth century, provincial dialects were perceived to be densely different from the speech of rulers, very real barriers to communication, closer to what we might call a separate language. While dialect speakers might understand "standard" speech, they could not understand even the neighboring shire's idiom. And elite speakers had limited understanding of regional speech outside their own locale. Thus "standard" speech was cosmopolitan in a very precise sense, lifting "refined" people out of their province and into a larger world through a language whose realm of "tacit Consent" was much wider.[19]

In the course of the 1830s and 1840s, however, the fear of mutual incomprehension disappeared. Instead, those fearing American English increasingly drew atten-

---

[16] Thomas Hamilton, *Men and Manners in America* (2 vols., Edinburgh, 1833), I, 12–13; Frances Trollope, *Domestic Manners of the Americans,* ed. Michael Sadleir (1832; reprint, New York, 1927), 38; James Fenimore Cooper, *The American Democrat* (1838; reprint, New York, 1931), 111; Charles Augustus Murray, *Travels in North America* (2 vols., London, 1839), II, 363.

[17] Hamilton, *Men and Manners in America,* I, 230.

[18] Pickering, *Vocabulary,* 9–10. Also see Jonathan Boucher, *Glossary of Archaic and Provincial Words* (London, 1832), xxiii.

[19] On the problem of dialect in France (where in 1863 one estimate was that one-quarter of the population spoke no French at all), see Eugen Weber, *Peasants into Frenchmen: The Modernization of Rural France, 1870–1914* (Stanford, 1976), 67–94. In Italy, according to Jonathan Steinberg, as late as 1861, "no more than 2 to 3% of the Italian population would have understood Italian." Jonathan Steinberg, "The Historian and the *Questione della Lingua,*" in *The Social History of Language,* ed. Peter Burke and Roy Porter (Cambridge, Eng., 1987), 198.

tion to the growth of regional dialects within the United States. The title of John Bartlett's 1848 *Dictionary of Americanisms* is actually a bit misleading; Bartlett was keenly aware of regional variation.

Samuel Kirkham's *English Grammar in Familiar Lessons* provides a good example. The best-selling book of its kind in the 1830s and 1840s, it indicated a knowledge of provincial idioms that earlier grammars lacked. *The keows be gone to hum, neow, and I'mer goin arter um,* was, to Kirkham, the New England way of saying *The cows are gone home, and I am going after them.* In the South, they said: *Is that your plunder, stranger?* instead of *Is that your baggage, sir?* Kirkham also included examples of dialect from Pennsylvania and New York. He was among the first American linguists to indicate some awareness of ethnic variation. While the Irish said *Let us be after pairsing a wee bit,* Kirkham noted, it was "correct" to say *Let us parse a little.*[20]

Behind this discovery of American provincialisms in the 1830s and 1840s was the betterment of travel and communication. The explosion of print, the building of roads, the spread of steam travel in the first decades of the nineteenth century helped change perceptions of regional speech in a number of ways. First, they eliminated the fear that the United States and Great Britain would create completely different languages. That in turn allowed for a redefinition of *dialect.* By the 1840s, provincial dialects in the United States were interpreted as vulgar variations of standard speech, which might raise questions of precision but did not promise fundamental incomprehension.

Finally, those same forces of communication and mobility meant further discovery of regional speech. John Russell Bartlett, who in 1848 compiled the first dictionary including western, southern, New England, and middle Atlantic seaboard regionalisms, got the idea for his book listening to dialects on an upstate New York canal. By 1859, when the second edition came out, Bartlett had spent three years working in Texas, New Mexico, and California. New popular literature also contributed. Regional humor emerged in the 1830s and 1840s—the southwestern stories about Davy Crockett and Sut Lovingood; the New England stories of Jack Downing—these books were full of dialect and absolutely central to the new recognition of American provincial speech. For more refined audiences, American travel literature including passages in dialect, from Anne Royall in the 1820s to Frederick Law Olmsted in the 1850s, also helped spread the same knowledge.[21]

The new interest in regional dialects was fed by politics as well as technology. The entrance of democracy into the political imagination had profound linguistic implications. To be sure, the actual horizon of early nineteenth-century democratic thinking did not stretch civic participation beyond white males. Nevertheless, the

[20] Samuel Kirkham, *English Grammar in Familiar Lessons* (Rochester, 1843), 206–7.

[21] [Anne Royall], *Sketches of History, Life, Manners, in the United States* (New Haven, 1826); Anne Royall, *Mrs. Royall's Southern Tour; or, Second Series of the Black Book* (3 vols., Washington, 1830–1831); Anne Royall, *Letters from Alabama on Various Subjects* (Washington, 1830); Frederick Law Olmsted, *A Journey in the Seaboard Slave States* (New York, 1856); Frederick Law Olmsted, *A Journey in the Back Country* (New York, 1860).

concept of democracy, of rule by the people, itself implied that the language of
rulers had to adjust to the language of citizens, that popular speech would vie with
Lockean precision as a linguistic norm. It became harder to ignore regional idioms,
harder in general to ignore any undisciplined language. Bounded speech now faced
a legitimation problem.

Everywhere, it seemed, wild, undisciplined language was erupting in the 1830s
and 1840s. Linguistic extravagance appeared at every turn, the disciplined language
of refinement ignored or laughed at. Tall talk, fantastic overstatement in the service
of self-aggrandizement, burgeoned in popular literature. Thus we hear the fictional
Davy Crockett claiming he could "walk like an ox, run like a fox, swim like an eel,
yell like an Indian, fight like a devil, spout like an earthquake, make love like a mad
bull, and swallow an Injun whole without choking if you butter his head and pin
his ears back." As important was the playful invention of extravagant vocabulary.
One could read in the 1847 *New York Tribune* of a stationmaster who had "ab-
squatulated with funds" or hear someone else talking about being "teetotaciously"
swallowed up. Finally, the use of plebeian idioms on the political stump—rustic
regionalisms, popular slang, and other vulgarities—tied the carnivalesque challenge
directly to the new politics. In the 1860s, after listening to a stump speech in
Galena, Illinois, a French aristocrat moaned that the "wild use of language" might
be inevitable in a democracy. The "American people," he thought, "especially here
in the West, love these raw, bloody, slabs of butcher's meat."[22]

Earlier writers like Witherspoon and Pickering had thought that Americanisms
must be wiped out. But by the 1840s, writers who recognized American regionalisms had no such illusions. Provincial dialects were inevitable. John Bartlett and
Samuel Kirkham simply hoped to keep refined English away from the con-
taminating "perversions" of popular speech.[23] While the older conservatives had
worked in a setting defined by fear of French radicalism, for the new conservatives
the reference point was Jacksonian democracy. For the former, Americanisms signaled a dismissal of moderate Anglo traditions. For the latter, American regionalisms were signs of the leveling of modern democracy.

But whether they feared incomprehension or wanted a buffer against the wild
language of popular speakers, all these writers wanted to save an Anglo-American
language. It was an expressly cosmopolitan attitude toward speech in general and
English in particular. ("*Nationality*," Pickering noted, "is a new word, and is not
to be found in the dictionaries.") Too deep an attachment to an American English
would cause profound loss.[24]

---

[22] Richard Dorson, ed., *Davy Crockett: American Comic Legend* (New York, 1939), 30; John Russell Bartlett,
Dictionary of Americanisms: A Glossary of Words and Phrases Usually Regarded as Peculiar to the United States
(Boston, 1859), 2, 474; Ernest Duvergier de Hauranne, *A Frenchman in Lincoln's America* (2 vols., Chicago, 1974),
I, 281–82, 285.

[23] See Bartlett, *Dictionary of Americanisms* (1848), xv, xviii.

[24] For some examples of this antinationalistic attitude toward language, see James Madison, *Letters and Other
Writings* (4 vols., New York, 1865), III, 172–73; Samuel Lorenzo Knapp, *Lectures on American Literature* (New
York, 1829), 9; and the comments by John Trumbull and John Marshall in American Academy of Language and

Pickering's 1816 essay stated the cosmopolitan presumptions quite precisely. It was not that Americans could not coin needed words nor that American authors had to defer to British. (Buried here is the notion that language is a human invention used to express our ideas.) But Americans wouldn't just accept any word from Scotland or Ireland, Pickering reasoned. Americanisms, similarly, should not be uncritically accepted elsewhere. Language, after all, had to be guarded. The ultimate point, to make sure it is not lost, was this—the English language was *not* national. Americans were "members of that great community of family which speaks the English language." The "final arbiters" of good English were "the body of the learned and polite of this whole community."[25]

Not everyone thought an American English signaled decline. "Let us then seize the present moment," wrote Noah Webster in 1789, "and establish a *national language, as well as a national government.*"[26] In fact, only a few were as bold as Webster (and he himself would become more timid in later years). Nevertheless, people like Webster, Thomas Jefferson, and William Cardell did champion the right of Americans to invent their own idiom.

These writers disliked what they saw as the carping criticism of conservatives. Noah Webster wrote a pamphlet responding to Pickering's book on Americanisms, claiming that Pickering had made hundreds of errors. The terms *brush, constitutionality,* and *presidential* were perfectly fine, according to Webster. So too were *demoralize* (in the sense "to become immoral"), *profanity,* and that often-attacked Americanism *lengthy.* Another writer in 1814 argued that a national language was "ours by right of conquest." Independence gave Americans the right to make their own laws, linguistic as well as political. British criticism was an "attempt to interfere with the privilege of speech."[27]

Practical and patriotic reasons combined to justify new language. Webster thought that British English was corrupt, that the distance between the two nations was too great for commonality, and, most important, that an American language would forge national bonds. Thomas Jefferson disliked the British criticisms of American speech and thought circumstances so different in the two countries that an "American dialect" was inevitable. Other southerners agreed, including Thomas Robertson, governor of Louisiana, and George McDuffie, later governor of South Carolina. Given "the novelty of our situation," McDuffie said, "we *must* innovate upon our vernacular language."[28]

Belles Lettres, *Circular No. III* (New York, 1822), 6, 10–11. While Edward Everett criticized British travelers who complained about Americanisms, he did not want any specifically "American" language to appear. See Allen Walker Read, "Edward Everett's Attitude towards American English," *New England Quarterly,* 12 (March 1939), 112–29.

[25] Pickering, *Vocabulary,* 20.

[26] Noah Webster, *Dissertations on the English Language* (Boston, 1789), 406.

[27] Harry Warfel, ed., *Letters of Noah Webster* (New York, 1953), 341–94; Lemuel Lengthy, "Americanisms," *Analectic Magazine,* 3 (May 1814), 404, 405.

[28] Webster, *Dissertations on the English Language,* 20, 21, 35–36, 405–6; Albert Ellery Bergh, ed., *The Writings*

For Webster and William Cardell, the new language would not come about unless it was actively pursued. Jefferson, on the other hand, thought an American
idiom would arise if not strangled in the crib by pedantic conservatives. This difference in part reflects different assumptions about language. Jefferson viewed language as a social custom. New language had to be invented to express new ideas.
It was for this reason that Jefferson disliked William Cardell's dream of a national
academy. Any effort to "fix" the language would be tragic. In what is almost a direct
paraphrase of Locke, Jefferson warned that "judicious neology can alone give
strength and copiousness to language, and enable it to be the vehicle of new ideas."[29]

William Cardell, however, was one of a group of linguists reviving notions of
philosophical grammar. For writers like Cardell, grammar was not arbitrary and convention but a blind guide.[30] That view was a return to the notion that syntax ultimately relied upon the universal rules of logic.

In 1820s America, this generated its own form of nationalism and revealed another aspect of the culture of invention. For Cardell, it was not that the United States
would create a distinct English, separate from Britain. Rather the United States was
uniquely placed to be the first nation to establish a truly rational language, one
grounded on philosophical grammar instead of arbitrary custom. Britain, moored
in its rank traditions, could not see the light. The United States, on the other hand,
was free, cut loose from history: "We are beginning in some degree, not only a separate nation, but another world, and opening a new destiny for the race of man."
For Cardell, the recognition of new truths would allow Americans to invent a new
language.[31]

This was the position of a number of linguistic nationalists of the 1820s. John
Sherman, in *The Philosophy of Language Illustrated* (1826), thanked God that he
belonged to a race of "*innovators*" and was a citizen of a republic "which had its
birth in *innovation*." In *The American System of English Grammar* (also 1826),
James Brown wanted readers to know that his goal was not merely linguistic independence from Britain. He hoped Americans might realize that language was "an
emenation from God" instead of an arbitrary custom. History could be overthrown
for a language of democracy and reason. James Fenimore Cooper, in the 1820s, argued that precisely because the United States had no commonly accepted cultural
capital or social elite, it was poised to adopt a far more "reasonable" English than
Britain. The "known laws of language" were replacing fashion as the standard.[32]

---

of Thomas Jefferson (20 vols., Washington, 1907), XIII, 340; American Academy of Language, *Circular No. III*,
10, 15–16, 25–26.

[29] American Academy of Language, *Circular No. III*, 10.

[30] William Cardell, *Essay on Language* (New York, 1825); William Cardell, *Philosophic Grammar of the English
Language* (Philadelphia, 1827).

[31] Cardell, *Essay on Language*, 30–31; American Academy of Language, *Circular No. III*, 13.

[32] John Sherman, *The Philosophy of Language Illustrated* (Trenton Falls, 1826), 7; James Brown, *The American
System of English Grammar* (Washington, 1826), 8; [James Fenimore Cooper], *Notions of the Americans* (2 vols.,
London, 1828), II, 161–69, esp. 167. Cooper repudiated nearly all these ideas one decade later in *The American
Democrat*.

Noah Webster's position varied over time. In 1789 he was a fervent linguistic nationalist. At the same time he argued that the basis of language was shared custom. By the first decade of the nineteenth century, however, he had discovered universal grammar, foreshadowing Cardell and the nationalists of the 1820s. Americans might produce a philosophically correct language in ways that British custom could not. But by the end of his life, Webster was back to arguing that the basis of language was universal spoken custom. And as Richard Rollins has shown, Webster's famous 1828 dictionary was not a nationalistic document. Webster was convinced that the United States and Britain would share a common language, in the 1820s telling one British traveler that there were but fifty differences in idiom between the two countries.[33]

In their nationalistic moments, writers like Webster, Cardell, and Jefferson tied the invention of new language to national pride. It is important to note, however, what sort of nationalism they were interested in. There was no trace of the proto-romantic sense of language and nation expressed by Johann Herder in the 1780s. Webster, Cardell, and Jefferson were late Enlightenment figures, and their linguistics was high Enlightenment.

Herder had argued that language and culture should define political formation. Language communities, rooted in custom, came first; the political state followed.[34] In his *Dissertations on the English Language,* however, Webster saw the new political institutions as the base point, the culture as what came after. Webster envisioned his national language as a way to cement bonds to the regime. Similarly, Jefferson thought that new language was generated by republican principles. And for the nationalistic grammarians, language was not an organic growth of a people, but something that could be radically altered by philosophic principles, principles capable of being put into practice because the United States had abandoned tradition. Whatever their differences, all those committed to more American speech placed culture in the service of politics.

This was a common form of Western nationalism in the late eighteenth and early nineteenth centuries, associated in particular with the French Revolution. Intellectually, it came from a reform tradition with a mentality just the opposite of Herder's. In the second half of the eighteenth century, the Frenchman Claude-Adrien Helvetius, the Englishman William Godwin, and the American Joel Barlow, among others, took eighteenth-century associationalism further than Locke himself had. Human beings were so malleable, they argued, that mores were the products of educational arrangements. It followed, and quite explicitly, that the form of government would shape the character of the people.[35]

---

[33] Webster, *Dissertations on the English Language,* 27; Noah Webster, *A Philosophical and Practical Grammar of the English Language* (New Haven, 1807), 5, 12–13, 120; Noah Webster, *Collection of Papers on Political, Literary and Moral Subjects* (New York, 1843), 371–72; Richard Rollins, *The Long Journey of Noah Webster* (n.p., 1980), 124–126; Captain Basil Hall, *Travels in North America* (3 vols., Edinburgh, 1829), II, 204.

[34] Johann Gottfried von Herder, *Outlines of a Philosophy of the History of Man,* tr. T. O. Churchill (1784; reprint, New York, 1966), 225–51, 374.

[35] Claude-Adrien Helvetius, *De l'esprit* (1768; reprint, Paris, 1988), 409; William Godwin, *Enquiry Concerning*

When connected to revolutionary politics at the end of the century, this thinking implied that the nation was *not* based on the inherited language of a people, but "on the freely expressed will of the inhabitants." This was a nationalism grounded on an ideological commitment to self-determination and preoccupied with "a homogeneous set of institutions and a centralized republican government." Such a conception of nationality did not mean language was trivial. It only meant that preexisting language was not the basis of citizenship. Indeed, like Webster, French revolutionaries in the 1790s began thinking of how they could eliminate *patois* and create a national language as support for the new republican government.[36]

This linguistic nationalism did not last beyond the 1820s, shattered by the explosive drama of Jacksonian speech. Even when Noah Webster argued for an American English, he could accept the effusion of regional jargon no better than his cosmopolitan opponents. The *absquatulate* or *galoot* of Alabama, the *burglarize* or *by golly* of New England, or the *git out* of the West—these words, and the conception of democracy they implied, flew in the face of a disciplined national speech that might both create a sense of American unity (an American "general will") and be a finely chiseled tool for presenting our ideas to fellow citizens. Jacksonian language games, on the other hand, conjured up a sense of democracy rooted in an existential respect for people as they are. By the 1840s, the philosophical grammarians faced a daunting problem: The facts of the language were making their linguistics unsteady.

Those writers ideologically tied to Enlightenment cosmopolitanism might best be termed "progressive conservatives" or "caretakers of progress." They combined a sense that language had to be watched, carefully controlled, and not split from the British with the notion that language was steadily progressing. Each custom would be better than the last but only if language continued to be carefully guarded by the refined and literate.

Those favoring an American English tied their sense of language to early nineteenth-century ideologies of nationalism most commonly associated with the French Revolution. They might best be called "constructive nationalists." These writers thought a national language would cement the new regime; and a republican regime, conversely, would encourage linguistic progress.

But while differing in crucial ways, both groups thought that we created language to better express our ideas. In other words, both understood language as a human invention used to represent the world. All conservatives and many nationalists continued to think of language as an arbitrary convention, just as Locke had. Nationalists like Cardell, who revived notions of philosophical grammar, did so to push the inventiveness of language even further. Human speech could for the first time

Political Justice (1793; reprint, Harmondsworth, 1985), 113–15; Joel Barlow, *Advice to the Privileged Orders in the Several States of Europe, Part II* (Paris, 1793), 65–66.

[36] Jacques Godechot, "The New Concept of the Nation and Its Diffusion in Europe," in *Nationalism in the Age of the French Revolution,* ed. Otto Dann and John Dinwiddy (London, 1988), 13–26, esp 16, 19. Michel de Certeau, Dominique Julia, and Jacques Revel, *Une politique de la langue* (Paris, 1975), 160–69.

escape history and autonomously invent a fully "rational" syntax. And linguistic progress was connected to progress elsewhere — language was a tool used to help control the world around us. Both cosmopolitans and nationalists understood language in terms of the West's culture of invention.

Between the 1830s and the 1860s, romantic language theory slowly altered debates about American English. The theory generated a very different sense of the ties between language and nation, one that was part of a rejection of Lockean notions of language. While earlier linguists thought of language as molded to the state, for romantics language and ethos were primary, defining what the state might be. In this sense, the national language was not "invented," as Webster and French revolutionaries had thought. It was the job of intellectuals to bring that language to light, to uncover, to *discover,* what was already there.

This theory refigured older debates about cosmopolitanism and nationalism. For most midcentury linguists, the new philology contributed to a belief that the American idiom was in reality the purest form of Anglo-Saxon English left on the earth. It denied the existence of American English and suggested deep connections between the mid-nineteenth-century United States and a glorious Anglo past. But for a few writers, notably Walt Whitman, the new linguistics could be stretched to speculate on the coming of an indigenous American idiom.

The new linguistics came to the United States between the 1830s and the 1850s. By the 1850s, philology was a remarkably popular subject among men and women of letters. The British author Richard Chenevix Trench published the popular Bible of the new thinking, *On the Study of Words,* in 1851. Four years later he followed with his *English: Past and Present.* And works like Maximilian Schele de Vere's *Outlines of Comparative Philology* and George Perkins Marsh's *Lectures on the English Language* were also well known. People like Nathaniel Hawthorne, Henry David Thoreau, and Ralph Waldo Emerson all studied the new philology.[37]

In theory, the linguistics was nationalistic. According to Schele de Vere, "the language of a people" was "the embodiment . . . of its spiritual life." Philology could trace "to the minutest detail" the "various mental qualities and moral instincts" of a people's idiom.[38] These instincts and idioms, moreover, were the product of long historical evolution. A language realized itself as it unfolded through time. Such notions, of course, can be traced back at least to Herder in the 1770s. This was not the elite cosmopolitanism of earlier American conservatives. Nor was it the constructive nationalism of Webster or Jefferson. It was, rather, a historical nationalism, one that presumed a deep and long-standing resonance between people and language.

---

[37] Adolph Benson, "James Gates Percival, Student of German Culture," *New England Quarterly,* 2 (1929), 603–24; John Wilson, "Grimm's Law and the Brahmins," *ibid.,* 38 (1965), 234–39; Philip F. Gura, *The Wisdom of Words: Language, Theology, and Literature in the New England Renaissance* (Middletown, 1981).

[38] Maximilian Schele de Vere, *Outlines of Comparative Philology* (New York, 1853), 87; also see Richard Chenevix Trench, *On the Study of Words* (1851; reprint, New York, 1866), 27–28.

This historical cast made etymology very important. The further back you went, the closer you got to the core. "The living import of a word lies in the root," Josiah Gibbs of Yale claimed. "He who has a clearer sense of the root, . . . will have a clearer sense of the meaning." The history of words would uncover the spiritual meaning of the people.[39]

Indeed, the "spiritual" was at the center of the new linguistics, more important even than nationalism. Here the new philology was expressly anti-Lockean. No longer were words mere conventions. Words were never, "however strong the seeming, mere arbitrary symbols of thought."[40] There was a *necessary* connection between word and idea, necessary because language was part of a spiritual order. This order was variously expressed as God, mind, spirit, reason, logos, the transcendental — but all the new philologists made the point in one way or another. Modern philology had to study the interior of words as well as their exterior. And mid-nineteenth-century philologists took for granted that this "interior" was religious, embodied in a people but more than simply a culture ethos. All the philologists, after all, knew that in the beginning was the Word (it is *logos* in the Greek original) and the Word was made Flesh.

It was the job of the etymologist, then, to uncover the hidden spirituality of language. This was necessary because time eroded the poetry of words. Conventions went stale, words that once buzzed with implication now seemed plain and common. Philology would recover the "uncanniness of the ordinary" packed in each word but now hard to see.[41]

This philological project was rooted in romantic objections to Lockean modes of thinking and the modern culture of invention. Language was no longer considered a human construction; truth was not understood in terms of crystal-clear ideas. Instead, for romantics, language was part of a transcendental order; and truth was an uncovering of what was there but hidden. As Hans Aarsleff has noted, in this strain of romantic Platonism, "to know is to remember."[42] Attention shifted from what humans created to a discovery (or recovery) of who they were. Truth was no longer conceived of as an accurate picture of our subjective ideas; it was now the revelation of an imminent order.

One of the more succinct statements of the new theory was Elizabeth Peabody's 1849 essay simply entitled "Language." Peabody chastised Horace Bushnell's *God*

[39] Josiah W. Gibbs, *Philological Studies with English Examples* (New Haven, 1857), 2; Schele de Vere, *Outlines of Comparative Philology*, 202–3. Also see Maurice Olender, *The Language of Paradise: Race, Religion, and Philology in the Nineteenth Century* (Cambridge, Mass., 1992).

[40] Benjamin Dwight, *Modern Philology: Its Discoveries, History, and Influence* (2 vols., New York, 1869), II, 278. Dwight argued that the "subjective period of perpetually self-measuring consciousness, and of cool anatomical self-criticism, as indicated . . . in the philosophy of John Locke, has happily now wellnigh passed away." *Ibid.*, II, 323. On the spiritual dimension in general, see *ibid.*, I, 141–47; Schele de Vere, *Outlines of Comparative Philology*, 25; Gibbs, *Philological Studies*, 3–6; George P. Marsh, *Lectures on the English Language* (New York, 1860), 260–63.

[41] See Stanley Cavell, *In Quest of the Ordinary: Lines of Skepticism and Romanticism* (Chicago, 1988), 153–78.

[42] Hans Aarsleff, *From Locke to Saussure: Essays on the Study of Language and Intellectual History* (Minneapolis, 1982), 38. I owe this whole paragraph to Aarsleff's discussion; see *ibid.*, 31–41.

in Christ for restating "the old and superficial theory, that language is, after all, arbitrary, the creature of convention." Instead, Peabody claimed, as Plato had claimed in the *Cratylus,* words "must have something of *a universal character."* Language was a "necessary product." It is what it is "precisely because it could not be otherwise." There was, Peabody added later in the essay, "a logos in the forms of things" that serve "as types or images of what is inmost in our souls." This form was embodied in grammar and words: The "outer world which envelops our being is itself language, the power of all language."

While Bushnell was correct in tracing "the national characteristics" of words, Peabody thought that he was wrong to stop there, for words could unveil the structure of the mind. "For what is language?" Peabody asked. "It is the picture and vehicle of all that has been present to the mind of Humanity, stretching back beyond all histories and other literatures; and its bearings are incalculable upon the discovery and retention of truth, as well as upon the discipline and activity of the human mind." Words were connected to an order imminent in the universe, which moved through custom but which was far more. It was not a question of inventing appropriate words but of discovering their hidden poetry, a poetry that was at bottom religious.[43]

The new philology shifted attention away from what Americans were creating and toward an understanding of their heritage. One of its key findings was that almost all of the so-called Americanisms were really old British provincial dialect. Indeed, the central and ironic discovery of this theoretically nationalistic philology was that in fact no national idiom existed. Schele de Vere would report in 1872 that "as yet there is no American Language." Marsh said the same thing in *Lectures on the English Language* (1860). The title of Alfred Elwyn's *Glossary of Supposed Americanisms* (1859) gave it away. "This little work," he wrote, "was undertaken to show how much there yet remains, in this country, of language and customs directly brought from our remotest ancestry."[44]

Another purpose was to contradict the criticisms of American words so prevalent in previous decades. According to Elwyn, the British travelers and writers who twitted us "upon the supposed peculiarity and oddity in our use of words" were just parading their own ignorance. But if Elwyn and the others critiqued earlier linguistic conservatives, they did not, as Jefferson had, defend the right of Americans to invent their own dialect. Rather the romantic philologists spoke of their realization of what the words in question actually were. "The simple truth is, that almost without exception all those words or phrases that we have been ridiculed for using, are good old English; many of them are Anglo-Saxon in origin, and nearly all to be heard at this day in England."[45]

[43] Elizabeth P. Peabody, "Language," in *Aesthetic Papers*, ed. Elizabeth P. Peabody (Boston, 1849), 215, 216, 220.
[44] Marsh, *Lectures on the English Language*, 66; M. Schele de Vere, *Americanisms: The English of the New World* (New York, 1872), 3; Alfred L. Elwyn, *Glossary of Supposed Americanisms* (Philadelphia, 1859), iii.
[45] Elwyn, *Glossary,* iii.

Writers like Elwyn and James Russell Lowell emphasized the ties between Old English and New England. *Aggravate,* for "irritate," Elwyn found in Forby's *Vocabulary of East Anglia. Hop-scotch* was in reality a mutation of *hop-score,* the latter widely heard in Hallamshire. A word like *squirm* was not really an American invention but from the south of England. Chaucer used *gab.* These philologists, moreover, did not just investigate vocabulary. As Maximilian Schele de Vere observed, the New England drawl was nothing more than "the well-known Norfolk 'whine.' "[46]

While New England speech was important, even a Brahmin like Lowell did not restrict himself to that dialect. Using *allow* for *affirm* ("I allow that's a good horse"), a locution prevailing "in the Southern and Middle States," Lowell found in Richard Hakluyt's sixteenth-century prose and even further back in Old English. As early as 1829 an article appeared in the *Virginia Literary Museum* attacking Pickering for not seeing "that many of the reputed Americanisms are common in the Provinces of England." The unnamed southerner who wrote that article was among the first to suggest that looking for the sources of words might change our understanding of them. Later, Schele de Vere, who taught at the University of Virginia, made the same point. Southern states in the seventeenth century got "a strongly marked vocabulary" from "her cavalier-settlers and countless indentured-servants," he wrote. These were "faithfully and with Southern conservatism preserved." Thus the southern *afeared* is just the old Saxon for *afraid; centrical* resisted the more modern *central;* and that notorious southernism *reckon* ("I *reckon* I'll go to the store") could be readily found in the King James Bible.[47]

How this retrieval of Old English was used to counter earlier criticism can be seen in the reinterpretation of the verb *to progress.* For this too was discovered to be a piece of forgotten English, widely used in Devonshire, from where, as Schele de Vere noted, "a great number of the early settlers" had come. *Progressing,* the activity, no longer seemed *just* American; it was now part of the Anglo-American way. James Russell Lowell could not resist sarcasm: "Surely we may sleep in peace now, and our English cousins will forgive us, since we have cleared ourselves from any suspicion of being original in the matter."[48]

While the most important part of the language was Anglo-Saxon, philologists also celebrated the capacity of the language to borrow from varied sources. Place names like *Harlem, Flushing,* and *Poughkeepsie* came from the Dutch, as did *boss, cookie,* and *Santa Claus.* From the Spanish came *cavort, negro,* and *vamoose. Loafer, noodles,* and *sauerkraut* were originally German. Even the Irish, while not contributing much yet, were expected to add to the language in the near future. In fact, the only noncontributors were African Americans. This last claim, while not

[46] *Ibid.,* 14, 51, 60, 110; James Russell Lowell, *The Poetical Works of James Russell Lowell* (5 vols., Boston, 1904), III, 1–79; Schele de Vere, *Americanisms,* 427.

[47] Lowell, *Poetical Works,* III, 53–54. The article from the *Virginia Literary Museum* is reprinted in M. M. Mathews, ed., *The Beginnings of American English* (Chicago, 1931), 99–112. Schele de Vere, *Americanisms,* 427, 431–32, 450, 530.

[48] Schele de Vere, *Americanisms,* 524; Lowell, *Poetical Works,* III, 45.

surprising in the mid-nineteenth century, would not be challenged in mainstream linguistics until the 1970s when such scholars as J. L. Dillard began arguing that Africanisms have made significant additions to American English.

Even Indian languages had made useful contributions. Not only words like *squaw, squash,* and *tomahawk;* even more important were the place names, terms like *Pawtucket, Potomac, Appomattox,* and *Susquehanna.* Indian words were safe largely because philologists could only imagine the natives as a doomed race. Indian place names were useful because they lent the United States a historic register philologists feared missing. Schele de Vere found it unfortunate that so many Indian names had been erased by the Anglo-Saxon. Indian place names, while "not legitimately included in a very strict definition of the term Americanism" were "almost the only really old things which we have, the only relics left to remind us that human beings roamed over our hills and floated on our waters before the Pilgrims landed at Plymouth." Tied to this was a sense of the alien as exotic. Indian names were "so musical and full of meaning, and ours so harsh and commonplace, that we should have been gainers by the exchange."[49]

That English would take so many words from other languages was meant to reflect on the English-speaking people. After all, it was argued, there was nothing new in this practice. English assimilated thousands of words from the French, Latin, and Greek after the Normans invaded in the eleventh century. Schele de Vere thought the English language "omnivorous." To Benjamin Dwight, the genius of the language was its ability to construct unity out of diversity. The "wonderful energy of its self-assimilating powers" revealed "its own individuality, as a language."[50]

If one feature of the language (and people) was its omnivorous assimilation of outside idioms, far more important was its terse, sinewy power. Images of power and strength pervade the romantic discussion of the English language, all based on the Anglo-Saxon roots of the tongue. While usually this was not explicitly associated with masculinity, such an association often seemed just below the surface. Occasionally, it could become explicit. Lowell, in this vein, called Lincoln's Gettysburg Address "truly masculine English." Another typical writer found the language's "strong aspirate, its open vowels, its close consonants, its army of monosyllables, its straightforward idioms" all representing "a race bold, daring and abrupt, full of enterprise, driving on its aim with an outbursting energy which no obstacles can bind."[51]

The new philology turned away from the earlier Lockean notions of arbitrary language and its commitment to the culture of invention. Words were now linked to historical mores that could not be altered by simply changing linguistic conventions. Words were expressive of lived traditions. At the same time, however, this theoretically nationalistic philology was in practice subverting any sense of linguistic nationalism. There was no American English.

---

[49] Schele de Vere, *Americanisms,* 11–12.

[50] *Ibid.,* 4; Dwight, *Modern Philology,* II, 298–99.

[51] Lowell, *Poetical Works,* III, 9; "The Claims of the English Language," *Southern Presbyterian Review,* 6 (Jan. 1853), 308.

Romantic philology ordered language in its own way. Etymology was destiny; our roots framed present possibilities. Received tradition, not imposed clarity, became the means of disciplining the language. Relying upon tradition, however, did not imply the wholesale rejection of modernity. Rather, it allowed philologists to interpret things like nineteenth-century "progress" as a traditional Anglo-American ideal. Romantic linguistics was a resource to capture and channel those explosive cultural forces swirling about at the center of the century.

The "nationalistic anti-nationalism" of romantic philology did three pieces of cultural work at the same time. First, wild extravagant speaking, the untamed speech of the early nineteenth century, was dismissed as an assault on Anglo-American mores. Popular literature was antitraditional. *Absquatulate* or *teetotatious* were ugly rejections of Saxon English. All the romantic philologists were disgusted by the new language games of the early nineteenth century. In this they did not differ at all from earlier defenders of refined speech like Witherspoon or Pickering.[52]

Second, the descriptions of English as "omnivorous" and "powerful" expressed support for the expansionism of the Anglo-Saxon peoples around the globe. Not only British imperialism but the western expansion that decimated the Indian population all seemed "natural" given the characteristics of the people and their language. There was just no question for George Perkins Marsh that contemporary English was already what Greek and Latin were to the ancients—the language heard all over the world. (He got his geography wrong here. Ancient Latin was not heard outside the Roman empire.)[53] The forceful energy associated with English, as well as its capacity to absorb from other sources, made it an ideal global idiom.

In this sense, the new linguistics remained cosmopolitan. But it was not the cosmopolitanism of an educated social stratum that Pickering espoused. It was an imperial cosmopolitanism of a chosen people. And here, the spiritual, supracultural aspect of the new linguistics was especially useful. As a number of the philologists had noted, nationalism was fine but language was far more than the values of a people. It was the spiritual *in* a people. The double edge of this theory, both individualizing a nation and expressive of a universal truth, was already contained in Herder's formulations some eighty years back.[54] In the mid-nineteenth century, it was easily used to support expansion. Anglo-Saxon peoples had certain universal traits that needed to be spread over the earth. This was history unfolding.[55]

The denial of American English served a third purpose as well. As the nation fell apart in the 1850s it was unclear what, if anything, northerners and southerners

[52] Marsh, *Lectures on the English Language*, 440–42; Schele de Vere, *Americanisms*, 573–77, 653–58.

[53] Marsh, *Lectures on the English Language*, 439–40. There was one romantic philologist who did not support political imperialism—Elizabeth Peabody. See Nina Baym, "The Ann Sisters: Elizabeth Peabody's Millennial Historicism," *American Literary History*, 3 (Spring 1991), 38.

[54] Marsh called the English language "cosmopolite" in just this sense. Marsh, *Lectures on the English Language*, 439. See also Trench, *On the Study of Words*, 144–45.

[55] J. G. Herder, *J. G. Herder on Social and Political Culture*, ed. and tr. F. M. Barnard (Cambridge, Eng., 1969), 165–77; Herder, *Outlines of a Philosophy of the History of Man*, 163–66.

held in common. Romantic linguistics suggested an answer. The English language, now understood as an expression of a people's spirit, was shared by all.

Nations are, as Benedict Anderson has noted, "imagined communities." Nationalities have to be invented, people convinced they belong. And those who at one point might see themselves as part of a nation at another stage will not. As Ernest Renan said in 1882, nationalism is a "daily plebiscite." But the *ideology* of historic nationalism, of a nationalism that is *not* imagined, but there, embedded in blood or language or custom, became important to the generation prior to Renan. For a writer like Jules Michelet, what was crucial was recovering the memory of the ancient French people. This was not a nationalism that thought culture should follow citizenship, a notion expressed by French ideologues in the 1790s and in 1789 by Noah Webster. Nor was it the nationalism of Renan in the 1880s or of roughly contemporary proponents of "Americanization" in the United States, people who freely admitted that nations were forged by getting people to forget what had divided them in the past rather than remembering common histories. Anderson points out that the historicist strain of nationalist thought, derived from Herder, became important in western Europe after the first blush of revolutionary nationalism had passed and while civil discord was prominent.[56]

Parallel forces were at play in the United States. When Lincoln referred in his first inaugural to the "mystic chords of memory" that bound the nation together, it must have struck most Americans—northern and southern alike—as a folly. This was a "nation" getting ready to war with itself. Nevertheless, the phrase expressed that same historically rooted nationalism of Michelet—and the historical philologists. Ironically, the denial of a new American English served nationalistic ends. Etymology told citizens that they *were* one, that their *roots,* quite literally, were the same. Here were those "mystic chords of memory" that Lincoln spoke of. It was probably the only ideology of nationalism possible in the 1850s and 1860s.

Despite their preoccupation with etymology, romantic philologists were far more ambivalent about modernity than later writers who developed their themes.[57] They did not repudiate Victorian notions of progress so much as try to channel them in particular directions. Some did press to stop linguistic change, but others thought it reasonable to "invent" new terms when the need arose.[58]

At moments like this, moments scattered in between their paeans to historical memory, the romantic philologists edged back toward the culture of invention. But instead of seeing linguistic invention as a social compact monitored by the cultivated, midcentury philologists proclaimed the poet the real maker of words. While

---

[56] Benedict Anderson, *Imagined Communities: Reflections on the Origin and Spread of Nationalism* (London, 1991), 187–206.

[57] I am thinking here of Martin Heidegger, who builds on a number of the themes of romantic philology.

[58] Marsh, *Lectures on the English Language,* 17; Dwight, *Modern Philology,* I, 141–44; Schele de Vere, *Americanisms,* 3–4; Trench, *On the Study of Words,* 130–72. Trench stated that the most common reason for new words was a new spiritual state of a people. When in "the appointments of highest Wisdom new moral and spiritual forces begin to work, and stir a society to its depths," new terms must be found to express this. God, in other words, not human invention, is the critical catalyst. Trench, *On the Study of Words,* 138–39.

this strain of thought rested in the background for most romantic philologists, when it took over it could even sustain the dream of an American English.

It did for Emerson. His commitment to an American idiom was not separate from his larger sense of the inventiveness of language.[59] But Emerson was not the one most interested in inventing an American English in the 1850s. That was the poet Walt Whitman.

Whitman had read books like Schele de Vere's *Outlines of Comparative Philology* and Trench's *On the Study of Words*. In the last half of the 1850s, Whitman sketched out two short essays on American English, wrote extensive notes for a lecture (never given) on the same topic, and collaborated on a book called *Rambles among Words,* a popularization of the new philology.[60]

In his writings on language, Whitman repeated a number of romantic themes. English was distinguished by being "composite" yet "united." It was vigorous, rough, and strong. Transcendental notions were evident. Language was not "arbitrary," as it was for the Lockeans, but the "most precious inheritance from all the legacies of the past." Nor did Whitman see truth as a matter of making clear pictures of our ideas for other people: "Whatever satisfies the soul is truth."[61]

But Whitman used these themes in his own way. "In America an immense number of new words are needed," he claimed. The "life-spirit of American States" had to be grafted onto the language. Whitman was quite sure of it: There had to be an American English.[62]

Whitman was far more interested in what had to be invented than in discovering what was already there. He took the creative side of romantic linguistics, that which made the poet the "maker" of new words, and expanded its importance so much that it obliterated the conservative sense of a language bounded by its history. Whitman was no etymologist, his politics wouldn't allow it. English "is not a fossil-language," he said, criticizing the other philologists, "but a broad fluid language of democracy."[63]

Whitman, in fact, was trying to transcend the very dispute between invention and discovery. Whitman spoke of easy movement from the past to the future, always, at least in the 1850s, with the accent on what was to come. The great poet "drags the dead out of their coffins," Whitman wrote, and says to the Past: "Rise and walk before me that I may realize you." It is in this vein that Whitman claimed that an American English did not yet exist but was in the process of being born. A democratic people would discover who they were through their very act of self-invention.[64]

---

[59] See Richard Poirier, *The Renewal of Literature: Emersonian Reflections* (New Haven, 1987), 33–36, 147–48.

[60] See Kramer, *Imagining Language in America,* 93–94; James Perrin Warren, *Walt Whitman's Language Experiment* (University Park, 1990); Mark Bauerlein, *Walt Whitman and the American Idiom* (Baton Rouge, 1991).

[61] Walt Whitman, *New York Dissected: A Sheaf of Recently Discovered Newspaper Articles by the Author of Leaves of Grass* (New York, 1936), 56; Walt Whitman, *An American Primer* (Stevens Point, 1987), 1, 8; untitled essay on language, printed in C. Carroll Hollis, "Whitman and the American Idiom," *Quarterly Journal of Speech,* 43 (Dec. 1957), 419–20; Walt Whitman, *Leaves of Grass* (1855; reprint, New York, 1959), 21.

[62] Whitman, *American Primer,* 9; Hollis, "Whitman and the American Idiom," 419.

[63] Hollis, "Whitman and the American Idiom," 419.

[64] Whitman, *Leaves of Grass,* 12. It might be most accurate to say that in Whitman invention swallows discovery.

Whitman did not proclaim himself the genius poet who would invent the new language. The true poet, he thought, was the people themselves. Whitman's job was to record a people making itself in language. But even here he differed from the historical philologists. For Whitman, far more than the other romantic philologists, tried to fashion a sense of language that embraced the new language games of nineteenth-century America. Whitman was intent on conceptualizing an unbounded language.

The "Real Dictionary" of the people was far more than those dead wordbooks collected by pettifoggers, Whitman thought. American English would not come into its own until we acknowledged all the energy and diversity of English as spoken. The words of fighters, gamblers, thieves, and prostitutes ought to be collected, he thought, the bad words as well as the good, for "many of these bad words are fine." He loved the words of barrooms, boatsmen, and technology, of politics and the body. The American language had to capture it all. "A perfect writer would make words sing, dance, kiss, do the male and female act, bear children, weep, bleed, rage, stab, steal, fire cannon, steer ships, sack cities, or do any thing, that man or woman or the natural powers can do." Those who couldn't turned "helplessly" to the "dictionaries and authorities."[65]

Whitman repeated the claim that English drew from all sorts of European tongues. But for Whitman, American English had a special edge, enriched as it was "with contributions from all languages, old and new." And while Whitman shared with the conservatives an appreciation for English borrowed from Indian languages, he was absolutely alone in suggesting in the 1850s that "hundreds of outré words" from slaves moved into the common speech of the nation. And even more surprising, Whitman thought that what he called "nigger dialect" would be critical to the future of American English. African-American accent in particular hinted at "the future modification of all words of the English language, for musical purposes, for a native grand opera in America."[66]

The one thing Whitman hated about American speech was its nasal twang. And like all romantic philologists, he thought pronunciation a direct reflection of the soul.[67] Since Whitman thought truly great language was music, it was imperative that the offensive "flat tones" vanish. Slave speech would help, Whitman thought, but so too would Italian opera (he was a fan) and women. All three would make the language more musical.

Whitman dreamed of a time when "women shall not be divided from men." He explicitly mentioned women as "equals" several times in his notes on language and

---

The only discovery possible is that which we have invented. This sense of discovery bears no relation to the philological notion that uncovering took place at the spiritual root and that this origin defines us. Also, this sense of invention bears no relation to the Lockean view of language as something invented to give us an accurate picture of reality. Is Whitman, despite his transcendental trappings, moving toward the ultimate "will to power," where self-invention simply announces itself unencumbered by Being, tradition, or reason?

[65] Whitman, *American Primer,* 7, 16–17.

[66] *Ibid.,* 2, 24.

[67] Whitman, *New York Dissected,* 60; see also Whitman, *American Primer,* 10, 12, 20. For the other philologists, see Schele de Vere, *Outlines of Comparative Philology,* 219.

spoke of women taking their place in "Politics, Business, Public Gatherings, Processions, Excitements." But if women (and slaves and opera) brought musicality into the language of white men, for women (no mention of blacks in this regard) it worked the other way as well. Women had to be as strong and forceful as the language. There was no love for gentility here. ("Sometimes I have fancied that only from superior, hardy women can rise the future superiorities of These States.") The language would be powerful, then, but far more explicitly than the conservative linguistics, not strictly speaking manly. It was the "glory and superb rose-hue of the English language" that it could become, according to Whitman, "the tough skin of a superior man or woman."[68]

Just as Whitman tried to transcend the invention/discovery dispute, he also pictured American English as both national and cosmopolitan at the same time. It was not the refined cosmopolitanism of a *philosophe*. Nor was it the imperial cosmopolitanism of a George Perkins Marsh. It was an earthy, rugged version, a version including the words of whores and slaves and loggers, of war and birth and sex. It included homoeroticism.[69] Nor was this, it should be added, a nationalism that envisioned the "people" as a unified entity. America was, in Whitman's own words, a nation of nations. *The Leaves of Grass,* he once told Horace Traubel, was a "language experiment," trying to catch the "new potentialities of speech" in America. For "the best of America," Whitman added, "is the best cosmopolitanism."[70]

In the 1850s, Whitman's was a minority view. But in the years after the Civil War, the idea of an unbounded language would become commonplace, although by no means universally accepted. Linguists turned to the colloquial, with succeeding generations trying to incorporate more and more variations of speech.[71] Literary modernists and postmodernists would argue that language experiments were crucial.

Everything wasn't permitted, of course. We still have our police—copyeditors, class idioms, stylistic customs, disciplinary constraints. That the language of a journal like this is patrolled with keen boundaries will surprise no one. But current borders must be erected on a field defined by an initial presumption that all language is equal, a field, in other words, that opens onto the democratic horizon.

With the appearance of the notion of democracy, the dialectic between fact and theory alters. Before Whitman, when theory strove to bind language, words outside did not challenge theory, they proved it. For John Witherspoon, provincialisms did not undermine Locke's theory of language, they rather reinforced its import—if imprecision was rampant, then there was ever more need for clarity. After Whitman, however, this changes. When language is connected to the democratic idea, those

---

[68] Whitman, *American Primer,* 13, 21.
[69] Michael Moon, *Disseminating Whitman: Revision and Corporeality in* Leaves of Grass (Cambridge, Mass., 1991).
[70] Whitman, *American Primer,* viii–ix.
[71] Daniel Boorstin, *The Americans: The Democratic Experience* (New York, 1973), 451–62; Edward Finegan, *Attitudes toward English Usage: A History of a War of Words* (New York, 1980).

facts of language lying outside a theory become a challenge. How dare you exclude provincialisms? Working-class speech? Vulgarities? African Americanisms? Facts undermine theory, exposing the limits of particular visions of democracy. That which is excluded must be legitimated as an exception to the general rule.

Contemporary post-structural theory celebrates linguistic freedom as the bursting of boundaries. In this it reveals itself to be on our side of the Whitman divide. But it is precisely this aspect of post-structural theory (and politics) that raises questions among its critics. Can such toleration sustain a national identity? Or will the language (and nation) just spin out of control, the whole disintegrated into the parts?

Post-structural dreams of escaping boundaries are often connected to a language theory claiming that crucial metaphors have a life of their own, that discourse always threatens to trap us. The grid of language imposes order on the world, suppressing the sheer diversity of reality. Roland Barthes puts it especially dramatically. Language, he claims, "is neither reactionary nor progressive; it is quite simply fascist." Since discourse always threatens to control us, undisciplined speech becomes an act of freedom. With post-structuralism, a new dialectic of invention and discovery is posed: The inventive play of language can only be set free through the persistent exposure (discovery) of language's limits.[72]

This translates into an effort to transgress borders. The goal is to let diversity emerge through an unequivocal respect for difference, an idea, of course, that is very Whitmanesque. But if respect for difference and the smashing of borders were aspects of Whitman's 1850s musings on American English, he differed in one important way from current theorists. Whitman did not see any contradiction between disorder and order, between the elaboration of difference and an embrace of the whole. He did not think that any conceptualization of American English, by the very virtue of its being a conceptualization, would inevitably constrict the language. His transcendentalism was critical here. For Whitman, a cosmic order held all. "The English language is grandly lawless like the race who use it," Whitman wrote. But then he caught himself: "or rather, [English] breaks out of the little laws to enter truly the higher ones." In the end there was unity.[73]

Contemporary post-structuralism draws on themes that Whitman was among the first to introduce — the elaboration of difference, the respect for unbounded language. But contemporary post-structuralism often rejects the other side of Whitman — the integrative side. The respect for other is emphasized while the gesture of embrace is suspect as subversive of difference. "Consensus," Jean-François Lyotard dryly informs us, "has become an outmoded and suspect value."[74] Post-structuralism's the-

[72] Roland Barthes, *A Barthes Reader,* ed. Susan Sontag (New York, 1982), 461. For other examples of the claim that linguistics or discourse overreaches the diversity of reality, see Michel Foucault, *L'ordre du discours* (Paris, 1971); Julia Kristeva, *Language: The Unknown,* tr. Anne M. Menke (New York, 1989), 325, 328–29; and M. M. Bakhtin, *The Dialogic Imagination: Four Essays,* tr. Caryl Emerson and Michael Holquist (Austin, 1981), 270–75.

[73] Whitman, *American Primer,* also see Nancy Rosenblum, "Strange Attractors: How Individualists Connect to Form Democratic Unity," *Political Theory,* 18 (Nov. 1990), 581–85.

[74] Jean-François Lyotard, *The Postmodern Condition: A Report on Knowledge,* tr. Geoff Bennington and Brian

oretical disdain for "wholism" or "totality" all too often encourages this very suspicion.[75]

No doubt Whitman's own solutions raise questions. I can't imagine his transcendentalism winning many contemporary adherents (to say the least). Similarly, his utterly unreflective mix of difference and nationalism invites scrutiny. But if the particulars are problematic, the project might still have something to say to us. For Whitman, unlike many contemporary writers, assumed that respect for difference could be complemented by a clasp to the bosom, that unregulated speech might be tied to a sense of belonging that even included nationalism. To understand this is to unpack Whitman's own claim that "the best of America is the best cosmopolitanism."

Is it possible that current theory has once again blinded us? That efforts to expose the limits of language have ironically limited our own sense of how people might live together—limited, in other words, our own democratic horizon? Perhaps the dance of language and linguistics will have to take a new turn, with facts, once more, speaking to theory. If this happens, we can be sure that it will also entail a new turn in modernity's unfolding dialectic of invention and discovery.

Massumi (Minneapolis, 1984), 66. Since American historians often associate "consensus" with broadly shared values and the absence of difference, it is worth pointing out that there are other ways to use the term. The jury, for example, suggests an alternative. A jury's task is to reach consensus on a specific issue. Being restricted to specific issues, juries do no obliterate the distinct forms of life of jurors. In fact, good juries recognize that respecting the different values of their members will help in reaching any agreement. Nor is a jury consensus one that simply exists. Jurors negotiate the agreement, although not everyone necessarily gets everything he or she wants. Almost any political alliance is a consensus of this sort. This, in fact, is the usage Lyotard was condemning.

[75] For a discussion of this problem from an epistemological standpoint, see Azade Seyhan, *Representation and Its Discontents: The Critical Legacy of German Romanticism* (Berkeley, 1992), 152–62. On the implications for politics, see Martin Jay, *Marxism and Totality: The Adventures of a Concept from Lukacs to Habermas* (Berkeley, 1984), 510–37; and Martha Nussbaum, "Human Functioning and Social Justice: In Defense of Aristotelian Essentialism," *Political Theory*, 20 (May 1992), 202–46.

One theorist associated with post-structural thinking who might be compatible with Whitman is Mikhail Bakhtin. While Bakhtin complained about certain notions of totality, he also talked about "open unity" in ways that sound like Whitman, seems to have thought of a national language as an "open unity," and at times hinted that unity and diversity might be combined only because there was a higher spiritual force. Gary Saul Morson and Caryl Emerson, *Mikhail Bakhtin: The Creation of a Prosaics* (Stanford, 1990), 55–56, 60–62, 236–37; M. M. Bakhtin, *Speech Genres & Other Late Essays*, tr. Vern W. McGee (Austin, 1986), 60, 100. Whatever Bakhtin himself might have thought, however, contemporary writers more often than not use his idea of the carnivalesque to the exclusion of any other, a tactic that emphasizes differentiation at the expense of the more complex Bakhtinian notions of the dialogic truth and open unity.

Columbia, Columbus, and Columbianism

Thomas J. Schlereth

In 1777, American poet Philip Freneau personified his country as "Columbia, America as sometimes so called from Columbus, the first discoverer." In 1846, shortly after the declaration of war with Mexico, Missouri senator Thomas Hart Benton told his Senate colleagues of "the grand idea of Columbus" who in "going west to Asia" provided America with her true course of empire, a predestined "American Road to India." In 1882, Thomas Cummings said to fellow members of the newly formed Knights of Columbus, "Under the inspiration of Him whose name we bear, and with the story of Columbus's life as exemplified in our beautiful ritual, we have the broadest kind of basis for patriotism and true love of country."[1]

Christopher Columbus has proven to be a malleable and durable American symbol. He has been interpreted and reinterpreted as we have constructed and reconstructed our own national character. He was ignored in the colonial era: "The year 1692 passed without a single word or deed of recorded commemoration."[2] Americans first discovered the discoverer during their quest for independence and nationhood; successive generations molded Columbus into a multipurpose American hero, a national symbol to be used variously in the quest for a collective identity.

This process in the public (rather than the professional) American history of Columbus can be traced over three chronological periods: first, Columbus as a feminine, classical deity, *Columbia,* an allegorical figure symbolizing liberty and progress; second, the masculine, fifteenth-century European, *Columbus,* who sanctioned nineteenth-century American Manifest Destiny and western expansionism;

Thomas J. Schlereth is professor of American studies at the University of Notre Dame.

In addition to the other scholars represented in this special issue, who critiqued an earlier version of this study at the *Journal of American History* seminar in February 1992 at the Newberry Library, I would also like to thank several individuals for their advice and assistance in preparing the published article: James Barrett, David Buisseret, Mary Jane Gormley, Frederick Hoxie, Wendy Clauson-Schlereth, Carroll Smith-Rosenberg, David Thelen, and members of the Institute for Scholarship in the Liberal Arts at the University of Notre Dame.

[1] Philip Freneau, "American Liberty, A Poem," in *The Poems of Philip Freneau: Poet of the American Revolution,* ed. Frederick Lewis Pattee (3 vols., Princeton, 1902), I, 143; Thomas Hart Benton quoted in Ronald Takaki, *Iron Cages: Race and Culture in Nineteenth-Century America* (New York, 1979), 154–55; Thomas Cummings quoted in Christopher Kauffman, "Columbian Societies," in *The Christopher Columbus Encyclopedia,* ed. Silvio A. Bedini (2 vols., New York, 1991), I, 160.

[2] Kirkpatrick Sale, *The Conquest of Paradise: Christopher Columbus and the Columbian Legacy* (New York, 1990), 331.

and third, Columbus as the major symbol of *Columbianism,* a late nineteenth-century form of patriotic Americanism that involved cultural and political hegemony and various ethnic and religious identities.[3]

Between the tercentenary of the Columbian landfall in 1792 and the World's Columbian Exposition of 1892–1893, Americans configured and contested Columbus differently as a national symbol. During this period a substantial material culture universe of Columbiana surfaced in American painting and philately, monuments and sculpture, civic iconography and national coinage, pageants and plays. In the postbellum United States Columbus became a multiple (at times a split) personality. Evidence of this last transformation is the simultaneous use of Columbus as a model for the country's largest religious fraternal association, as a symbol for an annual ethnic festival that later evolved into a national autumnal holiday, and as the official icon for the largest, most widely attended, and most international world's fair held in Victorian America.

By 1893 many Americans had wider access to the Columbus saga through different types of historical evidence and through new methods of communicating the meanings of that information than they had had in 1792. In the early national period Americans knew Columbus through oral tradition and through elementary schools, where they read prose and poetry about the discoverer. Midway through the nineteenth century, an explosion in the visual arts brought them in contact with Columbian imagery in various media. Later in the century, as participants or spectators, they might learn of Columbus through plays, pageants, or parades. In the early stages of this American public history of Columbia and Columbus, a small, professional elite (authors, congressmen, art patrons, publishers, artists) managed her/his history. Over the next decades other cadres—immigrant societies, religious fraternities, educational associations, veterans' organizations—developed Columbianism in order to shape their own identities. To other cultures, particularly African Americans and Native Americans, Columbus throughout the era primarily symbolized oppression.

This century-long process of "discovering" Columbus was only part of a larger, many-sided quest for an American national character. It was, in the words of Frederick Hoxie's introduction, a process whereby Americans "invented new identities, and recorded new histories."[4]

Nineteenth-century Americans involved in this process were selective in what they fashioned from the Columbian past. Columbus had done the same. He kept a log, secret from his crew, on the first voyage; on the second voyage he required his men

---

[3] Excellent surveys of the professional historiography on Columbus are provided in Foster Provost, *Columbus: An Annotated Guide to the Scholarship on His Life and Writings, 1750–1988* (Detroit, 1991); Simonetta Conti, *Bibliografia Colombiana, 1793–1990* (Genoa, 1991); and Alfred W. Crosby, *The Columbian Voyages, the Columbian Exchange and Their Historians* (Washington, 1987).

[4] Frederick E. Hoxie, "Discovering America: An Introduction," *Journal of American History,* 79 (Dec. 1992), 835.

to swear to and sign a deposition that an island they had reached (Cuba) was main-land Cathay; and when he wrote his own history of the first voyage, he chose his facts selectively. Nineteenth-century constructs of Columbus had their myopias as well. For example, Americans avoided thinking of him on land, other than at the first landfall. His historic achievement was usually reduced to the act of the first voyage. His triumphal return at Barcelona received its due, but not his failure as colonial governor in the Caribbean.

Precisely when and where the historical Columbus was first transformed into the allegorical Columbia is uncertain. Massachusetts Chief Justice Samuel Sewall could be credited with the first usage of "Columbia" (1697) as a synonym for the New World. By the 1730s, the *Gentleman's Magazine* referred to "Columbia, which is the Lilliputian name that answers our America." In the 1760s, the term came into use in early American poetry (popularized by African-American poet Phillis Wheatley in 1775), newspaper articles, engravings, magazine titles, place and ship names, songs, and political cartoons.[5]

The Columbian writings of Philip Freneau and Joel Barlow survive as the most important examples of this early American literature. In Freneau's poems, Colum-bus is transmuted from a personage of Italian birth and Spanish employ into the first American. In Barlow's *The Columbiad* (1807), the discoverer becomes a literary vehicle by which to prophesy the future of a brave, new American world.[6]

By 1792, the year of the Columbian tercentenary, American interest in the dis-coverer manifested itself in several ways. King's College, so named under the rule of George III, became Columbia in 1784 in order to demonstrate "both the rejection of England and the glorification of America." South Carolina made Columbia its state capital in 1786, the same year the *Columbian Magazine* began publication in Philadelphia (see Carroll Smith-Rosenberg's essay in this issue). In 1787, Yale tutor and later university president Timothy Dwight issued the first printed version of "Columbia," a song so popular in succeeding decades that many considered it the country's unofficial national anthem. Two years later the Society of Tammany or Columbian Order began as a New York City political and social organization. Joseph Hopkinson's "Hail Columbia" appeared in 1798.[7]

---

[5] E. McClung Fleming, "From Indian Princess to Greek Goddess: The American Image, 1783–1815," *Winter-thur Portfolio*, 3 (1969), 59; Albert J. Hoyt, "The Name Columbia," *New England Historical and Genealogical Register*, 40 (July 1886), 310–13; Julian D. Mason, Jr., ed., *The Poems of Phillis Wheatley* (Chapel Hill, 1989), 87–90; Kenneth Silverman, *A Cultural History of the American Revolution* (New York, 1976), 116–17, 214–17, 320.

[6] See Philip Freneau, "The Rising Glory of America," in *Poems of Philip Freneau*, ed. Pattee, I, 49–83; "The Pictures of Columbus, The Genoese," *ibid.*, 89–122; Joel Barlow, *The Vision of Columbus* (Paris, 1787), rewritten as *The Columbiad, a Poem* (Hartford, 1807), book 10. See also the writings of, for example, Walt Whitman, James Russell Lowell, Ralph Waldo Emerson, Sidney Lanier, Emma Lazarus, Paul Lawrence Dunbar, George S. Woodbury, and Harriet Monroe.

[7] David C. Humphrey, *From King's College to Columbia, 1746 to 1800* (New York, 1976), 270–72; Carroll Smith-Rosenberg, "Dis-Covering the Subject of the 'Great Constitutional Discussion,' 1786–1789," *Journal of American History*, 79 (Dec. 1992), 841–73; Timothy Dwight, *Columbia, a Song* (New Haven, 1940); Edwin P. Kilroe, *Saint Tammany or Columbian Order in the City of New York* (New York, 1913), 184; Vera Broadsky Lawrence, *Music for Patriots, Politicians, and Presidents: Harmonies and Discords of the First Hundred Years* (New York, 1975), 142–45.

The tercentenary—a modest, largely private, east-coast, urban affair—took place in this historical context. It was a historical commemoration by elites, for elites, and of elites. At a time when British Americans sought political disassociation from Britannia, Columbus/Columbia provided a non-British European ancestor. Baltimore unveiled the first public monument in the world to commemorate the discoverer, a forty-four-foot obelisk of brick covered with stucco. The Columbian Order in New York likewise raised an obelisk to Columbus, but it was temporary and puny (a mere fourteen feet) compared to that in Baltimore. The Sons of Tammany, nevertheless, raised their glasses high and often at a 1792 "Evening's Entertainment" with such toasts as "May the deliverers of America never experience that ingratitude from their country which Columbus experienced from his King" and "May peace and liberty ever pervade the United Columbian States." Jeremy Belknap, a founder and charter member of the Massachusetts Historical Society, directed and dominated Boston's October celebration. His long homily, titled "A Discourse Intended to Commemorate the Discovery of America by Christopher Columbus," contained several interpretive themes that would shape the popular American perception of Columbus as a heroic, intrepid explorer, a symbol of "enterprise and commerce."[8]

In the early republic, Americans began using Columbia as an eponym in their expanding geography. In 1791, for example, the Territory of Columbia, later the District of Columbia, was established as the permanent location of the federal government. A year later Capt. Robert Grant, in a ship named *Columbia,* made a territorial claim on a mighty western river (calling it the Columbia) for the United States in a region (later Oregon, Washington, Idaho) then disputed with the British. Britain eventually named its part of the contested terrain British Columbia. The ship *Columbia* in 1792 became the first American vessel to circumnavigate the globe, foreshadowing imperial voyages of a century later.

Use of the adjective *Columbian* became a commonplace shorthand by which one could declare public allegiance to the country's cultural pursuits and civic virtue. It was used in the titles of sixteen periodicals and eighteen books published in the United States between 1792 and 1825—for example, *The Columbian Arithmetician, A New System of Math by an American* (1811).[9] Columbian school readers, spellers, and geographies abounded, as did scholarly, literary, and professional societies—for example, the Columbian Institute for the Promotion of the Arts and Sciences, which later evolved into the Smithsonian Institution.

[8] Sons of Tammany quotations in Charles T. Thompson, "Columbus Day One Hundred Years Ago," *Chautauquan,* 16 (Oct. 1892–March 1893), 188–93. Jeremy Belknap, *A Discourse Intended to Commemorate the Discovery of America by Christopher Columbus: Delivered at the Request of the Historical Society in Massachusetts, on the 23rd Day of October, 1792, Being the Completion of the Third Century Since that Memorable Event* (Boston, 1792), 57. See also "The Last Columbian Century," *Harper's Weekly,* Aug. 17, 1889, p. 655; Charles Weathers Bump, "Public Monuments To Columbus," in *Columbus and His Discovery of America,* ed. Herbert B. Adams and Henry Wood (Baltimore, 1892), 69–88, reprinted in *Columbus,* ed. Anne Paolucci and Henry Paolucci (Whitestone, N.Y., 1989), 53–77; and Charles W. Cole, "Jeremy Belknap: Pioneer Nationalist," *New England Quarterly,* 10 (Dec. 1937), 743–51.

[9] Edward G. Porter, "The Ship Columbia and the Discovery of Oregon," *New England Magazine* (June 1892), 370–71. Sale, *Conquest of Paradise,* 340.

There was a brief national debate about changing the nation's official title from the "United States of America" to the "United States of Columbia," among other possibilities. In this conflict, a struggle over national identity not unlike the linguistic debates analyzed in Kenneth Cmiel's essay in this issue, various wordings were suggested. Samuel Latham Mitchell advocated "Fredonia," a coupling of the English *freedom* with a Latin ending. Washington Irving proposed "Appalachia" or "Alleghania." Renaming the whole country Columbia was an idea of the Massachusetts Historical Society.[10] But the Spanish colony of Nueva Granda declared its independence from Spain in 1819, the first South American country to do so, and officially identified itself as Colombia Grande (later the Republic of Colombia or simply Colombia).

Columbia's artistic presence in the new republic paralleled and at times exceeded the allegorical figure's impact on North American prose, poetry, and place names. In the Western iconographical tradition of representing the world's four known continents by female figures dressed to symbolize their individual lands, colonial America was "almost universally represented by the figure of an Indian Princess"— a barefoot maiden with insignia of feathered skirt and bonnet, a cape, a bow, and a quiver of arrows. By the 1780s, other representations appeared: Hercules (whom John Adams once proposed for the United States seal), Minerva (Roman goddess of wisdom), Liberty, and Columbia—the last a symbol with no precedent in antiquity but, in the estimate of E. McClung Fleming, "the most original, popular, and durable of [American] emblems inspired by classical mythology."[11]

Columbia acquired political attributes. She was frequently depicted with the liberty pole and cap, the American flag, shield, and eagle, the chain of states, the thirteen stars, and the dates of the Declaration of Independence and the Constitution. In contrast to the Indian princess (barefoot and often bare-breasted), the Caucasian Columbia was fully dressed in a modest white gown. Later, like Britannia (to whom she was a counter-symbol), she wrapped herself in the national colors. Columbia with the helmet, shield, and spear of Minerva was often used interchangeably with Liberty. In many engraved tableaux as well as in vernacular art forms, she appears with George Washington. (See figure 1.)

Columbia derived her name from an actual historical figure, but she was a historical symbol *sui generis*. The Indian princess personified an actual race of humankind who had first inhabited the continent, had symbolized the Western Hemisphere since the mid-sixteenth century, and could represent the Caribbean peoples Columbus had encountered in 1492; Columbia was a symbol newly created for a new republic. While based upon the Western tradition of gendering countries as female,

[10] George Stewart, *Names on the Land: A Historical Account of Place-Naming in the United States* (New York, 1945), 169–73; George A. Zabriske, "Why We Are Called Americans," *New York Historical Society Quarterly*, 27 (Oct. 1943), 85–86. Kenneth Cmiel, "'A Broad Fluid Language of Democracy': Discovering the American Idiom," *Journal of American History,* 79 (Dec. 1992), 913–36.

[11] Fleming, "From Indian Princess to Greek Goddess," 59. For an insightful analysis of "the multivocal nature" and interchangeability of Columbia and Liberty, see John Higham, "Indian Princess and Roman Goddess: The First Female Symbols of America," *Proceedings of the Antiquarian Society*, 100 (1990), I, 45–79.

Figure 1. *Liberty* [Columbia] *and Washington*, artist unknown. Oil on canvas windowshade (c. 1800–1810). *Courtesy New York State Historical Association, Cooperstown.*

she was the construct largely of male writers, artists, and politicians. By invoking Columbus through the icon of Columbia, they retained a European ancestor and prevented their newly born American identity from "bleeding into an American Indian identity." Even after their political severance from England, they "continued to associate an American identity with America's discovery by Europeans, not with the Americans who had been here all along."[12]

Columbia, as Linda Kerber has documented in her *Women of the Republic,* became the ideal republican mother: an abstract emblem of civic culture representing peace, liberty, the arts and sciences, and abundance. As Carroll Smith-Rosenberg argues in this issue, Columbia's provenance and usage also reveal the "ambivalence of America's iconographic feminization." In her analysis of the frontispieces for the *Columbian Magazine,* she notes that the conflated Columbus/Columbia androgyny was partially the simple repetition of a historical/classical trope. But she also argues

[12] I am indebted to Carroll Smith-Rosenberg for this insight; Smith-Rosenberg to Thomas J. Schlereth, June 1992.

it was a return of the repressed for the first generation of national identity builders who could not completely subjugate the feminine aspects of an earlier American republican identity or subjectivity. In time, however, other repression and ambiguity recurred; when Columbia appeared with "Concord, fair Columbia's son," the image began to take on masculine attributes in a problematic attempt to represent "a virile and virtuous American republic."[13]

The gradual transformation of feminine Columbia back into masculine Columbus took place over the course of the nineteenth century. Columbia never disappeared, but Columbus's reputation expanded. In the national pantheon, he assumed a place with Benjamin Franklin and, of course, Washington. Occasionally he was represented with new vernacular national images such as Brother Jonathan and Uncle Sam, but in his first major nineteenth-century role, he had the stage to himself as a providential New World discoverer. In this persona, he had several personality traits: He was a male conqueror, but not a *conquistador* like Hernando Cortez or Francisco Pizarro. He became a more romantic hero than British colonial discoverers such as Captains John Smith and John Cabot. Finally, he was seen as a more universal hero than regional explorers such as David Crockett or Daniel Boone.

Various eighteenth-century British authors, ranging from those who assembled the twenty-volume series *The World Displayed* (1759) — a work that many American children, including Washington Irving, grew up reading — to William Robertson in his more scholarly *History of the Discovery and Settlement of America* (1777), had featured Columbus (rather than Columbia) in their popular writings. While colonial American writers such as Cotton Mather (*Magnalia Christi Americana*, 1702), Thomas Prince (*Chronological History of New England*, 1736), and William Stith (*History of First Discovery and Settlement of Virginia*, 1747) acknowledged Columbus in their histories, the first issue (January 1758) of the *New American Magazine*, by "Sylvanus Americanus," appears to be the earliest extensive treatment of the discoverer in an American publication. Washington Irving expanded Columbus's American reputation enormously when he published the multivolume *A History of the Life and Voyages of Christopher Columbus* (1828). Translated into eight languages, the biography went through thirty-nine printings and editions in the United States and Britain and fifty-one more in Latin America and Europe during Irving's lifetime.[14]

Irving's unplanned discovery of the historical Columbus parallels Columbus's unanticipated discovery of a New World. Irving was best known in the United States for his *History of New York from the Beginning of the World to the End of the Dutch Dynasty by Diedrich Knickerbocker* (1809), written for the bicentenary of

---

[13] Smith-Rosenberg, "Dis-Covering the Subject of the 'Great Constitutional Discussion,'" 870, 871, 872. Linda K. Kerber, *Women of the Republic: Intellect and Ideology in Revolutionary America* (Chapel Hill, 1980), 265–89; see also Higham, "Indian Princess and Roman Goddess," 74–79.

[14] Perhaps the most erudite version of Washington Irving's *Life and Voyages* of the nearly two hundred editions and imprints published is John McElroy, ed., *The Complete Works of Washington Irving* (18 vols., Boston, 1981), IX.

Henry Hudson's European discovery of the New York watershed. By 1826 he had been abroad for over a decade, and literary critics at home were complaining he had abandoned the national quest for an indigenous American literature.

At the same time, Alexander Everett, the American ambassador to Spain, learned of the impending publication of a major collection of Columbian documents (known ultimately as *Colección de los viajes y descubrimientos*, 1825–1837) assembled over thirty-five years by Martin Fernandez de Navarrete. Everett thought the Spanish documents should be immediately translated into English for American readers. He wrote to Irving in France, inviting him to take on the task; Irving agreed to what he saw as a fast translation job. While working through Navarrete's documents, Irving decided instead to prepare the first full-scale English biography of Columbus for an American audience.[15]

Unfortunately, Irving neglected to use Navarrete's amassed documentary treasures either fully or carefully. He claimed to make his history "complete and accurate as to all information extant," but, as numerous twentieth-century critics (only a few in the nineteenth century) have pointed out, the work had serious flaws. Irving created conversations and monologues; he manipulated chronologies for dramatic effect; he staged scenes of dubious validity. Through Irving's dramatic narrative, numerous Columbian myths—for example, Queen Isabella's offer of her jewels to fund the first voyage, a near-fatal shipwreck off Lisbon, supposedly instant world recognition upon his return to Barcelona in 1494—reached a widening audience as Irving's work grew in popularity. The book quickly became "the essential inspiration for the vast array of popular histories and paintings and poems and plays that seem to fill the skies of the rest of the nineteenth century in such profusion."[16]

Irving's popular biography contained the details of his hero's split personality. Columbus the determined American explorer dominated the book, but glimpses of Columbus the misguided European imperialist also appeared. In chapter 46, for example, we have a succinct portrait of Irving's focus on Columbus as an American hero of epic proportions for an age of readers who relished both the epic and the heroic: Columbus was "a man of great and inventive genius. . . . His ambition was lofty and noble, inspiring him with high thoughts, and an anxiety to distinguish himself by great achievements. . . . Instead of ravaging the newly found countries . . . he sought to colonize and cultivate them, to civilize the natives . . . a visionary of an uncommon kind." In what John D. Hazlett calls "Irving's imperialist sub-text," however, we find hints of a flawed Columbus: an eventual participant in the Atlantic slave trade, an erratic colonial administrator, a religious zealot, a monomaniac with an obsession for the "gold of the Indies," and an enforcer of the Spanish *repar-*

[15] Mary W. Bowden, *Washington Irving* (Boston, 1981), 54–111; Jeffrey Rubin-Dorsky, *Adrift in the Old World: The Psychological Pilgrimage of Washington Irving* (Chicago, 1988), 219–23.

[16] Washington Irving, *A History of the Life and Voyages of Christopher Columbus* (London, 1828). Sale, *Conquest of Paradise*, 344. Compare Anon., review of *A History of the Life and Voyages of Christopher Columbus* by Washington Irving, *Athenaeum*, Feb. 22, 1828, pp. 131–33, with William L. Hedges, "Irving's *Columbus*: A Problem of Romantic Biography," *Americas*, 13 (Oct. 1956), 127–40, and with William Hedges, *Washington Irving: An American Study, 1802–1832* (Baltimore, 1965), 241.

timento, a labor system instituted by Columbus whereby he assigned or "distributed" Native American chiefs and their tribes to work for Spanish settlers.[17]

Although Irving exhibits an "ambivalence" toward what Hazlett sees as the darker Columbus, Irving is no revisionist interpreter. He explained away most of what would have been critique as resulting from the unsavory actions of his contemporaries and his followers: "slanderers, rapists and murderers who were driven by avarice, lust, superstition, bigotry and envy." His nineteenth-century readers likewise dismissed or ignored Columbus's actions as an enslaver of natives, a harsh governor, and a religious enthusiast. Irving's Columbus, "an heroic portrait" of an "American Hercules," became the standard account in American historiography for the next two generations. The book appealed to American readers on several levels. Irving created a Columbian saga that was "aesthetic, archetypical, and mystical." (He later wrote a *Life of Washington,* 1855, for which he constructed a fictional genealogy for the first president and relied upon Parson Weems's earlier myth making.) In the estimate of modern biographers, Irving "turned the story of Columbus into a work of art" wherein the discoverer could play several parts: the hero of a typical romantic novel so popular with antebellum Americans, a "modern Odysseus or a Faust casting a giant wager against fate, or a mythic American Adam, the First Man of the New World."[18]

The Irving biography widely influenced American school textbooks for the rest of the century. Such books concentrated on two elements of Columbus's history: his *passages,* that is, his transatlantic voyages of New World exploration; and his *personage,* that is, the character traits that made him an ideal New World man, an American worthy of emulation by the young.[19] As Ruth Miller Elson exhaustively documents, each of these emphases had important subthemes. For example, in undertaking the voyages (usually no differentiation was made among the four), Columbus's motives are adjudged as "purely scientific; they came from a knowledge of the figure of the earth 'much superior to the general notions of the age in which he lived.'" Furthermore, his course westward was both God-inspired and God-guided; for instance, when faced with a major storm on the first voyage, "Providence at length interposed to save a life of so much importance." In short, his achievement was simultaneously "the most important voyage ever undertaken since the history of man" and "the most important event of modern times."[20]

---

[17] Irving, *Life and Voyages of Christopher Columbus,* 348–53. John D. Hazlett, "Literary Nationalism and Ambivalence in Washington Irving's *The Life and Voyages of Christopher Columbus,*" *American Literature,* 55 (Dec. 1983), 560–75. Carla Rahn Phillips and William D. Phillips, Jr., *The Worlds of Christopher Columbus* (Cambridge, Eng., 1992), 217, 224, 253.

[18] Hazlett, "Literary Nationalism and Ambivalence," 564, 566. Jeffrey Burton Russell, *Inventing the Flat Earth: Columbus and Modern Historians* (New York, 1991), 56; Edward Wagenknecht, *Washington Irving: Moderation Displayed* (New York, 1962), 182–85. Rubin-Dorsky, *Adrift in the Old World,* xv–xvi.

[19] See Carla R. Phillips and William D. Phillips, Jr., "The Textbook Columbus: Examining the Myth," *Humanities,* 12 (Sept.–Oct. 1991), 27–30; Mario D. Fenyo, "Columbus and All That: 'Discovery' and 'Expansion' in American Textbooks," *Perspectives: American Historical Association Newsletter,* 24 (Dec. 1986), 14–16.

[20] Ruth Miller Elson, *Guardians of Tradition: American Schoolbooks of the Nineteenth Century* (Lincoln, 1964), 190–91.

American textbooks also projected Columbus as a model American. For example, he is usually depicted as a hero who transcends Old World nativism ("Although a European, Columbus, like Lafayette, is exempt from the national characteristics of his native land"). Textbook authors likewise dissociate him from "the avarice and cruelty of the Spanish in the New World," often claiming that "these qualities entered the New World with the Spaniards coming after Columbus." Several textbooks, ironically, bemoan a lack of appropriate Columbian recognition in their own country. Elson concludes, "The naming of America for anyone but Columbus is universally regarded as a manifest injustice."[21]

By the 350th Columbian anniversary in 1842, Americans began interpreting the role of Columbus (as distinguished from that of Columbia) in American history differently, in both visual and verbal forms. Some images of Columbus (a man never painted or drawn from life) had been done by American painters such as Benjamin West (*An Indian Cacique of the Island of Cuba,* 1794), by Edward Savage and David Edwin (*The Landing of Columbus,* 1802), and by illustrators in early editions of Irving's biography. Between 1840 and 1860, however, Columbus appeared increasingly often in large historical murals, public sculpture, and chromolithographs. Americans also discovered an additional use they might make of the Columbian past. Besides his being a providential discoverer, Columbus became a prototypical "westerning expansionist." This new image of his transatlantic adventures served as justification for the white American westward movement and conquest in the antebellum era. As the most famous champion of European expansionism, he was repeatedly enlisted by later Euro-Americans as they sought various "justifications for conflict"—with indigenous peoples, with the environment, with each other—over what they claimed as their national self-determination.[22]

In 1836 Congress commissioned four artists to fill in the large unoccupied mural spaces in the Rotunda of the Capitol. John Trumbull's famous panoramas—*The Declaration of Independence in Congress, Surrender of General Burgoyne at Saratoga, Surrender of Lord Cornwallis at Yorktown,* and *Washington Resigning His Commission to Congress*—were already on public view. Artists for the new murals could choose as subjects any individuals or ideas that illustrated events "civil or military of sufficient importance to be the subject of a national picture, in the history of the discovery or settlement of the Colonies . . . or the separation of the colonies from the mother country, or of the United States prior to the adoption of the federal constitution."[23] Two of the artists' choices celebrated European discovery: John Van-

[21] *Ibid.,* 191, 190.

[22] Hoxie, "Discovering America," 835; Takaki, *Iron Cages,* 154–55, 160–93. See also Patricia Nelson Limerick, *The Legacy of Conquest: The Unbroken Past of the American West* (New York, 1987); Richard Drinnon, *Facing West: The Metaphysics of Indian-Hating and Empire-Building* (Minneapolis, 1980); Richard Slotkin, *The Fatal Environment: The Myth of the Frontier in the Age of Industrialism, 1800–1890* (New York, 1985); and Peter Antelyes, *Tales of Adventurous Enterprise: Washington Irving and the Poetics of Western Expansion* (New York, 1990), 168–69.

[23] Lillian B. Miller, *Patrons and Patriotism: The Encouragement of the Fine Arts in the United States, 1790–1860* (Chicago, 1966), 56. On the import of the Capitol's influential iconography in the nineteenth century, see Barry

Figure 2. *Landing of Columbus at the Island of Guanahani, West Indies, October 12, 1492,* by John Vanderlyn (1842–1844). *Courtesy Office of the Architect of the Capitol.*

derlyn's *Landing of Columbus at the Island of Guanahani, West Indies, October 12, 1492* (1842–1844) and William Powell's *Discovery of the Mississippi River by De Soto, A.D. 1541* (1853); two commemorated European settlement: John Chapman's *Baptism of Pocahontas at Jamestown, Virginia, 1613* (1840) and Robert Weir's *Embarkation of the Pilgrims at Delfshaven, Holland, July 22, 1620* (1843).

Lillian Miller and William Truettner have persuasively argued that such paintings had their politics.[24] Expansionist congressmen such as Edward Everett, Gulian C. Verplanck, and Gouverneur Kemble served on various legislative committees overseeing the Capitol's artistic decoration. They and others exerted their influence as to what would be appropriately a national "history picture."

Many found John Vanderlyn's *Landing of Columbus* (figure 2) an exemplar of the type. Vanderlyn, a member of New York's Columbian Order and a contributor

---

Schwartz, "The Social Context of Commemoration: A Study in Collective Memory," *Social Forces,* 61 (Dec. 1982), 374–402; William H. Gerdts and Mark Thistlethwaite, *Grand Illusions: History Painting in America* (Fort Worth, 1988); and Ronald Paulson, "John Trumbull and the Representation of the American Revolution," *Studies in Romanticism,* 21 (Fall 1982), 341–56.

[24] See Miller, *Patrons and Patriotism,* 45–57; William H. Truettner, "Prelude to Expansion: Repainting the Past," in *The West As America: Reinterpreting Images of the Frontier, 1820–1920,* ed. William H. Truettner (Washington, 1991), 27–58; and Vivien Fryd, *Course of Empire: Art in the United States Capitol, 1815–1860* (forthcoming, 1992).

to its iconography in 1795, achieved his reputation by painting portraits such as that of Washington Irving in 1805. Joel Barlow commissioned Vanderlyn to illustrate *The Columbiad*, for which Vanderlyn painted *The Death of Jane McCrea* (1804; also called *The Murder of Jane McCrea*)—a lurid encounter wherein two Native Americans kill and scalp a young white woman.[25]

Native Americans figure in Vanderlyn's *Landing of Columbus*, but they are assuredly not in control (as they are in the McCrea death scene). In the center of Vanderlyn's neoclassical composition, Columbus strikes the pose of a New World proprietor; he is costumed in the Renaissance regalia of the aristocrat he was not at the time of the first landfall. Sword in one hand, conqueror's standard in the other, he takes it as a Caucasian right to *possess* (a verb frequently found in titles of paintings of the landfall) what he has found. In his wake, Native American peoples succumb or flee; the Pinzon brothers grudgingly concede his successful arrival; and a penitent mutineer bows on bended knee. To the far left, two of his crew jostle one another as they paw the sand for gold. No clergy accompanied Columbus on the first voyage, but Vanderlyn included a Franciscan monk holding a crucifix. That cross would follow crown is even more explicit in two of the other murals, Powell's *Discovery of the Mississippi River* and Chapman's *Baptism of Pocahontas*.

Charles W. Bump noted in 1892 that the Vanderlyn painting had become "familiar to every American by frequent engravings and lithographs, and more especially by being engraved on the back of the national bank note"; it was also used in advertisements, on souvenirs, and on an 1869 postage stamp. In 1892 the painting was on the two-cent stamp, one of fifteen commemoratives prepared by the federal postal service for the Columbian Exposition, but the engraver had purged the two fighting sailors from the design.[26] (In 1992 the United States Postal Service edited Vanderlyn's original image still further: Columbus and a half-dozen figures are on a twenty-nine-cent stamp for the World Columbian Stamp Expo '92 in Chicago, May 22–31, 1992.)

The commemorative stamp series of 1892 shows the several contexts in which nineteenth-century American artists interpreted Columbus as a historical figure: (a) the court, (b) the voyage, (c) the discovery, and (d) the humiliation. Not surprisingly, the largest number of Columbus paintings and sculptures produced by 1893 involve the admiral departing Spain, sailing the Atlantic, and discovering a new world and new peoples. A smaller number interpret his decade of petitioning the European monarchies (Portugal, Italy, France, England, Spain) to fund his expedition. Still less attention is given to his final three voyages, his disgrace, delusions, imprisonment, and death.

---

[25] Samuel Y. Edgerton, Jr., "The Murder of Jane McCrea: The Tragedy of an American *Tableau d'historie*," *Art Bulletin*, 47 (Dec. 1965), 481–92.

[26] Bump, "Public Monuments to Columbus," 55. The Vanderlyn painting appeared on the back of the $5 National Bank note of 1863–1875; on the note's front was an image of Columbus sighting land. Columbus was also on the front of the $1000 United States note of 1869–1880 and on the back of the $5 Federal Reserve note of 1914–1922. For an illustration of the 1892 stamp alteration, see United States Postal Service, *The Postal Service Guide to U.S. Stamps* (Washington, 1985), 61.

Figure 3. *Columbus before the Queen,* by Peter F. Rothermel (1842). *Courtesy National Museum of American Art, Smithsonian Institution.*

Philadelphia artist Peter F. Rothermel painted *Columbus before the Queen* (1842) as high drama. (See figure 3.) Rothermel perpetuates the apocryphal legend in which Isabella offers her jewels to finance the first voyage. Her hands are crossed on her breast (where rests a large pendant); she and Columbus eye each other with subtle ardor, which is not lost on King Ferdinand, whatever he may think of the Genoese's exploration schemes. Between queen and commoner is a terrestrial globe, possibly emblematic of their hoped-for "romantic complicity in New World discovery."[27]

Columbus's first voyage was in fact partially financed by the crown's plunder of Moorish possessions after the fall of Granada, not by Isabella's jewels. Few terrestrial globes existed in Columbus's era, but Rothermel showed a nineteenth-century artifact, complete with an elaborate meridian table; he thus reinforced the theme found in many nineteenth-century American descriptions and depictions of Columbus that his voyage was a navigational triumph of human empiricism. Finally, Rothermel, usually a realistic visual dramatist, had the stage set all wrong: Columbus first encountered the Spanish sovereigns, not in the mystical, ecclesiastical sanctuary of the painting, but at the royal compound at Cordoba; and he did so, not in his aristocratic Van Dyck plumage, but in the vernacular dress of a late fifteenth-century ship's pilot.[28]

Two popular variations on the Columbus-at-court theme involve his supposed cross-examination by a faculty council at the University of Salamanca and his stay with the Franciscans at La Rabida, a former Moor frontier outpost converted into a monastery. When depicting the Salamanca encounter, for example, Emanuel Leutze and a half-dozen other nineteenth-century painters reinforced the assumption that Columbus, equipped with his nautical acumen and his sea charts, maps, and world globe, disputed with and ultimately bested a learned coterie of clerical academicians; no such thing happened. Through such paintings and prose such as Irving's, argues Jeffrey Russell, an image of Columbus as a "bold young rationalist who overcame ignorant and intractable churchmen and superstitious sailors" became firmly "fixed in modern folklore."[29]

In many La Rabida tableaux, Diego, Columbus's legitimate son, listens in on debates among Columbus, the Franciscans, and local seamen on the feasibility of sailing west to reach the East. Diego's appearance is one of the few instances of the artistic record acknowledging the Genoese's personal past. To my knowledge, his illegitimate son, Ferdinand, born of Beatriz Enríquez de Arana in 1488, is never painted. Columbus usually appears without family, ancestry, or history, not unlike his namesake Columbia. Finally, the court, Salamanca, and La Rabida pictures all suggest another feature of Columbus as an American symbol: He is a lonely individualist, a man increasingly distant from (and superior to) European institutions.[30]

---

[27] Truettner, "Prelude to Expansion," 57; see also "The American School of Art," *American Whig Review,* 16 (Aug. 1852), 144; and Gerdts and Thistlethwaite, *Grand Illusions,* 32, 47, 52, 82.

[28] Truettner, "Prelude to Expansion," 57–58.

[29] For an exposure of the Salamanca hoax (the debate was not about the shape but the size of the earth) and an argument that it was not the Middle Ages but the nineteenth century (especially Washington Irving's biography) that perpetuated the flat earth error, see Russell, *Inventing the Flat Earth,* 5–6, 40–41, 52–54.

[30] Compare, for example, Peter Rothermel, *Columbus before the Queen* (1842); Emanuel Leutze, *Columbus before the Council of Salamanca* (1841); Luigi Gregori, *Columbus at the Gate of the Convent of La Rabida* (c. 1882); and Robert W. Weir, *Columbus before the Council at Salamanca* (1884). Ann Uhry Abrams, "Iconography: American Painting," in *Columbus Encyclopedia,* ed. Bedini, I, 322–23.

Figure 4. *The Return of Columbus and Reception at Court,* by Luigi Gregori (c. 1885).
Courtesy University Archives, University of Notre Dame.

Emanuel Leutze's *The Departure of Columbus from Palos in 1492* (1855), a typical embarkation picture by an American artist, implies a connection between European history and a yet-to-unfold American history. Columbus, even before discovery, confidently predicts that the passage of civilization is westward and that western Europeans (following the western sun of the painting's background) are predestined to undertake the passage. Columbus, as Truettner notes, "assumes the role of a minor divinity, the most legendary figure in New World iconography," a resolute prophet pointing toward a promised western land. Even as the anchor is weighed, the hero, standing in the center of the painting's composition above throngs of the fearful and disbelieving in the boats below, knows where he is going and why.[31]

Columbus-discovering-the-New-World paintings were the most frequent artistic interpretations of his history, but there were also several versions of his return. *The Return of Columbus and Reception at Court* (c. 1885), a mural by a little-known immigrant Italian artist, Luigi Gregori (1819–1896), was included in the Columbian Exposition postal series. (See figure 4.) In Gregori's panorama Columbus is center stage, and artifacts of the New World (nuts, spices, pineapples) lie at his feet — his gifts to two sovereigns of the Old World. To the right a court page holds a Caribbean

---

[31] Truettner, "Prelude to Expansion," 77; see also Nestor Ponce de Leon, *The Columbus Gallery: The Discoverer of the New World as Represented in Portraits, Monuments, Statues, Medals and Paintings* (New York, 1893), 147; William H. Truettner, "The Art of History: American Exploration and Discovery Scenes, 1840–1860," *American Art Journal,* 14 (Winter 1982), 4–31. See Barbara Groseclose, *Emanuel Leutze, 1816–1868: Freedom Is the Only King* (Washington, 1976).

parrot with exotic plumage. Columbus, however, holds the hand of one of his human trophies, a Taino Amerindian in full (but inaccurate) regalia, presenting him and five other Native Americans to their new rulers. The natives, bearing shields adorned with Northern Plains Indian pictographs and dressed with sleeveless Mandan shirts, carry metal-tipped weapons. (Gregori took no interest in portraying the Tainos correctly—any North American tribe could represent the Caribbean peoples whom Columbus enslaved.) The Tainos are shortly to be baptized—a fact reinforced by the mural's large number of clergy (twelve priests would accompany Columbus's second voyage)—and one of them will be given the Christian name Diego Colon, after Columbus. Behind the understandably anxious Indian group looms a massive fleet and a large crowd, seventeen vessels and about twelve hundred people, ready to sail in the wake of the discoverer. (On the second voyage Columbus would return with fifteen hundred Indians to be sold as chattel property in the Seville slave market.)

Visual interpretations of Columbus's arrest and removal as Spanish colonial governor on charges of tyrannical misadministration, his ignominious return to Spain in prisoner's chains, and his largely unnoticed death at Valladolid six years later were more frequently executed by European than by American artists. When American painters depict the humiliation of Columbus, he is portrayed as a lone visionary, a man betrayed by an ungrateful monarchy.[32] To nineteenth-century Americans, a dashing cavalier was preferred to a fallen hero, a triumphant explorer to a tragic colonial governor. Nowhere is this more evident than in the Columbian public statuary, monuments, memorials, busts, and decorative friezes with which Victorian Americans populated their city parks, civic spaces, and government buildings.

In 1844, the year of James Polk's election as president and of the opening of negotiations on the annexation of Texas, Congress dedicated a marble sculpture group, *Discovery of America* (also called the *Discovery Group*), on the Capitol's east front portico. The ensemble was executed in Naples by Luigi Persico. Columbus is clad in a totally inaccurate suit of European armor and carries aloft an orb labeled "America"; a seminude Native American female, the Indian princess of colonial America, crouches awkwardly by his side, ready to flee. While some contemporaries and later critics debated the sculpture's artistic merit (Nestor Ponce de Leon, writing in 1893, thought Columbus appeared ridiculous: "he looks like a warrior of the XVIIth century, playing baseball with a preposterously large ball"), other Americans viewed the marble group as an appropriate symbolization of their nation's manifest destiny and racial supremacy. For example, in 1845, James E. Belser, a Democratic congressman from Alabama, argued: "The artist, when he made Columbus the superior of the Indian princess in every respect, knew what he was doing. And when he likewise placed the ball in his hand he intended further to represent the power of civilization. . . ." To the legislator that orb symbolized

---

[32] For example, see Thomas Eakins's sketch of *Columbus in Prison* (Kennedy Gallery); and Abrams, "Iconography: American Painting," 323.

"freedom" which would "fill Oregon: it would fill Texas: it would pour like a cataract over the Rocky mountains, and, passing to the great lakes of the West, it would open the forests of that far distant wilderness to . . . the far shores of the Pacific."[33]

Randolph Rogers's massive bronze Columbus Doors for the east entrance to the Capitol Rotunda (1855–1859) drew higher praise than had Persico's sculpture, but they also presented a political ideology. (See figure 5.) A companion entry to Thomas Crawford's later portal depicting events in the life of George Washington and American Revolutionary War history, Rogers's Rotunda doors contained a tympanum and eight major panels devoted to the history of Columbus. In the doors' niches are sixteen statuettes of representatives of the Age of Discovery, among them Cortez and Pizarro. A bust of Columbus surmounts the America eagle above the tympanum depicting the 1492 landfall, clearly the most important event in the sculpture's narrative. Like Vanderlyn's mural and Persico's statuary, Rogers's tableaux present Native American Indians of 1492 "as awestruck, frightened primitives." The doors are also an intriguing historiographical study. The bronze heads include four female Native Americans representing America and six males associated with Columbus, among them Washington Irving. Lorenzo Ghiberti's bronze doors (1425–1452) on the Baptistry of San Giovanni in Florence, known as the *Gates of Paradise,* served as a model for Rogers's artistic interpretation of the man who, in the judgment of some, initiated the "Conquest of Paradise."[34]

By the quadcentenary, other cities in the United States had erected twenty-eight monuments to Columbus, more than in any other country. The monuments feature the discoverer atop pedestals, fountains, triumphal arches, socles, and freestanding columns. Most depict Columbus as independent, destined, and triumphant; he invariably appears as a young, clear-thinking conqueror, the prescient visionary of the first voyage, not the beleagued mariner of the last expeditions. He is frequently holding or viewing a world globe, sometimes surmounted by an American eagle.[35]

As Russell has documented, treatments of the discoverer in American historical writing were analogous to those in the visual arts. In popular histories such as those by Bishop Davenport and Emma Willard, Columbus becomes a modern rationalist whose 1492 voyage disproves the alleged medieval belief that the world was flat. Knowledge of a spherical earth was common to most medieval thinkers. Washington Irving, French writer Antoine-Jean Letronne, and other nineteenth-century writers popularized the "flat earth error," which supported the secular rationalism of various

[33] Ponce de Leon, *Columbus Gallery,* 125. James E. Belser quoted in Vivien Green Fryd, "Two Sculptures for the Capitol: Horatio Greenough's Rescue and Luigi Persico's Discovery of America," *American Art Journal,* 19 (no. 2, 1987), 21.

[34] Other men may be Bartolome de las Casas, Marco Polo, William H. Prescott, and Paolo Toscanelli; Millard F. Rogers, Jr., *Randolph Rogers: American Sculptor in Rome* (Amherst, 1971), 67. Sale, *Conquest of Paradise.*

[35] Bump, "Public Monuments to Columbus," 57, 60, 61; Ponce de Leon, *Columbus Gallery,* 75–128; William E. Curtis, "The Columbus Monuments," *Chautauquan,* 16 (Oct. 1892–March 1893), 138–46; Barbara Groseclose, "Monuments and Memorials," in *Columbus Encyclopedia,* ed. Bedini, II, 475–85. Several illustrations of American monuments are found in Sara Agnes Ryan, *Christopher Columbus in Poetry, History, and Art* (Chicago, 1917). Elsewhere Columbian memorials proliferated: 10 in the Caribbean, 2 in Mexico, 5 in South America, and, in Europe, 3 in France, 7 in Italy, and 9 in Spain.

Figure 5. The Columbus Doors, at the eastern entrance to the Rotunda, United
States Capitol. By Randolph Rogers (1855–1859). *Courtesy
Office of the Architect of the Capitol.*

"middle-class liberal progressives who projected their own ideals upon the heroes of the past." Columbus became such a hero to some American and European intellectuals engaged in the large controversy of the "war between science and religion." As David Noble writes in his foreword to Russell's *Inventing the Flat Earth,* "It was during the last years of the nineteenth century and the early years of the twentieth century, then, that the voyage of Columbus became such a widespread symbol of the futility of the religious imagination and the liberating power of scientific empiricism."[36]

For a large number of Italian-American immigrants and many Catholic Americans, however, Columbus served as an opposite symbol. He became an American ethnic saint in an era of unprecedented immigration. For him they created an American feast day, for him they sought official canonization by the Vatican, and with him as patron they created a para-ecclesiastical fraternal organization. As citizens of a disestablishment polity that had separated church and state but nonetheless fostered a national civil religion, such Americans now merged two faiths—Americanism and Catholicism—into a credo some called Columbianism.[37]

The uncertainty of Columbus's ethnic origins enabled many nationalities to name him as their own. Rival claims were put forth by Corsica, Khios, Majorca, Galicia, Portugal, France, and Poland; that the discoverer was Jewish has also had its champions. What Italian Americans claimed confidently during their nineteenth-century parades and pageants, however, is also the current professional historical consensus: Cristoforo Columbo was Genoese.

Celebration of various "Columbus Day" activities appears to have begun in the United States in the mid-1860s. In New York City, the first annual October sharpshooting contest (*Compagnia del Tiro Bersaglio di New York*), followed by a banquet and dance in honor of Columbus, may in 1866 have been the earliest such event. By 1869 the New York festivities also included a parade, a carnival, and the decoration of Italian ships in the harbor with Italian and American flags. San Francisco Italians first observed "Discovery Day" in 1869 on Sunday, October 17, but thereafter mounted their parade and pageant annually on October 12. By 1876, when the Italian Americans of Philadelphia erected a statue of Columbus at the Centennial Fair site in Fairmount Park and held their own Columbus Day parade, such historical commemorations were taking place annually in St. Louis, Boston, Cincinnati, and New Orleans.[38]

---

[36] Bishop Davenport, *History of the United States* (Philadelphia, 1831), 6; Emma Willard, *Abridged History of the United States* (New York, 1846), 22; both cited in Russell, *Inventing the Flat Earth,* 29. Russell, *Inventing the Flat Earth,* 29, 31; David Noble, "Foreword," *Inventing the Flat Earth,* x.

[37] Christopher J. Kauffman, "Columbianism," in *Columbus Encyclopedia,* ed. Bedini, I, 158–60; J. M. Dickey, *Christopher Columbus and the Monument Columbia* (Chicago, 1892); Henry B. Carrington, ed., *Columbian Selections: American Patriotism, For Home and School* (Philadelphia, 1892); Robert Bellah, *The Broken Covenant: American Civil Religion in a Time of Trial* (New York, 1975).

[38] See Roberta J. Park, "Private Play and Public Spectacle: Ethnic Sports and Celebrations in California, 1848–1915," *Stadion,* 12/13 (1986–87), 154–57; see also Frank Coppa, "Christopher Columbus in Historical Perspective," in *Columbus,* ed. Paolucci and Paolucci, 20–21; and "Columbus Day," in Hennig Cohen and Tristram Potter Coffin, eds., *The Folklore of American Holidays* (Detroit, 1987), 301–3.

History by parade and pageant, as several historians have documented, enjoyed enormous popularity among nineteenth-century Americans. American colonial and revolutionary war history events were the most revered and restaged topics, but seaport cities made use of their sites for other programs. In San Francisco, for example, the Columbian New World landfall was reenacted (albeit on the opposite ocean) at the city's waterfront, following a morning parade on Columbus Avenue. Favorite Columbus pageants and tableaux, wherever reenacted, included Phyllis M. Swinton's *Columbus The Courageous,* Yetta Klein and Florine Schwartz's *The Greatest Dreamer in the World,* and Emily Gibson's *New Worlds.*[39]

Columbus Day events promoted several types of historical consciousness. For Italian Americans, three were particularly important. Such civic ceremonies, especially the parades (which appropriated long stretches of a city as the stage for their historical dramas), became venues whereby the ethnic history of one constituency of the "new" immigrants could be publicly displayed in contrast to the well-established St. Patrick's Day parading of the "old" immigrants. Processing in honor of Cristoforo Columbo also meant identifying with nineteenth-century Italian-European history. Many viewed Columbus as a historical progenitor for a new nation in the Old World they had departed: the United Kingdom of Italy, proclaimed March 17, 1861. Understandably the major reason that the five million Italians who immigrated to the United States between 1876 and 1930 saw Columbus's history as their history was that he could be thought of as a *compatriotta,* the first American sojourner. Although he was not a permanent immigrant, he provided an authentic chapter in the American history of the nation they had newly adopted. In this way the collective rituals of Columbus Day paralleled other forms of Americanization among immigrants that James Barrett describes elsewhere in this issue.[40]

This ethnic embrace of one Italian hero was complicated by a growing interest in other symbolic figures. "Whether or not the very name 'America' derived from Amerigo Vespucci became a source of international debate for more than fifteen years after 1875." In addition to arguments over whether or not the Florentine Vespucci had discovered America, as proposed by German geographer Martin Waldseemüller in his *Cosmographiae Introductio* (1507), still other supposed discoverers such as the legendary Irish monk St. Brendan and the mythical Welsh prince Madoc were put forth in opposition to Columbus's priority.[41]

By the Columbian quatercentenary, however, it was Columbus, not Vespucci, who was the model American Catholic to many of his co-religionists in the United States. Parochial schools, orphanages, and hospitals were named after him. The

[39] See David Glassberg, *American Historical Pageantry: The Uses of Tradition in the Early Twentieth-Century* (Chapel Hill, 1990); Naima Prevots, *American Pageantry: A Moment for Art and Democracy* (Ann Arbor, 1990); and Susan G. Davis, *Parades and Power: Street Theatre in Nineteenth-Century Philadelphia* (Philadelphia, 1986). Hilah Paulier and Robert Schauffler, *Columbus Day* (New York, 1938), 201–58.

[40] James R. Barrett, "Americanization from the Bottom Up: Immigration and the Remaking of the Working Class in the United States, 1880–1930," *Journal of American History,* 79 (Dec. 1992), 996–1020.

[41] Michael Kammen, *Mystic Chords of Memory: The Transformation of Tradition in American Culture* (New York, 1991), 243. These disputes are documented with citations from the *New York Times,* Jan. 21, 1889, p. 5; Oct. 22, 1889, p. 9; Oct. 28, 1889, p. 9; and Nov. 3, 1889, p. 4, in Kammen, *Mystic Chords of Memory,* 750.

University of Notre Dame demonstrated the institution's commitment to Columbianism by commissioning Gregori to paint twelve murals in its Main Building tracing the history of "Columbus the Catholic"; *The Return of Columbus and Reception at Court* is part of that series. The Catholic Club of New York and the United States Catholic Historical Society issued a massive commemorative subscription tome, the *Columbus Memorial Volume* (New York, 1893), to honor their American secular saint.

To many nineteenth-century Catholics, the name Christopher Columbus seemed providential. Saint Christopher, "Christ-Bearer," was thought to have carried Christ on his shoulders across a formidable stream; he was the patron saint of both ferrymen and travelers. The earliest known chart of the New World, dedicated to Columbus by his friend and fellow sailor Juan de la Cosa, has a drawing on it of Saint Christopher. In Columbus's own actions and writings, there is ample evidence he frequently viewed his destiny as that of a "bearer" of Christianity to those whom he regarded as "pagan Indians." Corporate mogul Chauncey Depew, at the 1893 Columbian Exposition, praised this Christopher who bore "Christ across the sea," thus assuring "the salvation of the world, for the new continent was to be the home and temple of the living God."[42]

A movement to canonize Columbus, to secure ecclesiastical sainthood for the man whom some had already made a secular saint, came from various Catholic individuals and organizations in Italy and the United States in the middle of the nineteenth century. Italian-American organizations in the United States, some of the Italian ethnic press, and Knights of Columbus councils nationwide pressed the sainthood cause. They failed to convince the Vatican. Two obstacles stood in the way: Columbus's cohabitation with Beatriz Enríquez de Arana, which yielded a bastard son, Ferdinand, and a lack of proof of his performing verifiable miracles (an absolute requirement for canonization).[43]

To the Knights of Columbus, an American fraternal benefit society founded February 6, 1882, in New Haven, Connecticut, the papal decision was a severe disappointment. The knights, ultimately destined to become the largest body of Catholic laymen in the world, took Columbus as their patron. Their official historian explained they viewed the discoverer in much the same way as did the writer of an 1878 editorial in the *Connecticut Catholic:* "As American Catholics we do not know of anyone who more deserves our grateful remembrance than the great and noble man—the pious, zealous, faithful Catholic, the enterprising navigator, and the large-hearted and generous sailor: Christopher Columbus."[44] The founding council, most of whom were Irish Americans, apparently never entertained the idea of naming themselves after St. Brendan; for New Haven's Irish Catholics it had to be

[42] Quoted in Justus D. Doenecke, "Myths, Machines, and Markets: The Columbian Exposition of 1893," *Journal of Popular Culture,* 6 (Spring 1973), 538; also see Henry Paolucci, "Columbus the 'Christ-Bearer' (Christo-Ferens) and the Spanish 'Exodus' of 1492," in *Columbus,* ed. Paolucci and Paolucci, 42–52.

[43] Angelo Sanguineti, *La canonizzazione di Cristoforo Colombo* (Genoa, 1875); Osvaldo Chiareno, "La religiosita di Cristoforo Colombo e le polemiche sui tentativi per la sua canonizzazione," in *La lingua di Colombo e altri scritti di Americanisti* (Genoa, 1988), 27–50.

[44] "Christopher Columbus—Discoverer of the New World," *Connecticut Catholic,* May 25, 1878, p. 4.

Columbus. The "Sons of Columbus" was proposed first; the "Columbian Order" was also suggested, but the "Knights of Columbus" was quickly agreed upon in 1882.

To some knights, Columbus immediately provided an undisputable identity for all American Catholics, regardless of race or national background; to others, Columbus was a world hero against American nativism, a symbol providing "social legitimacy and patriotic loyalty." In the words of one knight, the cause of Columbianism was "the cause of Catholic civil liberty"; the discoverer symbolized that liberty. As Catholic descendants of Columbus, member knights were "entitled to all the rights and privileges due such a discovery by one of our faith."[45] In other words, the historical Columbus proved that their religious belief was no impediment to their American citizenship.

Discovering Columbus also gave Catholics in New England an alternative to that region's dominant interpretation of early American history. The first generation of knights, argues Christopher Kauffman, "viewed the discovery of America as a Catholic event, just as Anglo-Saxon Protestants viewed the landing at Plymouth Rock as a Puritan event. With the establishment of San Salvador Council No. 1 in New Haven, the Knights of Columbus were implicitly celebrating the landing of the *Santa Maria*, the Catholic counterpart to the Protestants' *Mayflower* and a ship which had arrived 128 years earlier."[46]

Operating from the premise that the discovery of America was "the first act of Catholic worship" in the New World, "a sacramental act," "the Catholic baptism of the country," the knights espoused a program of "citizen culture"—the ideal of "Columbianism." In order to promote this idea, they fought the American Protective Association and supported the Catholic University of America. Among their most distinctively Columbian projects was their commissioning of Columbus monuments such as Lorado Taft's Columbus Memorial Fountain (often called the *national* Columbian memorial) in front of Union Station in the District of Columbia.[47] With their headquarters in Hartford, they published their monthly *Columbiad* within the very precincts where Joel Barlow, a Connecticut wit, had, a century earlier, composed an early Columbian paean of that name.

Old-stock New Englanders and midwestern Scandinavians, however, contested Columbus as the nation's primal symbol. "Because of hostility directed at Italian immigrants," argues Michael Kammen, "strong resistence arose (starting in 1892) to making Columbus Day a legal holiday." As a *New York Times* editorial insisted in 1903: "Nobody needs a 'day off' every year to think about COLUMBUS and the discovery of America. . . . Nobody but our engaging friends of the Mafia would need all day in which to celebrate the feat of their compatriot."[48]

[45] Quoted in Christopher J. Kauffman, *Faith and Fraternalism: The History of the Knights of Columbus, 1882–1982* (New York, 1982), 16; see also *ibid.*, xii–xiii.

[46] *Ibid.*, 28.

[47] Maurice Francis Egan and John B. Kennedy, *The Knights of Columbus in Peace and War* (2 vols., New Haven, 1920), I, 47; Mary R. Dearing, *Veterans in Politics: The Story of the G.A.R.* (Baton Rouge, 1952), 407–8.

[48] Kammen, *Mystic Chords of Memory*, 242. *New York Times*, April 19, 1903, p. 8, quoted *ibid.*

Counter-Columbianism took other forms. Marie A. Brown claimed that Norse explorers discovered North America long before Columbus in *The Icelandic Discoverers of America; or, Honor to Whom Honor is Due* (1888). A Scandinavian Memorial Association had among its objectives the promotion of Leif Eriksson as the first American. Other Scandinavians, apparently to challenge the Columbian quatercentenary in 1892, planted the bogus Kensington rune stone on a Minnesota farm in the 1880s. New Englanders became fascinated with old Norse literature and history and, after a decade of controversy, erected a statue of Leif Eriksson in Boston in 1887, which was, in turn, countered by the Knights of Columbus who erected a statue to their champion on the grounds of the city's Cathedral of the Holy Cross in 1893.[49]

Within this context of ethnic, cultural, and political rivalries over the true history of the American genesis, the Grand Army of the Republic (GAR) joined various Italian-American organizations and the Knights of Columbus in a long campaign to introduce another national holiday (Decoration Day and Labor Day were also new to the era). In anticipation of October 1892, this Columbian coalition lobbied Washington for federal recognition of a "Columbus Day." Congress decided that the national day of celebration in the United States should take place October 23, since Columbus had arrived in the New World according to the Julian calendar (not the Gregorian calendar, which was instituted in 1582). That date in 1892, however, fell on a Sunday. Since all the promoters of the quatercentenary wanted to have patriotic Columbian exercises in the country's schools, a congressional joint resolution fixed Friday, October 21, as the commemoration day to be observed. By 1910 Columbus Day (moved back to October 12) became an official holiday in 15 states, 34 by 1938, and a official national holiday in 1964.[50]

The 1892 Columbus Day celebration was a patriotic extravaganza. In New Haven, Connecticut, six thousand Knights of Columbus marched in a morning parade with 36 bands and 11 drum corps; forty thousand people then assembled on the New Haven green, where three austere spires of New England Protestantism stood sentry, to listen to Columbian odes and oratory.

In his address, Rev. W. J. Maker, chancellor of the Diocese of Hartford, provided a litany of Columbian-Catholic ideology:

> Columbus—Columbia—what a name and what a nation. The one an emblem of truest Christianity: The other, a pledge of highest civilization . . . his flagship was named after the Virgin Mother of the Savior of mankind, Santa Maria. . . . The first act of the glorious admiral . . . was to plant the Cross of Christ on the shore, a symbol of his sacred commission to take possession of Columbia . . . as the viceroy of a Christian kingdom and representative of the faith of the Catholic Church.

---

[49] Oscar J. Falnes, "New England Interest in Scandinavian Culture and the Norsemen," *New England Quarterly,* 10 (June 1937), 211–42; Erik Wahlgren, *The Kensingston Stone: A Mystery Solved* (Madison, 1958).

[50] U.S. Congress, House, Committee on the Judiciary, *Columbus Day,* 61 Cong., 2 sess., April 19, 1910, pp. 1–25; U.S. Congress, House, Committee on the Judiciary, *Columbus Day,* 88 Cong., 1 sess., Dec. 18, 1963, pp. 1–45. On Anglo Noce, see Alfred K. Allan, "Forgotten Founder of Columbus Day," *Columbia,* 46 (Oct. 1966), 28–29.

. . . We enter the wake of the modern march of American progress . . . there is
no land, however far, fertile, or fortunate, like our beloved "Columbia."[51]

In New York City, the southwest corner of Central Park was officially renamed
Columbus Circle, a memorial erected by the Italians Resident in America was
unveiled — a column of Carrara marble with a statue of Columbus by Gaitano Russo
(only artists of Italian ancestry were invited to compete). (The city had denied the
Spanish-American community's petition to erect a Columbian shrine of their own
at the Eighth Avenue site; they were offered a "second-class place," which they refused.) GAR posts mustered out 10,500 New York schoolchildren for special class-
room exercises on the same day. In Washington, the national government issued the
country's first commemorative coin, a half-dollar memorial coin sold for a dollar to
raise money for the Columbian Exposition, and the commemorative postal series.[52]

Presidential candidates Benjamin Harrison and Grover Cleveland urged use of
the new Pledge of Allegiance to the flag as a way of observing the 1892 Columbus
Day and thereby honoring Columbus. The pledge originated as part of an 1888
campaign by the *Youth's Companion*, a national weekly children's magazine, to advance patriotism by encouraging the flying of the American flag in every school-
room. With support from the GAR and the U.S. Bureau of Education, the magazine
seized the opportunity of the quatercentenary's opening events to "invent a tradition" of American civic practice. Francis M. Bellamy, an ordained Baptist minister and
a *Youth's Companion* editor, coordinated the country's education officials into the
National Public School Celebration (NPSC), which devised a plan whereby American schoolchildren in October 1892 "would congregate in schools and churches to
celebrate Columbus's achievement and the Columbian Exposition designed to commemorate it." The NPSC provided American teachers with a complete, prepackaged
Columbus Day kit which included an address for Columbus Day ("The Meaning
of Four Centuries"), an ode ("Columbus's Banner"), and the song of Columbus
Day ("Columbia"). In an example of almost unprecedented national simultaneity,
twelve million American youngsters around the country joined a hundred thousand
Chicago schoolchildren on October 21, 1892, in saluting the flag and reciting a
twenty-three-word affirmation of loyalty as the city celebrated Columbus Day and
dedicated its world's fair.[53]

[51] "New Haven Celebration, Elm City in the Hands of the Knights of Columbus," *Connecticut Catholic*, Oct.
15, 1892, p. 1; quoted in Kauffman, *Faith and Fraternalism*, 81.
[52] Michele H. Bogart, *Public Sculpture and the Civic Ideal in New York City, 1890–1930* (Chicago, 1989), 60–61.
Dearing, *Veterans in Politics*, 408. Columbus, in profile, was featured on one side of the coin (according to a United
States Mint source, after a portrait in the Madrid Naval Museum) and the *Santa Maria* on the reverse. "The Columbian Issue of 1893 (#230–245)," in United States Postal Service, *Postal Service Guide to U.S. Stamps*, 61.
[53] Eric Hobsbawm and Terrence O. Ranger, eds., *The Invention of Tradition* (Cambridge, Eng., 1983) 1–13; for
the author's typology of "invented traditions," see *ibid.*, 9. "National School Celebration of Columbus Day: The
Official Program," *Youth's Companion*, Sept. 8, 1882, pp. 446–447, reprinted in Lovell Thompson, ed., *Youth's
Companion* (Boston, 1954), 391–401. "Dedication," *Chicago Tribune*, Oct. 22, 1892, p. 1; "The Parade," *ibid.*, Oct.
21, 1892, p. 6; Ellen M. Litwicki, "'The Inauguration of the People's Age': The Columbian Quadricentennial and
American Culture," *Maryland Historian*, 20 (Spring 1989), 47–58; Robert Knutson, "The White City — The World's
Columbian Exposition of 1893" (Ph.D. diss., Columbia University, 1956), 55–56; Robert W. Rydell, *All the World's
a Fair: Visions of Empire at American International Expositions, 1876–1916* (Chicago, 1984), 93.

Daniel H. Burnham, architectural impresario of the World's Columbian Exposition, claimed that the Columbus quatercentenary was the third most important event in American history, the other two occurring in 1776 and 1865. The fair, which attracted 24 million visitors in a nation of 63 million, was another chapter in the American quest for identity. The quest was manifested in numerous ways: *diplomatic identity* (the United States wrested the quatercentenary's international site from Spain and Mexico); *political identity* (a massive domed federal building and forty-two state buildings on the fair's grounds); *military identity* (a United States Army encampment, and the facsimile American battleship, USS *Illinois,* in Lake Michigan); *regional identity* (Chicago defeated Washington, D.C., New York, Minneapolis, and St. Louis to become the location of the fair).

Columbus, ever the protean American symbol, influenced many of these features of the American character in the 1890s. Columbia, Columbus, and Columbianism were all exhibited at the 1893 fair. Here too, in national as opposed to local or regional contexts, were revealed the problematic components of the Columbian myth, particularly as viewed by women and minorities. Here, for example, women and minorities contested the motivations of Columbus and the meanings of his "discovery."[54]

The early view of Columbus as a providential New World discoverer still enjoyed wide currency a century after Freneau, Barlow, and Belknap had molded him into a predestined and almost Yankee Protestant visionary and after Irving embellished this characterization with nationalistic overtones. In allegorical murals such as William Morris's *The Discoverer* (painted for the New York State capitol in Albany in the 1880s) and in countless orations at the fair, Columbus was proclaimed to be predestined, as was the nation. He was described in terms that appealed to the practical, goal-oriented, success-driven, Anglo-American mentality of the Gilded Age.[55] Columbus sought great wealth and commerce; so did *fin-de-siècle* Americans — to which the enormous materialism of the Columbian Exposition stood as overwhelming testimony. An international trade fair had no difficulty honoring a sea pilot seeking wider international trade.

In the late eighteenth century, Philadelphia publisher and businessman Mathew Carey used his *Columbian Magazine* to promote national expansion and commercial development. A century later, Columbus remained a model for the imperial ambitions of the United States, particularly in a city that was touting itself by the 1890s as both the Queen City of the West and the new American Seat of Empire.[56] The fair's Court of Honor, a stage set of Roman neoclassical architecture (see figure 6), paid tribute to Columbus while also evoking Columbia as a world power. Mary Lawrence's *Columbus Taking Possession,* a sculpture on a fourteen-foot pedestal in

[54] Jeanne Madeline Weiman, *The Fair Women* (Chicago, 1981), 523–50; Frederick E. Hoxie, *A Final Promise: The Campaign to Assimilate the Indians, 1880–1920* (Lincoln, 1984).

[55] Doenecke, "Myths, Machines, and Markets," 538.

[56] R. Reid Badger, *The Great American Fair: The World's Columbian Exposition and American Culture* (Chicago, 1979), 31–39; Thomas J. Schlereth, "A Robin's Egg Renaissance: Chicago Culture 1893–1933," *Chicago History,* 8 (Fall 1979), 144–55.

Figure 6. A view of the Basin and the Court of Honor, including Frederick W. MacMonnies's
The Triumph of Columbia (foreground) and Daniel C. French and Eward C. Potter's
quadriga, *The Triumph of Columbus* (center top), at the World's Columbian
Exposition in Chicago, 1893. *Courtesy Chicago
Historical Society, ICHi-02526.*

front of the Grand Basin entrance to the domed administration building, recalled
Vanderlyn's *Landing of Columbus* in the domed national Capitol. In sculpture as
in painting, Columbus was an imperial conqueror. Frederick W. MacMonnies's *The
Triumph of Columbia* or *Barge of State* dominated one end of the court's Grand
Basin. In a vessel vaguely reminiscent of a Spanish caravel, eight muscular maidens
representing the arts (Architecture, Sculpture, Music, Painting) and the industries
(Agriculture, Industry, Science, Commerce) propelled the ship of state, with Fame
at the prow and Time at the helm. An enthroned Columbia, torch in right hand,
navigated the course of empire. She gazed across the basin's miniature ocean to an
imposing Roman triumphal arch, atop which stood Daniel Chester French and Edward C. Potter's colossal quadriga, *The Triumph of Columbus*. In this ensemble,
a fourteen-foot-high Columbus drove an imperial chariot drawn by four powerful
horses led by women.

By 1893 Columbus, along with Columbia, had become a part of what scholars have called the civil or public religion of the United States. Columbianism, as an aspect of this civic faith of creed, code, and cult, added to its sacred texts (Irving's biography), feast days (October 12), credo (Pledge of Allegiance), hymns ("Hail Columbia"), and icons (Columbian statuary). In this context, the Columbian Exposition served as a summer-long civic liturgy, replete with invocations, dedications, odes, homilies, and benedictions. Some of the sacred scriptures were on public display in the full-scale replica of La Rabida monastery that served as a history museum; there were twenty-nine autographed letters of Columbus, one of his wills, and a copy of his *Book of Prophecies*. Ersatz relics, replicas of the *Niña*, the *Pinta*, and the *Santa Maria*, were anchored offshore in Lake Michigan. Steele MacKaye's proposal for a six-act spectacle of *The Great Discovery, or the World Finder* (for which Antonín Dvořák wrote his *From the New World* symphony) and Imre Kiralfy's historical production of *Columbus and the Discovery of America* also contributed to Columbianism's hagiology.[57]

Not all participants in the Columbian Exposition shared Columbianism's varied tenets. "We are doubtless aware that Columbus discovered America," argued Helen L. Bullock at the fair's World Congress on Women. However, "the greatest discovery of the nineteenth century is the discovery of woman by herself." Laura de Force Gordon, a lawyer from California, took the argument a step further: "The woman of the nineteenth century has discovered herself," she reiterated. "This discovery was of far greater import than Columbus's. . . . Her place in nature, no longer fixed by masculine dogmatism, shall be as broad and multifarious in scope as God shall decree her capacity and ability to accomplish."[58]

These arguments had real as well as rhetorical forms at the 1893 fair. The upper- and middle-class women who organized the Board of Lady Managers, the Women's Building, and the World Congress on Women pressed an agenda focused on the female future. Instead of celebrating Columbia, the republic's mother, or championing Columbus, the empire's father, they used the Columbian Exposition as a historical benchmark for citing past gender inequalities. Women at the fair also took a positive, progressive note. They demonstrated organizational and managerial skills, recognized past and present achievements by women in the arts and sciences, and in the process identified leaders who would play a role in the subsequent women's movement in the early twentieth century. A common manifesto fueled this varied activity: "In the Columbian Exposition, which celebrates a fifteenth-century fact," said Virginia C. Meredith, "the Board of Lady Managers stands for a nine-

[57] See Catherine L. Albanese, *Sons of the Fathers: The Civil Religion of the American Revolution* (Philadelphia, 1976); Robert Bellah, "Civil Religion in America," *Daedalus* (Winter 1967); Kauffman, "Columbianism," 159. Exhibition catalog: William Eleroy Curtis, *The Relics of Columbus: A Souvenir of Rabida* (Washington, 1893). On Steele MacKaye, see Glassberg, *American Historical Pageantry,* 167–68, 346–47; on Imre Kiralfy, see *ibid.,* 27, 30, 261.
[58] Helen L. Bullock quoted in David F. Burg, *Chicago's White City of 1893* (Lexington, Ky., 1976), 243; Laura de Force Gordon quoted in *ibid.,* 240–41.

teenth century idea. . . . [Its creation] may surely be considered a signal illustration of progress in the New World."[59]

Despite the requests of women such as Hallie Q. Brown of Wilberforce University, the Board of Lady Managers had no African-American members. No people of color sat on any of the fair's governing, funding, or advisory bodies. While African Americans repeatedly petitioned Congress for exhibition space both in the fair's main structures and in the state pavilions, the only official display allowed was the Hampton Institute educational program. Only a few members of Chicago's large black population were on construction crews or clerical staffs. Not without reason did an African-American newspaper in Cleveland label the Columbian White City "the great American white elephant," and Frederick Douglass, F. L. Barnett, and Ida B. Wells denounced it as a "white sepulcher."[60]

African Americans were unwillingly involved in the Columbian legacy from the beginning, but they were shown at the 1893 fair only in their 1492 roles, as were members of several other nonwhite cultures. As the exhibited rather than exhibitors, they were kept "in their place"; that is, they were located by the fair's white-controlled Department of Ethology in miniature villages, compounds, and reservations on the fair's midway. These living tableaux of colonialism, which historian Robert Rydell calls "the racist underpinnings of a utopian artifact," shared space with Hagenbeck's circus, wild animal acts, joyrides, and freak shows. The village displays reinforced American racial prejudices and ethnic stereotypes. The exhibits, often depicting people as curiosities (the Javanese) or trophies (the Sioux), were staged on what one contemporary called "a sliding scale of humanity." Nearest the White City were the Teutonic and Celtic races, represented by the two German and two Irish enclaves; the midway's middle contained the Muhammadan and Asian worlds; then, continued the observer, "we descend to the savages races, the African of Dahomey and the North American Indian, each of which has its place" at the remotest end of the midway.[61] Frederick Douglass, representing the Republic of Haiti, considered the Dahomean Village particularly repulsive; he saw his race represented there by the "barbaric rites" of "African savages brought here to act the monkey." In an address given at the fair's Colored Jubilee Day, Douglass castigated the exposition officials, declaring that the fact that blacks were outside the fair was "only consistent with the fact that we are excluded from every respectable calling."[62]

Native Americans experienced similar discrimination at the 1893 fair. Luigi Gregori had painted Columbus displaying his captured Tainos to Ferdinand and

---

[59] Virginia C. Meredith quoted in *ibid.*, 322.

[60] All quotations are from Elliot M. Rudwick and August Meier, "Black Man in the 'White City': Negroes and the Columbian Exposition of 1893," *Phylon*, 26 (Winter 1965), 354–61; see also F. L. Barnett, "The Reason Why," in *The Reason Why the Colored American is not in the World's Columbian Exposition*, ed. Ida B. Wells (Chicago, 1893), 63–81.

[61] Rydell, *All the World's a Fair*, 64–68, esp. 65. See also Robert Rydell, "The World's Columbian Exposition of 1993: Racist Underpinnings of an Utopian Artifact," *Journal of American Culture*, 1 (Spring 1978), 253–75; Hobsbawn and Ranger, eds., *Invention of Tradition*, 271.

[62] Frederick Douglass quoted in Doenecke, "Myths, Machines, and Markets," 543.

Isabella; exposition officials paraded the visiting duke and duchess of Veragua, Columbus's Spanish descendants, by the Native American "encampments" at the far end of the fair's midway. Donald Fixico, writing on the "American Indian Perspectives" of Columbianism, noted: "The end of the 1880s marked the ultimate defeat of native Americans and witnessed the emergence of their conquerors as a leading power in the world." A Potawatomi, Simon Pokagon, saw the Columbian legacy in similar terms. In Pokagon's judgment, Columbus and those who followed in his wake were arrogant intruders and avaricious trespassers. To Pokagon, the exposition meant only exploitation: "In behalf of my people, the American Indians, I hereby declare to you, the pale-faced race that has usurped our lands and homes, that we have no spirit to celebrate with you the great Columbian Fair now being held in this Chicago city, the wonder of the world."[63] Exposition organizers exhibited Native Americans in two contexts at the Fair. Frederick Putnam, director of Harvard's Peabody Museum, staged one display for the Department of Ethnology. Another was prepared by Thomas Morgan, commissioner of Indian Affairs. In the estimate of Richard Pratt, headmaster at the Carlisle Indian School, Putnam's living history ensembles of Indians from government reservations depicted Native Americans primarily as exotic savages, as relics of "a barbaric past." Emma Sickles, a former member of Putnam's staff, was equally offended by the "primitive presentations." In a long, but unsuccessful, newspaper campaign to close down the displays she wrote: "The exhibit of Indian life now given at the fair is an exhibit of savagery in its most repulsive form."[64]

Douglass, Wells, Pokagon, and Sickles represent important dissenting voices in Columbianism's varied choruses. There were others who questioned Columbus as an American symbol. In 1874 Aaron Goodrich, a maverick writer, produced *A History of the Character and Achievements of the So-Called Christopher Columbus,* a book that many historians credit as the first American attempt at debunking or demythologizing Columbus. Justin Winsor, the leading Columbus scholar in postbellum America, published his revision of Irving's interpretation as *Christopher Columbus and How He Received and Imparted the Spirit of Discovery* (1891, 1892), a study that raised significant questions about Columbus's motivation and meaning for American history. Critique also surfaced in the popular periodical press as the quatercentenary began. Eugene Lawrence, for example, writing in *Harper's New Monthly Magazine* in 1892, sought to revise Irving's "delightful biography," which "admits [Columbus's] faults but softens them into venial errors." Lawrence saw "the Columbus of history" as a medieval pirate and buccaneer, "a rude uneducated seaman" who introduced slavery into the New World. "He dreamed of golden palaces, heaps of treasure, and mines teeming with endless wealth." He was no saint for Lawrence: "Harsh, fierce, severe, the features of Columbus look down upon us

---

[63] Donald Fixico, "American Indian Perspectives," in *Columbus Encyclopedia,* ed. Bedini, II, 577–78. Simon Pokagon, "An Indian on the Problems of His Race," *Review of Reviews,* 12 (1895), 694–95; see also "The Future of the Red Man," *Forum,* 23 (1897), 698–708; *South Bend Tribune,* March 29, 1992, Section G, p. 1.
[64] Hoxie, *A Final Promise,* 88–90.

over the flight of four centuries, the symbol of his cruel age." William F. Poole, head librarian at Chicago's Newberry Library, argued Columbus was a historical accident, a man more avaricious than admirable. If the "discoverer" had not come upon the New World when he did, someone else would have early in the sixteenth century. To the erudite and urbane Poole, Columbus was a ruthless and unlettered opportunist.[65]

Such critiques challenged the influence of Columbianism in the 1890s. They foreshadowed the wider debate over Columbus's place in the national pantheon that would surface in the second half of the twentieth century; but the historical Columbuses (Columbias when American poetry, art, and architecture required neoclassical or Beaux-Arts personification) that Americans had constructed over the nineteenth century overshadowed these critical and dissenting positions. The Columbianism of *fin-de-siècle* America successfully conflated history and fiction, myth and reality, in its use of Columbus as a multipurpose national symbol.

What can be concluded about how Americans appropriated, adapted, or abandoned different aspects of Columbus's past between the tercentenary and quatercentenary? Did knowledge of the historical fifteenth-century Columbus impose any restrictions on the ways nineteenth-century Americans used him? Were there any significant restraints on the American Victorian interpreters of him as a national symbol?

To answer the last question first, it should be noted that many of his advocates had to ignore or minimize certain of his historical realities. For example, expansionists could not forget that he never saw the North American continent. Americanists had to remember that he sailed under the flags of several European nations, never under their own. Constitutionalists and supporters of religious freedom had to recognize that he served an autocratic monarchy that instituted a religious Inquisition that ruthlessly expelled Jews and Muslims. Nativists had to overlook his foreignness, Anglo-Saxons his Mediterranean ancestry, Protestants his Catholicism. Irish Americans had to deal with his Italian origins. Italian Americans and Anglophiles had to de-emphasize his allegiance to imperial Spain. African Americans and Native Americans could hardly condone his participation in the enslavement of people of color from two continents.

Within these complicated and conflicting contexts, nineteenth-century Americans argued with the historical evidence (often limited) and with each other about the meanings of Columbus. In this century-long process they fabricated several Columbuses, often according to their own historical imperatives. Why so?

[65] Justin Winsor, *Christopher Columbus and How He Received and Imparted the Spirit of Discovery* (Boston, 1891, 1892), 60. Eugene Lawrence, "The Mystery of Columbus," *Harper's New Monthly Magazine,* 84 (April 1892), 728–40; William F. Poole, "Christopher Columbus," *Dial,* 12 (April 1892), 421; William F. Poole, *Columbus and the Finding of the New World* (Chicago, 1892), 5–6, 18–19.

First, it should be remembered that the historical Columbus had almost as many public faces (Carla Rahn Phillips had devised a typology of seventy-one Columbus portraits that categorizes them into four distinct formats), career roles (seaman, chartmaker, caravel captain, colonial administrator), and titles (Dom Cristobal, Admiral of the Ocean Sea, Viceroy of All the Indies) as the multiple personalities that Americans created in their symbolic Columbus.[66] A man of many masks, Columbus took on many meanings. In addition to this protean quality, an element of mystery also surrounded the mythic hero. For example, today, as in Victorian America, several things still remain undiscovered about the discoverer: his exact ancestry; the precise date and place of his birth; when he first went to sea; where he actually landed in the New World; and where his mortal remains are buried.

The malleability of Columbus also made him a paradoxical symbol. His image appealed to a country that periodically bemoaned its lack of a distant past and alternatively boasted it was the first nation to transcend history.[67] To those anxious about the brief past of the United States, Columbus provided (by 1892) a four-century historical pedigree. For those who preferred to imagine the Republic as the first "new" nation, he represented to Euro-Americans the discovery of the greatest geographical "new" in modern times. The symbol of Columbus as the earliest and most ancient American mariner provided late eighteenth- and early nineteenth-century America with an emblem (Columbia) with which to counter Britannia and later Europa. The symbol of Columbus as the first modern American adventurer provided later Americans (well into the twentieth century) with an icon in whose image they would christen *new* communities, model cities, and space shuttles.[68]

The contrapuntal Columbus contained a final dualism. To the varied cadre that supported various forms of late nineteenth-century Columbianism—for example, Italian nationalists, the WASP managers of the 1893 fair, the Knights of Columbus, the Grand Army of the Republic—Columbus was simultaneously the last European and the first American. As an American Hercules, he held two worlds together.[69] Of course, to those who had been brought to America in slavery and to those who were, in fact, the first Americans, this Columbian image only meant oppression and conquest. To many nineteenth-century American immigrants, however, the dualities of being European and American characterized their immediate history. Columbus, thought by most of them to be the first European emigrant to America, represented to them success in both the Old and the New Worlds. Finally, to many white Americans (particularly those who considered themselves Americans by birth rather than by immigration), whether they were attempting to fashion a new nation

[66] Carla Rahn Phillips, "Iconography: Early European Portraits," in *Columbus Encyclopedia*, ed. Bedini, I, 315–21.

[67] See Michael Kammen, *People of Paradox: An Inquiry Concerning the Origins of American Civilization* (New York, 1973), 273–99.

[68] Gurrey Breckenfield, *Columbia and the New Cities* (New York, 1971); Charles B. Hosmer, *Preservation Comes of Age: From Williamsburg to the National Trust, 1926–1949* (2 vols., Charlottesville, 1981), 415–19.

[69] Abrams, "Iconography: American Painting," 321; Kauffman, *Faith and Fraternalism*, 160; Zvi Dor-Ner, *Columbus and the Age of Discovery* (New York, 1991), 330–31.

in the early decades of a new republic or, two generations later, bent on acquiring an American empire in an era of new nationalism, Columbus justified how they came to possess and occupy the lands and territories that they had acquired. Over the century, 1792–1892, Columbus, Columbia, and Columbianism served as important symbols in the nation's perennial search for self-identity. In various aspects of Columbus's individual character, many Americans found several representations of their national character.

Exploring a Cultural Borderland: Native American Journeys of Discovery in the Early Twentieth Century

Frederick E. Hoxie

During the early 1930s, a Salishan woman from the Colville Indian reservation in eastern Washington State began constructing her autobiography. In its opening sentences, she declared that "there are two things I am most grateful for in my life. The first is that I was born a descendant of the genuine Americans, the Indians; the second, that my birth happened in the year 1888. . . . I was born long enough ago to have known people who lived in the ancient way before everything started to change."[1]

Mourning Dove's words reach across a great divide in the experience of Native Americans in the United States. She belonged to the first generation of Indian people who saw that Euro-Americans were an inescapable presence on the continent and who had an opportunity to reflect on this fact for a broad audience. Like thousands of her ancestors, she experienced non-Indians, not as visitors on native land, but as a daily, conquering presence. But like few others, Mourning Dove had access to both the English language and modern technology and could therefore communicate her reactions widely. In this sense, Mourning Dove and her contemporaries were the first generation of Native Americans who could explore publicly the meaning of their predicament. Positioned as they were, between a remembered world of relative freedom and the grim realities of industrial society, people like the Colville author attempted to define ways in which their communities and their traditions might be valued in a new setting. They believed they could neither flee from white society nor contemplate an alternative world peopled only by Indians. For

Frederick E. Hoxie is director of the D'Arcy McNickle Center for the History of the American Indian at the Newberry Library.

I am grateful to David Thelen, Casey Blake, Susan Armeny, and my fellow authors in this volume for their encouragement and criticisms. In addition, I would like to thank the following colleagues for their suggestions and their careful reading of the text: Michael Grossberg, James Grossman, Harvey Markowitz, Jay Miller, Paul Murphy, Peter Nabokov, Gerald Vizenor, and Sarah McNair Vosmeier.

[1] Mourning Dove, *Mourning Dove: A Salishan Autobiography,* ed. Jay Miller (Lincoln, 1990), 3. For a discussion of the original text for this passage see *ibid.,* xxxv.

Mourning Dove's generation, the future depended on their ability to define and protect areas in American cultural and political life where the "ancient way" might somehow survive. Their efforts in the years between 1900 and 1930, which engaged them in fields as various as literature, anthropology, art, religion, and politics, were Native American journeys of discovery, journeys devoted to the search for a new home in a captured land.

Prior to Mourning Dove's birth, most Indians lived beyond the reach of highways and railroads. Even though tens of thousands of their forebears had died during two centuries of Euro-American invasion, most North American Indians living in the early nineteenth century encountered non-Indians only occasionally. Prior to 1800 relatively little sustained contact or social integration of the two societies took place. Their meetings were often dramatic but were nearly always brief: they crashed into one another on the battlefield or met formally at trading posts or in council. At the turn of the nineteenth century, the 5,000,000 non-Indians living in North America were clustered along the Atlantic seaboard and in the St. Lawrence and Rio Grande valleys, while most of the 600,000 Indians who had survived the colonial era sustained a separate existence in population centers in the Great Lakes region, the Plains, the Northwest Coast, and the Southwest. They lived out their everyday lives in communities that were overwhelmingly Indian in population and character.[2]

As Mourning Dove suggested, it was during the ensuing decades of the nineteenth century that "everything started to change." National expansion obliterated the physical distance separating Native America and areas of United States settlement. The United States population doubled nearly every twenty-five years between 1800 and 1900, while the number of indigenous people declined steadily. By the start of the twentieth century, the United States contained 76,000,000 non-Indians and only 250,000 Indians. These statistics paint only the outlines of a tragic historical narrative; they cannot describe the fervor of Euro-American "settlement" or the national chauvinism it unleashed.[3]

The conqueror's activities are relatively easy to trace, for the nation's continental expansion was supremely self-conscious. Unlike Christopher Columbus, who sailed from Spain in 1492 without soldiers or scientists, the explorers and settlers who enabled the United States to grow were supported by force and accompanied by professional academicians. The Italian admiral had not been prepared to study or even conquer a New World; nineteenth-century citizens of the United States heading into "Indian country" were. For Indians such as Mourning Dove, then, the arrival of the United States at their doorsteps produced a confrontation with a universe of ideas and expectations as well as an encounter with hostile strangers.

---

[2] Russell Thornton, *American Indian Holocaust and Survival: A Population History since 1492* (Norman, 1987), 90.

[3] Crude population figures obscure the fact that the nineteenth century was marked by the intermarriage of Indians and whites and by the rise of a large, non-Anglo-Saxon minority. The 250,000 represented people the U.S. Bureau of the Census classified as Indians, and the 76,000,000 included millions of African Americans, Asian Americans, and European immigrants.

The scientific classification of native traditions and material life was a central feature of the dramatic encounter with Indian communities in the nineteenth-century United States. Before 1850 this effort was carried out by individuals who were interested in recording the external appearance and behavior of tribal groups or describing the attributes of the "Indian race." The most famous of these early students were Thomas Jefferson, who excavated a prehistoric earthwork near his home, and Albert Gallatin, the "father of American ethnology," who compiled vocabularies of native languages. Despite their achievements, neither man was concerned with the history of a particular native community or the exploration of an individual tribe's linguistic philosophy. Instead, their concerns were general, and their studies were aimed at uncovering what they believed were characteristically Indian attributes and beliefs.[4]

A similar pattern was evident among the artists of the early nineteenth century. Except for George Catlin, who published his notebooks in 1844, most painters produced accurate renderings of native people and their possessions but paid little attention to tribal traditions and beliefs. Charles Bird King, who painted Indian delegations for the government in his Washington, D.C., studio, and Karl Bodmer, the Swiss illustrator who accompanied Prince Maximilian up the Missouri River in 1833, were typical of this trend. Other students of Indian life recorded physical characteristics (including cranial capacity) and folklore, but prior to midcentury there was little interest in the perspective of living native communities on history or recent events.[5]

At midcentury, however, as the pace of westward migration accelerated, scholars and collectors expanded their efforts to understand native communities. The publication of Lewis Henry Morgan's *League of the Ho De No Sau Nee* in 1851 (the first account of an Indian community's traditions based on extensive interviews with tribal members) marked the beginning of that acceleration of scientific activity as did the opening of the first Smithsonian Institution exhibits building later in the decade.[6] Although only one of the fifteen display cases inaugurating the Smithsonian's exhibits program contained American Indian materials, the collecting of native artifacts quickly became an institutional priority.

The Smithsonian's ethnological collection grew from 550 items in 1860 to more than 13,000 in 1873. For the remainder of the century, this pattern of enthusiasm spread quickly to other museums; displays of American Indian life became the basis for collection programs at the Peabody Museum of Archaeology and Ethnology at Harvard University (founded in 1866), the American Museum of Natural History in New York (opened in 1869), Chicago's Field Museum of Natural History

---

[4] Robert E. Bieder, *Science Encounters the Indian, 1820–1880: The Early Years of American Ethnology* (Norman, 1986), 205.

[5] See Brian W. Dippie, *Catlin and His Contemporaries: The Politics of Patronage* (Norman, 1990); and Robert F. Berkhofer, Jr., *The White Man's Indian: Images of the American Indian from Columbus to the Present* (New York, 1978), 88–89. Catlin's description of his travels among the Indians was a best seller in England and the United States. George Catlin, *Letters and Notes on the Manners, Customs, and Conditions of the North American Indians* (London, 1844).

[6] Lewis Henry Morgan, *League of the Ho De No Sau Nee* (Rochester, 1851).

(launched in the aftermath of the 1893 World's Columbian Exposition). These new institutions organized collecting and scientific expeditions that competed with one another in accumulating Native American artifacts and in laying the foundation for ethnological research in such new topics as language structures, kinship systems, and religious rituals.[7]

By the 1890s research on Native Americans began to occur as well in the graduate programs in anthropology, which had begun to spring up in the nation's new research universities. The rise of graduate programs in anthropology marked the final shift of Indianist scholarship from the realm of dedicated amateurs to that of professional scholars and signaled the transition of thinking about American Indians from generalized speculation to more rigorous, scientific analysis. By 1902 when President Morris K. Jesup of the American Museum of Natural History welcomed the International Congress of Americanists to the United States, America had become, in his words, "a new nation in science."[8]

Johannes Fabian, a modern critic of anthropological scholarship, has written that students of indigenous life have long perceived their subjects as "other men in another time." The engagement of Morris Jesup and his colleagues with Native Americans illustrates the dominance of this perspective among those who studied people like Mourning Dove. Jesup observed that modern technology had caused "even the remotest parts" of the world to be "touched and quickened by the genius and courage of the explorer." Americans, he noted, "have not been idle in the great field of discovery. . . . No more interesting study can occupy the mind of man of the present day than to know for a certainty how this great land was peopled, and the gradual advancement of the human race, from the far back up to the present."[9]

By calling research on Native Americans a "great field of discovery," Jesup was placing this intellectual enterprise within an American experience that coincided with "the advancement of the human race." For Jesup and his audience, the scientific discovery of the continent's indigenous traditions and beliefs provided an opportunity for them to incorporate Indian people into a progressive conception of human history that ran from ancient backwardness to modern achievements, "from the far back up to the present." As historian Curtis M. Hinsley, Jr., has written, "the museum process constructed a meaning of Indian demise within the teleology of manifest destiny." Indian cultures were, in Hinsley's phrase, "dehistoricized," and Indian people transformed into "other men." What Columbus's generation had begun, Jesup and his scientific colleagues were eager to continue.[10]

Because they believed Native Americans represented civilizations from "far back" in history, the new anthropologists also believed that they occupied "another time."

[7] See Douglas Cole, *Captured Heritage: The Scramble for Northwest Coast Artifacts* (Seattle, 1985), 10–12, 50, 165.

[8] *Proceedings of the International Congress of Americanists, 13th Session* (Easton, Pa., 1905), xx. See Regna Darnell, ed., *Readings in the History of Anthropology* (New York, 1974), 6–7, 420–21.

[9] Johannes Fabian, *Time and the Other: How Anthropology Makes Its Object* (New York, 1983), 143; *Proceedings of the International Congress of Americanists*, xx.

[10] Curtis M. Hinsley, Jr., "Zunis and Brahmins," in *Romantic Motives: Essays on Anthropological Sensibility*, ed. George W. Stocking, Jr. (Madison, 1989), 170.

Trapped in obscurity, Indians properly should not be thought of as fellow members of the modern world. Like the notion that Indians were historically backward, this sense that their cultures could not have a modern existence was shaped by evolutionary thinking as well as by the relative power scientist-discoverers held over their "discovered" subjects. Jesup's "new nation in science" had conquered a continent. Thus what Fabian observed of European scholars in Africa was no less true of Euro-Americans in "Indian country." Both groups were "under the spell of a . . . mendacious fiction . . . that interpersonal, intergroup, indeed, international Time is 'public time'—there to be occupied, measured, and allotted by the powers that be." Such a perspective allowed anthropologists in the United States to be dispassionate but sympathetic. Once discovered, Indians could become objects for "interesting study," but they should not be confused with human co-residents of the Republic.[11]

Ironically, then, the academic discovery of Indian beliefs and traditions, which Jesup so proudly celebrated before the International Congress of Americanists in 1902, fit neatly within an old tradition that classified native lifeways as both exotic and backward. Like a secret garden, the multiple features of Indian culture that scholars such as Jesup sought to understand in all their richness and complexity were defined from the outset as irrelevant to contemporary concerns.

Even Jesup's professionally trained colleagues shared this view. Franz Boas and his students, who were sympathetic to Indian traditions and assiduous in their scholarship, identified Indian culture with the past and sadly predicted the extinction of tribal traditions. Significantly, in 1924, when Elsie Clews Parsons solicited a series of fictional life stories from her anthropological colleagues, the portraits she received were all set in a world before extensive white contact. The resulting book displayed their collective assumption that the best way to present Native Americans was to isolate them from the continent's recent history. Native American traditions could be admired and examined, but their modern academic discoverers could be confident that indigenous cultures would not contribute to, or even survive in, the twentieth century. People such as Mourning Dove who found themselves discovered by settlers and scientists thus faced intellectual expectations that confined them to the outer margins of both history and society.[12]

The political structures Mourning Dove faced were similarly restrictive. During the years of the Salishan writer's youth, government policies for conquered Indian communities both quarantined and denigrated native traditions in an effort to promote general social progress. A letter written by an earnest schoolmaster at an eastern Montana Indian agency illustrates this administrative version of anthropological thought. It contained the following advice:

> There should be a board fence 12 feet high, enclosing a space 200 by 300 yards around the school buildings. There is now only a wire fence around the school

[11] Fabian, *Time and the Other*, 144.

[12] On Franz Boas and his students, see Frederick E. Hoxie, *A Final Promise: The Campaign to Assimilate the Indians, 1880–1920* (Lincoln, 1984), 141–45. Elsie Clews Parsons, ed., *American Indian Life* (1922; reprint, Lincoln, 1991).

yard, which is not over 50 feet from the front of the school buildings. Every Indian from the camp who wishes to, can converse with the pupils, and it cannot be prevented. The scenes of camp life, which are weekly presented to their view, are very detrimental to the pupils, and the camp gossip, which can not now be shut out, is a serious evil to them. With such a (board) fence they can be separated almost entirely from the demoralizing influences of the camp, and their progress towards civilization will be correspondingly accelerated.[13]

A proposal to wall a group of Indian children off from their parents to accelerate their "progress towards civilization" illustrates vividly the governing conviction that native life and modern life were incompatible. The Montana schoolmaster operated in a context of ideas and institutions that reinforced the separation of discoverer and discovered, thus confining native people to a prescribed place in American thought as well as on the American landscape.

The same year board fences were being recommended to insulate and educate children in Montana, Congress approved the General Allotment Act, which forcibly dismantled communally owned reservations and extended United States citizenship to tribal members. Employing the industrial imagery of the day, Amherst College president Merrill E. Gates (a prominent advocate of "humanitarian" Indian policies) described the new law as "a mighty pulverizing engine for breaking up the tribal mass." Gates and other reformers believed such splintered communities would more readily become "civilized."[14]

Jesup, Gates, and their colleagues thus provided the American public with an image of Indian people and Indian history that conformed to the power relationships of their day. The hegemony of their words and policies in the nineteenth century created the setting within which Native Americans such as Mourning Dove operated in the first decades of the twentieth century. That setting defined indigenous people as objects of a discovery process that stretched back four hundred years. They and their communities were positioned in the background of a national epic of conquest and progress.[15]

It is from that position of confinement that Mourning Dove and her generation spoke. Rejecting the idea of American progress and refusing to identify with her conquerors, Mourning Dove wrote with pride in her ancestry and with nostalgia for a shattered past. Far from welcoming those who taught her the English language she used in her stories, she grieved for what had been lost in the years after "everything started to change." At the same time, however, her use of English and the written word contradicted the idea that she was an artifact of a backward world hopelessly lost in the past. Despite their power, scientific sophistication, and moral rectitude, neither Jesup nor Gates could have explained the insistent tone or the

[13] *Report of the Commissioner of Indian Affairs* (Washington, 1887), 219.

[14] For Merrill E. Gates's comments, see Francis Paul Prucha, *The Great Father: The United States Government and the American Indians* (2 vols., Lincoln, 1984), II, 671. See also Hoxie, *A Final Promise*, 41–82.

[15] For my use of the term *hegemony*, see Jean Comaroff and John L. Comaroff, *Of Revelation and Revolution*, vol. I: *Christianity, Colonialism, and Consciousness in South Africa* (Chicago, 1991), 19–27.

nuanced prose of this outspoken Native American. They could not predict the message contained in her voice once she began to talk back to her discoverers.[16]

Burdened with the weight of scientific and physical domination, Mourning Dove appeared both defiant and willing to engage in an exploration of the non-Indian world. What was the source of this adventuresome pose? How did it alter the formulaic thinking of the curious scientists and bureaucrats who would spend so much time cataloging modern Indian life? And how would her "backtalk" and her explorations affect her contemporaries? The impact of Mourning Dove's generation can be measured by comparing their words with Jesup's and Gates's after one hundred years. Pronounced with confidence, Jesup's and Gates's words now sound hollow; celebrated as discoverers, Jesup and Gates now appear foolish. Mourning Dove's voice, on the other hand, seems to have risen in power and self-assurance. Echoed and repeated by others, her words and ideas helped form the basis for a new Indian identity, an identity that emerged from the Native American discovery of modern America.

Mourning Dove had been born to an interior Salish family whose life was frequently disrupted by American settlement in Idaho and eastern Washington. During the 1890s and afterwards, she was forced to attend missionary and government boarding schools and lived with a variety of relatives across the intermountain West. When she resolved to become a writer, Mourning Dove acted out of her own ambitions and experiences, but her decision echoed the determination of thousands of her contemporaries both to live in and to explore the new world that was rapidly intruding upon their communities. Because Mourning Dove was part of the first generation both to be "discovered" by science and the federal bureaucracy and to communicate to a wide audience, her career and those of her contemporaries sketch the outlines of what that discovery meant to people who could remember those "who lived in the ancient way before everything started to change."

Because nineteenth-century scholars and bureaucrats viewed Indians as people from another time, they did not recognize that even when conquered, Native Americans could still act and make choices. At the end of the nineteenth century, those choices were limited, but individuals continued to shape their own futures. Armed resistance was no longer an option for Indian people. Faced with a choice between accommodating themselves to their discoverers or completely withdrawing from further contact, Native Americans of Mourning Dove's generation selected a middle course. Examples of direct resistance to federal authority were rare, as were examples of complete noncooperation with researchers. Nonetheless, few communities welcomed the missionaries and government schoolteachers or shared Morris Jesup's enthusiasm for the "great field of discovery."

Individuals like Mourning Dove who found that they had been "discovered" confronted an array of people — scholars, politicians, bureaucrats, and businessmen —

---

[16] For discussion of "talking back," see Richard White, "Discovering Nature in North America," *Journal of American History*, 79 (Dec. 1992), 874–91.

who represented a combination of coercion and opportunity. The brute power of those outsiders crushed many native traditions. The very process of white settlement, for example, made many traditional subsistence methods impractical. Religious rituals, such as the Plains sun dance or Navajo curing rites, were swiftly outlawed by the government and condemned by missionaries. White authorities discouraged other ceremonial activities, such as vision quests and puberty rites, or rendered them impractical; Indians made still others secret to protect them from the curious.

On the other hand, the discoverers presented Indians with opportunities. Native Americans frequently perceived outsiders as a potential resource. If visiting scholars could violate sacred knowledge by condemning it and exposing it to the outside world, they could also publicize struggles against federal authorities or record local traditions that were in danger of being lost. Similarly, while the teachings of missionaries and schoolmasters could alienate children from their families, they could also provide those children with tools for reforming or combating the institutions that sought to regiment their existence. For example, Reuben Quick Bear, with the support of Catholic missionaries, brought suit against the commissioner of Indian affairs to allow tribal funds to be used for the local Catholic schools so that he could send his children there rather than to government institutions.[17]

Confronted with scientists, government officials, and the institutions they represented, indigenous people identified limited — but genuine — areas where they could participate in their discoverers' world, areas where whites and Indians could interact. Being discovered provided Native Americans with a limited set of tools for asserting and defining their presence in the modern world. In a sense, they saw avenues open before them for an *Indian* discovery of non-Indian America. Discovery thus presented Indians with interests and public positions from which they could launch their own voyages of exploration. Those voyages, in turn, would help both tribal communities and the larger public define a path leading from the "ancient way" to the twentieth century.

The voyages' starting point was frequently a version of Mourning Dove's statement that modern Indians "had known people who lived in the ancient way." Such an assertion — coupled with the fact that those ways were by definition American — set Native Americans apart from the rest of the population and transformed the native past from a source of shame (the beginning point for the "advancement of the human race") to a badge of distinction. Leaders such as Mourning Dove used the assertion of ancient origins as a rhetorical device to reverse the conventional understanding of discovery and to identify a unique Indian attribute for their audience. Mourning Dove positioned herself as the explorer — emerging from an ancient past no non-Indian could claim, she named objects and people from her distinctive point of view.

Other Indian writers of Mourning Dove's generation chose to present themselves as she did, writing in English both to assert and to celebrate an "ancient way." Best

---

[17] Prucha, *Great Father*, II, 776–79.

known among them was Charles A. Eastman (Ohiyesa), a Santee Sioux physician who published a partial autobiography, *Indian Boyhood*, in 1902 and followed it with nine other books that presented native life to a general audience. Born in 1858 in western Minnesota, Eastman spent his early childhood outside the orbit of white settlement. He lived a nomadic life, traveling with his relatives as far west as the Yellowstone River until 1872, when he was suddenly taken to a mission school. Eastman later recalled that his grandmother opposed his learning the white man's habits ("I cannot bear to see my boy live a made-up life"), but he recalled her own teachings to justify his decision to accommodate. He remembered that even though her "faith in her people's philosophy and training could not be superceded by any other allegiance," she had also held to the principle that "when you see a new trail, or a footprint that you do not know, follow it to the point of knowing."[18]

According to Eastman, his decision to explore the "new trail" of American education was an extension of his grandmother's ancient principles. He attended the Presbyterian Santee Normal Training School in Nebraska, Beloit College, Knox College, and Dartmouth College. Following his graduation from Dartmouth in 1887, he entered Boston University Medical School, receiving his M.D. in 1890. Despite his long immersion in white society, Eastman consistently focused on the continuities between his boyhood and his adult values. In his writings he carefully constructed a distinctly modern, yet Indian, point of view.

Eastman frequently cast himself as a modern tribal storyteller, a figure who, like the elders in an oral society, both described the old ways and gave them a contemporary twist. As he wrote in 1911 in *The Soul of an Indian*, "My little book does not pretend to be a scientific treatise. . . . So much has been written by strangers of our ancient faith and worship that treats it chiefly as a matter of curiosity. I should like to emphasize its universal quality, its personal appeal." His books carried out this objective. They included such titles such as *Old Indian Days, Indian Child Life*, and *Indian Scout Talks*.[19]

Significantly, his writing avoided identification with a particular tribal tradition, emphasizing instead a generalized and idyllic past. Not only did Eastman understand that his audience was largely uninterested in or ignorant of differences between tribes, but his principal objective was to counter the public's assumption that Indians were savage and backward. While later generations would detect a Victorian tone in his generalizations, they were offered as an antidote to the stereotypes he

---

[18] Charles A. Eastman, *Indian Boyhood* (1902; reprint, New York, 1971). For Eastman's grandmother's comments, see Charles A. Eastman (Ohiyesa), *From the Deep Woods to Civilization: Chapters in the Autobiography of an Indian* (1916; reprint, Lincoln, 1977), 28. Eastman's great-grandfather, Mahpiya Wichasta (Cloud Man), had been an early convert to Christianity, and his mother (who died soon after his birth) had had a white father, but his kinsmen continued to live away from white communities. His father was arrested for having taken part in the 1862 Minnesota Sioux uprising but was pardoned by Abraham Lincoln. (Thirty-eight others were executed.) For a modern biography, see Raymond Wilson, *Ohiyesa: Charles Eastman, Santee Sioux* (Urbana, 1983).

[19] For Eastman's comments, see David Reed Miller, "Charles Alexander Eastman, Santee Sioux, 1858–1939," in *American Indian Intellectuals*, ed. Margot Liberty (St. Paul, 1978), 64. Charles A. Eastman, *Old Indian Days* (New York, 1907); Charles A. Eastman, *Indian Child Life* (Boston, 1913); Charles A. Eastman, *Indian Scout Talks* (Boston, 1914).

Charles Alexander Eastman
(Ohiyesa)

so frequently encountered. For example, in *Indian Boyhood,* a record of the physician's "boyish impressions," a chapter on education begins with an attack on the idea that Indians had no system for training their children. "Nothing could be further from the truth," Eastman declared; "all the customs of this primitive people were held to be divinely instituted, and . . . were scrupulously adhered to."[20]

[20] Eastman, *Indian Boyhood,* preface n.p., 73, 87.

Charles A. Eastman's search for a way to present himself to his non-Indian audience is
reflected in the frontispieces of two of his books. The first (above), from *The Soul
of an Indian* (1911), accompanies a description of Native American religious
beliefs. The second (left), from *From the Deep Woods to Civilization:
Chapters in the Autobiography of an Indian* (1916), reinforces the
narrative structure of his life story. *Courtesy
The Newberry Library.*

Eastman and the other early Indian writers appeared at an opportune moment.
Despite the optimism of Morris Jesup and other museum collectors, the early twentieth century was marked by a current of disenchantment with a society many felt
was "overcivilized" and without moral content. As Mourning Dove and Eastman

were composing their stories, some white intellectuals were arguing that the size and complexity of industrial society separated individuals from the world around them. They portrayed modern Americans as alone and without purpose. Machines, bureaucracies, and newspapers did their work, organized their cities, and communicated with their neighbors, reducing industrial society to a place devoid of "authentic experience." This sentiment, which historian T. J. Jackson Lears has labeled "antimodernism," was both nostalgic and progressive; it looked to the past while attempting to reform current circumstances; it revealed a "vein of deep religious longing, an unfilled yearning to restore infinite meaning to an increasingly finite world." Such feelings surely lay behind the appeal of the early Indian writers, for several of them found that their descriptions of an idyllic ancient life won them an enthusiastic audience of white readers.[21]

By describing ancient traditions and recounting tales of their childhoods, Indian authors could both serve up satisfying, "authentic" experiences and preserve tribal traditions. For example, Zitkala-Sa (Gertrude Bonnin), a Yankton woman who attended Earlham College in Indiana and the Boston Conservatory of Music, published an essay in 1902 that contrasted the coherence of her Indian past with the superficiality of modern Christianity. "Why I Am a Pagan" described a visit the author had received from a fellow tribesman who had recently converted to the white man's faith. She wrote that the caller could to nothing but "mouth most strangely the jangling phrases of a bigoted creed," while she—authentically linked to her own past—thought only of "excursions into the natural gardens where the voice of the Great Spirit is heard in the twittering of birds, the rippling of mighty waters, and the sweet breathing of flowers." Aligning herself with this leafy scene, the Quaker-educated author declared, "If this is Paganism, then at present, at least, I am a Pagan."[22]

Zitkala-Sa published two collections of Indian tales celebrating the virtues of native culture, *Old Indian Legends* (1901) and *American Indian Stories* (1921); others of her generation followed a similar path. Mourning Dove published a novel, *Co-ge-we-a, the Half Blood* (1927), that contrasted virtuous Indians with corrupt whites and an anthology of Salish tales, *Coyote Stories* (1933). In 1916, Lucy Thompson, a Klamath woman from Oregon, published a general account of her tribe's history and folklore that emphasized its simplicity and described the ways in which outsiders had corrupted their beliefs. A decade later, Luther Standing Bear (who had attended the government boarding school at Carlisle, Pennsylvania, before embarking on a variety of careers, including a turn as a Hollywood actor) published a memoir, *My People, the Sioux.* His book carried an introduction by silent film star William S. Hart, who wrote of the Sioux, "philosophy was their life." Standing Bear replied to these expectations with a narrative that emphasized his own quiet

[21] T. J. Jackson Lears, *No Place of Grace: Antimodernism and the Transformation of American Culture, 1880–1920* (New York, 1981), 57. See also Curtis M. Hinsley, Jr., "Authoring Authenticity," *Journal of the Southwest,* 32 (Winter 1990), 462–78.

[22] Zitkala-Sa, "Why I Am a Pagan," *Atlantic Monthly,* 90 (Dec. 1902), 803.

virtues and the worth of Indian people. "The Indian has just as many ounces of brains as his white brother," Standing Bear wrote, and he noted that as a chief of his people, "I will do what is right and proper for them." In each of these collections and memoirs, the authors assumed the role of a storyteller who could assure white readers that the tale was authentic, not because it was scientific, but because it was personal. Mirroring the white craftsmen and nature lovers who stressed the meaning of their new hobbies over their content, the Indian authors posed as bearers of an ancient spirit in the modern age. Agreeing with Thompson that "so much said and written about the American Indians . . . is guessed at and not facts," Zitkala-Sa and the others came forward promising to deliver versions of their culture that could stand as authentic alternatives to the alienation of modern life. "These legends are relics of our country's once virgin soil," Zitkala-Sa wrote in 1901, adding that they provided evidence of the Indians' "near kinship with the rest of humanity and [point] a steady finger toward the great brotherhood of mankind."[23]

Eastman frequently noted the disparity between his inherited, Indian values and the conditions of modern society. According to the Santee writer, a reverence for the natural world and a charitable attitude toward relatives and neighbors were basic to native cultures, but precisely those values, he believed, were undermined by industrialization and organized religion. He argued this case in his books, as well as on the lecture circuit and in popular magazine articles that appeared (among other places) in *Boys' Life,* the magazine of the Boy Scouts of America. Eastman also presented his views at a New Hampshire summer camp he founded in 1915. He called the camp "the School of the Woods" and promised that all who enrolled would receive instruction from "a real Indian." He composed an eloquent summary of his position at the conclusion of his autobiography, *From Deep Woods to Civilization.* "I am an Indian," Eastman wrote, "and while I have learned much from civilization, for which I am grateful, I have never lost my sense of right and justice. I am for development and progress along social and spiritual lines, rather than those of commerce, nationalism, or material efficiency."[24]

As Eastman, Mourning Dove, and their contemporaries grew more comfortable with their roles as conveyors of ancient wisdom to modern audiences, they found that the presentation of traditional Indian culture could identify them as people worthy of respect. Like Thompson, who declared in 1916, "I deem it necessary to first tell you who I am," they employed "Indianness" to gain an audience and to

---

[23] Zitkala-Sa, *Old Indian Legends* (1901; reprint, Lincoln, 1985); Gertrude Bonnin (Zitkala-Sa), *American Indian Stories* (1921; reprint, Glorieta, N. Mex., 1976); Hum-ishu-ma (Mourning Dove), *Co-ge-we-a, the Half Blood: A Depiction of the Great Montana Cattle Range* (Boston, 1927); Mourning Dove (Humishuma), *Coyote Stories* (1933; reprint, New York, 1984); Lucy Thompson, *To the American Indian* (Eureka, Calif., 1916); Luther Standing Bear, *My People, the Sioux* (1928; reprint, Lincoln, 1975). Standing Bear, *My People, the Sioux,* xiv, 288, 276. See also Luther Standing Bear (Ota K'te [Plenty Kill]), *My Indian Boyhood* (1931; reprint, Lincoln, 1988); Luther Standing Bear, *Land of the Spotted Eagle* (1933; reprint, Lincoln, 1978); Luther Standing Bear, *Stories of the Sioux* (1934; reprint, Lincoln, 1988). For Thompson's comments, see Thompson, *To the American Indian,* 9. For Zitkala-Sa's comments, see Zitkala-Sa, *Old Indian Legends,* vi.

[24] Eastman, *From the Deep Woods to Civilization,* 195. For Eastman's summer camp, see Wilson, *Ohiyesa,* 151.

construct a verbal weapon they might employ against "modern" scientists and bureaucrats who threatened native interests or denigrated tribal communities.

Like the Native American writers, Indian men and women contemporary with Mourning Dove who collaborated with anthropologists and museum collectors to record tribal histories and to preserve examples of indigenous artistic expression sought to preserve ancient traditions. Frequently those individuals—such as George Hunt, who worked with Franz Boas at the turn of the century among the Kwakiutl of Vancouver Island, British Columbia; Chris (a pseudonym), who told his life story to Morris Opler at the Mescalero Apache reservation (New Mexico) in the 1930s; and James Carpenter, who assisted Robert H. Lowie in his research among the Crow between 1907 and 1930—were people of mixed ancestry who stood at the border of the local community. For example, Opler's Apache partner, Chris, the child of a Mescalero mother and a Chiricahua father, was born in 1880, "when such marriages were much rarer than they were later to become." Opler's estimation of the consequences of this dual parentage could readily be applied to others in Chris's situation: "Each tribe saw his idiosyncrasies as the result of his inheritance from the other group. These allowances and the lack of solid identification may well have encouraged deviation and experimentation."[25]

Other informants (such as the Omaha scholar, Francis La Flesche; the Lakota elder, Black Elk; and the Winnebago leader called Big Winnebago) were more fully centered in their home communities but had traveled widely among non-Indians and had developed an interest in the relationship between Indian traditions and the modern world. They sought both to relate ancient wisdom to contemporary conditions and to interpret their lives for a non-Indian audience. La Flesche spent most of his adult life in Washington, D.C., even though he had grown to adulthood among the Omahas in the decades after the Civil War. (He served as a runner in one of the tribe's last communal buffalo hunts.) In the early 1880s, he met the anthropologist Alice Cunningham Fletcher during her field research in Nebraska and became her partner in an impressive series of monographs. Black Elk traveled to Europe with Buffalo Bill Cody in the 1880s, and Big Winnebago spent a good part of his adult life as an itinerant workman along the rail lines of the upper Midwest. The latter two returned to their reservation homes in midlife and later formed partnerships with white scholars eager to record their memories of traditional culture. Their early experiences exposed them to the scale and technology of modern society, and like La Flesche, they chose to devote themselves to the preservation of indigenous traditions.[26]

Despite their diverse origins, all of these informants understood that by documenting their cultures, they were giving them greater permanence and elevating

[25] Morris E. Opler, *Apache Odyssey: A Journey between Two Worlds* (New York, 1969), 4.
[26] For a collaborative monograph, see Alice C. Fletcher and Francis La Flesche, *The Omaha Tribe* (2 vols., Washington, 1911). For biographical material, see Margot Liberty, "Francis La Flesche, Omaha, 1857–1932," in *American Indian Intellectuals,* ed. Liberty; John G. Neihardt, *Black Elk Speaks: Being the Life Story of a Holy Man of the Oglala Sioux* (New York, 1932); and Paul Radin, ed., *The Autobiography of a Winnebago Indian* (Berkeley, 1920).

them in the eyes of the outside world. In 1897 for example, Boas told Kwakiutl chiefs at Fort Rupert (Vancouver Island, British Columbia) that his partner George Hunt "would become the storage box of your laws and your stories." Similarly, Black Elk explained that he worked with John G. Neihardt because he believed that the poet's retelling of his great vision would preserve a part of Lakota culture. "What I know was given to me for men and it is true and it is beautiful," the old man told Neihardt. "You were sent to save it . . . I can teach you." La Flesche was more direct: "The misconception of Indian life and character so common among the white people has been largely due to an ignorance of the Indian's language, of his mode of thought, his beliefs, his ideals, and his native institutions." The Omaha scholar intended his career to be a response to this fact, for as a recent biographer has noted, La Flesche worked when "old restraints and restrictions upon the divulging of sacred traditions [became] — in the stark awareness of impending cultural loss — pitted against the value of preserving something at least for posterity."[27]

Collaborating with outsiders opened informants up to charges of opportunism, for even the most dedicated anthropologists approached native communities with their professional agendas foremost in their minds. And recorders of stories and histories usually had more than an academic interest in Indians; they were frequently accompanied by artifact collectors who worked closely with local traders and businessmen. Boas's meticulous research, for example, coincided with the ambitious effort of the American Museum of Natural History to bring monumental Northwest Coast carvings to New York City: Boas reminded Hunt in 1901, "under our present arrangement you must continue to collect." The 1937 comment of Boas's student, Robert Lowie, that Boas had "stimulated an enormous amount of high-grade recording by Indians" epitomizes the self-absorption of white researchers in this era. Even after three decades of field research, Lowie could not see that Indian colleagues

---

[27] For Franz Boas's comments, see Cole, *Captured Heritage,* 158; for Black Elk's comments, see Raymond J. DeMallie, ed., *The Sixth Grandfather: Black Elk's Teachings Given to John G. Neihardt* (Lincoln, 1984), 28; Francis La Flesche, *The Middle Five, Indian Boys at School* (Boston, 1900), xiv; Liberty, "Francis La Flesche, Omaha, 1857–1932," 53.

It is difficult to summarize dozens of examples of collaboration across North America. One example is War Eagle's invitation to the anthropologist Frank Speck in 1928 that the two of them write a description of the Delaware Big House ritual, a pivotal tribal event that had last been performed in 1924 and seemed on the verge of disappearing. War Eagle, a tribal leader whose father was Cherokee and whose mother was Munsee, had been born in 1880 and was determined to preserve this aspect of his community's past. See Frank G. Speck, *A Study of the Delaware Indian Big House Ritual: In Native Text Dictated by Witapanoxwe* (Harrisburg, 1931), 7–21. Another notable collaboration is described in James Mooney, *The Swimmer Manuscript: Cherokee Sacred Formulas and Medicinal Prescriptions,* ed. Frans M. Olbrechts (Washington, 1932). At Pine Ridge Agency, South Dakota, physician James R. Walker compiled a massive description of Lakota life with the assistance of community religious leaders. The religious leaders were convinced in part by the argument of George Sword, a Christian Sioux who, according to Walker, declared that "soon they would go from the world and all their sacred lore would pass with them unless they revealed it so it could be preserved in writing." James R. Walker, *Lakota Belief and Ritual,* ed. Raymond J. DeMallie and Elaine A. Jahner (Lincoln, 1980), 47. The Seneca scholar Arthur C. Parker (1881–1955) followed a career that does not fit neatly with others of his generation. Employed first as a field ethnologist by the Peabody Museum of Archaeology and Ethnology at Harvard University, Parker was named state archaeologist at the New York State Museum in 1906. In 1925 he became director of the Rochester Museum of Arts and Sciences.

shared his desire to preserve tribal knowledge. In his mind the influence had run in a single direction, from the scholars to the Indians.[28]

But the risk of being compromised by their involvement with selfish, non-Indian scholars did not prevent dozens of tribal members from participating in anthropological research. Their willingness to explore an intellectual relationship with outsiders made it possible for people like Fletcher, Boas, Lowie, Opler, and Neihardt to grasp the richness and complexity of North America's indigenous traditions. The partnership of native and non-native scholars, however uneven, created a common enterprise, the modern field of cultural anthropology, and provided tribal communities with a cadre of articulate friends who might represent them in the wider world. In the twentieth century, anthropologists would often repeat Boas's pledge to a group of Kwakiutl chiefs at Fort Rupert: "Wherever I can, I speak for you."[29]

Native Americans who found themselves discovered by outsiders in the late nineteenth century also found that their predicament allowed them to create new cultural expressions by combining elements of their own and their discoverers' traditions. This opportunity enabled them to produce new, and possibly more viable, versions of old activities. In the 1990s examples of those combinations are frequently evident in the world of native art. Native Americans explore traditional themes or tribal mythologies employing media as various as acrylic paint, videotape, or metal sculpture. These artists assert that their use of new technologies helps them bring ancient ideas into the present; new materials do not undermine the "Indianness" of their creations. Despite the popularity of this view, students of native culture continue to minimize the extent to which Indian art traditions are the product not only of interaction with non-Indian artists but of Native American artists' ongoing exploration of the commercial art market.

The first Native Americans to explore the world of professional painting were in Oklahoma. Soon after the turn of the century, as white settlers surged into central Oklahoma, a young Arapaho man, Carl Sweezy (1881–1953), began using butcher paper and house paint to record scenes from his own tribal history and to describe the rapidly changing landscape around him. "The way of the white people . . . seemed unsociable and lonely," Sweezy later recalled, so he focused on local family life, sacred rituals, and Arapaho social life to create the image of an appealing alternative. In a similar way, Shawnee artist Ernest Spybuck (1883–1949) recorded social and ceremonial scenes taking place in Oklahoma Indian communities near his home. Using watercolor, pencil, and ink, Spybuck created images of costumed dancers, lively tribal gatherings, and solemn religious meetings that are striking for their vivid color and meticulous detail. In their art, Sweezy and Spybuck defined a position much like that of Zitkala-Sa, Eastman, and Black Elk, for they stood be-

---

[28] For Boas's reminder, see Cole, *Captured Heritage*, 159. Robert H. Lowie, *The History of Anthropological Theory* (London, 1937), 133.
[29] Cole, *Captured Heritage*, 159.

Delaware Peyote Ceremony, by Ernest Spybuck (c. 1913). This depiction of the Big Moon
ceremony illustrates the syncretic nature of the new twentieth-century faith and
the dedication of the Native American communicants. A crucifix lies in front
of the leader, or "roadman," while the standing figure on the right
carries a book, possibly the Bible. Participants hold traditional
feather fans and gourd rattles, and a singer plays a water
drum. In the inset, worshippers emerge from the all-
night ritual to greet the dawn. *Courtesy
National Museum of the American Indian,
Smithsonian Institution.*

tween their ancient traditions and their modern white patrons, offering them an
appealing version of their Indianness.[30]

In the first decades of the twentieth century, Sweezy and Spybuck's audiences
were local, but by the 1920s other groups of Indian artists began to ally themselves
with white patrons and to display their work before critics and publics far beyond
their homes. In New Mexico and Arizona in the early twentieth century, anthropologists and travelers had occasionally purchased drawings from their informants and

[30] Margaret Archuleta and Rennard Strickland, *Shared Visions: Native American Painters and Sculptors in the Twentieth Century* (Phoenix, 1991), 5; Lee A. Callender and Ruth Slivka, *Shawnee Home Life: The Paintings of Ernest Spybuck* (New York, 1984), 7–10. For a review of Canadian Indian art in the same period, see Gerald R. McMaster, "Tenuous Lines of Descent: Indian Arts and Crafts of the Reservation Period," *Canadian Journal of Native Studies,* 9 (Winter 1989), 205–36.

hosts, but it was not until 1917 that the archaeologist Edgar L. Hewett began to commission paintings of Pueblo ceremonial life. Hewett began by supporting the work of Crescencio Martinez, who was from San Ildefonso, north of Santa Fe, but following the young man's tragic death in the flu epidemic of 1918, he turned to others. Interest from local Anglo artists, such as Ernest Blumenschein and Bert Phillips in nearby Taos, New Mexico, and the patronage of collectors such as Mabel Dodge Luhan, Mary Austin, and Alice Corbin Henderson encouraged Martinez's followers— Awa Tsireh (Alfonso Roybal) of San Ildefonso, the Hopi Fred Kabotie, and Otis Polelonema of Cochiti, New Mexico—to bring their work before a wider audience. By the early 1920s these artists were exhibiting their work in New York and Chicago.

In western Oklahoma, another combination of white patrons and ambitious young Indians brought a second group of native painters before a national audience. Encouraged by Susan Peters, a young Bureau of Indian Affairs teacher in Anadarko, six Kiowa students began showing their work and winning the attention of the rapidly growing community of Santa Fe collectors. In 1928 the six—Monroe Tsa Toke, Stephen Mopope, Spencer Asah, Jack Hokeah, James Archiah, and Bou-ge-te Smokey—enrolled in the University of Oklahoma to study with O. B. Jacobson. The connection brought them rapid fame. The group exhibited at the International Congress of Folk Arts in Prague, Czechoslovakia, in 1928 and three years later joined their southwestern counterparts and others at the Exposition of Indian Tribal Arts in New York City. The exposition show toured the United States and Europe for two years following its New York appearance.[31]

Exploring the professional art world and using their paintings to display the richness and beauty of tribal life, the Indian painters of the 1920s and 1930s asserted that their art embodied the survival of Native American traditions. Like the other Indian explorers of white America, they presented themselves to the non-Indian public as a bridge connecting an ancient past to the modern era. The enthusiastic public reception of their message set off a chain reaction among young would-be artists. The critic Elizabeth Shepley Sergeant wrote in 1923, for example, that "two writers, four artists, the School of American Research and all the Indian dealers in Santa Fe" claimed to have discovered the San Ildefonso artist, Awa Tsireh. "As a matter of fact," she observed dryly, "he probably discovered himself through his own observation of the work of his immediate precursor [Crescencio Martinez] . . . certainly the other boys and girls who are beginning to render the same subject matter in the same general style, have discovered themselves through Awa Tsireh."[32]

The exhibitions of the 1920s were the first to present living native artists whose bold images of ancient ways challenged the public's assumption that Indian people belonged to a backward, vanishing race, but writers unfamiliar with native communities were less insightful than Sergeant. Viewing dramatic paintings of Indian life, most commentators attributed the resurgence of native arts to a previously obscure

[31] See Dorothy Dunn, *American Indian Painting of the Plains and Southwest* (Albuquerque, 1968), 188–95, 198–201, 218–40.

[32] Elizabeth Shepley Sergeant, "An American Indian Artist," *Freeman,* Aug. 8, 1923, pp. 514–15.

ethnic genius. The *New York Times,* for example, noted that the 1931 Exposition of Indian Tribal Arts had brought a new generation of racial leaders to the fore. A review of the exhibition concluded, "Lo, the poor Indian . . . begins to emerge before our newly opened eyes, as artist. . . . Our problem child . . . is suddenly seen to be, in his own, a kind of genius passing our full comprehension."[33]

The success of Native American artists thus created an opportunity for tribal perspectives to appear and be appreciated. Indians who took advantage of that opportunity—the Kiowa six, Awa Tsireh, and others—operated within the limits of white expectations, but they persisted in asserting a new identity in which their distinctive traditions might find endorsement. Too often non-Indian patrons continued to view these artists as carriers of a primitive tradition—just as anthropologists overlooked the goals of their informants—but the artists' impact was unmistakable. Their success made it impossible to dismiss Native American traditions as simple curiosities.

Outside the world of art, the most dramatic combination of Indian and non-Indian traditions occurred within a new religious movement that emerged in Oklahoma in the 1890s. This innovation was far less popular with whites than the renaissance in Indian art, yet it won grudging acceptance in many quarters. The modern history of the Native American Church begins in 1881 when the construction of rail lines from Chicago and St. Louis south to the Rio Grande Valley allowed peyote, a hallucinogen that had been used in the valley for centuries in Lipan Apache religious rituals, to be transported to other parts of the country. Reservations occupied by recently relocated Plains Indian tribes lay along this new transportation route, and Lipan teachers apparently brought their ritual to those reservations first.[34]

As it spread across the Southern Plains, the ancient aspects of the peyote ritual were combined with elements of Christianity that had been introduced into Indian communities by missionaries. The result was a new ceremonial complex. Followers of the "peyote way" invoked Jesus in their ceremonies and prayed for hallucinogenic visions that would bring them into contact with Christian as well as native spiritual figures. With steady supplies of the peyote plant coming up from Texas by rail, Lipan, Kiowa, and Comanche religious leaders called "road men" spread their version of the ritual to neighbors and kinsmen across Oklahoma. They quickly generated support for what became a powerful new faith. Modeling their technique on that of the Christian missionaries who now opposed them, they also relied on trains and automobiles to spread their teachings to tribes across the United States and southern Canada. By 1899 groups on at least sixteen different reservations had embraced the new ritual.[35]

Emphasizing the importance of monogamy, sobriety, and hard work, road men won a wide following despite federal authorities' attempts to outlaw ritual use of the peyote plant. Early converts included educated young men such as Fred Lookout

---

[33] *New York Times,* Nov. 29, 1931, sect. 5, pp. 12–13, quoted in Dunn, *American Indian Painting,* 239.
[34] See Omer C. Stewart, *Peyote Religion: A History* (Norman, 1987), 62.
[35] David F. Aberle, *The Peyote Religion among the Navaho* (New York, 1966), 17.

of the Osage, who had attended Carlisle Indian School; Albert Hensley, a former chief of tribal police among the Nebraska Winnebagos; and a prosperous Crow farmer named Frank Bethune. In the nineteenth century, Indians met attacks on tribal religions with defiance, but tribal leaders were generally unable to stop government efforts to undermine their priests or to outlaw their ceremonies. In the twentieth century, however, the dynamic was very different, for the peyote road men defended themselves in terms non-Indians would recognize.

When faced with a move to outlaw peyote use in the new Oklahoma Territory, for example, Comanche leader Quanah Parker declared, "I do not think this legislature should interfere with a man's religion." In 1908 a similar proposal came before the new state of Oklahoma's constitutional convention. Sixteen native religious leaders testified in opposition to the prohibition, causing one white legislator to declare, "I have been almost overcome by the talk of these Indians and I do not believe any legislature wants to rob these Indians of their religious rights. . . . It is our duty to protect their rights — religious or otherwise." As a brake on the forces of prohibition, followers of the peyote ritual also incorporated themselves as the Native American Church, an organization formed "to foster and promote the religious belief of the several tribes of Indians in the State of Oklahoma." Groups in Nebraska, South Dakota, Montana, Wisconsin, and Iowa quickly followed suit. All of them argued that the American constitutional guarantee of the right to the free exercise of religion obligated the United States government to protect their worship services from harassment.[36]

Peyote leaders frequently emphasized the compatibility of their beliefs and the expectations of government officials. "We like church," the Ute peyotist William Wash wrote to officials at the Bureau of Indian Affairs, adding, "We want to meet every Sunday and have Church and pray and be good. . . . We want to rest on Sunday and then on Monday we want to work and farm." In 1908 Hensley, by then a Winnebago road man, responded to a government proposal to conduct scientific studies of the peyote plant by declaring that "it is utter folly for scientists to attempt to analyze this medicine." The Carlisle graduate asked rhetorically, "Can science analyze God's body? No."[37]

Like the Indian entrance into the commercial art world, the development of the Native American Church offered Indian people an opportunity to assert their perspectives in an arena sanctioned by whites. The defenders of peyotism discovered the power of political organization and constitutional rhetoric and turned them to the defense of an "ancient" rite; fitting themselves to the language of white piety, they asserted their distinctiveness while presenting themselves as loyal, Bible-reading Americans. Engagement in the new faith propelled the peyotists into a new world of organized religion and seven-day routines of work and worship, even as it

---

[36] Stewart, *Peyote Religion*, 75, 138, 224, 227–30.
[37] David Rich Lewis, "Reservation Leadership and the Progressive-Traditional Dichotomy: William Wash and the Northern Utes, 1865–1928," *Ethnohistory*, 38 (Spring 1991), 139, 134; Stewart, *Peyote Religion*, 157.

allowed them to construct and sustain a ritual complex that stood beyond the reach of science and the Office of Indian Affairs.

In addition to combining elements of their cultural traditions with pieces of the new world surrounding them, Native Americans of Mourning Dove's generation explored ways to use their discoverers' political institutions to defend Indian communities from external threats. These discoveries helped create other elements in twentieth-century native identity: the sense that sharp boundaries separated white outsiders and American Indians and the conviction that interests falling on the *native* side of those boundaries constituted a modern version of ancient traditions.

Among the first generation of native young people educated at boarding schools were hundreds of graduates who used their facility with English, their "civilized" appearance, and their understanding of American institutions to enter political life. They participated in tribal and village councils, circulated petitions attacking the policies of the Office of Indian Affairs, and employed the American legal system to pursue community objectives. Through such actions, the political leaders of a supposedly vanishing race began to define the legal limits of federal and state intrusion into their communities. This effort produced the insight that certain "rights" set Native Americans apart from other residents of the United States. That insight inspired tribal leaders to launch a campaign to defend their rights and to use existing political and legal institutions to reclaim control of community government and communally owned resources.

Examples abound of "returned students" challenging the authority of the Office of Indian Affairs. In northern Wisconsin, Reginald Oshkosh (a graduate of Carlisle and the son of Neopit Oshkosh, who was the Menominee's traditional chief) led the opposition to federal control over the tribe's vast timber reserves. Oshkosh conceded that lumbering on the reservation had brought employment to hundreds of his kinsmen, but he believed federal policy should produce more than wage labor. He declared the Menominee's goal was "to become independent and self-supporting and [to] terminate our relations as wards of the Government."[38]

Another Carlisle student became active in tribal affairs by writing letters to his kinsmen at Fort Yuma, Arizona, from his dormitory in Pennsylvania: Patrick Miguel, son of a Quechan leader whom the government insisted on calling "ex-Chief Miguel," also took on the local agent in 1899, warning him "not to touch the Indians again" or he would be reported to the Office of Indian Affairs. Upon Miguel's return to Yuma a decade later, he continued to advocate tribal self-government. Urging the Commissioner of Indian Affairs to authorize elections at the agency, he struck a conciliatory but insistent tone: "We believe the old Indians should be taught more by members of their own tribe, in a kindly way, to see and adopt the white man's laws and it is to this end the more progressive members of the tribe request that

[38] For Reginald Oshkosh's comments, see Brian C. Hosmer, "Creating Indian Entrepreneurs: Menominees, Neopit Mills, and Timber Exploitation, 1890–1915," *American Indian Culture and Research Journal,* 15 (Winter 1991), 15.

they be allowed to have a council and presiding officer to pilot the ship of state of the Yumas."[39]

In Indian Territory, Delos Lone Wolf, the Carlisle-educated nephew of the Kiowa chief Lone Wolf, returned from boarding school to discover that Congress had unilaterally abrogated its treaty with the tribe in order to open a tract of land for white settlement. Supported by cattlemen who wished to protect their leases on tribal land, Delos persuaded his uncle and other leaders to file suit in United States District Court seeking an injunction against the land sale. Acting on their behalf was a former Illinois congressman, William M. Springer, who had a law practice in Washington, D.C. The result of their efforts was *Lone Wolf v. Hitchcock* (1903), in which the Supreme Court pronounced the congressional abrogation constitutional. This defeat for Lone Wolf and the Kiowas accelerated the rate of federal seizure of tribal land, but it also indicated that Indian explorations of the American legal system had grown remarkably energetic. It sent a warning to federal officials that they should expect future opposition from other close-cropped boarding school graduates.[40]

The United States Court of Claims was the most popular legal forum for tribal leaders in the early twentieth century. Unlike efforts to block congressional decisions (actions that were frequently doomed from the start), using the Court of Claims was relatively safe—losses brought little additional hardship and wins could pay substantial benefits. Indian tribes had been barred from bringing suit in the Court of Claims in 1863, but individual groups frequently lobbied Congress for special legislation exempting them from this restriction. In 1881 Choctaws determined to win compensation for lands lost in Mississippi and Alabama a half-century earlier were the first to gain access to the claims process. Their success inspired others, and by World War I thirty-one claims had been brought to the court.

The steady but unspectacular pace of claims filings suddenly accelerated after 1920. The Teton Sioux opened the decade by winning approval for a resolution enabling them to bring to court their claim for the South Dakota Black Hills. They were quickly followed by dozens of other tribes so that during the next ten years more suits were filed than had been brought in the previous forty years. Responding to the new case load, the Government Accounting Office established an Indian Tribal Claims Section in 1926 to prepare financial data on pending suits. While it remains largely undiscussed by scholars, the history of these claims cases will surely reveal a pattern of political mobilization and the establishment of new ties between tribal leaders and their attorneys.[41]

---

[39] Ironically, Patrick Miguel had been sent to Carlisle Indian School as punishment for helping burn down some boarding school buildings at the Fort Yuma agency. For Miguel's comments, see Robert L. Bee, *Crosscurrents along the Colorado: The Impact of Government Policy on the Quechan Indians* (Tucson, 1981), 55, 59. Lewis, "Reservation Leadership," 139. For the successful career of another former Carlisle student, see Terry P. Wilson, "Chief Fred Lookout and the Politics of Osage Oil, 1906–1949," in *Indian Leadership*, ed. Walter L. Williams (Manhattan, Kans., 1984), 46–53.

[40] William T. Hagan, *United States–Comanche Relations: The Reservation Years* (New Haven, 1976), 263–64, 280.

[41] For a broad history of the early claims process, see Harvey D. Rosenthal, "Indian Claims and the American

In addition to the emergence of new leaders and the launching of new lawsuits, the first decades of the twentieth century witnessed the emergence of new Indian political pressure groups. They included the Black Hills Treaty Council, which first met on the Cheyenne River reservation in central South Dakota in 1911 to discuss the filing of a claim to restore the sacred Black Hills to the Sioux. In New Mexico, the All Pueblo Council conducted a widely publicized campaign to resist efforts by squatters and local politicians to reduce Indian landholding. At a meeting in 1922, the All Pueblo Council articulated a position common to many other groups when it declared that the Rio Grande communities had lived "in a civilized condition before the white man came to America" and called on the "American people" to help them preserve "everything we hold dear—our lands, our customs, our traditions." Combining an appeal to public morality with pride in their tribal past, the Pueblo leaders attempted to turn popular interest in their dances and traditions into political clout. By the end of the 1920s, appeals like that one were winning support from sympathetic non-Indians and enabling tribal leaders to carry on campaigns in every region of the United States.[42]

Other regional pressure groups included the Alaska Native Brotherhood and the Alaska Native Sisterhood, founded in 1912 and 1915, respectively. The brotherhood was led during the 1920s by the Tlingit Carlisle graduate William L. Paul, Jr., and together the two groups campaigned against segregation and discrimination in towns across the territory. Similarly, in 1919 the Northwest Federation of Indians launched efforts to protect the fishing rights of Puget Sound tribes; the Wampanoag Nation was founded in 1928 to serve as a representative body for scattered groups of Cape Cod Indians; and the Four Mothers Society was established by Redbird Smith and other conservative Cherokees to resist the expansion of white influence following Oklahoma statehood.

In the introduction to his memoir of boarding school life, *The Middle Five,* the Omaha scholar Francis La Flesche announced to his readers that the subjects of the stories he was about to tell were Indians who wore "civilized" costumes rather than "boy friends who knew only the aboriginal life. I have made this choice," he continued;

> not because the influences of the school alter the qualities of the boys, but that they might appear under conditions and in an attire familiar to the reader. The paint, feathers, robes and other articles that make up the dress of the Indian, are marks of savagery to the European, and he who wears them however appropriate or significant they might be to himself, finds it difficult to lay claim to a share in common human nature.[43]

Conscience: A Brief History of the Indian Claims Commission," in *Irredeemable America: The Indians' Estate and Land Claims,* ed. Imre Sutton (Albuquerque, 1985), 35–71. On the number of cases filed, see *ibid.,* 40.

[42] *Santa Fe New Mexican,* Nov. 6, 1922, quoted in Willard Rollings, "The Pueblos of New Mexico and the Protection of Their Land and Water Rights," in *Working the Range: Essays on the History of Western Land Management and the Environment,* ed. John R. Wunder (Westport, 1985), 3–24.

[43] La Flesche, *Middle Five,* ix.

Like La Flesche, the leaders and organizers who explored the non-Indian political world in the early twentieth century understood that the assertion of their rights and interests required the simultaneous construction of a new identity. Their discovery of a new place for themselves in American society required them literally to don a new costume even as it enabled them to defend their ancient traditions.

But La Flesche's recognition of the power of costume also suggests that, like the Hollywood producers and labor organizers described elsewhere in this volume, native leaders learned from the success of the new Indian identities that discovery could be a flexible process.[44] By removing his feathers to win an audience, La Flesche had conceded that those decorations had become "marks of savagery," tags in a silent cultural conversation. His book, like the work of so many of his Indian contemporaries, contained countless choices, poses, and trade-offs — each selected to link ancient traditions to the world that had engulfed him. The exploration of modern America thus produced both successful adaptations and frequent concessions to Indian and non-Indian audiences.

Like other discoveries, the Indians' twentieth-century explorations in modern America would have remained obscure and insignificant had they not been exploited by successive generations of thinkers, activists, and organizers. In each arena the pioneering efforts of writers, artists, anthropological informants, religious leaders, lawyers, and politicians began a discourse between Native Americans and the wider public and created fragile institutions to nurture future activity. Early Native American artists and writers established a market for their products, and that market alerted publishers and curators to the value of Indian expression in contemporary life. The proliferation of anthropology departments in colleges and universities continued in the 1930s and 1940s, creating both interest in, and a need for, accurate ethnographic presentations. Also in this era, Native Americans began studying in those departments. Pioneers into the world of anthropological scholarship, such as Edward P. Dozier and D'Arcy McNickle, made a more prominent Indian presence in university research programs possible. And while they were regularly embattled and not always successful, the formal institutions of the Native American Church, the growing number of Indian lawyers, the many intertribal organizations, and the emerging tribal governments of the 1930s promised that native voices would continue in these areas as well.[45]

Running parallel to these examples of the continuing Indian exploration of white America was a stunning rise in the native population. Beginning from a low point

---

[44] Michael Rogin, "Making America Home: Racial Masquerade and Ethnic Assimilation in the Transition to Talking Pictures," *Journal of American History*, 79 (Dec. 1992), 1050–77; James R. Barrett, "Americanization from the Bottom Up: Immigration and the Remaking of the Working Class in the United States, 1880–1930," *ibid.*, 996–1020.

[45] Edward P. Dozier (1916–1971) began his anthropological studies at the University of New Mexico in the 1930s, but he completed his Ph.D. in 1952 at the University of California, Los Angeles. D'Arcy McNickle (1904–1977), who had studied at the University of Montana and in Europe, was an adviser to Indian Commissioner John Collier during the New Deal. While he did not earn an academic degree in anthropology, he was active in the field. He was the founding chair of the Department of Anthropology at the University of Regina, Saskatchewan.

of 250,000 in 1890, the total number of enumerated Native Americans rose gradually during the first half of this century until in 1960 it exceeded 500,000. By the time Mourning Dove was beginning her autobiography, then, she understood that her life spanned a transition not to obscurity but to survival. Her tribe and her community were greatly outnumbered. They had suffered terribly at the hands of American settlers, but their future existence was no longer in doubt. Efforts like hers would not be preserved by antiquarians as Australians had recorded the dying words of the last Tasmanian but would constitute both testimony about a vanished time and an example for generations to come. The audience for Indian writers, artists, politicians, and activists could then include other Indians as well as outsiders.[46]

The Indians who explored the non-Indian world in the early twentieth century increasingly spoke to each other and, by the 1930s, considered how their various efforts might combine to form the basis for a modern Native American community. By finding places to be heard and appreciated in an alien world, they created ways of communicating with outsiders and, ultimately, with each other. The growing Indian population in the 1930s and 1940s gave them a sense of confidence and optimism that encouraged greater activism. With that activism came an understanding that artists, politicians, religious leaders, and others shared a common cultural tradition and a set of common interests; and as these insights were communicated among Indian leaders, a national Native American community began to take shape. In November 1944, tribal leaders from twenty-seven states gathered in Denver, Colorado, to found the National Congress of American Indians (NCAI). The new group's constitution declared that its purpose would be:

> to enlighten the public toward a better understanding of the Indian race; to preserve Indian cultural values; to seek an equitable adjustment of tribal affairs, to secure and to preserve Indian rights under Indian treaties with the United States; and otherwise to promote the common welfare of the American Indians.[47]

The origins and activities of the NCAI carry us far beyond the limits of this essay, but it is noteworthy that what became the most important Indian political organization of the twentieth century asserted from the outset that the common welfare of Native Americans required the preservation of cultural values, the defense of legal rights, and the education of the general public. One can see reflected in that assertion the efforts of writers, artists, anthropological collaborators, and politicians over the previous forty years. They had been the most successful in exploring areas where

---

[46] For a discussion of contemporary Indian attitudes toward the rising population, see Russell Thornton, *American Indian Holocaust and Survival: A Population History since 1492* (Norman, 1987), 182–85; and Kenneth R. Weber, "Demographic Shifts in Eastern Montana Reservation Counties: An Emerging Native American Political Power Base," *Journal of Ethnic Studies,* 16 (no. 4, 1989), 101–16.

[47] Hazel Hertzberg, "Indian Rights Movement, 1887–1973," in *Handbook of North American Indians,* Vol. IV: *History of Indian-White Relations,* ed. Wilcomb E. Washburn (Washington, 1988), 313.

The central role of men and women of mixed ancestry in the exploration process begs to be investigated. For one study of a "mixed blood" who played a central role in the construction of a modern Indian identity, see Dorothy Parker, *Singing an Indian Song: A Biography of D'Arcy McNickle* (Lincoln, 1992).

their community's vital interests might find recognition in the wider world and had been the most articulate in communicating their findings to others.

In 1933, at about the time when Mourning Dove was beginning to compose her autobiography, Luther Standing Bear, another boarding school graduate, wrote that if he had a child to educate and "was faced with the duty of choosing between the natural way of my forefathers and that of the white man's present civilization," he would "unhesitatingly set that child's feet in the path of my forefathers. I would raise him to be an Indian!" Standing Bear's statement not only repeats the familiar assertion that native culture can be a corrective to modern civilization, but it calls attention to other Indians—not only his fellow Sioux tribesmen—who share a common ethnic identity. His position was asserted in an English-language book and couched in romantic language that would also appeal to sympathetic whites; nonetheless the cry, "I would raise him to be an Indian!" stands in striking contrast to Morris Jesup's self-confident claim that the discovery of Indian culture could be incorporated into a tableau of progress. It marks both the discovery of an avenue for the powerless to participate in a hostile society and an understanding of how that participation could mark the advent of a new cultural identity.[48]

A recent round table in the *Journal of American History* devoted to the career of Martin Luther King, Jr., contained this description of the civil rights leader:

> Better than any other American, King embodied and projected the dream of creating a world in which people and ideas could travel as far and intermingle as freely as they wanted without hindrance from laws and customs erected to keep them apart. . . . [King] tried to draw separate worlds together by building borderlands between them where people and ideas could mingle instead of collide.[49]

The journeys of discovery launched by Native Americans in the first decades of this century were similar adventures into the cultural borderlands separating racial communities in the United States. The intellectuals, religious reformers, and political leaders who emerged in those years all struggled to define and defend areas where their voices would be heard by whites and yet remain recognizable to their kinsmen. In the cultural territories they discovered, Indians and non-Indians could interact with dignity and mutual respect. In the aftermath of their struggles, such borderlands have formed the heartland of a new Native American community.

The results of this process are still uncertain, but clearly American scholars no longer view Native Americans as "other men of another time." Rather, Indians are understood by anthropologists, by increasing numbers of their countrymen, and by each other as heirs to an ancient cultural tradition that was constructed by human beings and that has been altered by historical circumstance and individual innovation. Students of native life increasingly understand that the history of indigenous people, like the history of any community, is not locked into a tableau of progress;

---

[48] Standing Bear, *Land of the Spotted Eagle*, 258–59.

[49] David Thelen, "Becoming Martin Luther King, Jr.: An Introduction," *Journal of American History*, 78 (June 1991), 15.

it is confined solely by human ambition, interchange, and discovery. Similarly, there has been enormous growth in Indian organizations' and tribal governments' power in using the legal and political system to defend their vital interests. And with that growth of power, the choices available to individuals have multiplied.

Those who were once themselves the objects of exploration have challenged and replaced the nineteenth-century notion that the discovery of Native Americans could be contained by the rhetoric of progress. The Indian people who set off a century ago to explore the new world around them may have led us all away from the self-serving discoveries described in our textbooks and guided us instead toward a new conception of what it means to discover the peoples and institutions of this land.

Americanization from the Bottom Up: Immigration and the Remaking of the Working Class in the United States, 1880–1930

James R. Barrett

The scene is the athletic field at the Ford Motor Company's famous Model T assembly plant at Highland Park, Michigan, on the Fourth of July in the midst of World War I. The occasion is a graduation ceremony for the Ford English School, a language and civics program for the company's immigrant workers, part of Ford's ambitious Five Dollar Day corporate welfare program. The pageant incorporates a symbol that has acquired peculiar importance in Americans' self-image. While the ritual is heavy-handed and perhaps in rather bad taste, its importance lies in the meaning it holds for both the immigrant workers and their corporate sponsors. Ford's director of Americanization describes the scene.

> All the men descend from a boat scene representing the vessel on which they came over; down the gangway representing the distance from the port at which they landed to the school, into a pot 15 feet in diameter and 7½ feet high, which represents the Ford English School. Six teachers, three on either side, stir the pot with ten foot ladles representing nine months of teaching in the school. Into the pot 52 nationalities with their foreign clothes and baggage go and out of the pot after vigorous stirring by the teachers comes one nationality, viz, American.

Lest anyone miss the point, each of the workers emerges from the pot dressed in an identical suit and carrying a miniature American flag.[1]

James R. Barrett is professor of history at the University of Illinois at Urbana.

An earlier version of this paper was presented to the meeting of the Labor Migration Project in April 1989 at Bredbeck, Germany. I wish to thank Jenny Barrett, Carol Leff, Vernon Burton, David Brody, Dirk Hoerder, Marianne Debouzy, Catherine Collomp, Bruno Ramirez, James Grossman, Robert Wiebe, David Thelen, Fred Hoxie, and members of the Labor Migration Project, the University of Illinois Social History Group, and the Fellows' Seminar at the Newberry Library for their comments. I am particularly grateful to Mark Leff for his suggestions and encouragement. I also wish to acknowledge the Newberry Library for its support in the form of a Lloyd Lewis Fellowship and to thank Youn-jin Kim and Toby Higbie for their research assistance.

[1] Clinton C. Dewitt, "Industrial Teachers," in U. S. Bureau of Education, *Proceedings, Americanization Conference, 1919* (Washington, 1919), 119. See also Howard Hill, "The Americanization Movement," *American Journal of Sociology*, 24 (May 1919), 633–34; and Stephen Meyer, "Adapting the Immigrant to the Line: Americanization in the Ford Factory, 1914–1921," *Journal of Social History*, 14 (1980), 67–82. On the symbol of the melting pot, see Werner Sollors, *Beyond Ethnicity: Consent and Descent in American Culture* (New York, 1986), 76–101.

Scenes like this one, perhaps without its contrived drama, were occurring in factories, public school rooms, and settlement houses throughout the United States in
the early twentieth century. Between 1880 and 1924, the year immigration was se-
verely restricted, more than twenty-five million immigrants poured into the
country; they transformed the face of America's laboring population. From the late
nineteenth century on, in a movement that gathered momentum after the turn of
the century, teachers, settlement house workers, and professional patriots aimed to
"Americanize" these immigrants, to guide and hasten the process of acculturation
by which they might embrace the values and behavior of mainstream America.
During and immediately after World War I, the movement became a kind of crusade as employers, nationalist groups, and various state and federal agencies sought
to remold the values and behavior of immigrant workers and their families.[2]

But what did it mean to be Americanized and who was fittest and best placed
to do the Americanizing? Typically, the term *Americanization* has had conservative
connotations. It conveys a unified notion of what it meant to be American and more
than a hint of nativism. It was something the native middle class did to immigrants,
a coercive process by which elites pressed WASP values on immigrant workers, a form
of social control. That side of Americanization was very real, particularly during the
era of World War I and the Red Scare. But it is a rather narrow understanding of
Americanization. I employ the term critically, to suggest the broader acculturation
of immigrants, the day-to-day process by which they came to understand their new
situation and to find or invent ways of coping with it. Americanism was, in fact,
a contested ideal. There were numerous understandings of what it meant to be an
American, divergent values associated with the concept, and so, many ways that an
immigrant might "discover" America.

Ethnic culture certainly persisted in the New World, and immigrants employed
older cultural values and behavior in facing the problems of urban industrial society.
Immigration historians have emphasized the striking diversity and complexity of
American society, demonstrating that there is not one American story, but many
of them that must be told in relation to one another. But if we wish to understand
how working-class formation took place in the midst of great ethnic, cultural, and
racial diversity and change, then we must study the widespread contacts and interaction between workers from diverse ethnic and racial backgrounds, the gradual acculturation of new immigrants, and the transformation of immigrant worker consciousness.

We need an analytical framework that acknowledges the very uneven and continual quality of American working-class formation, shaped by constant migration,

[2] John Higham, *Strangers in the Land: Patterns of American Nativism, 1859–1925* (New York, 1971), 234–63;
John F. McClymer, "The Americanization Movement and the Education of the Foreign-Born Adult, 1914–1925,"
in *American Education and the European Immigrant, 1840–1940,* ed. Bernard J. Weiss (Urbana, 1982), 96–116;
John F. McClymer, *War and Welfare: Social Engineering in America, 1890–1925* (Westport, 1980), 105–52; Rivka
Shpak Lissak, *Pluralism and Progressives: Hull House and the New Immigrants, 1890–1919* (Chicago, 1989), 3–4,
74–81; Ruth Hutchinson Crocker, *Social Work and Social Order: The Settlement Movement in Two Industrial
Cities, 1889–1930* (Urbana, 1992), 213–14; and Edward G. Hartmann, *The Movement to Americanize the Im-
migrant* (New York, 1948).

and allows us to do more than simply describe instances of interethnic class cooperation, one that also enables us to explain how and why they occurred. Such an analysis
would incorporate the sequential character of the process and the element of cultural continuity noted by immigration historians but would also assess the impact
on the newcomers of existing working-class culture and organizations. The arrival
of these immigrants and the prospect of integrating them into existing communities
and institutions represented as much of a challenge to the maturing working class
as it did to employers and the state. Through formal and informal efforts, working-
class people, themselves from quite diverse backgrounds, introduced and explained
American society to the immigrants.

This process undoubtedly occurred in many ways and in many settings for various
age, gender, and occupational groups in immigrant communities — at the dancehall
or on the street corner, at a club meeting, in a city park, in a movie theater, or in
a saloon.[3] Labor organizations were not necessarily involved. For my purposes here,
however, "bottom" refers to wage-earning people, and by "Americanization from the
bottom up," I mean the gradual acculturation of immigrants and their socialization
in working-class environments and contexts — the shop floor, the union, the radical
political party. These settings provided immigrants with alternatives to the world
view and the values advocated in programs sponsored by employers and the government. They absorbed alternative views from their own ethnic communities, from
cosmopolitans of various sorts, and from an earlier generation of older immigrant
and native-born workers. Immigrant workers constructed their own identities, embracing those perspectives and ideas that made sense to them, rejecting those that
seemed to be at odds with what they recognized as reality. Conceptualizing the
"remaking" of the working class in the early twentieth century as the interaction
between two historical generations and class formation itself as an Americanization
from the bottom up provides a new perspective on both working-class and immigration history.

The notion of historical generations illuminates this relationship between workers
either native-born or long resident in the United States and recent immigrants who
were still constructing new identities and coming to terms with life in the United
States. Used in this way, the term *generation* refers to a cohort with comparable historical experiences, rather than the biological generations in any particular immigrant community.[4]

---

[3] Kathy Peiss, *Cheap Amusements: Working Women and Leisure in Turn-of-the-Century New York* (Philadelphia, 1986), 11–33; Susan Glenn, *Daughters of the Shtetl: Life and Labor in the Immigrant Generation* (Ithaca,
1990), 159–60; David Nasaw, *Children of the City: At Work and Play* (Garden City, 1985), 68–73; and Roy Rosenzweig, *Eight Hours for What We Will: Workers and Leisure in an Industrial City, 1870–1920* (Cambridge, Eng.,
1983), 148–50.

[4] Karl Mannheim, "The Problem of Generations," in *Essays on the Sociology of Knowledge,* ed. Paul Kec-
skemeti (New York, 1952), 276–322; Alan Spitzer, "The Historical Problem of Generations," *American Historical
Review,* 78 (Dec. 1973), 1353–85; David Montgomery, *Workers' Control in America: Studies in Work, Technology,
and Labor Struggles* (New York, 1979), 9–10; and John Bodnar, *The Transplanted: A History of Immigrants in
Urban America* (Bloomington, 1985), 85–93.

Two fairly distinct generations of workers lived in many American industrial communities between the end of the nineteenth century and the 1920s. The first consisted of native-born and "old" immigrant workers and their children—British, Germans, and Irish, with smaller numbers of Scandinavians, English-speaking Canadians, and others. By the late nineteenth century, these workers had not only had years of industrial and urban experience, they had also created institutions and developed and popularized ideas that they used to cope with the rigors of wage labor. They had organized and now led trade unions, Knights of Labor assemblies, co-ops, and labor parties. To use E. J. Hobsbawm's famous phrase, they had learned "the rules of the game."[5] They might be steeped in their own ethnic cultures, as were the Irish and Germans as late as the early twentieth century. But they also had experience in dealing with other ethnic groups, and though some retained a measure of prejudice, they often recognized the value of interethnic cooperation.

By the turn of the century, a new generation of workers, drawn to the United States largely from eastern and southeastern Europe, shared the cities and industrial towns with these older, more experienced groups and their American-born children. By the end of World War I, these "new immigrants" were joined by black and Mexican migrants to create a new working-class population. Few of these newcomers were ignorant peasants recently uprooted from the land and casting about in the city, disoriented and demoralized, but all of them faced major adjustments if they were to cope with life in large factories and in city neighborhoods.[6] To some degree, they relied on the material and cultural resources of their own ethnic communities, but for good or ill, they had also to contend with the structures already in place, those created by the earlier generation of industrial workers, who played major roles in acculturating and socializing the newcomers.

Various forms of old-country radicalism and social mobilization shaped the development of labor radicalism in the United States. The precise content of such cultural and ideological continuity varied in important ways from one ethnic group to another, but we might think about such continuity as part of what might be termed either *ethnocultural* or *segmented* class formation. I use the phrase ethnocultural class formation to underscore the fact that some immigrant workers did indeed create viable working-class cultures with distinct institutions, political ideas, forms of socialization, organizations, and strategies. But they tended to do this *within* their own ethnic communities, often developing such cultures partly on

[5] E. J. Hobsbawm, *Labouring Men: Studies in the History of Labour* (London, 1968), 344–45.

[6] Ewa Morawska, *For Bread with Butter: The Lifeworlds of East Central Europeans in Johnstown, Pennsylvania, 1890–1940* (New York, 1985), 22–62; Caroline Golab, *Immigrant Destinations* (Philadelphia, 1977), 75–100; Victor Greene, *The Slavic Community on Strike: Immigrant Labor in Pennsylvania Anthracite* (South Bend, 1968), 13–32; Glenn, *Daughters of the Shtetl*, 1–7; Peter Gottlieb, *Making Their Own Way: Southern Blacks' Migration to Pittsburgh, 1916–1930* (Urbana, 1987), 1–62; John Bodnar, Roger Simon, and Michael P. Weber, *Lives of Their Own: Blacks, Italians, and Poles in Pittsburgh, 1900–1960* (Urbana, 1982), 29–54; and James R. Grossman, *Land of Hope: Chicago, Black Southerners, and Migration, 1916–1930* (Chicago, 1989). Bodnar, *The Transplanted*, emphasizes the *transformation* of immigrant culture and everyday life over cultural continuity. See James R. Barrett, "The Transplanted: Workers, Class, and Labor," *Social Science History*, 12 (Fall 1988), 221–31.

the basis of Old World experiences and then adapting them to the conditions of the New.

The phrase segmented class formation suggests a different vantage point on the same process. Class formation in the United States was segmented in the sense that it took place simultaneously in various ethnic communities. But describing workers' cultures within each ethnic community is not enough, especially since ethnic socialization often had exclusivist strains that inhibited broader working-class solidarity. Especially by the early twentieth century, *American* working-class formation was of necessity interethnic, emerging from the mixture of people from diverse backgrounds and depending on contact across ethnic boundaries. We should be looking rather carefully at the relations *between* the generations of immigrant workers and the various ethnic working-class communities, not simply telling the story of each group of ethnic workers.

In industrial communities throughout the country during the late nineteenth century, skilled German, British, Irish, and native-born male workers built strong craft unions and settled into comfortable communities. The cultures they built, based on associational life and home ownership, were imbued with notions of class, but they were largely defensive in nature. New immigrants might be viewed with as much suspicion as bosses. Where they were organized, these skilled workers used their leverage to protect their standards and prerogatives, but even with no union organization at all, they might achieve some of the same security by employing ethnic and kinship connections to secure work and to retain their hold on the better jobs. Through their craft unions, churches, fraternal organizations, and other institutions, they created their own cultural worlds, ones that often left little room for newcomers.[7]

These older native-born and immigrant workers often embraced a "social republicanism" that fused notions of economic and social reform with democratic nationalist ideals. Indeed, the concept of a distinctive working-class republicanism has even been advanced as a kind of synthesis for labor history. But there are several problems with employing republicanism to reintegrate the story of American workers in the wake of the massive immigration at the turn of the century. It is questionable whether even the earlier generation of immigrants all understood republicanism in the same sense as native-born workers. The traditions with which many of the earlier immigrants identified were those of 1848, not those of 1776; both those traditions had more to do with nationalism than with internationalism and

---

[7] Linda Schneider, "The Citizen Striker: Workers' Ideology in the Homestead Strike of 1892," *Labor History*, 23 (Winter 1982), 47–66; Linda Schneider, "Republicanism Reinterpreted: American Ironworkers, 1860–1892," in *A l'ombre de la Statue de la Liberté: Immigrants et ouvriers dans la République Américaine, 1880–1920*, ed. Marianne Debouzy (Saint-Denis, 1988), 211; Rosenzweig, *Eight Hours for What We Will*, 65–90; Richard J. Oestreicher, *Solidarity and Fragmentation: Working People and Class Consciousness in Detroit, 1875–1900* (Urbana, 1986), 30–67, 172–214; David Emmons, *The Butte Irish: Class and Ethnicity in an American Mining Town, 1875–1925* (Urbana, 1989); and James R. Barrett, *Work and Community in the Jungle: Chicago's Packinghouse Workers, 1894–1922* (Urbana, 1987), 38–44, 119–31.

class solidarity. Finally, whatever the republican consensus that may have obtained among earlier immigrants, it had clearly fragmented by the turn of the century.[8]

Nor was such ideology always progressive in content. The same defensive mind-set that might impart great cohesion and solidarity for resistance against employers and state authorities could also manifest itself in exclusionary impulses that shaped responses to new immigrant workers. A common reaction to labor's decline in status during the late nineteenth and early twentieth centuries, for example, was the demand for immigration restriction that enjoyed great popularity among not only the native-born but also many Irish and British and some German labor activists. Even as an instrumental approach to problems of unemployment or low wages, the demand for restriction revealed an exclusionary quality to workers' thinking, and it sometimes betrayed a narrow, nativist conception of "labor" shared not only by American Federation of Labor (AFL) craft unionists but also by Knights of Labor activists and even socialist militants.[9]

In its extreme form, that perspective infused the anti-Chinese movement that swept the West and other parts of the country in the late nineteenth century. Here the element of race added an enduring and explosive quality to the mixture of defensive sentiments characterizing conservative and even some radical workers. Some Socialist party leaders, for example, held profoundly racist attitudes toward Asian, black, and many immigrant workers and strongly supported immigration restriction.[10]

Immigrant socialization in working-class settings could perpetuate this negative strain of thought and feeling: Older immigrants and natives passed their own prejudices on to the newcomers. Irish immigrants, who had been in job competition with Asians and blacks for more than a generation before eastern European immigrants arrived and who had themselves suffered discrimination and violence at the hands of nativists, often developed racist attitudes and repertoires of behavior. Inside the labor movement, the Catholic church, and the political organizations of

[8] Leon Fink, *Workingmen's Democracy: The Knights of Labor and American Politics* (Urbana, 1983); Eric Foner, "Class, Ethnicity, and Radicalism in the Gilded Age: The Land League and Irish-America," *Marxist Perspectives*, 1 (Summer 1978), 6–55; Richard Schneirov, "Political Cultures and the Role of the State in Labor's Republic: The View from Chicago, 1848–1877," *Labor History*, 32 (Summer 1991), 376–400; David Brundage, "Irish Land and American Workers: Class and Ethnicity in Denver, Colorado," in *"Struggle a Hard Battle": Essays on Working-Class Immigrants,* ed. Dirk Hoerder (DeKalb, 1986), 46–67; Sean Wilentz, "Against Exceptionalism: Class Consciousness and the American Labor Movement, 1790–1920," *International Labor and Working-Class History*, 26 (Fall 1984), 1–24; David Montgomery, "Labor and the Republic in Industrial America: 1860–1920," *Le Mouvement Sociale*, 110 (1980), 211–15.

[9] Nick Salvatore, "Some Thoughts on Class and Citizenship," in *A l'ombre de la Statue de la Liberté*, ed. Debouzy, 215–30; Catherine Collomp, "Les organizations ouvrières et la restriction de l'immigration aux Etats-Unis à la fin du dix-neuvième siècle," *ibid.,* 231–46; Catherine Collomp, "Unions, Civics, and National Identity: Organized Reaction to Immigration, 1881–1897," *Labor History,* 29 (Fall 1988), 471–74; and A. T. Lane, "American Unions, Mass Immigration, and the Literacy Test: 1900–1917," *Labor History*, 25 (Winter 1984), 5–25.

[10] David Roediger, *The Wages of Whiteness: Race and the Making of the American Working Class* (London, 1991), 71–112, 179–80; Gwendolyn Mink, *Old Labor and New Immigrants in American Political Development: Union, Party, and State, 1875–1920* (Ithaca, 1986), 228–35; Collomp, "Unions, Civics, and National Identity," 463–64; Alexander Saxton, *The Indispensable Enemy: Labor and the Anti-Chinese Movement in California* (Berkeley, 1971); Lawrence Glickman, "Inventing the 'American Standard of Living': Gender, Race and Working-Class Identity, 1880–1925," paper, 1991 (in James R. Barrett's possession). My thanks to Lawrence Glickman for allowing me to cite his unpublished work.

many working-class communities, the Irish occupied vital positions as American-izers of later groups.[11] Racism was a learned value, deeply ingrained in the world views of many workers by the end of the nineteenth century; it was passed on to immigrants along with values enhancing class solidarity.

The AFL's craft unionism was, of course, exclusionary by definition; keeping non-members out of the labor market through control of hiring was its *raison d'être*. In the context of mass immigration, craft organization reinforced any nativist tenden-cies derived from other sources. The contempt some craft unionists had for new immigrants and women was often based more on their cultural, gender, ethnic, or racial "otherness" than on any threat they posed to the livelihood and living condi-tions of skilled workers and their families. But these two aspects of the newcomers' image — otherness and lack of skill — fused. When they did, exclusion from a trade might be based not simply on the question of skill but either implicitly or explicitly on race, ethnicity, or gender. To overdraw the point, it was possible to be a "good union man" and at the same time a racist, a nativist, and a chauvinist.

The earlier generation, then, sometimes reacted to new immigrants defensively, seeking to exclude them from the labor market and from the broader working-class community. Yet the older, entrenched generation often could not afford to shut out the newcomers. Relations between the two generations occurred in a context of mas-sive technical and economic upheaval, something like a second industrial revolu-tion. The American working-class population was transformed in the course of the early twentieth century precisely because the economy and the nature of work itself were also being transformed. In some sectors of the economy, for instance, the building trades, where skills were still required and complex work rules hung on, craft unions might retain control over the labor market. In many industries, how-ever, such unions faced a sustained crisis throughout the late nineteenth and early twentieth centuries. The desperation of their struggle to retain some control over the work process and jobs varied considerably from one trade to another, but most skilled workers felt the pressure. Most of the literature about this problem has fo-cused on the control struggles of the skilled, yet many old-line AFL unions did reach out to unskilled immigrants in these years, if only because the transformation of the labor process and the labor market left them little choice.[12]

The ongoing social transformation and the related technological revolution in in-dustry presented the labor movement with an enormous challenge, one with both social and organizational dimensions. The integration of the newcomers into the labor movement called not only for new forms of organization, new organizing strategies, and new strike tactics, but also for a new means of socializing and accul-turating the new people, a "remaking" of the working class between the turn of the century and the Great Depression. That involved the organized efforts of unions

[11] Roediger, *Wages of Whiteness*, 133–63; Kerby A. Miller, "Green over Black: The Origins of Irish-American Racism," paper, 1969 (in Barrett's possession). My thanks to Professor Miller for allowing me to cite this fine work.

[12] Montgomery, *Workers' Control in America*. On the countervailing pressures of skill dilution and nativism and the consequent efforts of American Federation of Labor (AFL) craft unions to integrate less skilled immigrants, see Robert Asher, "Union Nativism and the Immigrant Response," *Labor History*, 23 (1982), 325–48.

and other labor organizations, myriad informal contacts between workers in various settings, and a long struggle with management for the loyalty of the immigrant worker.

We know most about the impulse for immigrant acculturation that came from the native middle class in public school classrooms, settlement houses, and factories. Because most of the new immigrant's waking hours were spent at the workplace, much of his or her learning about what it meant to be an American occurred there. Certainly employers had their own lessons to teach. They experimented with English instruction and citizenship classes during the early years of this century and took a special interest in the movement during the labor shortage and unionization of the World War I era.[13]

Henry Ford launched the most ambitious of these plans at his Highland Park Model T plant as part of the Five Dollar Day plan, which, beginning in 1914, combined assembly-line technology with a shorter work day, incentive pay, and an elaborate personnel management system. Accepting prevailing Progressive notions that environment shaped one's behavior and attitudes, Ford engineers established a Sociology Department to remake the lives of their immigrant workers and win them over to thrift, efficiency, and company loyalty. Case workers fanned out into Detroit's working-class neighborhoods, ready to fight for the hearts and minds of the immigrant auto workers. They investigated each worker's home life as well as his work record, and one could qualify for the Five Dollar Day incentive pay only after demonstrating the proper home environment and related middle-class values. Thus the company sought to show workers not only the "right way to work" but also the "right way to live." In describing the work of his Sociology Department, Ford argued that "these men of many nations must be taught American ways, the English language, and the right way to live." (And he meant business. When about nine hundred workers of Greek or Russian extraction missed work to celebrate Orthodox Christmas—on the Julian calendar, hence thirteen days after Christmas on the Gregorian calendar—he summarily fired them all. "If these men are to make their home in America," he argued, "they should observe American holidays.") Other companies established similar plans: meat packers, steel mills, farm implement manufacturers, textile plants, and others. By the spring of 1919, there were at least eight hundred industrial plants sponsoring their own classes or working in conjunction with the YMCA and other agencies to put on evening or plant classes.[14]

---

[13] Herbert Gutman, *Work, Culture, and Society in Industrializing America: Essays in Working-Class and Social History* (New York, 1976), 7–9, 22–25; and Hartmann, *Movement to Americanize the Immigrant*, 165–73.

[14] W. M. Roberts, "Promotion of Education in Industry," in U.S. Bureau of Education, *Proceedings, Americanization Conference*, 145; Stephen Meyer, "Adapting the Immigrant to the Line," 67–82; and Stephen Meyer, *The Five Dollar Day: Social Control in the Ford Motor Company, 1908–1921* (Albany, 1981), 123–64, esp. 151, 156. For other company programs, see David Brody, *Steelworkers in America: The Nonunion Era* (New York, 1969), 190–97; Gerd Korman, "Americanization at the Factory Gate," *Labor and Industrial Relations Review*, 18 (1965), 396–419; Lizabeth Cohen, *Making a New Deal: Industrial Workers in Chicago, 1919–1939* (Cambridge, Eng., 1990), 163, 165; and, for a more general discussion, Stuart Brandes, *American Welfare Capitalism, 1880–1940* (Chicago, 1976), 58–60, 78–79, 116–17; and Daniel Nelson, *Managers and Workers: Origins of the New Factory System in the United States, 1880–1920* (Madison, 1975), 144–45.

Of course, learning also went on at work outside the structured programs. The workplace was by its nature an authoritarian environment, and foremen and other supervisors were always "teaching" immigrants—to do what they were told, to act promptly, to keep working. There was one phrase "every foreman had to learn in English, Polish, and Italian," recalled William Klann, a Ford Motor assembly foreman: "'Hurry up.'" The verbal abuse of immigrant workers for which steel mills and some other factories were notorious derived in part from the heartfelt prejudices of lower-level management, but it was also a crude effort to teach the immigrant "who was boss." Blast furnaces, rolling mills, slaughterhouses, and freight yards were brutal places where the foreman or straw boss undoubtedly felt obliged to assert his authority with whatever force seemed justified. He too had a lesson to teach the immigrant, in this case a lesson about power in the workplace.[15]

But there were other teachers—older, more experienced, sometimes politicized workers, who conveyed different notions of what was right or wrong in the workshop and in the United States as a society. Immigrants learned restriction of output and other aspects of a new work culture from their workmates and, according to David Montgomery, "exchanged portions of their traditional culture, not for the values and habits welfare plans sought to inculcate, but for working-class mores."[16] Immigrant strikers' frequent demands for humane treatment and for the discharge of abusive foremen suggest the importance of such socialization. Clearly, immigrants themselves were constructing identities and embracing values that reflected situations they faced in the workplace.

Not all workplace conversations were concerned with work itself. Nor did all one's lessons come from earlier immigrants. Some had broader implications that might be conveyed by more experienced and sophisticated workers from within one's own community. Something like the ethnocultural class formation that characterized the "old immigrant" communities in the late nineteenth century was occurring in "new immigrant" communities in the early twentieth. Here too workers developed the ideas, organization, institutions, and movements commonly associated with the phrase "working-class culture." Once again such cultures were built in part on Old World experiences and values, but they were soon tailored to American industrial settings. Sicilian peasants and artisans who created Italy's "red towns" and then carried a radical oral tradition to Tampa, Chicago, and New York are examples of this phenomenon, as are the Jewish socialists of the ghettos of eastern Europe and America or the Finnish leftists of the Mesabi Range. Comparable radical minorities

[15] Meyer, *Five Dollar Day*, 56; Nelson, *Managers and Workers*, 81; "Family Records" [1919], 23, box 120, Mary Heaton Vorse Papers (Archives of Labor History and Urban Affairs, Wayne State University, Detroit); Andrea Grazziosi, "Common Laborers, Unskilled Workers, 1890–1915," *Labor History*, 22 (Fall 1981), 512–44; Richard Edwards, *Contested Terrain: The Transformation of the Workplace in the Twentieth Century* (New York, 1979), 30–34, 63–65; David Montgomery, *The Fall of the House of Labor: The Workplace, the State, and American Labor Activism* (New York, 1987), 92–93; Cohen, *Making a New Deal*, 167–68; Brody, *Steelworkers in America*, 28; Gerd Korman, *Industrialization, Immigrants, and Americanizers: The View from Milwaukee, 1866–1921* (Madison, 1967), 62–63.
[16] Montgomery, *Workers' Control in America*, 43; Montgomery, *Fall of the House of Labor*, 89–91; Glenn, *Daughters of the Shtetl*, 154–60.

flourished throughout America's eastern European ethnic communities and in workplaces around the country.[17]

John Wasko of United States Steel's Homestead Works might have been one of these people. By 1919 he had been in the country only seven years, but he was already married with two children and a home. He had taken out his first papers and spoke English fluently. He learned the language and a number of other things down in the anthracite mines. There he had seen the United Mine Workers of America handle all the common complaints he encountered in the mill—arbitrary and abusive foremen, unpaid overtime, and phony pay scales—and it was a lesson learned well. Wasko read several Slavic-language papers and New York City's socialist *Call* every day. When the organizing started in the mill, he knew what to do, and he "spread the principles of trade unionism among his fellow countrymen."[18]

Stjepan Mesaroš, a twenty-year-old Croatian immigrant, met a man like Wasko when he arrived for his first day on the job at Berk's slaughterhouse in Philadelphia. He was overwhelmed by what he found there and in the streets of his neighborhood. Among the many mysteries was the verbal abuse meted out to a young black man with whom Stjepan shared his duties. Noticing a Serbian laborer who seemed to spend every free moment reading Serbo-Croatian pamphlets and newspapers, Stjepan took a chance and asked him about it. Almost sixty years later, he recalled the conversation which took place amidst the blood of the slaughterhouse and changed the course of his life. "The Serb sat down next to me and explained that both bosses and workers were prejudiced against black people. 'You'll soon learn something about this country,' he said. 'Negroes never get a fair chance.'" The next day the Serb brought a newspaper clipping in to work.

> The picture showed the Berk family on its way to vacation in Florida for the winter. The picture showed the young men in white pants and shoes and the young ladies in white summer dresses. The whole family was boarding a Pullman parlor car. The explanation proceeded in Serbo-Croatian.
> "What's Florida?" I asked.
> "That's a place that's warm in the winter. . . ."
> "Who goes there?"
> "You can see who goes, only bosses."

[17] Gutman, *Work, Culture, and Society*, 3–76; Donna Gabaccia, *Militants and Migrants: Rural Sicilians Become American Workers* (New Brunswick, 1988); Bruno Cartosio, "Sicilians in Two Worlds," in *A l'ombre de la Statue de la Liberté*, ed. Debouzy, 127–38; Gary Mormino and George Pozetta, *The Immigrant World of Ybor City: Italians and Their Latin Neighbors in Tampa* (Urbana, 1987); Irving Howe, *World of Our Fathers: The Journey of the East European Jews to America and the Life They Made* (New York, 1976), 287–304; Steven Fraser, *Labor Will Rule: Sidney Hillman and the Rise of American Labor* (New York, 1991); Moses Rischin, *The Promised City: New York's Jews, 1870–1914* (New York, 1970), 162–68; Michael G. Karni, "Finnish Immigrant Leftists in America: The Golden Years, 1900–1918," in *"Struggle a Hard Battle,"* ed. Hoerder, 199–266; "Interview with Leo Laukki, Chicago, July 10, 1919," folder 15, box 21, David J. Saposs Papers (State Historical Society of Wisconsin, Madison); Mary Cygan, "Political and Cultural Leadership in an Immigrant Community: Polish-American Socialism, 1880–1950" (Ph.D. diss., Northwestern University, 1989); and Joseph Stipanovich, "Immigrant Workers and Immigrant Intellectuals in Progressive America: A History of the Yugoslavian Socialist Federation, 1900–1918" (Ph.D. diss., University of Minnesota, 1977).

[18] "Interview with John S. Wasko, Homestead," folder 8, box 26, Saposs Papers.

"But the boss [the foreman, as I understood the setup] is still here."
"The Berks just hire him to run the factory. They get all the money."[19]

The Serb described the sort of life that came with the requisite amount of money, and the young Croatian was astounded by the wealth he heard described. Did Stjepan wish to know how this was all possible? The Serb handed him some Socialist Labor party pamphlets and soon after gave him other reading matter of the sort favored by self-educated worker radicals around the world—not just on politics but on popular science, temperance, health foods, atheism. Such literature conveyed more than a formal political ideology—socialism—it also incorporated a new world view. This too was Americanization, but not the sort that employers or most adult educators had in mind when they used the term. Stjepan had discovered America.

Stjepan Mesaroš's slaughterhouse conversation raises the important question of how other immigrant workers discovered the significance of race in American life. The black migrants arriving from the Deep South in the war years and the 1920s were part of the same generation as the new immigrants, and the two groups had a great deal in common. Yet we know very little about the relations between them or for that matter about the more general problem of the evolution of racism among white workers. It seems likely, however, that racial attitudes were part of the legacy that older, more Americanized workers passed on to newcomers. In some cases, these might have included the sort of enlightened perspective displayed by Stjepan's Serbian friend. The anarchist Luigi Galleani often wrote in the Italian-language press about the problem of white racism and concluded that in America the proletariat's motto should be "Not race struggle but class struggle." Surely there were others like these men. More often, however, recent immigrants encountered the hostile attitudes toward blacks that had developed among the Irish and other older groups in the late nineteenth century, exacerbated by the competition for jobs and resources in the early twentieth. The fact that newer immigrants played little part in the race riots of the World War I era suggests that it took some time for them and their children to make these prejudices their own, but their prominent presence in post–World War II racial conflicts demonstrates that many learned their lessons only too well.[20]

The results of Stjepan's friendship with the Serb and his later career also suggest another context for Americanization—radical working-class politics. Stjepan joined a South Slav branch of the Socialist Labor party and later the Communist party. He changed his name to Steve Nelson, learned to read the party press in English, with the help of a young German-American radical, and studied public speaking, organizing methods, economics, Marxist philosophy, and labor history at party

[19] Steve Nelson, James R. Barrett, and Rob Ruck, *Steve Nelson, American Radical* (Pittsburgh, 1981), 16.

[20] Rudolph J. Vecoli, "'Free Country': The American Republic Viewed by the Italian Left, 1880–1920," in *A l'ombre de la Statue de la Liberté*, ed. Debouzy, 75–76; Miller, "Green over Black"; Roediger, *Wages of Whiteness*, 133–63; Barrett, *Work and Community in the Jungle*, 202–24; Dominic Pacyga, *Polish Immigrants and Industrial Chicago: Workers on the South Side, 1880–1922* (Columbus, 1991), 212–27; Arnold Hirsch, "Race and Housing: Violence and Communal Protest in Chicago, 1940–1960," in *The Ethnic Frontier: Essays in the History of Group Survival in Chicago and the Midwest*, ed. Peter D'A. Jones and Melvin Holli (Grand Rapids, 1977), 350–55.

schools in New York and Moscow. He became a union organizer and later an organizer of the unemployed. He worked in Detroit, Chicago, and the anthracite coal fields of eastern Pennsylvania. During the Spanish civil war he served as commissar of the American Abraham Lincoln Battalion, fighting for his own notion of democracy. Jailed for his political activities during the McCarthy era, he left the Communist party in 1957 but remained a committed socialist.

The Communist party gave Nelson more than language and speaking skills. It brought him into contact with educated and politically committed young people from a wide range of ethnic backgrounds, provided him with a key to understanding the world around him, and gave him a vision of a new and better world. Ironically, Steve Nelson's Americanization came in the context of a revolutionary party, a path he trod with a small but important group of immigrant radicals.

The early Socialist party was ethnically segmented through a system of foreign-language federations and socialist culture was often ethnic culture, but immigrant socialists were not isolated either from one another or from their native-born counterparts. Many recognized that the party's long-term viability rested on links between foreign and native-born radicals, on creating an American mass movement. In each ethnic community, whether it was preponderantly new immigrants or old, small groups of radicals assumed a disproportionate significance in the acculturation of immigrant workers. Already sympathetic to the goals of the movement, perhaps a bit more articulate or cosmopolitan than their workmates, they provided labor activists with invaluable links to the immigrant communities. As newspaper editors, street-corner speakers, and organizers, they carried the socialist message into their communities in a language workers could understand, and in the process they provided a framework within which the individual immigrant could comprehend the American political and economic system and her or his place in it.[21]

The Communist party in the 1920s was a bit different from earlier socialist organizations. In the mid-twenties, the Communists made a conscious decision to "Americanize" the party (their term). They dissolved language federations, shifted immigrant activists into neighborhood branches, shop nuclei, and other ethnically mixed mass organizations, and even asked foreign-born comrades to change their names. During the Popular Front of the late 1930s, Americanization was even more elaborate. Proclaiming that "Communism Is Twentieth Century Americanism," Earl Browder and other party leaders consciously cultivated an American image, using patriotic symbols and language to convey their message. The new line came easily to second-generation immigrants who eagerly identified themselves as American radicals. A veteran of this movement later recalled beginning to feel "like we were really part of the American Scene. We were looking for some kind of legitimation

[21] Julianna Puskás, "Hungarian Immigration and Socialism," in *A l'ombre de la Statue de la Liberté*, ed. Debouzy, 145–50; Mary Cygan, "Political and Cultural Leadership"; Mary Cygan, "Polish American Socialism as an Americanizing Force," paper presented at the American Historical Association convention, Cincinnati, December 1988 (in Barrett's possession); Robert Park, *The Immigrant Press and Its Control* (New York, 1922), 107–9; Timothy L. Smith, "Introduction," in Ivan Molek, *Slovene Immigrant History, 1900–1950: Autobiographical Sketches* (Dover, 1979), xix–xx; and David Shannon, *The Socialist Party* (Chicago, 1967), 43–48.

John Fitzpatrick, Chicago Federation of Labor president, addresses a large crowd of packinghouse workers on Chicago's south side during the World War I organizing drives. *Courtesy Chicago Historical Society, ICHi-10294.*

of our feeling about becoming even more American. Browder came along and sort of articulated this."[22]

Labor organizations striving to organize in the era of mass immigration also became contexts for acculturation. Indeed, when organizers reached out to the newcomers — and this happened rather more often than we have realized during the early twentieth century — they had little choice but to engage the immigrants in a dialogue about unionization. Too often union drives are thought of in purely institutional terms — as attempts to build up organizations. Surely, this was the goal and sometimes the end result. But each of these efforts was a process of socialization as well, an effort to convey to the immigrants basic values as well as the structure and function of unions and other working-class organizations. To some degree, this was simply a matter of "selling the union," and this effort itself was important. In coal mining, steel production, clothing manufacturing, slaughtering and meat

[22] On the "Americanization" of the Communist party in the mid-1920s, see Theodore Draper, *American Communism and Soviet Russia: The Formative Period* (New York, 1960), 272–75; and Irving Howe and Lewis Coser, *The American Communist Party: A Critical History, 1919–1957* (Boston, 1957). On the Americanism of the Popular Front, see Fraser Ottanelli, *The Communist Party of the United States: From the Depression to World War II* (New Brunswick, 1991), 83–105; Harvey Klehr, *The Heyday of American Communism: The Depression Decade* (New York, 1984), 167–206; Maurice Isserman, "The 1956 Generation: An Alternative Approach to the History of American Communism," *Radical America,* 14 (March–April 1980), 43–51; George Watt interview by Maurice Isserman, Jan. 7, 1978, in Maurice Isserman's possession, quoted in Maurice Isserman, *Which Side Were You On? The American Communist Party during the Second World War* (Middletown, 1982), 9–14.

packing, and other industries, organizers, business agents, and shop stewards had to convey to the immigrants the specific goals, strategies, and structures of the labor movement. But they also conveyed the values and ideas that gave the movement its rationale, its soul. What in the union's appeal attracted immigrants more than official programs? Why were they willing to make the sorts of sacrifices that were clearly necessary to sustain organization in the face of staggering odds? Such questions might help us begin to sketch out some of the characteristics of immigrant workers' mentalities in the early twentieth century.

There were several elements to labor's version of Americanism. Not surprisingly, activists frequently emphasized basic civil liberties, particularly free speech, and encouraged immigrants to speak up and defend their rights. Nor were these ideals abstract. In coal company and steel mill towns and in many other industrial communities, labor's ability to organize depended on the maintenance of such rights, and immigrants frequently learned the values of these freedoms in the midst of organizing activities, strikes, and demonstrations. Workers' notions of these rights, moreover, were often much broader than the law itself. They tended to reflect rights that were more idealized than real. "It is time that some people learned," wrote a West Virginia miner in the midst of the 1921 coal strike, "that working men have some rights under the Constitution, among them the right to organize for mutual protection, the right of collective bargaining and the right to quit work when conditions surrounding their employment become unbearable. And these rights we are going to maintain at any cost." Another miner wrote to President Warren Harding the same year to complain that "the coal operators are depriving the coal miners of the right to belong to the labor organization which is their inherent right given to all citizens of the United States." A steelworker who termed his forty-one years in the mill "slavery and persecution" claimed that the long work day and poor conditions were "against the Constitution."[23]

Organizers frequently invested their material demands with the power of democratic rhetoric and patriotism by speaking of an American standard of living, by which they meant higher wages, shorter working hours, and decent working conditions. Reference to the "American" standard could be and sometimes was used to exclude newcomers, as in the case of the working-class agitation against Chinese immigrants. But it could also be the basis for integrating newcomers and imparting the basic values of the movement, while establishing a legitimacy in the eyes of the public at large. During World War I, the "American standard of living" provided the unions with a patriotic image and immigrant workers with the prospect of an ideal American life for themselves and their children. "We cannot bring up our children as Americans on 15 and a half cents an hour," a Polish stockyards worker argued, "We cannot live decently. Our wives, our children, our homes demand better wages."[24]

[23] John Hutchinson to Editor, *United Mine Workers Journal,* June 15, 1921, p. 21; David Allan Corbin, *Life, Work, and Rebellion in the Coal Fields: The Southern West Virginia Miners, 1880–1922* (Urbana, 1981), 242; "Interview with Mike Connolly, Pittsburgh" [1919], folder 9, box 26, Saposs Papers.
[24] Glickman, "Inventing 'The American Standard of Living'"; Peter Shergold, *Working-Class Life: The Amer-*

Finally, many labor activists embraced the concept of cultural pluralism, if only in the interests of labor solidarity, and tried to impart this value to immigrants. What this might have looked like at the level of the local union is suggested by the scene at a meeting of Local 183, which included all women working in the Chicago stockyards, regardless of race, nationality, or trade. When the young Irish chairwoman called for a discussion of grievances, a young black woman complained that a Polish member had insulted her. The chairwoman asked both to come forward.

> "Now what did yez call each other?"
> "She called me a Nigger."
> "She called me a Pollock first."
> "Both of yez oughta be ashamed of yourselves. You're both to blame. But don't you know that this question in our ritual don't mean that kind of griev-e-ances, but griev-e-ances of the whole bunch of us?"[25]

Ethelbert Stewart, the United States commissioner of labor, observed labor's version of Americanization as it unfolded in Chicago's slaughterhouses and meat packing plants during the early years of this century. Here ethnic hostilities had been rife, and ethnic communities tended to be dominated by charismatic "clan leaders" who fought the unions for influence over the immigrants. Since the workers' worlds were organized largely on the basis of nationality, the union "represented the first, and for a time the only, point at which [the immigrant] touches any influence outside of his clan. . . . The Slav mixes with the Lithuanian, the German, and the Irishman—and this is the only place they do mix until, by virtue of this intercourse and this mixing, clannishness is to a degree destroyed, and a social mixing along other lines comes into play." In the anthracite coal fields, labor economist John R. Commons noted, "foreigners were given over to the most bitter and often murderous feuds among the ten or fifteen nationalities and the two or three factions within each nationality. . . . When the union was organized all antagonisms of race, religion and faction were eliminated. The immigrants came down to an economic basis and turned their forces against the bosses." "The only effective Americanizing force for the southeastern European," Commons concluded, "is the labor union."[26] Later conflicts suggest that Commons was too optimistic, but there was no question that the union's focus on common grievances helped to break down ethnic barriers. Why? Immigrants themselves were the critical element in this process. They responded better to unions than to official programs because the unions stressed issues that were vital to the welfare of ethnic communities but simply could

ican Standard in Comparative Perspective, 1899–1913 (Pittsburgh, 1982); Barrett, Work and Community in the Jungle, 142–46; Mary McDowell, "The Struggle for an American Standard of Living," in Mary McDowell and Municipal Housekeeping, ed. Caroline Hill (Chicago, 1938), 62–66, esp. 66.

    [25] Howard Wilson, Mary McDowell, Neighbor (Chicago, 1928), 100; Alice Henry, The Trade Union Woman (New York, 1905), 56; Alan Dawley, Struggles for Justice: Social Responsibility and the Liberal State (Cambridge, Mass., 1991), 257–60.

    [26] For Ethelbert Stewart's 1905 statement, see Barrett, Work and Community in the Jungle, 139; Winthrop Talbot, ed., Americanization (New York, 1917), 307, 305, 177–78; Peter Roberts, The New Immigration (New York, 1912), 195.

The radical Industrial Workers of the World (IWW) conveyed their own analysis of American society to immigrant workers in numerous languages. *Courtesy Charles H. Kerr Publishing Co., Chicago.*

not be resolved without looking beyond their boundaries to class-based organization.

Besides teaching immigrants interethnic solidarity, unions did more than any civics lesson to impart the principles and methods of democratic government by relating them to practical matters: wages, hours, and working conditions. For most immigrants, introduction to the American political and economic system came not through night-school classes but through discussion and debate at union meetings (with interpreters), informal conversations with fellow workers, and labor movement publications (often printed in various languages). And the union's version of

Americanism was likely to be different from the one conveyed in employer programs, emphasizing the free expression of one's opinions and the importance of standing up with fellow workers to demand one's rights.[27]

This kind of socialization took great effort but could yield impressive results. After they had hired Polish, Slovak, and Hungarian organizers and made contacts in the various ethnic communities around the turn of the century, the United Mine Workers of America quickly gained a loyal following among recent immigrants. During World War I, one laborers' local of the Stockyards Labor Council recruited more than ten thousand Polish and Lithuanian butcher workmen inside a month's time. Council organizers found that once the immigrants understood the unions' goals, they were easier to organize than the native-born and the more skilled and generally made better union members. William Z. Foster drew similar conclusions from his experiences in steel. At the end of World War I, the National Committee for Organizing Iron and Steel Workers swept through the thoroughly open-shop steel mill towns, penetrating deep into the immigrant communities and conveying the union message to workers in their own languages.[28]

The huge numbers can easily overshadow the vital element here—the human agency of the immigrants themselves. They fashioned their identities out of their own experiences, the language and ideas they brought with them, and those they confronted in such union campaigns.

Americanization, whether official or labor, was also fundamentally shaped by issues of gender. Concentrated in precisely those professions—teaching, settlement house work, public health—that brought them into close contact with immigrant families, women assumed major roles at the highest reaches of the corporate and government bureaucracies that provided the Americanization movement with its structure, ideas, and legitimacy. Thousands of them taught English and civics in evening school, settlement house, Young Women's Christian Association (YWCA), and factory programs, conveying the Americanization message. But the message itself encoded notions of domestic orthodoxy and other gender values in English primers, loyalty parades, and citizenship plays. In its early stages, when it chiefly emphasized naturalization and the right to vote, the movement focused almost entirely on men. When Americanizers did begin to address women, it was because of their key role in child rearing and for fear of the dangers posed by the "un-Americanized mother." Long after woman suffrage, Americanizers placed far more emphasis on the im-

[27] Wilson, *Mary McDowell*, 99; William M. Leiserson, *Adjusting Immigrant and Industry* (New York, 1924), 234–45; Neil Betten, "Polish-American Steelworkers: Americanization through Industry and Labor," *Polish American Studies*, 33 (Autumn 1976), 31–42; David J. Saposs, "The Problem of Making Permanent Trade Unionists Out of the Recently Organized Immigrant Workers," 1919, folder 5, box 21, Saposs Papers; Talbot, ed., *Americanization*, 112–13.

[28] Greene, *Slavic Community on Strike*, 157–58; Barrett, *Work and Community in the Jungle*, 195–96; Brody, *Steelworkers in America*, 214–62. The contention that immigrants were easier to organize and more loyal in strikes recurred often in David Saposs's interviews with union officials in the period immediately after World War I. See "Digest of Interviews with Trade Union Officials" [1919], 3–4, folder 15, box 21, Saposs Papers; "Interview with Dennis Lane, president, Amalgamated Meat Cutters and Butcher Workmen of North America," folder 2, box 26, Saposs Papers; and other interviews in boxes 21 and 22, Saposs Papers.

migrant mother's role in the home than on her duties as a citizen. She was urged to maintain the new American standard of living in diet, hygiene, and infant and child care and to be mindful of her crucial role in producing a second generation of "true Americans."[29]

Working-class Americanizers made their own approaches to immigrant women. Organizing them presented special problems, some created by the changing occupational structure of women's work in the early twentieth century, others by the patriarchal values of the immigrant household and the labor movement itself. Yet the proportion of the female labor force in unions doubled during the first two decades of the twentieth century, and the Women's Trade Union League (WTUL), a coalition of working women and middle-class reformers, played a particularly important role in socializing immigrant women. In organizing garment workers, the league employed activists from the communities involved and printed leaflets in various languages. During and after the garment strikes of 1909 and 1910, Jewish and Italian organizers visited women in their homes to explain the issues involved in the strikes and the importance of unions. The Chicago WTUL set up neighborhood committees to organize social and educational events, a tactic that was later used in immigrant neighborhoods in New York. Chicago teachers' union volunteers assumed a function comparable to that of "home teachers" in the official Americanization movement, bringing English to immigrant women in their own homes. The New York league produced a labor-oriented English primer, *New World Lessons for Old World Peoples,* in Lithuanian, Italian, Yiddish, Bohemian, and English. It contained illustrated stories "designed to provoke lively discussion and to stimulate students to think out their own answers to the various questions surrounding unionization." Most of the characters were women living in immigrant neighborhoods and facing situations that the students themselves might encounter. The texts emphasized women activists and their accomplishments and in this way provided realistic role models. These immigrant women learned English in a way that developed important values of class solidarity and personal relationships that they relied upon in later organizing and strikes. "For the WTUL," Colette Hyman concludes, "teaching English was a point of entry into these women's lives through which lessons of unionism could be taught. It was the first step in female institution-building among immigrant women."[30]

[29] Higham, *Strangers in the Land,* 239–42; John McClymer, "Gender and 'the American Way of Life': Women in the Americanization Movement," *Journal of American Ethnic History,* 10 (Spring 1991), 5–6; U.S. Labor Department, Naturalization Bureau, *Suggestions for Americanization Work among Foreign-Born Women* (Washington, 1921); McClymer, "Gender and 'the American Way of Life'"; Harriet P. Dow, "Home Classes for Foreign-Born Women," in *Proceedings, Americanization Conference,* 128–35; and George J. Sanchez, "'Go after the Women': Americanization and the Mexican Immigrant Woman, 1915–1929," in *Unequal Sisters: A Multi-Cultural Reader in U.S. Women's History,* ed. Ellen Carol DuBois and Vicki L. Ruiz (New York, 1990), 257.

[30] Colette Hyman, "Labor Organizing and Female Institution Building: The Chicago Women's Trade Union League," in *Women's Work and Protest: A Century of U.S. Women's Labor History,* ed. Ruth Milkman (Boston, 1985), 35–36; Agnes Aitkin, "Teaching English to Our Foreign Friends, Part II: Among the Italians," *Life and Labor,* 1 (Oct. 1911), 309; Violet Pike, "New World Lessons for Old World Peoples, Lesson VI: Joining the Union," *ibid.,* 2 (March 1912), 90; Nancy Schrom-Dye, *As Equals and as Sisters: Feminism, the Labor Movement, and the*

World War I and the years immediately following represented a watershed in the Americanization process. Labor's own notions about Americanism stood out in bold relief against the war's backdrop. The massive immigration of the preceding decade had produced a remarkably diverse population who might come to see their chances for a decent life in America embodied in labor's efforts. In this context, interethnic and often interracial organizing was vital to union efforts. The economic effects of the war—increased demand, labor shortages, and steep inflation—sharply raised the issue of living standards and mutual sacrifice for the good of the war effort. In the process the war greatly strengthened unions' bargaining position and ability to organize and raised questions of democratic ideology, providing union organizers and immigrant workers with a vocabulary with which to express their grievances and aspirations.

Because of large war orders and labor shortages, both employers and the government sought to co-opt the labor movement into the war effort and avoid strikes, while inflation provided workers with incentive to organize. An ideological dimension was less tangible but probably just as important. In the interests of stimulating sacrifice and hard work on the part of immigrant workers, employers and government agencies couched their propaganda in a democratic idiom. For their part, labor activists sought to appropriate such democratic rhetoric and symbols in the name of labor. More than ever before, the plight of the immigrants, their status as workers, and their vision of the labor movement became part of a discourse on Americanism. The concept was hotly contested, and the immigrants were very much at the center of this symbolic struggle.[31]

For their part, the unions, seizing on the war situation to launch ambitious organizing drives in non-union basic industry where most of the immigrants were employed, framed their appeals in patriotic terms. The March 17, 1918, issue of the *United Mine Workers Journal* put the issue forcefully:

> If this war is waged for the destruction of political autocracy, we demand . . . the elimination of industrial autocracy in this country. The workers demand a voice in the conditions of their service, in all sections of the country; thus shall they be assured that this is indeed their war.

The National Committee for Organizing Iron and Steel Workers geared its campaign around this theme and drove it home repeatedly at mass meetings and in publications produced in various languages. Ironically, it was the recent immigrant rather than the native-born worker who was most receptive to the democratic rhetoric. The committee's large red, white, and blue campaign badges were favorites in

---

Women's Trade Union League of New York (Columbia, Mo., 1980); Elizabeth A. Payne, *Reform, Labor, and Feminism: Margaret Dreier Robbins and the Women's Trade Union League* (Urbana, 1988), 85–86; Leiserson, *Adjusting Immigrant and Industry*, 297–331; and James R. Barrett, "Women's Work, Family Economy, and Labor Militancy: The Case of Chicago's Packinghouse Workers, 1900–1922," in *Labor Divided: Race and Ethnicity in United States Labor Struggles, 1835–1960*, ed. Robert Asher and Charles Stephenson (Albany, 1990), 260–62.

[31] See David Montgomery, "Nationalism, American Patriotism, and Class Consciousness among Immigrant Workers in the United States in the Epoch of World War I," in *"Struggle a Hard Battle,"* ed. Hoerder, 327–51.

the immigrant neighborhoods. Far from being abstract, David Brody concludes, "The democratic theme made unionism comprehensible." A Polish steelworker made the connection between trade unionism and democratic war aims in rather more eloquent terms: "just like a horse and wagon, work all day. . . . For why this war? For why we buy Liberty Bonds? For the mills? No, for freedom and America — for everybody. No more horse and wagon. For eight-hour day."[32]

Similar scenarios unfolded in many industries throughout the country. During a 1919 conflict at Scovill Manufacturing in Waterbury, Connecticut, a strike leaflet framed the issue in patriotic terms. "Where is the democracy our boys gave their lives for? Wake up American workers; can't you see that we have another kaiser, another von Hindenburg, another czar who is conspirating to destroy humanity?" The workers, most of them of Italian or eastern European parentage, demanded a decent "American wage" and frequently used democratic and patriotic language in expressing their grievances.[33]

In steel, coal, and metal mining, in meat packing, in textile and garment manufacturing — across the whole spectrum of American industry — unions or loose federations of unions launched large organizing drives designed to integrate the new, unskilled immigrants. In the short run, the efforts were remarkably successful and union membership doubled between 1917 and 1920. In steel, the strongest bastion of the open shop, earlier organizational efforts had failed repeatedly, though the new immigrants were certainly active in several of those efforts. During World War I, the National Committee for Organizing Iron and Steel Workers launched an ambitious organizing drive and had garnered more than 100,000 workers, most of them recent immigrants, by the spring of 1919. In textiles and clothing and in many other industries, the emergence of the so-called "new unions" represented efforts on the part of an earlier generation of activists or of radicals *within* the various "new immigrant" communities to integrate the second generation of immigrant workers into the movement by creating new sorts of unions with new organizing and strike strategies. A massive strike wave, the largest in American history to that point, involving more than a million strikers per year for several years, accompanied this organizing, and many of the activists who led the strikes emerged from radical subcultures in the various ethnic communities.[34]

Union locals, national unions, and city labor federations across the country launched educational programs for new immigrant members. These incorporated

---

[32] David Brody, *Labor in Crisis: The Steel Strike of 1919* (Philadelphia, 1965), 73; Brody, *Steelworkers in America,* 221, 223; Betten, "Polish-American Steelworkers," 36–38; Montgomery, *Fall of the House of Labor,* 384–85.

[33] Fernando Fasce, "Freedom in the Workplace? Immigrants at the Scovill Manufacturing Company, 1915–1921," in *A l'ombre de la Statue de la Liberté,* ed. Debouzy, 107–21, esp. 116.

[34] Brody, *Steelworkers in America,* 214–30; Frank Serene, "Immigrant Steelworkers in the Monongahela Valley: Their Communities and the Development of a Labor Consciousness" (Ph.D. diss., University of Pittsburgh, 1979); Emmons, *Butte Irish,* 255–91, 340–97; Barrett, *Work and Community in the Jungle,* 188–239; David J. Goldberg, *A Tale of Three Cities: Labor Organization and Protest in Patterson, Passaic, and Lawrence, 1916–1921* (New Brunswick, 1989); Montgomery, *Workers' Control in America,* 93–101; David Montgomery, "Immigrants, Industrial Unions, and Social Reconstruction in the United States, 1916–1923," *Labour/Le Travail,* 13 (Spring 1984), 104–9.

A class analysis of war from the Industrial Workers of the World (IWW) in the *Industrial Pioneer*, June 1925. *Courtesy Charles H. Kerr Publishing Co., Chicago.*

not only English and civics instruction but also courses in economics, political economy, history, and literature taught by lawyers and college professors as well as labor activists and socialist elected officials. Sam Levin, business agent of the Amalgamated Clothing Workers' Chicago Council, explained why it was essential to teach such classes from labor's perspective:

> it is not sufficient to tell the workers that they are entitled to all profit since they create all wealth. They know this, but it is important to tell them how each individual institution of our political and economic system is composed, how it

works, and how it is possible to improve upon it, and whether it is possible or necessary to abolish it.[35]

The successful wartime organizing among very recent immigrants and the related
strike wave raise two crucial questions that deserve a great deal more research. The
first has to do with the immigrants themselves: What do these phenomena suggest
about their thinking? The second is equally vital: What happened to this impressive
movement?

One might begin to think of the consciousness characterizing many of the new
immigrants of the early twentieth century as a sort of transitional mentality, an
amalgam of Old World traditions, values, and behaviors with new working-class
ideas, forms of organization, and strategies. Whatever the content of the transition,
it was neither linear nor inevitable. Perhaps it was a sort of conversation in the immigrants' own minds and between older voices and newer ones, which were still not
quite clear. There was undoubtedly an infinite variation to such thinking, beginning
with differences between various ethnic groups and ranging down to the personality
of each individual immigrant. Each person embraced multiple identities shaped by
her or his experiences as a woman or man, an Italian or Pole living in a particular
type of community in the United States, working in a particular industry. But conceptualizing consciousness as transitional lends the analysis a dynamic and fluid
dimension and suggests that such identities were not entirely idiosyncratic, that they
were created within a specific historical context that is vital to explaining them. It
also directs our attention away from particular ethnic communities and toward the
relationship between ethnicity and class identity.

The transitional quality of the unskilled immigrants' world views is suggested in
part by the words and the symbols they chose. Employers were described as "czars"
or "Kaisers"—unjust rulers without the support of their subjects—and the police as
"Cossacks," a particularly apt word for the mounted officers mobilized in steel mill
towns and ethnic working-class city neighborhoods in the World War I era. The
strong support for the Polish army in immigrant neighborhoods and the centrality
of nationalism in the political discourse of eastern European immigrants both suggest continuing ideological links with the Old World. Many immigrants lacked what
might be termed an "industrial lexicon" and found it difficult to even describe their
work to folks back home without resorting to Old World metaphors and analogies.
Yet these same immigrant workers often led their parades and picket lines with the
American flag, marched in their own American military uniforms, and employed
patriotic rhetoric to attack their employers and express their grievances, especially
during World War I. Increasingly integrated into the working-class movement, they
were becoming proletarians by the war years.[36]

---

[35] *Report of Proceedings of the Thirty-Ninth Annual Convention of the American Federation of Labor, Atlantic City, New Jersey, June 9–23, 1919* (Washington, 1919), 135–44; Glenn, *Daughters of the Shtetl*, 4–5, 218–22; J. M. Budish to David J. Saposs, Nov. 16, 1918, folder 7, box 1, Saposs Papers; Sam Levin interview by David J. Saposs, Dec. 26, 1918, folder 15, box 21, Saposs Papers.

[36] James R. Barrett, "Comment: Polish Immigrants and the Mentality of the Unskilled Immigrant Worker,

But if there was a gradual transformation in the consciousness of unskilled recent immigrants, reflected in the changing strategies and social composition of the labor movement, then what happened to the new movement that was emerging in these years? Labor history, like other fields of social history over the past two decades, has tended to steer away from the analysis of particular events and toward the delineation of processes and trends. Yet specific events are often crucial to explaining historical change. Working-class fragmentation, for example, is too often thought of as an eventuality rather than a problem to be explained with reference to a particular historical situation that shaped the process. In this case, the war, which had first brought dramatic breakthroughs in the integration of recent immigrants into the labor movement, also set the stage for the political reaction to follow. Several short-term factors in the postwar years devastated the immigrant-based movement that had provided a context for Americanization from the bottom up, fragmenting the impressive wartime movement along ethnic, racial, and political lines.[37]

In the midst of a serious depression, which had a particularly disastrous effect on the new unions of unskilled immigrants, employers attacked in one industry after another between late 1919 and early 1922. Among the strikebreakers in many of these conflicts were the most recent migrants to join the labor force, southern blacks and Mexicans. Race emerged as the decisive division within many working-class communities, and employers clearly manipulated this development to deepen racial tensions. Race riots broke out in two dozen American cities and towns in 1919, leaving any dream of an interracial labor movement in tatters.

In the wake of war, the Americanization campaign took on a distinctly nativist cast and a patriotic frenzy. Ritual and symbolism had a peculiar importance to both government and corporate Americanizers. As nationalism and the fear of subversion grew, the government and employers put more effort and resources into the crusade to turn foreign-born workers into citizen patriots: On July 4, 1918, in cities across the country, federal agencies and voluntary organizations staged giant patriotic celebrations featuring dozens of ethnic groups demonstrating the gifts they had brought with them to the New World and affirming their loyalty to the government. The Flag Day Program at Wilson and Company's Chicago meat packing plant was typical of the events staged in industrial establishments. The drive for one-hundred-percent Americanism began with a brass band, a parade, and patriotic songs; thousands of loyalty leaflets were distributed. But the corporate programs were not notably successful. At Wilson's plant disappointed organizers noted that few of the

1900–1922," *Polish American Studies*, 46 (Spring 1989), 100–107; Adam Walaszek, "Was the Polish Worker Asleep? Immigrants, Unions, and Workers' Control in America, 1900–1922," *ibid.*, 74–79; Adam Walaszek, "'For in America Poles Are Like Cattle': Polish Peasant Immigrants and Work in America, 1890–91," in *A l'ombre de la Statue de la Liberté*, ed. Debouzy, 95–105; Montgomery, "Nationalism, Patriotism, and Class Consciousness"; Fasce, "Freedom in the Workplace?" 116–18.

[37] James R. Barrett, "Defeat and Decline: Long-Term Factors and Historical Conjunctures in the Decline of a Local Labor Movement, Chicago, 1900–1922," paper presented at the Perspectives on Labor History Conference, State Historical Society of Wisconsin, Madison, March 9, 1990 (in Barrett's possession); Dawley, *Struggles for Justice*, 235–36.

immigrants joined in the songs, presumably because they did not know the words, and the leaflets, all of them in English, went unread. By 1919 Ford had traded its melting pot and elaborate welfare program for an extensive network of spies and a practice of firing workers for disloyalty to the nation or the corporation. Employers saw these programs as part of a broad effort to inoculate immigrant workers against the dangers of bolshevism and other forms of radicalism. They called their new offensive, which mixed lockouts, industrial espionage, and private armies and police forces with welfare plans and company unions, the "American Plan."[38]

State and local governments' own version of one-hundred-percent Americanism involved the widespread use of injunctions and mounted police to quell strikes. Workers usually lost these struggles, and the new organizations that had provided the context for integrating the new immigrants were demolished. During the Red Scare, federal and local authorities raided meeting places, closed down presses, seized organizational records, and jailed or simply deported immigrant activists, decimating the ranks of radical labor in immigrant communities. Never more than a tiny minority in any immigrant community, the radicals had played key roles in organizing and leading the mass strikes of recent unskilled workers, and they linked immigrant communities to trade unions, the Industrial Workers of the World (IWW), the Socialist and Communist parties, and other organizations that provided alternative forms of socialization for people who were still trying to understand the society in which they found themselves.[39] The Red Scare amounted to a kind of enforced Americanization.

Again labor radicals contested the term's meaning. The Farmer-Labor party's 1920 platform demanded democratic control of industry, abolition of imperialism, public ownership and operation of railroads and mines, the legal right to collective bargaining, the eight-hour day, unemployment compensation, and government old-age pensions. The document also called for its version of one-hundred-percent Americanism:

> Restoration of civil liberties . . . including free speech, free assemblage, right of asylum, equal opportunity, and trial by jury . . . amnesty for all persons imprisoned because of their patriotic insistence upon their constitutional guarantees, industrial activities or religious beliefs. . . . As Americanism means democracy, suffrage should be universal. We demand full, unrestricted political rights for all citizens regardless of sex, race, color, or creed.[40]

[38] Higham, *Strangers in the Land*, 234–63; Gary Gerstle, *Working-Class Americanism: The Politics of Labor in a Textile City, 1914–1960* (Cambridge, Mass., 1989), 43–46; Dawley, *Struggles for Justice*, 257–60; Brody, *Steelworkers in America*, 190–98; *National Provisioner*, Sept. 25, 1920, pp. 18–20, 25–26, 42–43; Barrett, *Work and Community in the Jungle*, 243–63; Meyer, *Five Dollar Day*, 169–89; Goldberg, *Tale of Three Cities*, 148–62; Korman, *Industrialization, Immigrants, and Americanizers*, 148–66; Ronald Edsforth, *Class Conflict and Cultural Consensus: The Making of a Consumer Society in Flint, Michigan* (New Brunswick, 1987); Montgomery, "Nationalism, Patriotism, and Class Consciousness," 334–35; Montgomery, *Fall of the House of Labor*, 438–39, 454–57.

[39] William Preston, Jr., *Aliens and Dissenters: Federal Suppression of Radicals, 1903–1933* (New York, 1963), 88–117, 208–37; Robert K. Murray, *Red Scare: A Study in National Hysteria* (New York, 1964); and Dawley, *Struggles for Justice*, 243–51.

[40] *American Labor Year Book, 1923–24* (New York, 1924), 143. For comparable rhetoric, see "Labor's Fourteen

But the Red Scare undeniably enhanced the more general development of nativism and other forms of intolerance that split the working class and the labor
movement in the early 1920s. Already on the defensive, unions made fewer efforts
to reach new immigrant and black migrant workers as nationality, race, and patriotism once again became sources of identification for many native-born and old immigrant workers. Indeed, the resulting fragmentation represented the social basis
for labor's organizational decline in the course of the 1920s.

It might be tempting to think of the 1920s as a period of triumph for more conservative notions of Americanism, as a time when ethnic workers were culturally and in-
stitutionally integrated through the rise of a mass consumer culture and corporate
welfare programs, but the reality was much more complex. Certainly elements of
the new mass culture penetrated blue-collar ethnic communities and the burgeoning ghettos of northern cities, but often what emerged was a fusion of new and
old. Likewise, corporate programs and the daily routine of work in giant mass-
production factories spawned a new workplace culture and collective identity, especially among second-generation immigrants, but the values actually created were
seldom those promoted by the companies involved. When the corporate welfare
system collapsed and jobs disappeared in the Great Depression, traditional sources
of support in immigrant communities were overwhelmed, and workers turned increasingly toward government programs, self-organization, and protest, first
through unemployed councils and later through the industrial union movement
that ultimately produced the Congress of Industrial Organizations (CIO).

This rhetorical and symbolic Americanization was also very real for workers who
experienced the bloody union struggles and the fight to maintain democracy from
the late thirties through World War II. The second generation in immigrant communities came of age during those struggles, and there was never any question that
they thought of themselves as American workers. Political discourse was once again
dominated by a democratic idiom, a working-class Americanism.[41]

Points," *Survey*, Nov. 30, 1918, p. 265; *New Majority*, Jan. 18, 1919, pp. 8–9; Illinois Federation of Labor,
Proceedings of the Convention, 1918 (Springfield, 1919), 134–59.
   [41] Gerstle, *Working-Class Americanism*; Cohen, *Making a New Deal*; and Thomas Gobel, "Becoming American: Ethnic Workers and the Rise of the CIO," *Labor History*, 29 (Spring 1988), 173–98. See also the story of Dobie
Dobrejcak in Thomas Bell's novel *Out of This Furnace* (Pittsburgh, 1976), 259–413.

Disorientation and Reorientation: The American Landscape Discovered from the West

Patricia Nelson Limerick

In the month of September, in the year 1972, I traveled from the Pacific Coast to the Atlantic Coast, from southern California to southern New England. To the East of Arizona lay wilderness, and the exotic names of that wilderness both chilled and lured me: Tennessee, Virginia, the District of Columbia, Philadelphia, and, most alarming of all, Manhattan. In the course of this journey, I discovered the eastern United States, an event as consequential to me as it was insignificant to the residents.

As I drove across Oklahoma, crossing what I later learned was the ninety-eighth meridian, discovery joined up with its usual partner, disorientation. The air became humid, clammy, and unpleasant, and the landscape turned distressingly green. The eastern United States, I learned with every mile, was badly infested with plants. Even where they had been driven back, the bushes, shrubs, and trees gave every sign of anticipating a reconquest. Even more remarkable was that millions of people lived in this muggy, congested world, and they considered it *normal*.

On my transcontinental journey of discovery, people I met along the way were impressed by the large number of books I had managed to fit into a small car. In retrospect, I am more struck by the books that I did not own and had not read. In 1972, my VW Bug did not contain Henry Nash Smith's *Virgin Land* (1950), Hans Huth's *Nature and the American* (1957), Arthur A. Ekirch's *Man and Nature in America* (1963), Leo Marx's *The Machine in the Garden* (1964), William H. Goetzmann's *Exploration and Empire* (1966), or Roderick Nash's *Wilderness and the American Mind* (1967).[1] Those standard scholarly writings on the discovery of the

Patricia Nelson Limerick is professor of history at the University of Colorado, Boulder.

I would like to thank William Wei and Gail Nomura for their critical readings of this essay, and Claire Priest, Stephen Sturgeon, and Clark Whitehorn for their help with sources.

[1] Henry Nash Smith, *Virgin Land: The American West as Symbol and Myth* (Cambridge, Mass., 1950); Hans Huth, *Nature and the American: Three Centuries of Changing Attitudes* (Berkeley, 1957); Arthur A. Ekirch, Jr., *Man and Nature in America* (New York, 1963); Leo Marx, *The Machine in the Garden: Technology and the Pastoral Ideal in America* (New York, 1964); William H. Goetzmann, *Exploration and Empire: The Explorer and the Scientist in the Winning of the American West* (New York, 1966); and Roderick Nash, *Wilderness and the American Mind* (New Haven, 1967). A later book on the discovery of landscape matched these books in its exclusive attention

American landscape would have puzzled me as deeply as did the landscape of the eastern United States, and for many of the same reasons.

At that time, the study of American responses to landscape ran on an east-to-west track, following the physical and mental migrations of white English-speaking men. In the conventional view, the process of discovery reached completion when the maps had their blank spots filled in and literate white Americans had seen all the places worth seeing. What the discoverers explored was wilderness, a kind of pristine natural landscape in which Indians lived more as symbols than as three-dimensional human beings. In the same spirit, the authors of the reigning texts in this field took for granted a norm of a green, plant-filled landscape, a norm that they shared with nineteenth-century American explorers of the American West. In 1972, with these premises locked into place, and with the problem of point of view seemingly settled, one could write comfortably and complacently about this subject.

In 1992, comfort and complacency have fled the field. The east-to-west process of exploration now must compete with a recognition of Indian prior presence, as well as of northward movements from Mexico, southward movements from Canada, and eastward movements from Asia. The notion of a pristine wilderness is deservedly in tatters; the discoverers now appear as late arrivals in an already fully occupied and much affected landscape. Thanks to various environmental messes and crises of scarce resources, the celebration of a completed process of discovery, ending in a landscape known, mastered, and put to good use, seems at best silly and at worst dangerous. The assumption that "normal" means green and well watered has lost credibility; through pollution and over-allocation of what once seemed to be abundant supplies, the residents of the eastern United States have created for themselves a number of the dilemmas in water scarcity long familiar to the West.

The new, improved, "revised standard" orthodoxy on the discovery of landscape shows no mercy in bringing its charges against the old orthodoxy. The conventional studies concentrated wholeheartedly on the thinking of English-speaking, westward-moving, literate, record-keeping, middle- and upper-class, pre-twentieth-century, white men. Offered as studies of American attitudes toward landscape, the standard works were in fact investigations into the minds of a minority. In the late twentieth century, such exclusivity in scholarly inquiry is no longer tenable.

And at this point, the 1992 orthodoxy comes to an abrupt halt. Working on this essay led me to a full recognition of how the new assumptions—that scholarship can no longer be exclusive or parochial—escort one to the edge of one's ignorance and then leave one to contemplate the vacancy. I recognize that human beings discovered the American landscape from all directions: east to west, from Europe and Africa; south to north, from Mexico and South America; west to east, from Asia and the Pacific Islands; and from a variety of directions, for Indian people whose arrival took place in another time frame entirely. And yet almost all of what I know

---

to the east-to-west movements of white men: Patricia Nelson Limerick, *Desert Passages: Encounters with the American Desert* (Albuquerque, 1985).

on the subject pulls me back into the old framework of the east-to-west movement of white men. In twelve years' residence on the East Coast, I had assimilated all too successfully. I had learned a lot about American explorers, who were indeed an interesting group. I could hold forth for hours on the attitudes and experiences of Meriwether Lewis, William Clark, Zebulon Pike, Stephen Long, John C. Frémont, John Wesley Powell, Clarence King, and the other big names of exploration. I could speak at length on the responses of emigrants to the scenery they saw on the overland trail, on the utilitarian appraisals of landscape by miners, cattlemen, farmers, loggers, and city builders, on the development of a tourist industry based on the aesthetic commodification of landscape, and on the rise to visibility of John Muir, Aldo Leopold, Edward Abbey, and the various celebrators of nonutilitarian value in landscape. At the end of this mega-lecture, I would have shown how much I remained loyal to a number of the flaws of the old school of landscape studies. White men would still be the principal, virtually the only, players in my story; and my framework would remain stuck on the east-to-west track of perception.

This is not my first encounter with the puzzles of an intellectual revolution that is something short of complete. In *The Legacy of Conquest*, I undertook to offer a model of western American history that recognized and respected the multiplicity of points of view in the region's past. Earnestly resolving to move outside the world view of westward-moving white Americans, I nonetheless wrote a chapter on Indian people that concentrated on Euro-American perception of and action toward natives and only briefly remarked on internal Indian points of view. My discussion of Asian immigrants concerned itself with white hostility to Asian people and campaigns for their exclusion. Despite my impatience with older, white-centered tellings of Western history, in much of *The Legacy of Conquest*, my fine resolution to see the world from a variety of points of view ran into serious complications in practice; it therefore had the usual short life of New Year's resolutions and other seasonal fits of self-improvement.[2]

In his study of narrative and history, Robert Berkhofer offers an extended critique of *The Legacy of Conquest* precisely on these terms, considering the text as an example of the "problem of point of view" encountered by multiculturalism. "At bottom," Berkhofer concludes, "Limerick's advice on how to combine actors' and historians' viewpoints into a single text still privileges the historian's viewpoint over those of the actors."[3] Berkhofer's critique offers me some consolation by taking my case to be representative. I seem to have arrived at the status of a kind of poster child for the narrative problem of multiculturalism. Resolving to write a version of American history that incorporates the perspectives and experiences of various cultures and classes ranks as one of the world's easiest intellectual acts. Acting on the resolution, however, ranks among the toughest.

---

[2] Patricia Nelson Limerick, *The Legacy of Conquest: The Unbroken Past of the American West* (New York, 1987).

[3] Robert Berkhofer, "A Point of View on Viewpoint in History," draft manuscript in author's possession, 17.

Still, in the spirit of optimistic resolutions, I have a clear vision of where scholars in the discovery of landscape would want, eventually, to arrive. Future studies would include, at the least, these ten elements:

(1) the geologic, climatic, botanical, and zoological qualities of a particular place;

(2) the indigenous people's world views and the values they invested (and may well continue to invest) in the landscapes of their home;

(3) the impact of the native people's actions in creating a landscape that was neither purely natural nor wholly human-made;

(4) the perceptions and actions of intruders, explorers, invaders, colonizers, and conquerors, responding to places that were at once new to them and familiar to the original residents;

(5) the second-generation experience of those born to the colonizers—the perspective of the invaders' children, to whom the new and exotic area had become home;

(6) the continuing arrival of both new residents and impression-gathering travelers, who may well have felt a sense of discovery, whether or not that sense of originality seemed legitimate to the residents who preceded them;

(7) the ways in which these various groups saw each other—as legitimate residents, illegitimate invaders, enrichers, despoilers, improvers, or devastators of the landscape, or as quaint figures or eyesores in the view;

(8) change and continuity in the physical components and arrangements of the landscape over time;

(9) the ongoing process of discovery and rediscovery, as people with different concerns, needs, and assumptions found and find new meaning in landscapes, even when those landscapes, by an earlier judgment composed of equal parts of cheer and gloom, seemed to have been fully discovered, known, mastered, and thereby reduced in interest; and

(10) an evaluation, in the historian's best judgment and with subjectivity fully acknowledged, of what this all adds up to—a kind of balance sheet of gains and losses: gains that can be sustained and gains that prove temporary; injuries and losses where repair and recovery are imaginable; and injuries where repair and recovery are beyond imagination.

This is a thorough and sensible model, and it is one that I would like to be practicing in the early twenty-first century. I am grateful to other scholars who have already field-tested pieces and parts of this model.[4] But in 1992, my relationship to this handsome, evenly numbered approach consists mostly of yearning. I do not know enough about the history of any one place to go through the ten elements thoroughly and carefully. Instead, for the purposes of this essay, I will focus on the

---

[4] The books that come closest to matching this model are William Cronon, *Changes in the Land: Indians, Colonists, and the Ecology of New England* (New York, 1983); William deBuys, *Enchantment and Exploitation: The Life and Hard Times of a New Mexico Mountain Range* (Albuquerque, 1986); and Richard White, *Land Use, Environment, and Social Change: The Shaping of Island County, Washington* (Seattle, 1980).

fourth element, the perceptions and behavior of recent arrivals responding to land-scapes that were new to them. To dramatize the fact that the east-to-west movement was only one part of the process of discovery, I will follow the west-to-east vector of exploration. This will, therefore, be an investigation of the discovery of North American landscapes by some Asians and Asian Americans, a tracking of the responses of people moving west to east across the Pacific and into the interior.

Why am I still using the word discovery? How can I say that arriving Chinese discovered California in the nineteenth century? What possible sense could it make to refer to the Japanese and Japanese-American discovery of the arid interior of the American West during their coerced relocation during World War II?

Columbus, we can now say by rote, could not have *discovered* the Western Hemisphere because native people already lived here. The problem lies in the assumption that to qualify for true discovery, the explorer must come upon a place that is without previous occupants. But we now take it as our premise that the European discoverers found people as well as places. For an experience of discovery, the place involved does not have to be new to everyone; it has to be new to the discoverer. The encounter is, of course, reciprocal; when Columbus discovered the Indians, the Indians had the chance to discover Columbus. Sometimes, as in my own discovery of the eastern United States, the residents can be thoroughly unmoved by the event. But however the natives respond, the person encountering a new place is having an experience of some significance. This does not mean that the act of discovery has *introduced* significance into a place where there was none before; that arrogant assumption was, after all, what went wrong with the word discovery. But why not undercut the *hubris* of the old idea by defining discovery simply as a group's first encounter with a place new to them? While this definition may lack the self-dramatization of discovery on the grand (and misguided) old model, it gives a down-to-earth meaning to a formerly flighty concept.

It was an easy undertaking to resolve to reverse directions and to track the west-to-east discovery of the American landscape. The resolution made, the easy part ended. With no Asian or Asian-American equivalents to *Virgin Land, The Machine in the Garden, Exploration and Empire,* and *Wilderness and the American Mind,* disorientation was the next stop on this journey.[5] This was not to be the sort of pleasant intellectual excursion in which one comfortably reviews, appraises, and critiques the work of one's predecessors in a field of inquiry. Under these circumstances, the analogy between literal, geographical discovery and metaphorical, intellectual discovery became instantly too close for comfort. Simply raising the question of Asian

---

[5] Of the various surveys of Asian American history, only Ronald Takaki, in *Strangers from a Different Shore: A History of Asian Americans* (New York, 1989), makes repeated references to perceptions of landscape; those references are, however, scattered through the text and not pulled together in a systematic discussion of the issue. The issue of landscape is rarely mentioned in, for example, Roger Daniels, *Asian America: Chinese and Japanese in the United States since 1850* (Seattle, 1988) or Sucheng Chan, *Asian Americans: An Interpretive History* (Boston, 1991). Lucy M. Cohen, *Chinese in the Post–Civil War South: A People without a History* (Baton Rouge, 1984) and Robert Seto Quan, *Lotus among the Magnolias: The Mississippi Chinese* (Jackson, Miss., 1982), for instance, make virtually no mention of the immigrants' response to the Southern landscape.

and Asian-American responses to the American landscape, I was out of my turf, traveling without landmarks, maps, or guidebooks, yearning for the familiar and predictable company of Meriwether Lewis, William Clark, John C. Frémont, and the rest. I will confess to beginning this project with the response typical of mainstream scholars taking up a new topic in ethnic history: Perhaps there is so little written about this topic because there are no sources. And yet even when one confines oneself to published primary and secondary sources, there proves to be a considerable amount of material.

True to the patterns of Euro-American discoverers, I had a language problem, rendering me dependent on the kindness of interpreters and translators. I do not read Chinese or Japanese; an untranslated source is a source marked Off Limits to me. Also true to earlier patterns of Euro-American discovery, the territory that seemed so disorienting to me was in fact a territory familiar to others who traveled in it long before my arrival. How on earth did Asians and Asian Americans see the American landscape? In answering that question, hundreds of thousands of Asian and Asian-American people had a considerable head start on me.

Neither Chinese nor Japanese immigrants are, in any direct way, my people. The descendant of Danes whose conversion to the Church of Latter-day Saints brought them to Utah, I come from a rather different line of immigration. To the people of the Mormon past, Utah was a promised land, a new Jerusalem, a sacred place. While I and my immediate family have lapsed far from Mormonism, I show some signs of having held onto a vision of the American West as sacred space. The investment of human life and emotion in particular places, I believe, gives those places transcendent meaning. In American life, this way of thinking—and feeling—is most often evoked by battlefields. At a site where many people gave up their lives, few have to struggle to grasp the idea that the place has been permanently changed, even sanctified, by death. But I would remove the "death-in-battle" requirement from the definition of sacred ground. Where people have labored, suffered, struggled, or even just survived, they have planted seeds of memory as directly as farmers sow crops, and memory has its roots in the soul.

The landscape thus has a number of layers, all demanding the scholar's attention: rock and soil; plants and animals; humans as a physical presence, manifested in their physical works; *and* humans as an emotional and spiritual presence, manifested in the accumulated stories of their encounter with a place. Our attention and curiosity here cannot be exclusive. One can glimpse the full power of a place only in the full story of human presence there. Thus, exclusive attention to the movements, actions, and impressions of Anglo-Americans is equivalent to the arbitrary editing of a scripture, skipping entire chapters and devoting disproportionate attention to a few featured verses. The complete story of the investment of human consciousness in the American landscape requires attention to the whole set of participants—indigeneous people as well as invaders, eastward-moving Asian-American people as well as westward-moving Euro-American people. With anything less, the meaning of the landscape is fragmented and truncated.

Take into account a wider range of points of origin and points of view, and the most prosaic and pedestrian landscape lights up with meaning. Recently, taking a taxi from the San Francisco Airport and chatting with the cabdriver, I was suddenly knocked into silence by a glimpse of the sign for the Tanforan Race Track in San Bruno. With a subdued borrowing from the traditions of Las Vegas signage, the Tanforan sign tries to convey cheer and festivity. The effect on me was exactly the opposite, and yet Tanforan was a name I would not have recognized two months ago. Since then, I have read narratives of Japanese-American people who were held captive at Tanforan at the start of World War II, forced to live in stalls and stables recently vacated by horses. At Tanforan, they were still near their bay area homes, but they were living in a place that bore no resemblance to home. The stories of life at Tanforan capture the misery and injustice of forced relocation. To a person who knows these stories, even a person rushing by on a highway, a glimpse of the Tanforan sign says instantly: "You are near a place where the human soul was tried and tested."

Reading the stories of Tanforan makes it impossible to avoid identifying with the ordeal of Japanese Americans. The people who were placed there in 1942 can never forget Tanforan. After reading their stories, neither can I. Those of us moved by the name Tanforan, or by the other place names that appear in this essay, constitute a minority, a tiny fraction of the American population. This is a state of affairs that *can* change with a broader, more generous, more inclusive definition of the discovery of landscape.

In 1900, the young Chinese immigrant John Jeong arrived in San Francisco. Riding with others in an open carriage, he was halfway to Chinatown when "some white boys came up and started throwing rocks at us." Welcome by rock throwing was an intense and memorable opening encounter with the social landscape of the West Coast, and it was a lesson reinforced repeatedly after arrival. The "boundaries" of Chinatown, one old man remembered, were marked by city streets: "from Kearny to Powell, and from California to Broadway. If you ever passed them and went out there, the white kids would throw stones at you." Discovery, in these places, came down to learning the boundaries of safety and mapping one's way through a landscape of risk. This risk extended beyond the coastal cities and into the rural interior. In the Sacramento / San Joaquin Delta, except for the all-Chinese town of Locke, the small towns mirrored the dangers of the city: "The whites would attack you with stones when you walked through some of these towns," Bing Fai Chow remembered. "We never dared to walk on the streets alone then—except in Locke. This was our place."[6]

---

[6] John Jeong, quoted in *Longtime Californ': A Documentary Study of an American Chinatown*, by Victor G. Nee and Brett de Bary Nee (Boston, 1974), 73; Wei Bat Liu, quoted *ibid.*, 60; Bing Fai Chow, quoted in *Bitter Melon: Stories from the Last Rural Chinese Town in America*, by Jeff Gillenkirk and James Motlow (Seattle, 1987), 64.

A landscape so sharply divided between safety and danger, refuge and risk, actively discouraged discovery. Just as important, a preoccupation with finding work and doing work drained both mental and physical energy. "I was always at work," Suen Hoon Sum remembered. "I worked all over the place! . . . It was very easy for a year to go by. Year after year you did the same thing—pick fruit and trim fruit trees." At the California placer mines, in railroad construction camps, on farms and orchards, work swallowed time and energy. Looking for work meant constant travel, but it was not the sort of travel that encouraged one to see the sights. Necessity monopolized attention, and the discovery of the landscape took second place to the discovery of the job. "We went everywhere looking for work," Jone Ho Leong told an interviewer, but the responses she felt to the many places that she saw did not register in the interview.[7]

And indeed, I thought at first, why should they? Beginning this essay, it was my operating assumption that the conditions of immigrant, working-class life—inadequate housing, uncertain food, constant work, inequitable rewards for that work, racial harassment, and campaigns for exclusion—made a self-conscious, aesthetic response to landscape into a luxury few could afford. It made perfect sense to me that the immigrants would appraise, explore, and read the western American landscape in terms of jobs and income. But this assumption has become more and more doubtful. The proposition that immigrant workers had little response to landscape begins to seem more and more an artifact of my puzzlement at reckoning with unconventional sources, as well as a product of my assumption that because *I* would have been too fatigued to respond to the landscape, all the Asian immigrants would have been in a similar state.

Still, asking the question, "But what did they *think* of the landscapes they saw?" gets the scholar few direct answers. Denied an answer often enough, one begins to recognize the narrow limits of the intellectual turf and the kinds of sources that have traditionally fallen within the category of the discovery of landscape. The boundaries of this turf have been set by the particular conditions of American national expansion into contiguous territory. In the context of territorial conquest, the discoverers were commissioned agents of their national government, explicitly directed to report on their findings; they could concentrate on discovering landscapes, and not on finding jobs, because discovery *was* their job. Agents of territorial conquest, in other words, kept a lot of records, and historians are thus inclined to define those records as the "normal" source for responses to landscape.

Contrary to white fears of the "yellow peril" or Asian invasions, neither China nor Japan had much reason to send advance scouts for conquest into North America. Nineteenth-century Chinese immigrants no doubt had interesting mental responses to the coastline, valleys, cities, mountains, and deserts of the United States, but they were not acting as official information gatherers for their home nation; they had no assignment to record their responses in the official public reports

---

[7] Suen Hoon Sum, quoted in Gillenkirk and Motlow, *Bitter Melon*, 56–59; Jone Ho Leong, quoted *ibid.*, 102.

that, in the Anglo-American tradition, have made up the literary record of discovery.

"The Chinese themselves left few records of their perceptions and experience," Sucheng Chan notes in *This Bittersweet Soil,* and that fact makes a guessing game of an inquiry into their thinking. Moreover, when Chan remarks that "no [Chinese] landowning-literati class established itself in America," one is suddenly made aware of the enormous role of leisure and privilege in creating the possibility of an aesthetic, self-conscious, recorded response to landscape. A "landowning-literati class" is indeed the source of much of the Anglo-American literature of discovery of landscape; even the wilderness-loving John Muir married into a family of orchard-owning Californians. Without a margin of assured subsistence, without the opportunity for contemplation and introspection, without a way to enter one's memories into a permanent, written source, a group's response to a new geography can be close to impossible for posterity to hear.[8]

This dilemma offers an opportunity to broaden the turf of inquiry, to look for evidence of the experience of discovery, first, in "unconventional" literary sources and, second, in action and behavior. In the first category, one turns to the walls of the Angel Island immigration facility, opened in 1910 in San Francisco Bay. Those walls held poems written by immigrants, which have recently been transcribed and translated by Him Mark Lai, Genny Lim, and Judy Yung. In these poems one finds ample evidence that a people who might initially seem inarticulate to the historian were charged with intense and profound responses to the American landscape. Angel Island in often-foggy San Francisco Bay served as a focal point in the Chinese discovery of the landscape. Many immigrants spent weeks, even months, on the island, enduring prolonged interrogations and inspections.

Many of the Angel Island poems used the landscape as an analogy for the experience of being stranded and kept waiting:

> Green waters surround a green hill on four sides.
> Ascending to a high place, one does not see the shore.

In this poem and many others, the writer found in the island setting a direct mirror for emotion:

> At times I gaze at the cloud- and fog-enshrouded mountain-front.
> It only deepens my sadness.

The remoteness and separation of the island from the mainland mirrored the social reality of exclusion:

> The Western styled buildings are lofty;
> But I have not the luck to live in them.

Other poems drew a contrast between the landscape of home and the landscape of a remote place of confinement:

[8] Sucheng Chan, *This Bittersweet Soil* (Berkeley, 1986), xx, 369.

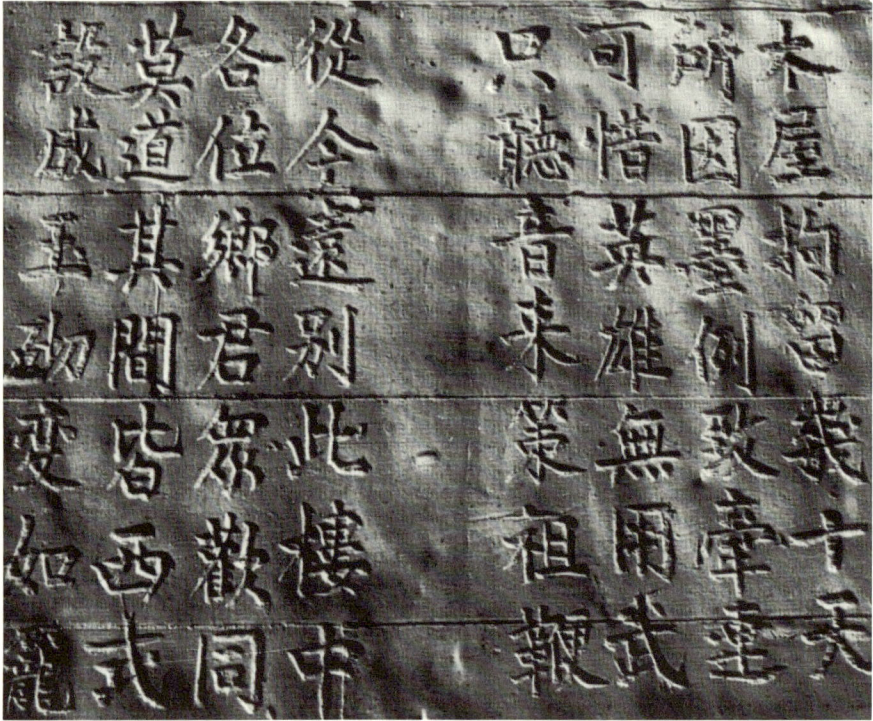

A poem engraved on a barracks wall at Angel Island immigration facility in San Francisco Bay, which opened in 1910. Many Chinese immigrants were detained there for weeks or even months; some expressed their feelings by carving poems into the wooden walls. *Photograph courtesy Chris Huie.*

> I left the village behind me, bade
> farewell to my father and mother.
> Now I gaze at distant clouds and mountains,
> tears forming like pearls.

In these poems, the authors crafted internal feeling and external setting into one experience. The elegance of their readings of the landscape provides us with a useful reminder for the whole subject. On those occasions when it seems to us that Asian immigrants had no response to the landscape, there is a good chance that we are confronting a failure of records, and not a failure of response.[9]

The record of action and behavior can speak with considerable clarity about discovery. Consider, for instance, the Chinese role in expanding California agriculture.

---

[9] Him Mark Lai, Genny Lim, and Judy Yung, *Island: Poetry and History of Chinese Immigrants on Angel Island, 1910–1940* (San Francisco, 1980), 122, 54, 40, 92. See also Marlon K. Hom, *Songs of Gold Mountain: Cantonese Rhymes from San Francisco Chinatown* (Berkeley, 1987).

In a study of the Chinese in the Monterey Bay area, Sandy Lydon gives discovery a gritty, down-to-earth meaning. The Chinese, Lydon writes, "quickly saw the agricultural potential in the marginal lands of the region." They "saw resources" that Americans and Europeans "could not" see. Americans looked at mustard plants growing wild in California and saw a nuisance; the Chinese looked at the same mustard plants and saw the abundant raw material for a valued spice. The Americans saw willows as the sign of a useless swamp; the Chinese saw willows as the sign of fresh water and fertile land, once it was "cleared and drained." This "ability to see the potential in the most mundane things," Lydon concludes, "may be the greatest contribution of the Chinese immigrants to the history and development of the Monterey Bay Region—they showed the Yankees and Europeans the infinite *possibilities* that the region offered."[10]

As the word "contribution" suggests, this line of argument has its risks. It is not simply a question of whether an ethnic group reaches its peak of significance when it contributes to the economic growth of the American nation. In the late twentieth century, environmentalism has added another puzzle to the concept of contribution, a puzzle that points directly to the unfortunate distance separating environmental history from ethnic history. Given the recognition of the various ways in which economic development exacted a heavy price from the physical environment, is a group's active role in the reshaping of landscape and the domination of nature still an occasion for congratulations? In most of the texts of Asian American history, the question still waits for recognition.

Until quite recently, environmental historians paid little attention to ethnic history; they focused their inquiries on the attitudes and behavior of white men. There may well have been some logic in that choice. If one's principal interest is in the impact of human action on physical places, then it makes sense to track the attitudes and behavior of people in power. The patterns of change in landscape often reflect the choices and preferences of the segment of society that carries economic and political power. Nonetheless, a full study of the human relationship to landscape cannot confine itself to a powerful elite. Workers, often minority workers, provided the essential labor of environmental change, and members of minorities often absorbed a disproportionate share of undesirable environmental impacts, whether in the siting of dumps or in the deploying of pesticides; yet environmental history and ethnic history have been very separate enterprises. The citing of Chinese contributions to the transformation of western landscapes provides only one among many case studies in the challenge of finding the common ground between these fields.[11]

---

[10] Sandy Lydon, *Chinese Gold: The Chinese in the Monterey Bay Region* (Capitola, Calif., 1985), 22–24, italics in the original. For other views on whether immigrants sought and valued landscape similar to what they had left, see Sylvia Sun Minnick, *Samfow: The San Joaquin Chinese Legacy* (Fresno, Calif., 1988), 23; and Chan, *Bittersweet Soil*, 159.

[11] The overlap between environmental issues and racial and ethnic issues is getting much more attention recently; see especially Robert D. Bullard, *Dumping in Dixie: Race, Class, and Environmental Quality* (Boulder, 1990).

One can easily understand how the habit of celebrating contributions began. Huang Zunxian was the Chinese consul general in San Francisco in the early 1880s, facing the challenge of the newly passed Chinese Exclusion Act. "When the Chinese first crossed the ocean," Huang Zunxian wrote in a poem, "They were the same as pioneers. . . . Dressed in tatters, they cleared mountain forests." Thanks to their efforts, "wilderness and waste turned into towns and villages." Zhang Yinhuan, Chinese minister to the United States in the late 1880s, wrote, the "barren areas around San Francisco" had become "a metropolis" where "wonderful structures now reach the clouds." "How," Zhang Yinhuan asked, "could all this have been accomplished without the efforts of the Chinese?"[12]

Celebrations of the Chinese contribution to the economic development of the American landscape originated in a framework of defending the Chinese against their enemies and defamers. This mode of defensive congratulations extended into the writing of history. In California, Jack Chen writes, the Chinese "played a big role in bringing irrigation to a million acres of California farmland by 1890. This was a vital contribution to fruit and vegetable farming." "With bone and muscle," Sylvia Sun Minnick writes of Chinese laborers in the Sacramento / San Joaquin Delta, "they moved the earth, built the levees and rearranged" the Delta. And yet, before its transformation into what Minnick calls "an agricultural wonderland," the Delta had been a wildlife wonderland. The Chinese, Minnick writes, "transformed the flat [Central Valley] floor into grazing and workable farm land." Before it grew crops, the Central Valley grew carpets of wildflowers that dazzled John Muir and others. Should the loss of wildlife and wildflowers, as well as the costs of imposing intensive, irrigated agriculture in a semiarid landscape, figure in the writing of the history of the Chinese in California?[13]

The Chinese immigrants "tunneled through mountains, cleared forests, reclaimed swamps, and helped to open up the American West for settlement," Shih-Shan Henry Tsai writes. To this proclamation, the environmentally sensitive reader of the late twentieth century may well respond "Too bad" rather than "Hurrah." This is not only a matter of putting environmental history into some relationship with ethnic history; it also involves the relationship between different categories of ethnic history. A reader of Tsai's sentence might be equally troubled by the impact that the "opening up" of "the American West for settlement" had on Indian people. The question is an enormous one: What place did Asian immigrants occupy in the broadest picture of the conquest of both nature and natives in North America?[14]

If environmental history has now redefined much of this rearranging of the American landscape as disruption and injury, how do we appraise the Chinese "con-

[12] Huang Zunxian, "Expulsion of the Immigrants," in *Land without Ghosts: Chinese Impressions of America from the Mid-Nineteenth Century to the Present*, ed. R. David Arkush and Leo O. Lee (Berkeley, 1989), 62; Zhang Yinhuan, "Chinese in America," *ibid.*, 73.
[13] Jack Chen, *The Chinese of America: From the Beginnings to the Present* (San Francisco, 1981), 89; Minnick, *Samfow*, 25, 53.
[14] Shih-Shan Henry Tsai, *The Chinese Experience in America* (Bloomington, 1986), xi.

Wright's Tunnel, in the Santa Cruz Mountains, was completed in April 1880 by Chinese
work crews after two and a half years of difficult labor interrupted by two
disastrous explosions. *Courtesy University of California,
Santa Cruz, Special Collections.*

smell of burnt human flesh. In our times, the rediscovery of the landscape hinges
on just such recognitions as this one. Never the simple, pristine, virgin place of the
European imagination, the landscape is now knee-deep in stories, many of them
forgotten and ready for rediscovery. Some of the stories, like the construction of
Wrights Tunnel, shake the soul.

tribution" to that disruption? Sandy Lydon's story of the building of a railroad across the Santa Cruz Mountains grounds this abstract question in an unsettling reality. Compared to the Sierra Nevada, the mountains of the coastal range between Santa Cruz and San Jose are, in Lydon's words, "small and round, covered with redwoods and Douglas fir. On closer inspection, however, the Santa Cruz Mountains are dark, brooding, mean, little mountains, twisted and gnarled by the faults which run their entire length." To cross these mountains, the South Pacific Coast Railroad required a number of tunnels, including a very long tunnel at the summit, and Chinese labor proved essential for that project.[15]

Begun in late 1877, the Wrights Tunnel at the summit took two and a half years to complete. In the excavation, the Chinese crews encountered both coal gas and oil, "creating an extremely volatile and dangerous situation." In February of 1879, oil in the tunnel caught fire, and with the tunnel acting "like a huge cannon," an explosion threw workers against the walls. A dozen wounded Chinese men were brought out of the tunnel, and five of them died. The Chinese for a time refused to work in this dreadful place, but when they returned, the problem with gas and oil continued. In November of 1879, in another explosion and fire, twenty-four of the Chinese workers in the tunnel "were killed outright and the remaining were badly burned." An observer described the horror of the scene: "The stench of burning flesh, combined with the escaping gas, is almost overpowering anywhere near the portal. The cabins are filled with mutilated Chinamen, some shrieking with the excruciating pain they are undergoing; others praying in their native tongue to their countrymen to kill them and put an end to their sufferings."[16]

Completed in April 1880, the Wrights Tunnel leaves any simple formulation of the Chinese relationship to the American landscape properly and productively muddled. The violence done to the humans surely outweighs the violence done to the Santa Cruz Mountains. And yet any gesture of celebrating the Chinese for this "contribution" to the growth of the Santa Cruz economy trivializes their sufferings and deaths. This, like many other cases of the impact of Asian labor on the landscape, is a richer story if we see it as a case study in both the domination of nature and the abuse of labor.

With its grueling details and multiple meanings, the story of the tunnel in the Santa Cruz Mountains puts a spotlight on the meaning of the rediscovery of landscape for scholars today. As a college student in Santa Cruz, I crossed over these mountains dozens of times. The landscape struck me as pleasant, pretty, and really quite untouched and natural. The area had, as far as I knew, the usual stories of American pioneers setting up homesteads, founding small towns, cutting down trees, and building roads and railroads. Crossing the mountains near the Wrights Tunnel, it never occurred to me that I was in the neighborhood of tragedy. I never knew that I was passing a site where the "price of progress" had registered in the

[15] Lydon, *Chinese Gold*, 93.
[16] *Ibid.*, 95–99.

In the late nineteenth and early twentieth centuries, the Japanese immigrant encounter with the American landscape matched some of the patterns of the Chinese encounter. Like Chinese immigrants, the Japanese discovered a landscape of restriction—in prohibitions on alien land ownership, in housing segregation, and in episodes of harassment when they crossed certain boundaries of space and behavior. Like Chinese immigrants, the Japanese created urban neighborhoods and also played a major role in California rural life, both as migrant workers and as independent farmers.

Even though they were pressed hard by necessity and work, many Japanese immigrants recorded, often in poetic form, their response to the landscape. Gail Nomura has written a memorable portrait of Teiko Tomita, a woman who lived first in the Yakima Valley and later in the area near Seattle. Working in the fields or working in garment factories, Tomita crafted her experiences into *tanka*, Japanese poems "consisting of thirty-one syllables arranged in five lines of five, seven, five, seven, and seven syllables successively." Tomita's poems leave a vivid record of the experience of farmwork in the hot Yakima Valley summers:

> As we busily pick beans
> Even the breeze stirring
> The weeds at our feet
> Feels hot

The transformation of "desert and sagebrush into fertile fields of alfalfa, onions, tomatoes, beans, and melons" might be a dramatic one, but Tomita recognized "the tenuous hold on success" that those fields represented:

> Sagebrush desert to fertile plain
> A transformation, I hear,
> But when the windy season comes
> There's no transforming the sandstorm

Poems like Tomita's were not the artifacts of a literary elite; as Nomura notes, "one did not have to be highly educated or uniquely gifted to compose" them. Stephen Sumida points out in another essay on localism in Asian-American writing that responses like Tomita's, grounded in intense encounter with a particular place, are by no means the exception. There were, and are, a number of Japanese American community newspapers publishing poems, and many of those poems concerned the physical and social landscape of the immigrants' lives. "For the immigrant in Asian American literature," Sumida writes, "definition of the self and identification of his or her actual culture in America depend critically on locale."[17]

While some Japanese immigrants moved into the Western interior and encountered its deserts before 1941, the relocation policy of World War II forced Japanese-

---

[17] Gail M. Nomura, "Tsugiki, a Grafting: A History of a Japanese Pioneer Woman in Washington State," in *Women in Pacific Northwest History: An Anthology,* ed. Karen J. Blair (Seattle, 1988), 208, 213, 207; and Stephen H. Sumida, "Hawaii, the Northwest, and Asia: Localism and Local Literary Developments in the Creation of an Asian Immigrants' Sensibility," *Blue Funnel Line (Seattle Review),* 11 (Spring/Summer 1988), 10.

Manzanar from Guard Tower: Summer Heat (1943), by Ansel Adams.
Courtesy Library of Congress.

American residents of California, Oregon, and Washington into a coerced west-to-east movement. "Eastward I go only by force; westward I go free": those familiar words of Henry David Thoreau are usually quoted to reinforce the standing of the American West as a place of openness and freedom.[18] The relocation of the Japanese and Japanese Americans gives Thoreau's cheerful words a different, and deeper, meaning. Moreover, the oral histories and autobiographical writing that record the experience of the concentration camps provide a rich source of information on the response to landscape. On the matter of the politics of landscape representation, it is, however, worth noting the sources that do *not* exist. At the time of evacuation, "by military orders," John Armor and Peter Wright note in a collection of camp photographs by Ansel Adams, "'Japanese' were forbidden even to own cameras." While some exceptions were made, most photographs of the camps were taken by *hakujun* (white) photographers.[19]

The pain of forced relocation dramatized the degree to which the landscapes of the West Coast had been transformed into home both for first-generation Japanese

[18] Henry David Thoreau, "Walking," in *Walden and Other Writings,* ed. Brooks Atkinson (New York, 1950), 607.

immigrants (issei) and their American-born children (nisei). "We had bought a house and my husband had been happy just to smell the trees in the garden up until we were evacuated," Kamechiyo Takahashi remembered. "Even mowing weeds gave us pleasure." As her family prepared to leave its home outside Sacramento, Mary Tsukamoto said, "There were tears everywhere; Grandma couldn't leave her flowers, and Grandpa looked at his grape vineyard. We urged him to get into the car and leave." Tsukamato's family took its last look at "the snow-clad Sierra Nevada mountains that we had loved to see so often." Aesthetic ties to landscape came, of course, in the same package as economic ties: "I had already planted seedlings on fifty acres of land," Masao Hirata remembered, "and all our money was invested in the farm." Picked up by the Federal Bureau of Investigation (FBI) as a "dangerous enemy alien," Hirata "worried about my wife and my six little children whom I had left behind. I also worried about the land already planted with seedlings. You can't imagine how I felt at that time." Seized by the FBI on the evening of December 7, 1941, and held in Missoula, Montana, Yoshiko Uchida's father wrote frequent letters home, asking "often about his garden."[20]

Japanese-American families had in the space of a few decades transformed the West Coast from a newly encountered landscape to home. When Yoshiko Uchida stood in the mess hall line at the Tanforan Assembly Center and felt "degraded, humiliated, and overwhelmed by a longing for home," she was not yearning for a far-off, ancestral, foreign home in Japan, but for a familiar, domestic, residential landscape in Berkeley, California.[21]

As a midpoint between home and the detention camps in the western interior, most of the issei and nisei went first to a set of temporary camps near the coast. Fairgrounds and racetracks were transformed overnight into assembly centers. Stables for livestock were instantly redefined as homes for humans; stalls for horses became "apartments" for families. "The government moved the horses out and put us in," Osuke Takizawa said. "The stable stunk awfully." Often only linoleum or a thin coat of paint covered the manure-saturated floorboards. "I understand that we are going to live in the horse stalls" at the Santa Anita Race Track, the diarist Charles Kikuchi wrote. "(Move over Seabiscuit!)"[22]

The guards "treated us as if we were a herd of horses or cows," Tome Takatsuki said. "Suddenly you realized," Mary Tsukamoto said, "that human beings were

[19] John Armor and Peter Wright, *Manzanar* (New York, 1988), xviii–xx. Forbidden to photograph certain features of the camp, Ansel Adams found creative ways of fudging. He was not permitted to take photographs of the guard towers, and so he took a photograph *from* that vantage point, entitling it, "Manzanar from Guard Tower: Summer Heat." See Armor and Wright, *Manzanar,* 154.

[20] Kamechiyo Takahashi, quoted in *The Issei: Portrait of a Pioneer, an Oral History,* ed. Eileen Sunada Sarasohn (Palo Alto, 1983), 181–82; Mary Tsukamoto, quoted in *And Justice for All: An Oral History of the Japanese American Detention Camps,* by John Tateishi (New York, 1984), 11–12; Masao Hirata, quoted in *Issei,* ed. Sarasohn, 162–63; Yoshiko Uchida, *Desert Exile: The Uprooting of a Japanese American Family* (Seattle, 1982), 50.

[21] Uchida, *Desert Exile,* 71.

[22] Osuke Takizawa, quoted in *Issei,* ed. Sarasohn, 183; John Modell, ed., *The Kikuchi Diary: Chronicle from an American Concentration Camp, the Tanforan Journals of Charles Kikuchi* (Urbana, 1973), 49, 51.

being put behind fences just like on the farm where we had horses and pigs in corrals." When the veterans of relocation said that they had been treated like animals, this was often more fact than metaphor. Consider the barbed-wire fences that framed the landscape at the camps. Deeply associated with the legends of the "frontier" West, barbed wire was originally designed to set boundaries for and to control the movements of cattle. The assembly centers along the coast and the relocation centers in the interior thus twisted both the use and meaning of barbed wire. Deployed, along with guard towers and armed guards, to remind Japanese Americans that they were prisoners, barbed wire became a symbol with new meanings in regional and national history. It was a symbol that the relocatees read clearly and directly. "The barbed wire fence," Charles Kikuchi wrote, "reminds us that we are on the inside." Mitsuye Yamada masterfully mocked the rationale of the fence in a poem called "Block 4 Barrack 4 'Apt' C":

> The barbed fence
> protected us
> from wildly twisted
> sagebrush

"Of one thing I was sure," Monica Sone remembered. "The wire fence was real. I no longer had the right to walk out of it."[23]

If we place the relocatees' encounter with the assembly and relocation centers within the category of the discovery of the American landscape, that field gains new relevance, depth, and tragedy. Forced from their homes, the issei and nisei did not know their destination; the experience had all the elements of uncertainty and disorientation associated with journeys of discovery. Deposited at the assembly centers, they could read the terms of their immediate future in the landscape: the stables redefined as barracks made the attack on human dignity a fact of daily life, and the barbed wire and guard towers made the suspension of freedom a visible message in the landscape.

In the summer and fall of 1942, the federal government sent the issei and nisei on their coerced west-to-east journey of discovery. In some cases, the trip from assembly center to concentration camp took them past their former homes, with an agonizing nearness to a familiar landscape to which they could not return. Ben Takeshita remembered "asking the MP when we got on the train if when we came to San Mateo [Takeshita's home], we could open the shade and look? And he said no, definitely no. I remember him watching to make sure I didn't open the shades." Yearning for home, Takeshita "consciously count[ed] the bells, you know, the railroad crossings, trying to figure out if this was San Mateo and . . . trying to listen to every little thing that might help me identify it."[24]

---

[23] Tome Takatsuki, quoted in *Issei,* ed. Sarasohn, 199; Mary Tsukamoto, quoted in *And Justice for All,* by Tateishi, 12; Modell, ed., *The Kikuchi Diary,* 156; Mitsuye Yamada, *Camp Notes and Other Poems* (Berkeley, 1976), 27; Monica Sone, *Nisei Daughter* (Seattle, 1979), 177.

[24] Ben Takeshita, quoted in *And Justice for All,* by Tateishi, 244. See also Uchida, *Desert Exile,* 103.

The guards' insistence on drawn shades, at night and in areas they judged to be sensitive territory, made for a curiously interrupted encounter with the western landscape, a journey punctuated by blackouts. Transported from Washington to Idaho, Monica Sone passed through "the Hood River region along the Columbia River"; "we all pressed our faces against the windows and drank in the extravagant beauty," admiring the mountains and "the tumbling blue river." The guards then closed the shades. In the morning, "the scenery had changed drastically overnight." Beauty, in Sone's eyes, had vanished. The land was "parched" into "gray-brown wrinkles out of which jagged boulders erupted like warts. Wisps of moldy-looking, gray-green sagebrush dotted the land."[25]

Even with the opportunity to watch the landscape change in stages, the shift from the comparatively green West Coast to the semiarid or arid interior was an unsettling shock for most of the relocatees. "After the lush greenness of the Willamette Valley" in coastal Oregon, Minoru Yasui's party arrived near Twin Falls, Idaho. When they saw "the sterile, dusty desert which was to be our home 'for the duration,' many sat on the baggage in the middle of nowhere and wept." To the relocatees, the landscape was a study in vacancy: "No houses were in sight, no trees or anything green — only scrubby sagebrush and an occasional low cactus, and mostly dry, baked earth." Except for two camps in Arkansas, all the sites chosen by the War Relocation Authority were in arid or semiarid places: Minidoka, Idaho; Heart Mountain, Wyoming; Amache (or Granada), Colorado; Topaz, Utah; Poston and Gila River, Arizona; Manzanar and Tule Lake, California. Arid places thus brought a response of distress and disorientation at camps all over the West. At Heart Mountain, Amy Uno Ishii remembered, her party "looked up there at the camp that was to be our home," and "most of the people who got off the train shed tears like you've never seen before," facing a landscape with "no trees, nothing green."[26]

Most of the camps were in areas with frequent winds. In building the camps, the land had been recently bulldozed and the original ground cover destroyed. The conditions were thus perfect for blowing sand and dust. "You couldn't open your mouth," Amy Uno Ishii remembered of the Heart Mountain dust storms, "because all the dust would come in. You could just barely see, and the only way to keep your eyes clean was just to cry and . . . let the tears wash your eyes." At Manzanar, California, on the eastern side of the Sierra Nevada, Yoriyuki Kikuchi remembered, "when the wind blew, it was terrible. . . . Everybody resented being put in such a place, especially when they were suffocated in sand." George Fukasawa arrived at Manzanar in the middle of one of the "very common" windstorms. The residents he saw "had goggles on to protect their eyes from the dust, so they looked like a bunch of monsters from another world or something. It was a very eerie feeling to get into a place under conditions like that." At the Utah camp ("Topaz: The Jewel

[25] Sone, *Nisei Daughter*, 190–91.

[26] Minoru Yasui, quoted in *And Justice for All*, by Tateishi, 76; Amy Uno Ishii, quoted in *Japanese American World War II Evacuation Oral History Project, Part I: Internees*, ed. Arthur A. Hansen (Westport, 1991), 80, 67.

of the Desert," according to the masthead of the official camp newspaper), Miné Okuba and Yoshiko Uchida chose the same metaphor to describe the meeting of people with dust: "everyone looked like pieces of flour-dusted pastry"; "we looked as if we had fallen into a flour barrel." Monica Sone summed up the experience of arrival for many people: "We felt as if we were standing in a gigantic sand-mixing machine as the sixty-mile gale lifted the loose earth up into the sky, obliterating everything." When the Sone family found its assigned room, it offered little refuge: "The window panes rattled madly, and the dust poured in through the cracks like smoke."[27]

At these various dust-choked camps, the American landscape was not laid out serenely, passively awaiting and accepting discovery. On the contrary, it was on the offensive, actively intruding on the observer, "dust and sand entering nostrils and ears, lodging between teeth, a horrible feeling." Sweeping could be a full-time job, as the poorly constructed barracks walls put up a weak fight against invasion by the landscape. A poem written by Toyo Suyemoto Kawakami captures the sense of domestic space invaded:

> The floor is carpeted with dust, wind-borne
> Dry alkali, patterned by insect feet.
> What peace can such a place as this impart?

The dust, the wind, the sky, the heat, and the cold played enormous roles in shaping people's experience of the camp environment. With the impact on the body, mind, and senses of these uncontrollable forces, one simply has to abandon the idea of the landscape as scenery, experienced primarily through the eyes and appraised and judged from a reflective, abstract distance.[28]

In the process of dissolving the division separating visual experience from other encounters of the senses, the case study of the relocation camps also invites a recognition of the shifting boundary between natural and human-made landscapes. The dust and wind were certainly "natural," but the bulldozing of the ground exacerbated the interaction of wind and dirt. Similarly, in the eyes of the internees, the rows and rows of barracks made a perfect match in desolation and bleakness to the desert landscape. Walking in the Manzanar camp, Jeanne Wakatsuki Houston saw a view composed of both natural elements and the products of human action: "I would hike past row upon row of black barracks, watching mountains waver through that desert heat." The built landscape could be as disorienting as the geological landscape; at Topaz, for instance, "all the blocks looked alike." Long "after we settled in," Toyo Suyemoto Kawakami remembered, "camp residents would occasionally

[27] Amy Uno Ishii, quoted in *Oral History Project,* ed. Hansen, 67; Yoriuki Kikuchi, *ibid.*, 206; George Fukasawa, *ibid.*, 236–37; Uchida, *Desert Exile,* 109; Miné Okuba, *Citizen 13660* (Seattle, 1983), 123; Sone, *Nisei Daughter,* 192.

[28] Amy Uno Ishii, quoted in *Oral History Project,* ed. Hansen, 67; Toyo Suyemoto Kawakami, "Camp Memories: Rough and Broken Shards," in *Japanese Americans: From Relocation to Redress,* ed. Roger Daniels, Sandra C. Taylor, and Harry H. L. Kitano (Salt Lake City, 1986), 28.

lose their sense of direction at night and wander into a barracks not their own, much to their embarrassment and that of the occupants." "All residential blocks looked alike," Miné Okubo put it; "people were lost all the time."[29]

Nature and the War Relocation Authority seemed to have joined forces to construct landscapes designed to break the spirits of the prisoners. In these bleak circumstances, the determination of the issei and nisei to improve their settings was and is genuinely astonishing. In our times, it has become a set piece to say that people whom we once thought of simply as victims did, in fact, act to shape their own worlds. The efforts of the issei and nisei to reshape their landscapes gives that now familiar phrase fresh and vivid meaning.

At the assembly centers and the concentration camps, the residents took the first opportunity to plant gardens of flowers and vegetables. At Manzanar, Jeanne Wakatsuki Houston noted, "gardens had sprung up everywhere, in the firebreaks, between the rows of barracks—rock gardens, vegetable gardens, cactus and flower gardens." At the Tanforan Assembly Center, Yoshiko Uchida wrote, the residents "made good use of the manure-rich soil, cultivating flowers for pleasure and vegetables to supplement their camp diet." Besides individual gardens, the camps also had farms producing many of the vegetables the residents consumed.[30]

Living under conditions at once infuriating, disorienting, and demoralizing, many of the residents nonetheless pitched into the project of discovering and realizing the potential of these grim landscapes. At Topaz, one of the most discouraging desert sites in the country, "despite reports that the alkaline soil was not good for agriculture purposes, in the spring practically everyone set up a victory garden." Watering these gardens was no easy matter. "In the evening," Miné Okuba remarked, "there was the usual bucket brigade from the laundry buildings to the garden."[31]

The gardens were testimony to the powerful work ethic of the issei and nisei. They were also, in part, a response to necessity. The food in the mess halls was often unappealing, and sometimes even dangerous; many residents experienced frequent stomach problems from spoiled food. Used to a diet rich in vegetables, the issei and nisei found gardening and farming a route to better health. Indeed, this could be a matter of life and death. Mabel Ota's father, a diabetic, "had always raised all kinds of vegetables in the backyard, fresh vegetables," Ota said, "because they were so essential to his diet." Placed at the Gila River camp, he endured a "terrible" diet; "the food," Ota was sure, "was related to my father's death."[32]

---

[29] Jeanne Wakatsuki Houston and James D. Houston, *Farewell to Manzanar* (Boston, 1973), 31; Toyo Suyemoto Kawakami, quoted in *Japanese Americans*, ed. Daniels, Taylor, and Kitano, 27; Okubo, *Citizen 13660*, 136.

[30] Houston and Houston, *Farewell to Manzanar*, 72; Uchida, *Desert Exile*, 87. While the gardens were the most visible, outdoor sign of this effort to recreate normality, a similar campaign went on indoors. Descriptions of the building of furniture and the partitioning and reshaping of the barracks rooms occur in almost all camp narratives; see, for example, Sone, *Nisei Daughter*, 195–96; and Okuba, *Citizen 13660*, 137.

[31] Okuba, *Citizen 13660*, 192–93.

[32] Quoted in *And Justice for All*, by Tateishi, 111.

Miniature landscapes shaped from sand were a traditional Japanese art form known as *bon-kei*.
This art was recalled and revived in the Amache internment camp near Granada,
Colorado. From Allen H. Eaton, *Beauty behind Barbed Wire*
(New York, 1952). *Courtesy HarperCollins.*

The pressures of the work ethic and the demands of health do not, however, explain the gardens. A powerful set of aesthetic and spiritual motivations, derived
directly from Japanese culture, were also at work. Okuba noted that, at the Tanforan
Assembly Center, "Everyone knew the camp was not a permanent one." Would the
gardeners still be there when the flowers bloomed and the vegetables became ripe?
The harvest was clearly not the only point of these gardens. Leaving the Fresno assembly center, Mary Tsukamoto noted that "the whole camp was transformed," with
"so many beautiful flowers and vegetables, so lush and green." "Who but Nihonjins
(Japanese)," she asked, "would leave a place like that in beauty?"[33]

At Tanforan, "a group of landscape architects decided to build a lake to beautify
the camp." Transformed "from a mere wet spot," the site became "a miniature
aquatic park, complete with bridge, promenade, and islands." At Manzanar,
gardeners "built a small park, with mossy nooks, ponds, waterfalls and curved
wooden bridges." Walking in that park, Jeanne Wakatsuki Houston remembered,
"you could face away from the barracks, look past a tiny rapids toward the darkening
mountains, and for a while not be a prisoner at all."[34]

A distinctively creative response to the setting went beyond the planting of
gardens. At the Amache camp in Colorado, one woman arrived in the midst of the

[33] Okuba, *Citizen 13660*, 98; Mary Tsukamoto quoted in *And Justice for All*, by Tateishi, 14.
[34] Okubo, *Citizen 13660*, 98–99; Houston and Houston, *Farewell to Manzanar*, 72.

usual sandstorm. Mrs. Minomiya remembered a traditional art using sand, "the making of miniature landscapes, or *bon-kei*." Under her guidance, Amache became a center in the creation of remarkable landscapes and seascapes, sculpted in small trays. Residents at various camps hunted for *kobu,* any "curious natural wood growth," hand rubbing the ones they found into often stunning sculpture. At the Minidoka camp in Idaho, the residents adapted traditional flower arranging to sagebrush, the dominant plant in the area. Indeed, "special gardens" of sagebrush "were developed, largely by thinning, and clumps of it were trimmed as decorative features of the landscape." In examples like these, distinctive cultural responses to landscape were at work. The issei and nisei found beauty, and coaxed it into visibility, in ways seldom seen in Anglo-American responses to arid lands.[35]

And yet, in other ways, issei and nisei seemed to match the Anglo-American notion of a desert as an unfortunate landscape in need of major reconstruction by human enterprise. In Idaho, the camp newspaper recorded a familiar determination to master an uncooperative landscape. We can, the *Minidoka Irrigator* said, "have but one resolve; to apply our combined energies to the grim task of conquering the elements and converting a wasteland into an inhabitable community." The familiarity of the phrasing here was fully intended: "Our great adventure is a repetition of the frontier struggle of pioneers against the land and its elements." It is, of course, important to note that the camp newspapers were supervised, and sometimes censored, by the War Relocation Authority staff. When the *Irrigator* proclaimed the camps' compatibility with white American expansion, or when the newspaper at Amache adopted the name the *Pioneer,* one does not know exactly whose ideology is revealed.[36]

A decade ago, writing a book on attitudes toward the western deserts, I adopted the notion that a distaste for dry places and an urge to remake deserts into gardens were distinctive, perhaps even unique, cultural properties of Anglo-Americans. It was thus a useful surprise for me to find such a similarity of response in the issei and nisei. As American citizens and natives, of course, many of the nisei had adopted American points of view on the use of nature. They had, moreover, grown up with comparatively green settings, irrigated farms or well-watered urban yards. "Most of us were born in this country," Jeanne Wakatsuki Houston reminds us; "we had no other models."[37]

And yet the proposition—that some of the nisei had picked up the Anglo-American ideology of lands conquered by pioneers and deserts made to bloom—

[35] Allen H. Eaton, *Beauty behind Barbed Wire: The Arts of the Japanese in Our War Relocation Camps* (New York, 1952), 16–19, 32–35. Eaton also provides descriptions and photographs of gardens; see 24–25, 50–53, 56–57, 74–75, 92–95.

[36] *Irrigator,* quoted in Robert C. Sims, "Japanese Americans in Idaho," in *Japanese Americans,* ed. Daniels, Taylor, and Kitano, 107.

[37] Limerick, *Desert Passages;* Houston and Houston, *Farewell to Manzanar,* 72. Despite different cultural origins, Anglo-American teachers and anthropologists at the camp sites were equally repelled by the setting; see, for example, Rosalie H. Wax, *Doing Fieldwork: Warnings and Advice* (Chicago, 1971), 67–68; and Eleanor Gerard Sekerak, "A Teacher at Topaz," in *Japanese Americans,* ed. Daniels, Taylor, and Kitano, 40.

Arranging sagebrush at the internment camp in Minidoka, Idaho. From Allen H. Eaton,
Beauty behind Barbed Wire (New York, 1952). *Courtesy HarperCollins.*

only partially explains the camp residents' response to aridity. Like other Asian immigrants, the issei had their own reasons to be unsettled by deserts and to take up the project of making the landscape green. Most Asian immigrants came from humid places. The prefectures of southern Japan, the place of origin for most Japanese immigrants, had an annual rainfall of at least forty inches a year, and as much as eighty inches a year. The rainfall for much of southern China, the place of origin for most nineteenth-century Chinese immigrants, was close to eighty inches a year. Asian immigrants did not need to borrow their discomfort with arid lands from Anglo-Americans; they had their own reasons to lament the absence of trees, to flinch at the rarity of the color green, to size up the prospects for manipulating the water supply, and to throw themselves into the enterprise of coaxing at least a small part of the desert into becoming a garden. Before World War II, a number of Japanese immigrants had farmed in places like California's Imperial Valley and Washington's Yakima Valley; the camps were not their first encounter with the challenges facing agriculture in arid lands.

The "Jeffersonian agrarian dream" is a stock item in the conceptual tool chest of landscape studies. The gardens in the concentration camps, as well as the earlier Chinese and Japanese vegetable gardens and farms throughout California, offered a powerful statement that the term "agrarian dream" could carry the adjectives "Chinese" and "Japanese" as well as "Jeffersonian." Originating in a very different set of historical and cultural circumstances, the Chinese agrarian dream and the Japanese agrarian dream joined up with the American version in bringing an ideal of order and productivity to bear on the "wild" American landscape. But those dreams were tested under very different conditions. Federal legislation gave official support to the American agrarian dream, while the Chinese and Japanese versions had to persist in spite of racial harassment, official obstacles to land ownership, and, for the Japanese, an involuntary relocation.[38]

To recognize the Japanese and Chinese agrarian dreams is not, of course, to claim an essentially agrarian character for these populations. As Sucheng Chan reminds us, "Though the Chinese who came to California [in the nineteenth century] were peasants, they had not come to farm; they took up cultivation because they needed to feed themselves" and because they "discovered . . . that farming could often provide a more steady income than mining for gold." People with other skills entirely found few opportunities to use them. Wong Yow, a resident of the town of Locke in the Sacramento Delta, remarked:

> I had just finished learning to be a carpenter in China, so I was ready for that. Instead, I went to work in the orchards, picking pears and trimming trees. . . . There was plenty of work to do if you were interested in doing farmwork. . . . I

---

[38] On the Japanese and Japanese-American agrarian dream, see Valerie J. Matsumoto, *Sustaining Fruit: Family, Farm, and Community among Japanese Americans, 1919–1982* (Ithaca, forthcoming, 1993); and David Masumoto, *Country Voices: The Oral History of a Japanese American Family Farm Community* (Del Ray, Calif., 1987).

never did get to use my carpentry skills. It just wasn't done. . . . [Chinese people] weren't expected—I guess allowed—to do anything else.[39]

Many issei and nisei people saw farming and gardening as, at best, a temporary expedient. "A countless number of times," Akemi Kikumura's mother remembered of her husband, "he wanted to throw away the pruning shears and study." "My occupation is now a gardener," Iwato Itow told an interviewer, "and working the soil is the one thing I wanted to get away from." Asian-American society, like Anglo-American society, was divided into rural and urban groupings, and very different definitions of familiar landscapes characterized those two groups. When the older residents of a Japanese-American farming community in Del Ray, California, remark that they "were *inaka* (country)" and "enjoyed living out," they remind us that rural consciousness and urban consciousness both cut across ethnic boundaries and offer a not-always-perceived common ground to people who, whatever their national origin, see themselves as "country" or "city" people.[40]

The politics of Asian-American agrarianism are complicated in ways that go beyond the problem of an essentialist cultural character. To be rural and to be Asian American can, in the context of an industrializing and urban nation, be a double dose of restricted power and opportunity. The image of the simple, docile, close-to-the-earth farmer can cross cultural boundaries here. Consider the remark of Bess Tuck, "librarian and local historian" of Granada, the Colorado town next to the Amache camp: "The Japanese were really very good about the whole thing [coerced relocation]. They took immediately to farming the camp and did quite a bit of landscaping." Interpreting the gardens from the outside, Bess Tuck and I take opposite paths; she seems to see a symbol of compliance where I see a symbol of defiance, a visible statement of unbroken will. But the topic remains an unsettling one. It is, for instance, a peculiar experience to examine Allen Eaton's book, *Beauty behind Barbed Wire.* The descriptions and photographs of gardens, *kobu,* miniature landscapes, and sculpted sagebrush are stirring and inspirational; the first pages of the book are not. In the "Foreword," Eleanor Roosevelt praises "the remarkably fine spirit" of "our Japanese Americans," shown in "the gardens–which I can testify were truly beautiful even in camps where the desert surrounded them." Eaton's book, Roosevelt writes, "show how well the War Relocation Authority did its work, one of the achievements of government administration of which every American citizen can be proud." Allen Eaton concurs, noting his intention "to share with the reader a part of the distinguished record of the War Relocation Authority . . . ; it is one of the finest achievements in American war- and peacetime government administration." By this point, one's response to the gardens, art, sculpture, and crafts of the prisoners is thoroughly muddled: if one admires the gardens, is one inadvertently

[39] Chan, *Bittersweet Soil,* 79; Gillenkirk and Motlow, *Bitter Melon,* 44.

[40] Akemi Kikumura, *Through Harsh Winters: The Life of a Japanese Immigrant Woman* (Novato, Calif., 1981), 49; Iwato Itow, quoted in *And Justice for All,* by Tateishi, 145; Masumoto, *Country Voices,* 81.

"An Early Bit of Landscape at Poston, Arizona." Japanese Americans interned in the arid camps shaped their own landscapes. From Allen H. Eaton, *Beauty behind Barbed Wire* (New York, 1952). *Courtesy National Archives.*

joining Roosevelt and Eaton in a round of applause for the institution that provided the challenges for the gardeners to meet?[41]

Precisely because of the interpretive complications they present, the camp gardens are an important chapter in the study of the application of agrarian ideals to

[41] Bess Tuck, quoted in "Return to Amache," by George Lurie, *Denver Magazine,* 12 (May 1982), 36; Eaton, *Beauty behind Barbed Wire,* xi–xii, xiii. The question of the gardens also returns us to the unsettled border territory between environmental history and ethnic history. In works such as Donald Worster, *Rivers of Empire: Water, Aridity, and the Growth of the American West* (New York, 1985) and James Earl Sherow, *Watering the Valley: Development Along the High Plains Arkansas River, 1870–1950* (Lawrence, Kans., 1990), environmental historians offer a quite stern judgment of the unintended consequences and the inappropriateness of irrigated agriculture in deserts. Should that appraisal apply to the camp gardens, or do the smallness of scale and injustice of the circumstances mitigate the judgment?

the landscape. On a number of counts, the study of attitudes and behavior toward the American landscape is deepened and enriched by attention to Asian-American history. The friction created when new arrivals arrive with high expectations and confront less-than-ideal places, the appraisal of and behavior toward arid lands, the variations in agrarian dreams, the split in perception and power between rural and urban populations, the necessity for leisure and a comfortable margin of subsistence in the aesthetic appreciation of landscape, the sense among rural Americans that they are losing ground, unable to recruit children to stay on the farms: on these counts and many others, the similarities and differences between Anglo-American and Asian-American experiences, not to mention Indian, Mexican-American, and African-American experiences, present an open range of scholarly opportunity. In all these cases, the encounter with landscape was also a complex and often conflict-ridden encounter with other groups of people. Refought, with the historian's mind serving now as the place of contest, these struggles for the right to shape and to interpret the American landscape give a new life to what was, not long ago, a set and routinized scholarly subject.

"We knew America was huge, but we didn't know it was this huge," Amy Uno Ishii remembered of her trip to Heart Mountain, Wyoming.[42] Her perception of vast space matches the response of many Euro-Americans to the landscapes of this continent. But her destination—a clump of barracks tightly bounded by barbed wire—reminds us that many racial and ethnic minorities, as well as working-class whites, discovered a landscape of restriction, even in the midst of the widest and most open spaces. Under those circumstances, the discovery of possibilities had to alternate with the discovery of injustice and inequity, as indeed it does in the scholarly rediscovery of this issue.

Starting from very different points on the planet's surface, traveling west and traveling east, Anglo-Americans and Asian Americans met, and meet, in the American landscape. In the eighteenth century, the area along the upper Missouri River was a center of Plains Indian life, as the Mandans planted gardens along the river bottom and as the Lakota moved in from the east. In 1804, in the archetypal Anglo-American voyage of westward discovery, Lewis and Clark camped near a site that would later become the town of Bismarck and the capital of North Dakota. Seventy years after Lewis and Clark's visit, George Armstrong Custer's wife, Elizabeth, spent the anxious summer of 1876 at Fort Abraham Lincoln, near Bismarck, where she received the news of her husband's death. Sixty-five years later, when the FBI made its first sweeps through the Japanese communities on the West Coast, many of the "dangerous enemy aliens" were separated from their families, taken to North Dakota, and held at Fort Lincoln, now relocated on the other side of the river. Far from being the middle of nowhere, central North Dakota is now layered with experiences and perceptions, anticipation and anxiety, arrivals and departures. With this layering of history, the area around Bismarck has become a kind of common

---

[42] Amy Uno Ishii, quoted in *Oral History Project*, ed. Hansen, 67.

ground, between the westward-moving participants in conquest and the eastward-moving participants in a coerced relocation, with both groups appearing as unlikely intruders into the land of the Mandan and the Lakota.

In a similar pattern, the Owens Valley in interior California was first the home of the Paiute Indian people. In the 1860s, it was colonized by white farmers and ranchers. Those residents were in turn displaced in a bureaucratic conquest, as the city of Los Angeles and the Bureau of Reclamation acquired land and water rights in the valley and drained its water. When Los Angeles took the water, the community of Manzanar in the Owens Valley was abandoned, leaving the land available for use as a relocation camp in World War II. Here, too, the layering of experiences creates a site shaped by cycles of conquest and heavily invested with human memory. And yet we have usually fragmented the history of landscapes like this one, telling in very separate volumes the story of the Paiutes and their conquest, the white colonization of the valley, the aesthetic responses of writers like Mary Austin, the maneuverings of the water developers, and the creation of the Manzanar concentration camp.[43]

In 1943, the Chinese anthropologist and sociologist Fei Xiaotong toured the United States and compared what he saw with his childhood in China. In his home, "there were more places for ghosts than for people." Americans lived in another world entirely. "How," he asked, in the United States, "could ghosts gain a foothold . . . ? People move about like the tide, unable to form permanent ties with places." Fei Xiaotong could not, he said, "get used to people today who know only the present moment." Indeed, he confessed to feeling "a little sorry for people raised in a world without ghosts."[44]

In 1992, we can no longer think of the United States as "a world without ghosts." The landscapes of North America are heavily invested with human memories, and the tangle of those memories provided both common and contested ground for the people of various origins whose descendants now populate this nation. Life "melds past, present, and future" into one "multi-layered scene, a three-dimensional body," Fei Xiaotong wrote. "This is what ghosts are."[45] This "multi-layered scene" is what the American landscape now presents for our exploration. That enterprise requires historians to engage in a constant process of disorientation and reorientation, taking part in the pleasures, the discomforts, and the conflicts of discovery.

[43] The first study to come close to a united narrative of this sort is John Walton, *Western Times and Water Wars* (Berkeley, 1992).

[44] Fei Xiaotong, "The Shallowness of Cultural Tradition," in *Land without Ghosts,* ed. Arkush and Lee, 177–80.

[45] *Ibid.*, 178.

Making America Home: Racial Masquerade and Ethnic Assimilation in the Transition to Talking Pictures

Michael Rogin

In 1890, when Philip Krantz and Abraham Cahan were starting a Yiddish-language socialist newspaper (the *Arbeiter Zeitung*), Cahan proposed initiating the venture with an article on cannibalism in Africa. Krantz, wholly focused on promoting socialist doctrine on New York's Lower East Side, objected. Cahan was also a socialist and went on to edit the *Jewish Daily Forward* for half a century. But just as he had moved from Russian to Yiddish to reach Jewish immigrants in their own language, so he believed that African cannibalism would attract an audience for Krantz's "Our Program."[1]

Cahan had read the article he proposed to translate and publish, "Life Among the Congo Savages," in *Scribner's Magazine.* This journal offered its readers fiction by such writers as Henry James, Sarah Orne Jewett, and Robert Louis Stevenson; political articles (Theodore Roosevelt's account of leading his white and black troops up San Juan Hill appeared within the decade); and displays of exotic peoples. The newspaperman turned explorer, Henry M. Stanley, was often featured. Closer to home, Jacob A. Riis's "How the Other Half Lives," his tour through the urban jungle, appeared four months before the article on Congo savages. The documentary, classificatory invasion Frederick E. Hoxie locates as part of imperial expansion was discovering not only exotic non-Europeans but urban immigrants as well. Cahan himself, "discovered by [the] . . . renowned . . . literary Columbus," William Dean Howells, as Theodore Dreiser put it, soon published stories in English about the Lower East Side. *Scribner's* genteel readers could make the connection between Riis's "street Arabs," children sleeping on the city streets, and the "benighted savages in the heart of Africa"; between the "dark hallways and filthy cellars, crowded, as is every foot of the street, with half-naked children" at home, and the "cannibal orgies" in the Dark Continent; between the savage "craving for . . . human flesh,"

Michael Rogin is professor of political science at the University of California, Berkeley.

Thanks to Elizabeth Abel, Ann Banfield, Kim Chernin, Casey Blake, David Thelen, and the contributors to this issue of the *Journal of American History* for comments on an earlier draft of this essay.

[1] Ronald Sanders, *The Downtown Jews: Portraits of an Immigrant Generation* (New York, 1987), 104–9.

the cries of "Nyana! Nyana! (Meat, meat)," and the "pigmarket" in the Jewish quarter where "crowds . . . pushing, struggling, screaming, and shouting in foreign tongues, a veritable Babel of confusion," buy everything except the forbidden flesh that gives the market its name. Just as the nineteenth-century cartoons and racial doctrines turned Irish into Africans, so the multiethnic New York slums brought savagery to the heart of civilization.[2]

Jews, to be sure, were more the objects of sympathy in *Scribner's,* cannibals the objects of horror, but reform impulse jostled exotic display both in the article about Cahan's prospective readers and in the article he translated for them. After all, Stanley told readers of *Scribner's* that pygmies, who ate everything in sight, human flesh included, "were the intellectual equals of about fifty per cent of the modern inhabitants of any great American city of today." Although Stanley was reducing immigrants to pygmies, he was conversely elevating African savages, for he insisted, "I see no difference between the civilized and the pygmy!" "Let light shine upon the trackless region," Stanley concluded. "Some will survive the great change and . . . prove themselves to be very much like the rest of humanity."[3]

The progress Stanley imagined from savagery to civilization would catch up Riis's other half as well. The *Arbeiter Zeitung's* "Cannibalism in Africa"—for Cahan won his dispute with Krantz—was a step neither toward Cahan's Jewish socialism nor toward Stanley's universal civilization but toward Americanization. Just as the *Forward's* famous *Bintel Briefs,* letters from readers sharing their concerns, introduced Jewish immigrant workers to daily life in America, so "Life Among the Congo Savages" introduced them to American culture. Discovering savages, they were discovering America. Thanks to Cahan, they began to move from being the objects, to being the reading subjects, of exotic interest, from what they shared with cannibals to what they shared with readers of *Scribner's.*

Far from discovering something new in the period of mass immigration, Cahan—as Ronald Takaki shows—had come upon the oldest American story. He was creating a line of descent from the first self-styled children of Israel in the New World to the Jewish immigrants who followed them. Like those first settlers, the Jews would be discoverers. The discovery and appropriation of native peoples, peoples defined by and ripped from their relationship to their land, stands at the origins of the United States. Genocide and slavery notwithstanding, these native peoples

[2] Herbert Ward, "Life Among the Congo Savages," *Scribner's Magazine,* 7 (Feb. 1890), 135, 152–54, 186; Frederick E. Hoxie, "Exploring a Cultural Borderland: Native American Journeys of Discovery in the Early Twentieth Century," *Journal of American History,* 79 (Dec. 1992), 969–95; Jacob A. Riis, "How the Other Half Lives: Studies among the Tenements," *Scribner's Magazine* 6 (Dec. 1889), 655, 657, 659; Sanders, *Downtown Jews,* 197–204; Amy Kaplan, *The Social Construction of American Realism* (Chicago, 1988), 109; L. Perry Curtis, *Apes and Angels: The Irishman in Victorian Caricature* (Washington, 1971). Sanders identifies Henry M. Stanley as the author of the article Cahan translated, but Stanley's *Scribner's* article (see note 3) was published the year after the first issue of the *Arbeiter Zeitung.* Ward's travel account, which centers on cannibalism as Stanley does not, must be the essay in question. It appeared one month before Cahan's translation.

[3] Henry M. Stanley, "The Pygmies of the Great African Forest," *Scribner's Magazine,* 9 (Jan. 1891), 3, 8, 17. On Henry M. Stanley, see Maria Torgovnick, *Gone Primitive: Savage Intellects, Modern Lives* (Chicago, 1990), 26–33.

were neither forgotten nor simply kept at a distance. Their discovery generated, in Hoxie's terms, not so much dialogue as invention, the invention of America.[4]

Discovery establishes priority, less of one colonizing power over another than of the colonizer over the peoples already living on the land. Discovery bestows rights over the heretofore undiscovered people. Discovery makes the discovered into passive objects, the discoverers into autonomous subjects. But, as "Life Among the Congo Savages" illustrates, the discovered are objects not only of concrete utility but also of symbolic fascination.

Their society built on the land of Indians and with the labor of slaves, early Americans created a national culture on that material foundation. The two originary forms of that culture were the captivity narrative, the first and most popular secular American writing and the source of both classic American literature and the frontier myth, and blackface minstrelsy, the first and most popular form of American mass entertainment. Indian literature and blackface, moreover, expressed both racial aversion and racial desire. Both promoted identification with native peoples as a step in differentiation from them.[5]

In both forms, reversion to primitivism fashioned American identity. Racial cross-dressing turned Europeans into Americans not only on Frederick Jackson Turner's mythological frontier but also in the cities, where blackface made white Americans out of Irish immigrants on the "cultural borderland" (to adapt a phrase Hoxie has used) between the Anglo-Saxon and colored races. My concern here is with the extension of that pattern to the period of mass immigration at the turn of the twentieth century, and to the central, mass-cultural, Americanizing instrument, motion pictures.[6]

Like Irish immigrants in the mid-nineteenth century, Jewish movie producers, vaudeville performers, and songwriters occupied an insecure position between whites and peoples of color. Hollywood movies imagined the ideal America that the moguls and their immigrant audience aspired to enter; racial cross-dressing acknowledged the ambiguous racial status they occupied. It at once provided access to the depth of feeling and infantile behavior attributed to African Americans and, since blackface was only skin deep, demonstrated the Europeans' difference from them. Making visible the significance of race in the continuing creation of American

---

[4] Ronald Takaki, "*The Tempest* in the Wilderness: The Racialization of Savagery," *Journal of American History,* 79 (Dec. 1992), 892–912; Frederick E. Hoxie, "Discovering America: An Introduction," *ibid.,* 837.

[5] From the enormous body of work on which this paragraph draws, I cite here only Richard Slotkin, *Regeneration through Violence: The Mythology of the American Frontier, 1600–1860* (Middletown, 1973); Richard Slotkin, *The Fatal Environment: The Myth of the Frontier in the Age of Industrialization, 1800–1890* (New York, 1985); Robert Toll, *Blacking Up: The Minstrel Show in Nineteenth-Century America* (New York, 1974); Alexander Saxton, *The Rise and Fall of the White Republic: Class Politics and Mass Culture in Nineteenth Century America* (London, 1990); Eric Lott, *Blackface Minstrelsy and the American Working Class* (New York, forthcoming); and David R. Roediger, *The Wages of Whiteness: Race and the Making of the American Working Class* (London, 1991).

[6] "The wilderness . . . strips off the garments of civilization and arrays [the colonist] in the hunting shirt and moccasin. . . . The outcome is . . . a new product that is American," wrote Frederick Jackson Turner in "The Significance of the Frontier in American History," the 1893 paper reprinted in Frederick Jackson Turner, *The Frontier in American History* (New York, 1920), 4. Hoxie, "Exploring a Cultural Borderland."

identity, racial masquerade pointed to white privilege. Since the sources of white advantage in the slaughter of Indians, the enslavement of African Americans, and the exploitation and exclusion of Asians were too terrible to acknowledge directly, racial masquerade also released the tension. Narratives about jazz age music emancipated it from its African-American roots. Sentimentality confused the question of whose grievances merited redress. Humor exploited racial stereotypes, but it also played with the hypocrisy of racial divisions, sometimes stopping short of full disclosure, sometimes going all the way.

The immigrant urban entertainers operated within a continuing tradition when they invented Americanizing forms. Werner Sollors's *Beyond Ethnicity* shows that tradition as pervasive, breaking down the distinction between early settlers in what became the United States and immigrants. The colonists were ethnics like their successors, argues Sollors, caught between inherited, ancestral, Old World, Old Testament, blood-based, Hebrew particularism and New World, New Testament, melting pot, spiritual universalism. Reincarnating the Turner thesis in postmodern, urban form, Sollors stands with "consent," as he labels it, against "descent." But though he sides with the children, preferring their universalism to their parents' particularism, he calls attention to generational conflict, the loss of the old home in making the new, as the pathos of Americanization.[7]

Replacing the Puritan/immigrant opposition with the one between consent and descent, however, gives freedom too large a field. Sollors does not sufficiently stress that the discovery of racial difference is part of Catholic and Jewish immigrants' inheritance from the colonists. Facing nativist pressure that would assign them to the dark side of the racial divide, immigrants Americanized themselves by crossing and recrossing the racial line. Their discovery of racial inequality propelled the United States beyond ethnicity, I will argue, by transforming ethnic descent into an American national identity.

Sollors observes the role of musical metaphors — symphony, harmony, orchestra — in symbolizing the melting pot. In the songs of Irving Berlin, Al Jolson, George Gershwin, Sophie Tucker, and many others, music was not simply a metaphor for the melting pot, but an instrument of it. Melting pot music has much in common with nineteenth-century theories about American English. Nineteenth-century language theorists believed that American English combined an organic discovery of the past with the construction of a nationalist identity (Sollors's descent and consent) by celebrating the expansionist power of national culture, what Kenneth Cmiel calls "the imperial cosmopolitanism of a chosen people."[8] My subject is the use of race in that process.

In a 1914 afterword to *The Melting Pot*, the 1908 intermarriage play that fixed its title on the United States, Israel Zangwill wrote, "However scrupulously and

---

[7] Werner Sollors, *Beyond Ethnicity: Consent and Descent in American Culture* (New York, 1986), 4–5.

[8] Kenneth Cmiel, "'A Broad Fluid Language of Democracy': Discovering the American Idiom," *Journal of American History*, 79 (Dec. 1992), 930.

justifiably America avoids intermarriage with the negro, the comic spirit cannot fail to note spiritual miscegenation which, while clothing, commercializing, and Christianizing the ex-African, has given 'rag-time' and the sex-dances that go with it, first to white America and then to the whole white world." "Spiritual miscegenation" created an authentic American national music, wrote the jazz critic Henry O. Osgood in 1926; his examples were Stephen Foster's blackface "My Old Kentucky Home" and "Old Folks at Home," and "Dixie," which he described as "written by a minstrel, Dan Emmett, for a minstrel show." "The property today of all the English-speaking peoples of the world," Osgood continued, minstrel songs like these "were on the song sheets supplied to the crowds that assembled in Pretoria and Johannesburg, South Africa, to welcome the Prince of Wales."[9]

Minstrelsy was the world-wide sign of American identity because it made Americans. The 1939 musical, *Babes in Arms,* shows the process at work.[10] The babes in arms are children of retired vaudevillians. Putting on *Babes in Arms* to revive the family fortunes, which had been killed by talking pictures, they get their chance on Broadway through a minstrel number. "My daddy was a minstrel man," Judy Garland begins her song. "I'd like to black my face," she sings in blackface, "and go again down memory lane with an old-fashioned minstrel show." This, the central spectacle in *Babes in Arms,* offers all the pleasures of the traditional minstrel show, with Tambo and Bones routines, Mickey Rooney's dialect imitations, and a mass, blackface production number. Talking pictures, descended from vaudeville and entertaining genteel America, here pay homage to the blackface origins of American mass entertainment.

Spectacle has a higher purpose than mere pleasure, however. "Hi there, Yankee, Give me a thankee, You're in God's Country, now," sings Rooney in the movie's finale. "We've got no Duce, Got no Fuehrer, We've got Garbo and Norma Shearer" celebrates Hollywood as the patriotic alternative to authoritarian, European politics. Mentioning the acquisition of Greta Garbo, the song alludes to the melting pot that transformed Germans and Italians from supporters of dictatorship to democratic moviegoers. The myth is enacted by national couples (one man wears a yarmulke) as Rooney welcomes them as Yankees and invites them to dance. In this production number, called "God's Country," racially based nationalisms of descent confronted a spiritually based, inclusive, American nationalism. But there were no African Americans among Dan Emmett's or Mickey Rooney's minstrels, and none appear among the dancing couples in the movie's melting pot conclusion. American nationalism may be spiritual, not racial, from a European perspective, but race is the instrument of spirit from an American one.

Babes in Arms speaks for a motion picture industry that replaced, or rather incorporated, the frontier myth and the minstrel show as it became the agent of American-

[9] Israel Zangwill, *The Melting Pot* (New York, 1914), 207; also quoted in Sollors, *Beyond Ethnicity,* 71; Henry O. Osgood, *So This Is Jazz* (1926; reprint, New York, 1978), 55n.
[10] *Babes in Arms,* dir. Busby Berkeley (MGM, 1939).

Figure 1. Al Jolson as the "Mammy singer" in *The Jazz Singer*. © 1927
Turner Entertainment Co. All rights reserved.

ization. Like the Yiddish press and antebellum, urban blackface, early one-reelers
were often sites of immigrant, working-class self-presentation. But the Jewish
moguls who came to dominate Hollywood in the 1920s repudiated "the slum tradition in the movies" (in Adolph Zukor's phrase). As Neal Gabler has shown, they
constructed an imaginary America for themselves and their mass audience. Dissolving divergent class, regional, and ethnic histories into a unifying American
dream, the moguls propelled themselves from Hebraic particularism to American
universalism.[11]

Although Americanization was not the subject of most of the moguls' movies,
when the immigrant Warner brothers, Harry, Al, Jack, and Sam, made the first
talking picture, *The Jazz Singer*, they told their own story. Choosing melting pot
music against the wishes of his father, Cantor Rabinowitz, the jazz singer exchanges
his inherited Jewish identity for an American one. Speaking and singing in the new

[11] Neal Gabler, *An Empire of Their Own: How the Jews Invented Hollywood* (New York, 1988); Lary May,
Screening Out the Past: The Birth of Mass Culture and the Motion Picture Industry (New York, 1980); Michael
Rogin, Ronald Reagan, *The Movie and Other Episodes in Political Demonology* (Berkeley, 1987), 190–235; Miriam
Hansen, *Babel and Babylon: Spectatorship in American Silent Film* (Chicago, 1991). For Adolph Zukor's phrase,
see *ibid.*, 64.

sound medium, Jakie Rabinowitz acquires a new name, Jack Robin, and a gentile dancer, Mary Dale. Jack's refusal of his inherited cantorial identity kills his father; in the film's climax, Jack first sings Kol Nidre, the chant for Yom Kippur, the day of atonement, over his father's dead body, then "My Mammy" to his mother, his girl friend, and the audience at the Winter Garden theater. (See figure 1.) Although *Beyond Ethnicity* would not lead one to expect it, the Jewish jazz singer Americanizes himself by appearing in blackface. His racial cross-dressing enacts the pleasures and dangers surrounding not only race and ethnicity but also domestic and technological change. The first talking picture at once celebrated its technological breakthrough and allied the medium with parricide. In *Beyond Ethnicity*, domestic loss is the price of becoming American. But racial cross-dressing supplies "the Mammy singer" not only with a gentile wife but also with an American past, as plantation nurture replaces the east European home and mother left behind. In his relation to technology and domesticity, the immigrant turns into a representative American. He has to make technology serve the home because its promise of freedom — in car, radio, and motion picture — invaded traditional American family life. And the jazz singer's lost and found domestic haven defuses the threat from the career-oriented, sexually available New Woman by transforming her from threat to support for domesticity.[12]

The problematic of the first talking picture shaped other movies made during the transition to sound, when the technological revolution that ended silent pictures coalesced with the end of mass immigration, when nativist prejudice against ethnic urbanity confronted the new morals and forms of entertainment of the jazz age. I look at four movies made between 1927 and 1930 and united by racial cross-dressing — an urban melodrama, a musical review, a musical family melodrama, and a musical comedy set in the West. *Old San Francisco* (1927) was one of the five movies issued before *The Jazz Singer* that had occasional sound effects and a synchronized musical score. In these films, Warner Brothers introduced its new film sound system, Vitaphone. Directed by Alan Crosland, who later shot *The Jazz Singer,* its racial cross-dressing extends the European immigrant / white / black triangle of eastern cities (and of *The Jazz Singer*) to the Chinese, Irish, and Old California Spanish of the West. *The King of Jazz* (1930), an expensive, part-color musical and vaudeville review, starred Paul Whiteman, the most popular band leader of the jazz age. In this movie, jazz is a white man's music with black roots that turns immigrants into Americans. *The Singing Fool* (1928), Warner Brothers' part-silent, part-talking, part-singing blackface sequel to *The Jazz Singer,* shifts the focus of Al Jolson's first movie from crossing ethnic boundaries to crossing gender boundaries. Starring the first mass entertainment idol of the twentieth century, *The Singing Fool* was the top box office hit of the 1920s. Finally, *Whoopee!* (1930) returns Indians to the ethnic intermarriage story by way of blackface, redface, and

---

[12] *The Jazz Singer,* dir. Alan Crosland (Warner Brothers, 1927). This paragraph summarizes Michael Rogin, "Blackface, White Noise: The Jewish Jazz Singer Finds His Voice," *Critical Inquiry,* 18 (Spring 1992), 417–53. For Werner Sollors's amusement at urban Irish blackface spoofs of the tragic Indian, see Sollors, *Beyond Ethnicity,* 132–38.

gender destabilization. Starring Eddie Cantor, it was among the most successful movies of 1931.[13]

Romantic triangles in these movies do not establish fixed points of rivalry in the traditional Freudian pattern, but rather resemble the complex triangularity among liminal American identities that Carroll Smith-Rosenberg describes. She analyzes popular writings of the late 1780s to reveal the process of negative identification that fixes and unfixes the identity of the white middle-class male. But whereas her anxious texts fear destabilized identities, the circuits of desire in Americanization films deliberately mobilize identity exchange — between colored and white, man and woman, ethnic and American.[14]

Like Irish blackface minstrelsy a century earlier, films such as these were one way in which, to quote James Barrett, "immigrant workers discovered the significance of race in American life." There were, Barrett shows, alternative modes of acculturation, some racially inflected and others not, in which workers themselves were more than spectators.[15] But no full account of the immigrant discovery of America can avoid the creative role first of Irish and then of Jewish Americans at the blackface point of production. Leaving aside the question of how mass audiences responded, one can see, for example, the difference between racial cross-dressing as a vehicle for ethnic self-assertion and as a vehicle for ethnic self-denial in the contrast between Cantor's *Whoopee!* and Jolson's *Jazz Singer.*

The entertainment business anywhere might be expected to celebrate acting as the vehicle for changing identities, but the ethos of American self-making suggests that to watch these American films, as audiences before us did, is also to discover America. Five movies (including *The Jazz Singer*), however significant and widely seen, do not establish the dominance of a pattern. They rather provide evidence for the pattern's existence and — the primary purpose of the analysis that follows — begin to elucidate its character.

Repudiating 1920s nativism, these films celebrate the melting pot. Unlike other racially stigmatized groups, white immigrants can put on and take off their mark of difference. But the freedom promised immigrants to make themselves over points to the vacancy, the violence, the deception, and the melancholy at the core of American self-fashioning. The films make us wonder: Do cross-dressing immigrants buy freedom at the expense of the imprisonment of peoples of color? Or does that freedom itself look less like consent and more like the evasion of crimes, less like making a new self and more like endless disguise?

[13] *Old San Francisco*, dir. Alan Crosland (Warner Brothers, 1927); *The King of Jazz*, dir. John Murray Anderson (Universal Pictures, 1930); *The Singing Fool*, dir. Alan Crosland (Warner Brothers, 1928); *Whoopee!*, dir. Thornton Freeland (Samuel Goldwyn, 1930). Thanks to William Nestrick for his copy of *The King of Jazz*.

[14] Carroll Smith-Rosenberg, "Dis-Covering the Subject of the 'Great Constitutional Discussion,' 1786–1789," *Journal of American History*, 79 (Dec. 1992), 841–73.

[15] James R. Barrett, "Americanization from the Bottom Up: Immigration and the Remaking of the Working Class in the United States, 1880–1930," *Journal of American History*, 79 (Dec. 1992), 1006.

Old San Francisco brings together two staples of early twentieth-century popular fiction and film, the ethnic intermarriage plot and the yellow peril melodrama. Dolores Vasquez, granddaughter of an Old California rancher, and Terrence O'Shaughnessy, son of a San Francisco Irish American, fall in love. The villain, Chris Buckwell, who endangers Dolores's property and her virtue, is exposed during the film as a Eurasian passing as white. *Old San Francisco* may seem like straightforward propaganda for Oriental exclusion, for the Supreme Court decision of the 1920s making "Orientals" ineligible for American citizenship. But that view, adopted in occasional recent attention to the movie, fails to account both for the sympathy shown the Chinese at the beginning of the film and for the orientalist ambience that permeated 1920s Hollywood: movie palaces (like Grauman's Chinese Theatre in Hollywood itself), narrative themes, set decor, costumes, and other objects of eroticized consumption and exotic display. Hollywood orientalism could bring once-forbidden pleasures to the mass movie audience as long as actual Asian Americans were kept out. Instead of illustrating a "social contradiction" between Oriental exclusion and Hollywood's orientalist turn, *Old San Francisco* shows how the one was the enabling condition for the other. Redistributing its initial sympathy for the exploited Asians and Spanish, *Old San Francisco* condemns the Asian racial passer and blesses mobility across ethnic lines. It thereby appropriates orientalism, not for miscegenation, prostitution, and dangerous drugs, but for the libidinized American home.[16]

As *Old San Francisco* begins, the urban Chinese and rural Spanish are equally victims of Anglo enterprise, greed, real estate speculation, and political corruption. Masquerade and sexual desire across group lines turn that opening upside down. As an Anglo, Buckwell confined the Chinese to Chinatown and threatened Old California Spanish property, the latter threat a stand-in for the American taking of Mexican and Indian land. Masquerading as a pious Christian to enter the Vasquez ranch, Buckwell seizes, not the ranch, but Dolores. That sexual violation allows the girl to "penetrate his secret," for when he raises and lowers the cloak over his face, an intertitle announces, "the heathen soul of a Mongol stood revealed."

In turning the Chinese from victims to agents of greed, *Old San Francisco* joins the Oriental exclusionist politics of the California labor and progressive movements.[17] As the attack on Chinese labor slid from the capitalists who employed the Chinese to the Chinese themselves, so the movie reveals the apparent Anglo capi-

[16] *Takao Ozawa v. U.S.*, 260 U.S. 178 (1922); cited in Ronald T. Takaki, *Strangers from a Different Shore: A History of Asian Americans* (Boston, 1989), 208. See Edward Said, *Orientalism* (New York, 1978); William K. Everson, undated program notes, *Old San Francisco* file, Clippings Collection (Pacific Film Archive Library, University Art Museum, University of California, Berkeley); Norman K. Dorn, "San Francisco from Gold Rush to '06 — Warner Bros. Film Revival," *San Francisco Chronicle*, Sept. 9, 1973, pink section, p. 15, *ibid.*; Gina Marchetti, *Romance and the "Yellow Peril": Race, Sex, and Discursive Strategies in Hollywood Fiction* (Berkeley, forthcoming), ch. 1, 2; Nick Browne, "American Film Theory in the Silent Period: Orientalism as Ideological Form," *Wide Angle*, 11 (Oct. 1989), 26–30, esp. 30; Matthew Bernstein, *Walter Wanger: "Independent" in Hollywood* (Berkeley, forthcoming), ch. 4; Michael Rogin, "The Great Mother Domesticated: Sexual Difference and Sexual Indifference in D. W. Griffith's *Intolerance*," *Critical Inquiry*, 15 (Spring 1989), 522–28; Hansen, *Babel and Babylon*.

[17] Alexander Saxton, *The Indispensable Enemy: Labor and the Anti-Chinese Movement in California* (Berkeley, 1971).

OTTO LEDERER   RICHARD TUCKER   BOBBIE GORDON   EUGENIE BESSERER

WARNER OLAND   MAY McAVOY   WARNER OLAND

ANDERS RANDOLF   AUDREY FERRIS   NAT CARR   MYRNA LOY   WILLIAM DEMAREST

Figure 2. Warner Oland as Chris Buckwell in *Old San Francisco* (center right) and as Cantor Rabinowitz in *The Jazz Singer* (center left), from a 1927 souvenir program.

Warner Oland, cast as the cantor father in *The Jazz Singer,* plays the Oriental villain in *Old San Francisco. The Jazz Singer*'s souvenir program featured two pictures of Oland (the only actor besides Jolson so honored), one as evil Oriental and the other as patriarchal Jew. (See figure 2.) The double casting points to traits united in the Jewish patriarch that are split between Buckwell and Grandfather Vasquez. Oland's two roles suggest the orientalist connections between the stereotyped races — between Oland as Mongol and the Jewish moguls, for example. But *The Jazz*

talist as an Oriental. The surveyors who invade the Vasquez ranch are Buckwell's agents, revenging his failed invasion of the Vasquez woman. As the source of the threat shifts from white to Asian, the target shifts from property in land to property in women. Putting yellow faces on what it had earlier depicted as an Anglo menace, *Old San Francisco* endorses what it had first bemoaned, the passing (in both senses) of the California Spanish. Grandfather Vasquez's prophecy that "the city will bury us beneath an alien civilization" is at once fulfilled and reversed: the movie transfers alienness from Anglos who endanger Spanish to Orientals who menace whites. Instead of threatening the independent freehold and traditional culture, the "alien civilization" threatens white female virtue. Instead of burying Old California, the alien civilization will itself be buried in the film's climax, the San Francisco earthquake.

Hollywood movies of the 1920s and 1930s typically portrayed Latins as "lazy peasants and wily señoritas." *Old San Francisco* and *The Jazz Singer,* by contrast, repudiated nativist prejudice against Latins and Jews. Setting Terrence's love for Dolores against Buckwell's lust, *Old San Francisco* blesses attraction across ethnic lines. As in other ethnic intermarriage movies of Hollywood's early years, sympathy is distributed between the older generation's resistance and the younger generation's desire. Whichever side they ultimately choose, generational conflict movies acknowledge the pull of Old World ties.[18]

Old San Francisco scores its victory for love when the force keeping the lovers apart is no longer the parental victim (who dies failing to protect his granddaughter) but the racial villain. The Oriental passing as white takes the place of the Spanish grandfather in the triangle with the granddaughter and Irish lover. Once illegitimate desire moves from property to sex and is exposed as racial passing, the Spanish girl can marry the Irish boy and embrace American enterprise. Grandfather Vasquez's insistence that "blood will tell" and that his granddaughter should marry her Spanish suitor, Terrence's rival, falls to the younger Spaniard's cowardly inability to defend granddaughter and ranch. But far from repudiating blood for love, Sollors's descent for consent, *Old San Francisco* illustrates the process Michel Foucault has described that substitutes one exclusion for another, as feudally based blood exclusiveness is replaced with democratically based exclusion of Chinese blood. *Yellow* may be a term of character in the West, distinguishing some Spaniards, like some Anglos, from others. But the term also denotes an Oriental racial trait that crossdressing cannot hide.[19]

[18] Patricia Erens, *The Jew in American Cinema* (Bloomington, 1984), 64–164; Rogin, "Blackface, White Noise," 422–28; Ana M. Lopez, "Are All Latins from Manhattan? Hollywood, Ethnography, and Cultural Colonialism," in *Unspeakable Images: Ethnicity and the American Cinema,* ed. Lester D. Friedman (Urbana, 1991), 406–13. For the reference to "wily señoritas," see *ibid.,* 406–7.

[19] Michel Foucault, *The History of Sexuality,* vol. I: *An Introduction,* trans. Robert Hurley (New York, 1978), 124. Sollors acknowledges the shift from aristocratic blue, to racialized black, blood but fails to see how that transfer of taboos calls into question his subsumption of race by ethnicity. Thus his enthusiasm not simply for the intermarriage praised in Zangwill's *Melting Pot* but also for the playwright's "spiritual miscegenation" collapses racial expropriation into ethnic romance. See Sollors, *Beyond Ethnicity,* 38, 71.

Singer's blackface links Jews and blacks in order to separate them; *Old San Francisco* rejoins the Chinese passing as white to his own people.[20]

As in *The Jazz Singer,* racial masquerade transfers value from traditional, patriarchal family to melting pot America. *The Jazz Singer* blesses Jewish blackface, whereas *Old San Francisco* condemns racial passing. But the cross-dressing Chinese villain hides the movie's own racial transfer: Asian masquerades as white in the story, but the actor playing the Asian passing as white is himself white passing as Asian. Buckwell's "unknown origins" are the shadow underside of the humble beginnings of the Jacksonian self-made man and of the typical movie mogul.

The specter of miscegenation, defused when the racially ambiguous Jew dons blackface and thereby moves from the "Oriental" to the white category, takes over *Old San Francisco.* The California law prohibiting miscegenation defined it as intermarriage between the white race and the "negro, mulatto, or Mongolian."[21] Racial cross-dressing facilitates intermarriage, not between whites and people of color, but between whites divided by ethnic lines. Put more exactly, racial masquerade moves white ethnics from a racially liminal to a white identity. Racial cross-dressing in both films collapses the division separating Anglos from some other Americans, but it allows Spanish and Jew in by keeping Asian and black out. Buckwell's crime is not passing; it is the threat to white womanhood from his Oriental blood.

Buckwell's Chinese concubine, revealed with the exposure of his identity, marks the shift from Asian victims to Asian villains. She inherits the sexual menace of the Eurasian femme fatale. The dark, sultry Dolores is whitened by contrast with Buckwell's concubine, who helps kidnap her, and sympathy for Dolores as Spanish granddaughter is replaced by sympathy for her as victim of Asian desire. As sexual melodrama covers over the dispossession of Mexican land, so the expression of materialism as menace shifts from Anglo commercial speculation to Chinese opium, jewelry, and depravity.

When he is exposed as Oriental, Buckwell carries Dolores to a Chinatown opium den and house of prostitution. Dolores is stripped of the mourning black she had put on for her grandfather, dressed in bridal white, and displayed for sale. Rotated before Oriental eyes, touched by Oriental hands, Dolores four times tries to escape from the closed room. The camera follows her in four different directions, each time to find an Asian blocking the door.

New York's Chinatown, wrote Jacob Riis, was "honey-combed with scores of the conventional households of the Chinese quarter: the men worshippers of Joss, the women all white, girls nearly always of tender age, worshipping nothing save the pipe that has enslaved them body and soul." That is to be Dolores's fate. In actuality Chinese girls were the victims of the Chinatown traffic in women, a product of the grossly unbalanced sex ratio perpetuated by the Chinese exclusion laws. *Old San*

---

[20] *"Jazz Singer* Souvenir Program," in *Souvenir Programs of Twelve Classic Movies, 1927–1941,* ed. Miles Kreuger (New York, 1971), 13. On Jewish orientalism, see Rogin, "Blackface, White Noise," 440.
[21] Takaki, *Strangers from a Different Shore,* 102.

Francisco, like the yellow peril pulp novels from which it derived, turned the victimized woman white.[22]

Victimization Americanizes and thus whitens Dolores, and the movie discovers whites as the true victims. Ancestors are either impotent, if Spanish, or monstrous, if Chinese. But just as her grandfather could not preserve her Spanish blood, so her lover cannot protect her white blood. Terrence's Irish brogue, intrusive in the early titles, disappears as he "becomes acclimated," in the words of *Variety.*[23] Nonetheless, even as American, he is powerless against the mass of Asians. Dolores prays to God, and He sends the San Francisco earthquake. A mad, Old Testament–quoting derelict had earlier called God's curses down on Buckwell and mammon; as Buckwell is being crushed, he sees the prophet again. The jeremiad directed against Buckwell as agent of modern materialism is fulfilled against the Asian as white slaver.

Prayer and divine intervention also save Cecil B. De Mille's heroines, infected by leprosy passed from a Eurasian seductress in *The Ten Commandments* (1923) and by atheism in *The Godless Girl* (1928).[24] Sign that the individual male subject is helpless on his own, these *di ex machina* invoke the power, not of God, but of Hollywood. Orchestrated crowd scenes of panic and the sight and sound of crashing, burning buildings testify to the authority of Hollywood special effects. Profane technological progress threatened the Vasquez ranch; the miracles of modern technology rescue the Vasquez woman.

Earthquake and fire destroy Chinatown, the modern Sodom and Gomorrah. Chinatown is a melting pot, the crucible in whose burning interior a new American identity forms. Though this Christian meaning is not intended by the film, the redemptive sacrifice of Chinatown gives birth to the American family. Having filmed Chinatown's destruction from inside and within, the camera pulls back for an aerial view of "the cleansed streets of the modern quarter" built on Chinese-American ruins. The aerial perspective turns into a shot from the point of view of Dolores and Terrence, as they look out over the city. Removed from the urban carnage, they constitute the American family, for the camera cuts from their distant perspective to the baby in their arms.

Spanish and Chinese no longer share pariah status as the victims of American progress. Civilization has confiscated the productive property of Chinese and Old California Spanish, but the Spanish daughter has gained a compensatory domestic space. There, like other Americans, she enjoys orientalist property — jazz records, for example — in consumption and display. As the teeming crowds of immigrants are destroyed, the individualist, rural Spanish move into the American home. Observers

---

[22] Riis, "How the Other Half Lives," 155; William F. Wu, *The Yellow Peril: Chinese Americans in American Fiction, 1850–1940* (Hamden, 1982); Takaki, *Strangers from a Different Shore,* 14, 41, 121–23. For the identification of the 1927 pulp novel by Allie Lowe Miles from which Darryl Zanuck wrote the screenplay for *Old San Francisco,* see Dorn, "San Francisco from Gold Rush to '06," 15.

[23] Review of *Old San Francisco,* June 29, 1927, in *Variety Film Reviews, 1907–1980* (16 vols., New York, 1983), III, n.p.

[24] *The Ten Commandments,* dir. Cecil B. De Mille (Famous Players–Lasky, 1923); *The Godless Girl,* dir. Cecil B. De Mille (C.B. De Mille Productions, 1928).

of the reformed, urban scene, the melting pot couple are no longer interactive members of it.[25] They stand for the movie's spectators, whose position they have achieved. The medium is the message, for just as the special effects of Hollywood prove more powerful than Buckwell's makeup, and his masquerade hides Hollywood's own, so the sign of achieved Americanization is passively to observe the spectacle of making Americans. The Warner brothers were preparing to move that story closer to their home, in *The Jazz Singer.* The proceeds of *Old San Francisco's* first night in New York went to benefit the Hebrew Orphan's Asylum.[26]

Old San Francisco expels one alien to incorporate another; *The King of Jazz* appropriates African-American music to Americanize immigrants and exclude blacks. The link between the Dark Continent and the melting pot, to which Abraham Cahan's translation of *Scribner's* article about cannibalism pointed, becomes explicit in *The King of Jazz.* Part of the tradition that runs from blackface minstrelsy through *The Jazz Singer* and *Babes in Arms, The King of Jazz* makes Americans out of American entertainment. Since that entertainment is American thanks to its African-American origins, "the melting pot of music" in *The King of Jazz* digests and expels its own beginnings. Asian Americans are a visible presence in *Old San Francisco;* their elimination comprises the plot. African Americans are an absent presence in *The King of Jazz* because their exclusion sets the movie in motion. But closeness is the precondition for separation in both movies, the method by which the properties of one group are expropriated for another. The property in *Old San Francisco* is Old California / Spanish / Indian land and orientalist eroticism; in *The King of Jazz* it is African-American labor and emotional expression.

Antebellum blackface minstrelsy grounded American popular culture in expropriated black production. Since myths of minstrelsy's origins insisted on the authenticity of blackface imitations, they revealed what Eric Lott has recently labeled the reciprocal problems of love and theft. Black and white closeness (the precondition for the authenticity of blackface) raised the specter of interracial love, whose material basis was the sexual exploitation of slave women, but whose transgressive feature in minstrelsy, an originally all-male, transvestite entertainment form, was homoeroticism. But to create distance by excluding actual blacks from performance raised the specter of theft; its material basis was slave labor.[27]

The popular music of the jazz age, deriving from ragtime, New Orleans bands, and other black performance styles, inherited minstrelsy's obsession with origins. An obligatory black man who made rudimentary noises, in the jazz myth of origins,

[25] Cf. Lawrence W. Levine, *Highbrow/Lowbrow: The Emergence of Cultural Hierarchy in America* (Cambridge, Mass., 1988), 171–84, 197–200.

[26] Mordaunt Hall, review of *Old San Francisco,* June 22, 1927, in *New York Times Film Reviews* (6 vols., New York, 1970), I, 372.

[27] Eric Lott, "Love and Theft: The Racial Unconscious of Blackface Minstrelsy," *Representations* (no. 39, Summer 1992), 23–50. On the origins of minstrelsy in Jacksonian mass politics and culture, see Saxton, *Rise and Fall of the White Republic,* 165–82.

gave the music its name; for Paul Whiteman, he was "that jazzy darky player, named James Brown and called Jas." Minstrelsy had begun as a ribald, vulgar popular cultural form, and that is how the opponents of jazz saw it. Defending itself against that accusation, the melting pot music of the jazz age (not to be confused with the jazz of King Oliver, Jelly Roll Morton, or, though they played alongside blackface acts for white audiences in segregated clubs, Fletcher Henderson and Duke Ellington), stressed the distance jazz had traveled from its primitive, African, slave roots.[28]

Advocates of jazz age music argue that whites transformed black raw material into art. "Our whole present music is derived from the negro," Gilbert Seldes insisted in 1924. Negroes simply were their primitive music, writers in the mass-circulation magazines and newspapers explained. Whites did the skilled labor of musical arrangement and intelligent performance. "The negro side" of jazz, as Seldes put it,

> expresses something which underlies a great deal of America—our independence, our carelessness, our frankness, and gaiety. In each of these the negro is more intense than we are, and we surpass him when we combine a more varied and more intelligent life with his instinctive qualities. . . . The greatest art is likely to be that in which an uncorrupted sensibility is *worked* by a creative intelligence.

Having resolved the problem of theft by assigning labor to whites, Seldes gave an illustration: "Nowhere is the failure of the negro to exploit his gifts more obvious than in the use he has made of the jazz orchestra . . . no negro band has yet come up to the level of the best white ones, and the leader of the best of all, by a little joke, is called Whiteman."[29]

Paul Whiteman was the acknowledged king of jazz, and, like "King Jazz," all the "Jazz Kings" celebrated in the 1926 *Literary Digest* article of that title were white. Like Seldes, Whiteman insisted on the African origins of jazz. But in his autobiography and in music critic Henry Osgood's book on jazz, mostly anonymous African Americans (none are named by Osgood) supply the prehistory of the music, replaced by named, white performers when the author reaches what he calls jazz.[30]

"Jazz is the spirit of a new country, . . . the essence of America," the music "of the common people," Whiteman proclaimed. Standing against an imitative, "highbrow," Europe-oriented culture, it inherited the American nationalism of Walt Whitman, Nathaniel Hawthorne, and Edgar Allan Poe. "Americans—and the term included Slavs, Teutons, Latins, Orientals, [were] welded into one great mass as if

---

[28] Paul Whiteman and Mary Margaret McBride, *Jazz* (New York, 1926), 122; Samuel B. Charters and Leonard Kunstadt, *Jazz: A History of the New York Scene* (New York, 1981), 246. On the relationship of the jazz age to jazz, see Rogin, "Blackface, White Noise," 447–49, and the sources there cited.

[29] Gilbert Seldes, *The Seven Lively Arts* (New York, 1957), 98–100. The first version of this book was published in 1924.

[30] "King Jazz and the Jazz Kings," *Literary Digest*, Jan. 30, 1926, pp. 37–42; Whiteman and McBride, *Jazz*, 3–4, 17, 176, 265; Osgood, *So This Is Jazz*; William Weaver, "Jazz in Jackets: Cultural Commodification in the Jazz Age," seminar paper, Johns Hopkins University, 1988 (in Michael Rogin's possession).

by the giant machines they tended," wrote Whiteman. Jazz, removed from its origins in African-American labor and community, gave these machine age workers their leisure-time release. Since only Americans could express the national music, "the most important item in the jazz equipment is that each player shall be American"; while Whiteman included "the nationalized citizens" of foreign ancestry in his band, he, like all other white band leaders of the 1920s, excluded African Americans.[31]

Whiteman performed that exclusion in his 1924 concert at Aeolian Hall in New York City (according to one historian, second only to talking pictures in importance for 1920s popular music) and in *The King of Jazz*. The concert, announced Isaac Goldberg, the biographer of George Gershwin, was an "Emancipation Proclamation, in which slavery to European formalism was signed away." Whiteman was emancipating jazz from enslavement not just to Europeans but also to black Americans. He took his orchestra, as the movie reviewer Creighton Peet put it, "into the sacred precincts of Aeolian Hall in an attempt to make an honest woman of Jazz, at that time a cheap and notorious wench." The orchestra played "The Livery Stable Blues," complete with imitation barnyard noises, to show how far the music had traveled, in Whiteman's account, "from the day of discordant early jazz to the melodious form of the present." This "crude jazz of the past" was counterposed to George Gershwin's "Rhapsody in Blue."[32]

Exclusion reinforced expropriation. "The Livery Stable Blues" came from "an old Negro melody," Whiteman acknowledged. But he endorsed a judge's dismissal of a copyright infringement suit brought against the Original Dixieland Jazz Band (ODJB), the mendaciously named white group whose hit record of that song launched the jazz age. "As to the moral aspects of the theft, there aren't any," Whiteman concluded. The ODJB served not only to deflect the accusation of theft away from Whiteman but also to move his band one safe step further from the African-American original.[33]

Advanced technique plays a similar distancing function in *The King of Jazz*. Just as the prologue to *Old San Francisco* announces the Anglo displacement of the Spanish, Whiteman's prologue introduces the white appropriation of Africa. It does so in a cartoon that, Whiteman explains, will show how he became king of jazz. The scene opens on the rotund, immaculately dressed band leader "big game hunting in darkest Africa." When a lion chases Whiteman and is about to devour him, the white hunter takes out a violin and plays. The lion begins to dance; instead of swallowing Whiteman, his wide open mouth speaks the word Al Jolson had made famous, "Mammy." Africans and snakes dance as Whiteman continues to play. Far from being their own product, music calms the primitives. It turns them into plan-

[31] Whiteman and McBride, *Jazz*, 15, 19, 27–28, 122–27, 178, 237.

[32] Arnold Shaw, *The Jazz Age: Popular Music in the 1920s* (New York, 1987), 47–53; Isaac Goldberg, *George Gershwin* (New York, 1931), 136; Creighton Peet, "The Movies," *Outlook and Independent*, May 14, 1930, p. 72; Whiteman and McBride, *Jazz*, 94–99.

[33] Whiteman and McBride, *Jazz*, 178–79.

tation, blackface mammies. A soothing, nurturing mouth naming the black nurse of white boys and men replaces the lion's devouring orifice. Jazz, which here domesticates Africans into creatures on which white men feed, is the trophy the white hunter brings back from Africa.

Having served their originary function, African Americans are, with two exceptions, excluded from the musical numbers and vaudeville sketches that constitute *The King of Jazz*. One appearance repeats a genteel version of the opening cartoon. Jazz combines the most primitive and the most modern elements, intones a voiceover, "for jazz was born from the African jungle to the beating of voodoo drums." The camera shows first a blacked-up, nearly nude, male dancer, then white female ballroom performers, finally Gershwin's "Rhapsody in Blue." The primitive male dancer is segregated from the women whose pleasure he inspires. For the libidinal character of jazz flirted with sexual transgression along not just gender (pleasure for respectable women) but also racial lines.

Jazz, the product of "musical miscegenation" (in Isaac Goldberg's phrase), could not afford to be seen as promoting interracial sex. The "Mammy" aspect of jazz spilled over into sexual excitement, and the only moment in *King of Jazz* where an actual black person appears flirts with the sexual risk, only to neutralize it. Whiteman, filmed from behind and apparently alone, conducts from a park bench as white couples dance; the number is called "Public Park." Each band member sings and dances with a girl on his arm. Whiteman turns around in the middle of the scene to reveal a little black girl on his lap. Repeating the paternalist racial relation established in the opening cartoon, the interracial couple is safely set off, as white father and black child, from the adult, dancing partners. Peet had wondered to what sort of child Whiteman's "honest woman" jazz would give birth. Paternalist miscegenation produces a musical baby that is not the offspring of interracial, sexual exploitation but the catalyst of romance between whites.[34]

The place of African Americans in *The King of Jazz*, culturally routine, provoked no critical comment. Attending instead to the film's trick photography, reviewers divided on whether the photographic effects (Whiteman's band emerges, for example, from his briefcase) enhanced or detracted from the music. But all praised the opening cartoon and the "Melting Pot" finale, for the new technology and the new music joined together in the film's climax to make Americans.[35]

In a scene perhaps borrowed from the graduation ceremony at the Ford Motor Company's Highland Park Model T assembly plant that James Barrett describes, Whiteman stirs a giant steaming pot. A voice-over declaims, "America is a melting pot of music, where the melodies of all nations are fused into one great new rhythm." Suitably costumed singers and dancers perform their national music, one

[34] Isaac Goldberg, "Aaron Copland and His Jazz," *American Mercury*, 12 (Sept. 1927), 63–64; Peet, "Movies," 72.
[35] Richard Dana Skinner, review of *The King of Jazz, Commonweal*, May 21, 1930, p. 80; Peet, "Movies," 72; review of *The King of Jazz, Variety*, May 3, 1930, *Variety Film Reviews*, III, n.p; review of *The King of Jazz, Nation*, May 28, 1930, p. 633; review of *The King of Jazz, Time*, May 12, 1930, p. 64.

Figure 3. The Paul Whiteman band in redface. *Courtesy Whiteman Collection, Williamsiana Collections, Williams College Archives.*

group after another. Ethnic insignias identify English, Italians, Spanish, Scots, Germans, Irish, Mexicans, Russians, and Poles (or Jews). "The incredible pressure was bound to blow off the lid" of machine-tending, ethnically diverse, industrial America, Whiteman wrote in his autobiography, "and it might conceivably plunge a whole nation into nervous prostration or insanity." Instead of the lid blowing off the melting pot of music after the nine different ethnic performances, out from the enormous base of the pot dances a chorus line of American cowgirls. (Figure 3, another version of Americanization, shows Whiteman and his band dressed as Indians.) "For sheer spectacle, the Melting Pot finale can't be beat," enthused *Photoplay.* The movie ends with couples from the different nations (one man wears a yarmulke) dancing to American music.[36]

Israel Zangwill's cauldron melted down Old World metals to produce a stronger alloy. But Whiteman's "restorative," "brewing in New Orleans . . . to the national

[36] Barrett, "Americanization from the Bottom Up," 996. Mordaunt Hall, review of *The King of Jazz,* May 30, 1930, in *New York Times Film Reviews* (6 vols., New York, 1970), I, 623; Whiteman and McBride, *Jazz,* 15; "King of Jazz," *Photoplay,* 38 (June 1930), 56, in *Selected Film Criticism, 1921–1930,* ed. Anthony Slide (Metuchen, 1982), 157.

nerve complaint," invokes a cooking pot as well as a crucible. The cooking pot, instead of being a cauldron in which cannibalism devours civilization, harks back to the maternal origins of melting pot imagery. The breasts and lap of New World nature, in eighteenth-century visual and linguistic depictions, gave birth to a new American man. From that vantage point, the finale of *The King of Jazz* inverts the prologue, for jazz turns the devouring lion's mouth into the vehicle for cooking up a new, American stew, making Americans out of the separate ingredients of the old.[37]

But African Americans, like the Asian Americans of *Old San Francisco,* are the melting pot medium; like them, they are not included in the final message. No African or Caribbean nation enters the melting pot of music; no dark skins (as in *Old San Francisco,* all the Mexicans are white) dance as members of their own nations or in the American melting pot. By the compensatory cultural logic of the jazz age, Whiteman's music has nothing to do with jazz.

All the movies discussed here played variations on themes in *The Jazz Singer;* the central subject of *The Singing Fool* was gender. *The Jazz Singer,* I have elsewhere argued, feminized its protagonist. Singing in blackface the price of success, the loss of home that joined immigrant to native-born, mobile American, the jazz singer crossed the border not only between white and black but also between desire for and identification with the woman. If *Old San Francisco* foreshadowed the first talking picture's ethnic example, *The Singing Fool* followed its gender example. Perhaps because blackface domestic tragedy drained of its ethnic particularism had a wider appeal, *The Singing Fool* was the top box office success of its time. Jolson's Jewishness, *The Jazz Singer*'s subject, is barely acknowledged, but it is the condition of the gender cross-dressing.[38]

In minstrel ideology, blackface wildness invoked Africa, and blackface nostalgia invoked the lost plantation. Minstrel consciousness not only repressed the savagery experienced by slaves on plantations; it also appropriated for voluntary immigrants and migrants to the New World the longing for home of the single group of Americans stolen from their Old World homes. Jolson sings loss in his first movie, moreover, to facilitate gain. Blackface spectacle looking backward, to Jewish mother and Russian/plantation home, projects narrative progress forward for the immigrant son. The balance shifts from gain to loss in *The Singing Fool.* The entertainer who had used blackface to move from Jew to American and to sing "My Mammy" now uses it to become mammy and to mourn the loss of his child.

The Singing Fool's opening shots invite us into Blackie Joe's, the cabaret where Al Stone, the singing waiter, performs. The peephole through which prospective

---

[37] Sollors, *Beyond Ethnicity,* 75–99; Whiteman and McBride, *Jazz,* 17.
[38] On feminization in *The Jazz Singer,* see Rogin, "Blackface, White Noise," 441–44. Box office figures are from William K. Everson, *American Silent Film* (New York, 1978), 373–74.

Figure 4. The Al Stone family in *The Singing Fool*. © 1928 Turner
Entertainment Co. All rights reserved.

guests are inspected marks the speakeasy as illicit; the mobile camera is the film
audience's peephole, moving up to, in, and around the hidden room. The first
image of Molly, shot from below, shows her lying on a dressing room bed with one
long, thin, bare leg crossed over the other. The intrusive, voyeuristic camera
fetishizes the showgirl leg as the sign of female sexuality. Sexual aggression is assigned to the woman, however, not simply employed to display her. Molly's foot will
crush the sheet on which Al has written her a song.

Silent for its opening, *The Singing Fool* switches to sound for Al to sing that song.
As in *The Jazz Singer*, Jolson introduces his first song in *The Singing Fool*'s initial
lip-synched talking sequence. Both scenes display the famous voice and patter to
celebrate talking pictures and to make Jolson's sound the instrument of his success.
Song raises the Jolson character to stardom in both movies and wins him his girl.
Louis Marcus, a producer in Blackie Joe's audience, gives Al his chance. The naming
of the fatherly producer as Jewish moves ethnicity from the jazz singer and his family
to a show business impresario.

But in *The Singing Fool,* paternal permission, removing the barrier between the
son and his object of desire, proves a deeper obstacle to romance than paternal pro-

hibition in *The Jazz Singer*. The exchange of looks between Molly and Al that registers their desire follows Molly's interception of an approving look from Marcus to Al. She kisses Al after he sings "It All Depends on You," the song she had originally rejected; the kiss is a performance for the producer. Molly brings Al to Marcus; the three form a triangle, Molly between the two men. Audience and producer approval have created desire in Molly, but it is triangulated desire.

Molly marries Al only because Marcus has come between them. Her lover replaces the producer in the next section of the film. Montage reviews real-life Jolson hits as a voice-over announces, "In the following four years, Al wore out eight pianos, rhymed 'Mammy' with 'Alabammy' 981 times—and did more for Dixie than Robert E. Lee." But the arm that reaches out to a close-up of Molly's face, pinches her cheek and pulls her off screen, is revealed to belong to another man. As eager son and cuckolded husband, Al borders on the ridiculous.

The triangle introduced in the next scene, Al, Molly, and their child, makes Al the vehicle for pathos. Al embraces and caresses Sonny Boy; cut to Molly alone in bed. (See figure 4.) Al sings "Sonny Boy" to the toddler and puts him to sleep; Molly primps alone before her mirror. Molly refuses Al's kisses and terms of endearment; the child enters the bedroom to interrupt their fight. Sonny Boy goes to his father; Al, carrying the child back to his bedroom, sings "Sonny Boy" again. Cut to Molly alone in bed, back to Al rocking Sonny Boy. In the next scene, Al calls home from the cabaret to discover that Molly has taken Sonny Boy and left him.

The most successful film of the jazz age inverts the stereotypical sex roles. Wife wants sex; husband wants affection. Wife has lover; husband has child. Wife looks nonmaternal, with exposed legs and no breasts; husband rocks baby. Wife leaves home for lover and career; husband mourns the loss of his child.

When Al returns to his empty house, *The Singing Fool* reverts to silence for the first time since his opening song. In *The Jazz Singer*, a paternal "Stop!" silenced the jazz singer, interrupting the romance between mother and son. In *The Singing Fool* too a transgressive maternal relationship is punished, but this one features Al, not as son who wants mother, but as mother who wants son. Success entails loss in the plots and in the lost sound of these films. But whereas the jazz singer wanted both Jewish mother and jazz, the singing fool (like many career women) wants both career and child.

Moving back and forth between silence and sound to show Al's penultimate farewell to his son and to register his decline and the recovery of his career, *The Singing Fool* climaxes when Al learns that Sonny Boy is dying. Al, the nursing father, holds the child to his breast; he sings "Sonny Boy" and rocks him to sleep. Carrying the dying child in his arms, Al is Uncle Tom in Edwin Porter's film version of *Uncle Tom's Cabin*, carrying the dead little Eva.[39] Cut to Molly, slim and alone, all in white. The jazz singer killed his father by becoming a blackface singer rather than a cantor. The singing fool, by contrast, is an innocent; an abandoning mother destroys his home and is to blame for the death of their son.

---

[39] *Uncle Tom's Cabin*, dir. Edwin S. Porter (Edison, 1903).

The jazz singer Americanized himself through blackface, not just by choosing New World entertainment over Old World ritual but also by providing the emotional form to mourn the loss of the old. Blackface, I have argued, was the transitional object whose emotional linkage to a world left behind facilitated movement forward and away. Conflating Jewish and plantation home, blackface linked agrarian (immigrant and American) past to urban, industrial future.[40] Blackface provides the emotional climax, the catharsis, of *The Jazz Singer; The Singing Fool,* to that same purpose, withholds blackface (after the opening shot of the blackface performer) until the film's final scene.

"I'll feel better if I try to work," says Al, and he begins to apply burnt cork. He puts it on slowly, covering neck, nose, cheeks, top of head. As the catatonic Al, paralyzed by grief, disappears under the cork, a close-up shows his expressive, sad, blacked face, lips exaggerated, holding back tears. The hit of the first Vitaphone program was Giovanni Martinelli performing "Vesti la Giubba," and the great tenor's clown-costumed, whiteface, rendition of Pagliacci's grief may well have encouraged Warner Brothers to make *The Jazz Singer* and *The Singing Fool.* In celebrating performance as vehicle for emotional intensity, Hollywood celebrated itself, with a self-consciousness about losing self-consciousness that complicates descriptions of classic Hollywood's illusionistic, narrative realism. Blackface gives full expression to the feelings that would otherwise lock Al in frozen melancholia. Faking cheerfulness when he relinquishes Sonny Boy and nonchalance when he is rescued from starvation, catatonic when Sonny Boy dies, Al cries real tears for the first time in blackface performance. The jazz singer's acting is the vehicle for changing identities in order to Americanize; the singing fool's acting recovers the feelings of abandonment concomitant to the change. The line "I still have you, Sonny Boy" anticipates the theft of the child by the mother and later holds onto a son present only in the ability of talking pictures to make absence present and thereby memorialize loss. The singing fool's performance facilitates authenticity, but at the expense of those supposed to have closer access to feeling, African Americans and women.[41]

The Singing Fool was probably a woman's film, like the 1930s weepies that followed it. Women were a larger film audience than men. If Rudolph Valentino was the object of women moviegoers' sexualized, maternal gaze, the singing fool offered maternal mouth and breast. Just as the Valentino cult disturbed traditional defenders of male sexual privilege, so *The Singing Fool,* challenging film theorists' stereotypes of the male gaze, reproached the sexually aggressive, dominating man. But *The Singing Fool's* target was less the traditional man than the new woman. The feminized man wins sympathy at the expense of the sexual, abandoning

40 Rogin, "Blackface, White Noise," 444–49. On transitional objects, see D. W. Winnicott, *Playing and Reality* (New York, 1982), 1–25.

41 Richard Koszarski, "On the Record: Seeing and Hearing Vitaphone," in *Dawn of Sound,* ed. Mary Lea Bandy (New York, 1989), 18. Cf. David Bordwell et al., *The Classical Hollywood Cinema* (New York, 1985), 3–39.

woman. If *The Singing Fool* is an early version of male feminism, then it is a precursor of *Kramer v. Kramer.*[42]

Blackface is the method of Al's maternalization. The portrayal of the black man as mother not only (as in *Uncle Tom's Cabin*) reproaches the white woman who refuses to play that role but also makes the black man nurture whites. Blackface operates as vehicle for sexual as for ethnic mobility by offering freedom for whites at the price of fixedness for blacks. The white man plays with a nurturing, emotional identity that fixes black man, like white woman, as mother and child. The forbidden liaison between black man and white woman is realized in the black man as mammy. Cross-dressing, as *Old San Francisco* also testifies, is not reversible across race and gender lines.

In *The Jazz Singer,* the Jolson figure escapes ethnic imprisonment. Cantor Rabinowitz, fixed in a traditional identity, sings Kol Nidre as ritual. His grown son, ethnic only in performing the sacred number, can take or leave his ethnicity; in *The Singing Fool,* he may seem to leave it behind. But Jewishness also placed a limit on the gentile dreams Jolson could interpret to his mass audience. A liminal figure, he was not permitted full, patriarchal authority. For the Jew to perform his transitional functions in classic Hollywood, linking immigrant to American and man to woman, he had to know his place. That is the message of the comedy that brings together ethnic and sexual cross-dressing, blackface and the myth of the West: Eddie Cantor's *Whoopee!*

Whoopee! begins where *The King of Jazz* ends, with a western production number. Instead of dancing out of a melting pot, cowgirls join with cowboys to form the spokes of a human wheel. But Busby Berkeley's wagon wheel explicitly performs the function the melting pot pretends not to do; like drawn-up covered wagons, the wheel excludes those outside its circle. The first outsider is Henry (Eddie Cantor), a hypochondriacal Jewish weakling out of place in the West. The second is Wanenis, the Indian in love with Sally, the white girl whose marriage to Sheriff Bob the wagon wheel number celebrates. Indian and Jew come together, like Asian and Spaniard in *Old San Francisco,* as those threatened by American progress.

Unlike *Old San Francisco,* however, *Whoopee!* dwells on the relationship between the excluded rather than substituting one group for the other. The comic tie between Indian and Jew places *Whoopee!* in a tradition of Jewish/Indian spoofs, from Yiddish theater and vaudeville to *Blazing Saddles* (1974), productions that typically mock the white man's tragic, noble savage, intermarriage story. The first movie in which Cantor starred, *Whoopee!* may also derive from Cantor's friendship with the part-Cherokee "cowboy," Will Rogers, who wrote the introduction to Cantor's autobiography. The jazz singer, first successful in San Francisco, exemplifies the Turner

---

[42] Hansen, *Babel and Babylon,* 245–94; *Kramer v. Kramer,* dir. Robert Benton (Columbia, 1979).

Figure 5. Eddie Cantor in redface advertising *Whoopee!* in the *New Yorker,* Oct. 6, 1930.

thesis, for he loses his ethnic particularism on the frontier. When the Jew goes West as vaudeville Jew, as Eddie Cantor, he at once facilitates and subverts the melting pot.[43]

Whoopee! disturbs not just ethnic and racial boundaries but, like *The Singing Fool,* sexual ones as well. Cantor's stereotypical Jew is a timid neurasthenic. If the high intermarriage plot brings together white girl and noble savage, the low one makes Henry the target of sexually aggressive ("I like weak men") Nurse Custer.

Whoopee! makes humor from the outsider status of Indians and Jews. Indian burlesque was a vaudeville feature; Cantor's first job was in a review called *Indian Maidens.* "I'm only a small part Indian," Wanenis tells Henry. "How small?" "My grandfather married a white girl." "So did mine," responds Henry. He speaks as a white man, but since Jews were Oriental, racially stigmatized, and themselves the

<hr>

[43] Sollors, *Beyond Ethnicity,* 131–48; Charles Musser, "Ethnicity, Role-Playing, and American Film Comedy: From *Chinese Laundry Scene* to *Whoopee* (1894–1930)," in *Unspeakable Images,* ed. Friedman, 62; Ella Shohat, "Ethnics-in-Relation: Toward a Multicultural Reading of American Cinema," *ibid.,* 230, 245; *Blazing Saddles,* dir. Mel Brooks (Warner Brothers, 1974); Eddie Cantor, as told to David Freedman, *My Life Is in Your Hands* (New York, 1928). (I am indebted to Mark Slobin for directing me to this source.) *Whoopee!* is also an early example of the male buddy film, pairing a straight, macho man with a clownish feminized cross-dresser (Dean Martin and Jerry Lewis, Bing Crosby and Bob Hope). See Rebecca Bell-Mettereau, *Hollywood Androgyny* (New York, 1985), 23.

protagonists of intermarriage plots, the joke has a double edge. Is or is not this "half-breed," as Henry calls himself, a member of the group into which Wanenis wants to marry? "I've gone to your schools," Wanenis explains to Henry, who asks, "An Indian in a Hebrew school?"[44]

Whoopee! also makes fun of the opposite crossover, the Indianization of whites, by making its Dances with Wolves a Jew. After a captivity narrative spoof places Henry and Sally among the Indians, Wanenis's father ("Old Black Eagle, not old man Segal," sings Cantor to the tune of "Old Man River") invites Henry to join his tribe. Disguised as an Indian ("Me big chief Izzy Horowitz"), Henry adopts a Jewish accent to haggle over the price of an Indian blanket and doll he is selling to a rich white man. The message is that Jews would have gotten a better price for their land. Ads for *Whoopee!* show Cantor wearing Indian feathers, but, as in the movie, red-face does not disguise but rather calls attention to the Jew wearing the costume. (See figure 5.) Claiming to be an Indian fire chief, Henry holds a Pueblo wall scaler and his nose: "Here's my hook and ladder."[45]

Degrading physical humor and violations of bodily integrity spread from ethnic jokes to sexual relations. Henry takes pills and receives injections from Nurse Custer. He and the rich white man roll around on the ground examining each other's surgical scars. When the half-naked Wanenis appears in Indian feathers, Henry subjects him to a minute, intimate, physical inspection. These plays with the grotesque body, borrowed from blackface minstrelsy and Cantor's vaudeville shows, mock genteel romance. But the male body contact becomes respectable in the service of intermarriage. "Making Whoopee," the song whose ridiculous pun joins Indian war dances to sexual play, comes down on the side of marriage. Conjugal fidelity disciplines indiscriminate heterosexual pleasure in the song's lyrics, polymorphous, homoerotic perversity in the movie's subtext.[46]

In response to Black Eagle's invitation to join the tribe, Henry reinstates the intermarriage plot by bringing up Pocahontas. "Pocahontas saved John Smith," responds Black Eagle. Henry asks, "Why didn't he do something for his brother, Al?" Before viewers have time to reflect on the failure of Pocahontas (and by extension, that of the melting pot) to save Al Smith from anti-Catholicism in the 1928 presidential election, Henry goes on, "And I don't mean Al Jolson." Cantor, like Jolson, achieved stardom through blackface, so the reference to the two Als is a reference to cross-dressing and the situations that provoke it.[47]

Blackface is the fulcrum at the center of Cantor's multiple cross-dressings. "I brought my negro friend up north," Cantor wrote of his blackface persona, by

---

[44] Sollors, *Beyond Ethnicity*, 132–38; Cantor as told to Freedman, *My Life Is in Your Hands*, 82; Musser, "Ethnicity, Role-Playing, and American Film Comedy," 64.

[45] Musser, "Ethnicity, Role-Playing, and American Film Comedy," 62, 43; ad for *Whoopee!*, *New Yorker*, Oct. 6, 1930, p. 87.

[46] Cantor as told to Freedman, *My Life Is in Your Hands*, 29–30; Lott, "Love and Theft."

[47] Al Smith was Cantor's ghetto boyhood hero, "as if the lady of the statue of liberty had sent her own son to receive these poor, bewildered immigrants," the actor wrote in his autobiography. Cantor as told to Freedman, *My Life Is in Your Hands*, 44.

"add[ing] an intellectual touch to the old-fashioned darkey of the minstrel shows." Cantor's trademark character was "the cultured, pansy-like negro with spectacles"; Cantor and the "whitest black man I ever knew," the African-American blackface vaudevillian, Bert Williams, appeared as "Sonny and Papsy." As a blackface performer Cantor was ambiguously male/female and black/white; he played Salome in drag and moved from man to woman to black eunuch in a slave harem in *Roman Scandals*.[48]

As it facilitates intermarriage in *The Jazz Singer*, so blackface brings *Whoopee!*'s Indian and white lovers together. Henry, helping Sally escape her wedding to Sheriff Bob, hides in an oven. When the stove is lit, he explodes out in blackface. Like Whiteman's lion, Jolson's mammy, and the prototypical, exaggerated blackface mouth, the oven associates blackface with primitive orality. The disguise fools Sheriff Bob and encourages Sally to confess her love for Wanenis. Promoting anarchic violence against the forces of law and order, blackface also facilitates intermarriage in the low plot. Cantor sings "My Baby Just Cares for Me" in blackface and sings it again sans cork to Nurse Custer to end the film. Transforming Jew from frightened melancholic into trickster, blackface shifts the meaning of "cares for" from nursing to sex. When Sheriff Bob tries to wipe Henry clean, he leaves him with what look like Orthodox Jewish earlocks and beard.

Racial cross-dressing promotes ethnic intermarriage in *The Jazz Singer* and *Old San Francisco; Whoopee!* may seem to bless racial intermarriage as well. Indians, to be sure, were not universally the targets of intermarriage taboos. As the John Smith/Pocahontas story attests, Indian/white intermarriage was one way to provide the white presence in the New World with a native ground. But racist hostility extended to Indians. "My one drop of Indian blood makes your people hate me," Wanenis explains to Sally. *Whoopee!*'s spoof of the one-drop theories of racial contamination flourishing in the jazz age acknowledges the racial prejudice buried in *The Jazz Singer* but dominant in *Old San Francisco* and *The King of Jazz*.

As in the intermarriage melodramas, Black Eagle wants Wanenis to return to the ways of his people, and the combination of traditional loyalty and white prejudice seems to doom the romance. But faced with the love between Wanenis and Sally, Black Eagle reveals that Wanenis has not even a drop of Indian blood; a parodic descendant of James Fenimore Cooper's Oliver Effingham, he is a foundling the chief raised as his own child. Wanenis may not know it, but, like Henry, he has been masquerading as an Indian. As in Rudoloph Valentino's *Sheik*, the dark object of female desire is white beneath his mask. In *Whoopee!*, as in *The Jazz Singer*, there is racial cross-dressing, not miscegenation. The amalgamation that gives birth to a distinctively American culture substitutes for the mixing of blood.[49]

---

[48] *Ibid.*, 113–15, 122–23, 159–60; *Roman Scandals,* dir. Frank Tuttle (Samuel Goldwyn, 1933); William D. Routt and Richard J. Thompson, "Keep Young and Beautiful: Surplus and Subversion in *Roman Scandals," Journal of Film and Video,* 42 (Spring 1990), 17–35. Thanks to Vivian Sobchack for this reference.

[49] James Fenimore Cooper, *The Pioneers* (New York, 1823); Marchetti, *Romance and the "Yellow Peril,"* 22–27.

Turning Wanenis white is parodic; unlike *Old San Francisco* or *King of Jazz*, *Whoopee!* does not eliminate the racial in favor of the ethnic group. Nor does it, like the other movies discussed here, put technological innovations in the service of new identities. Even the dance numbers, Busby Berkeley's first Hollywood productions, are, like the movie as a whole, self-mocking.[50] *Whoopee!*, with its blackface and redface masquerades, remains in the technologically more primitive, anti-illusionistic, vaudeville and early silent movie tradition.

Nonetheless, *Whoopee!* also participates in the racialist tradition it ridicules. By making savages noble and confining the Jew to slapstick, *Whoopee!*'s plot privileges the racial over the ethnic minority, but its method has the opposite effect. Cantor's stereotyping may edge into anti-Semitism, but it is the vehicle for Jewish performance. Like the vaudeville routines and Vitaphone shorts of Lou Holtz, George Burns, Gregory Ratoff, and George Jessel, Cantor's performance participates in a recognizable, authentically Jewish milieu. No Indian, by contrast, will recognize himself in the cardboard straight men for Jewish humor. Wanenis has not a drop of Indian blood, and the actors playing Indians are palefaces, too.

Cantor's blackface does not even pretend to depict real blacks. *Whoopee!*'s blackface is Jewish, its redface (Cantor aside) is goyish—to borrow Lenny Bruce's distinction between mocking, physicalized signifiers and pious, disembodied ones—for the film privileges an urban minority voice over the racially based, melting pot myth of the West in *The King of Jazz* and *Old San Francisco*.[51] In the other movies, race is the vehicle for ethnic assimilation; in this one it supports ethnic self-assertion.

Cantor gains power over his ethnicity by turning it into performance.[52] Signifying on his Jewishness, playing with the stereotype rather than challenging it, is also a sign of the narrow constraints within which he could assert his ethnicity. The sexual cross-dressing implied in Jewish neurasthenia and male horseplay may point either to polyphony or (as in *The Singing Fool*) to the limits of Jewish liminality. But however one evaluates the transgressions in *Whoopee!*'s ethnic and sexual carnivalesque, the movie—it is necessary to say—provides no vehicle for nonwhite self-expression. Bad taste is its virtue, but *Whoopee!* plays with, mocks, and operates wholly inside the ethnic, sexual, and racial hierarchies of jazz age America.

Blackface carried Cantor from the slum to the stars. But it "had become an inseparable part of my stage presence," Cantor wrote in *My Life Is in Your Hands*, "and I feared that the day might come when I could never take it off. I would always be Eddie Cantor, the blackface comedian, but if I ever tore the mask off I'd be nobody at all." Resolving that "I was not going to be a slave to a piece of burnt cork for the rest of my acting days," Cantor convinced Florenz Ziegfeld to let him appear in whiteface. Unlike African Americans, inadvertently invoked by Cantor's refusal to

---

[50] Cf. Routt and Thompson, "Keep Young and Beautiful," 24–27.

[51] Lenny Bruce's Jewish/goyish monologue is legendary. I heard it in Chicago c. 1960.

[52] Musser, "Ethnicity, Role-Playing, and American Film Comedy," celebrates ethnic performance as a vehicle for American self-making. Although I have learned and borrowed from Musser's rich essay, which I read after completing a draft of my own, he takes a sunnier view of the material.

be a slave, the white man in blackface could change the color of his skin. "It was the first time I felt revealed to the audience and in personal contact with it," Cantor confessed. In Cantor's first, whiteface skit a doctor subjected him to an invasive physical exam. The comedian connects it to a later scene, "in essence" the same, that turns on his Jewish identity. Cantor's free association moves him from the stage doctor's to the audience's hands. *The Jazz Singer* escapes his Jewish past in blackface. Cantor, thanks to blackface, can finally reveal himself to the mass audience as a Jew.[53]

Like the jazz singer, however, the urban Jew finds a southern home. Cantor's autobiography ends with "the slum boy of the tenements" preparing to make the stage production *Whoopee!* and, "a modern pioneer," buying a house in Great Neck, Long Island. Cantor's neighbor is Nathan S. Jonas, "an imposing gentleman with a trace of southern aristocracy" who has planted a "boxwood garden reminiscent of southern estates" and developed "one of the most beautiful and exclusive country clubs in America." "Space and time are the slaves that tremble under the wand of wealth," writes Cantor, and those modern slaves allow the financier to "return to the simple and primitive" pastoral life. Cantor is incorporated into the family homecoming, for the boy who at the age of two had "floundered in the streets of New York, fatherless and motherless" writes that he is "now sitting in a flower-laden bower with my parents. Mr. and Mrs. Nathan S. Jonas have become father and mother to me."[54]

If Cantor's autobiography lacked the comic courage of *Whoopee!*'s convictions, the Marx brothers supplied it. Cantor's plantation refuge could well have been the Long Island estate the polyglot immigrants invade in *Animal Crackers* (1930), where Groucho, taking off on Henry M. Stanley, plays Geoffrey T. Spalding, "the noted explorer returning from Africa." ("Hurray for Captain Spaulding, the African explorer; did someone call me *schnorrer?*") "I wish I was back in the jungle, where men are monkeys," says Groucho. Then, in a "program . . . coming to you from the House of David," the barbershop quartet of Groucho, Chico, Harpo, and Zeppo lament and replace their lost home. They mangle — not the version of "Swanee River" that helped launch the jazz age, written by one east European Jew and performed in blackface by another, not Gershwin and Jolson's "Swanee"— but the original Stephen Foster minstrel ballad, "Old Folks at Home."[55]

[53] Cantor as told to Freedman, *My Life Is in Your Hands*, 40, 44, 186–87.

[54] *Ibid.*, 292–95.

[55] *Animal Crackers*, dir. Victor Heerman (Paramount, 1930). Charles Musser described the barbershop quartet, inspiring me to see *Animal Crackers* again and discover that the Marx brothers had already written this article. (See Musser, "Ethnicity, Role-Playing, and American Film Comedy," 66–67.) That *Animal Crackers* was in part a deliberate parody of *My Life Is in Your Hands* is indicated by Chico's Irish chiropodist tune, "My fayt is in your hands."

Index